NEONOMICON

ALAN MOORE story & script
JACEN BURROWS art
JUANMAR color

THE COURTYARD

ALAN MOORE story
JACEN BURROWS art
ANTONY JOHNSTON sequential adaptation
ALAN MOORE consulting editor
JUANMAR color

WILLIAM CHRISTENSEN editor-in-chief
MARK SEIFERT creative director
JIM KUHORIC managing editor
KEITH DAVIDSEN director of sales
DAVID MARKS marketing director
ARIANA OSBORNE production assistant

Alan Moore's NEONOMICON COLLECTED. September 2011. Published by Avatar
Press, Inc., 515 N. Century Blvd. Rantoul, IL 61866. ©2011 Avatar
Press, Inc. Neonomicon, The Courtyard, and all related properties TM &
©2011 Alan Moore. All characters as depicted in this story are over the
age of 18. The stories, characters, and institutions mentioned in this
magazine are entirely fictional. PRINTED IN CANADA.

www.avatarpress.com
www.twitter.com/avatarpress
www.facebook.com/avatarpresscomics

AVATAR ™

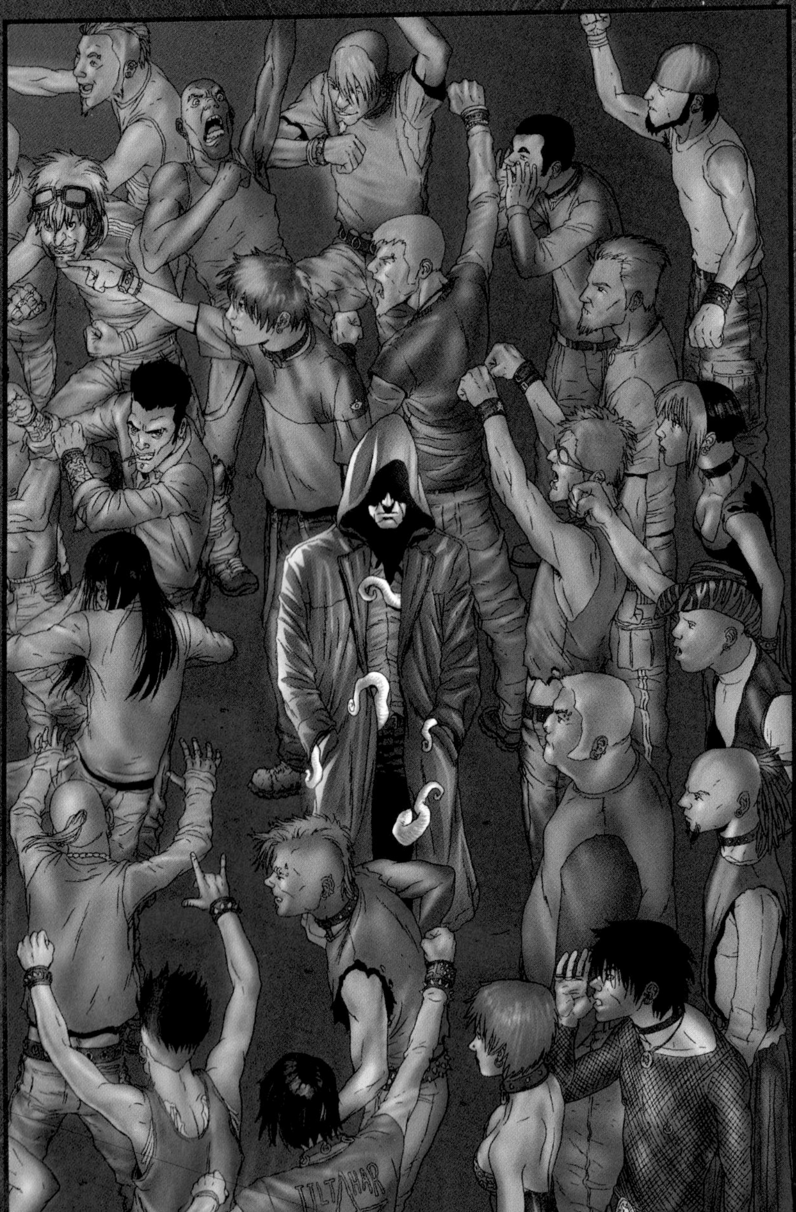
ULTHAR

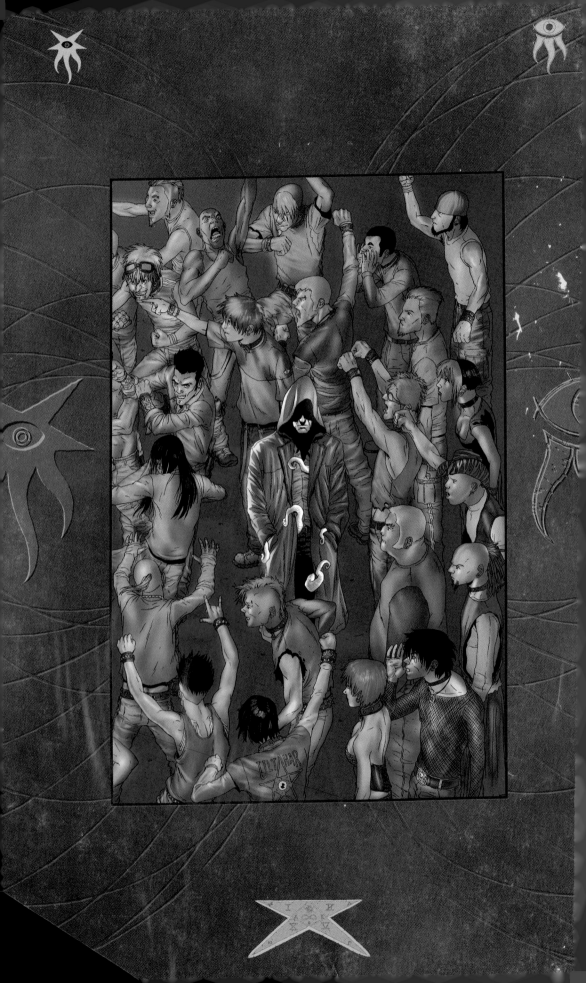

THE COURTYARD
Chapter 1

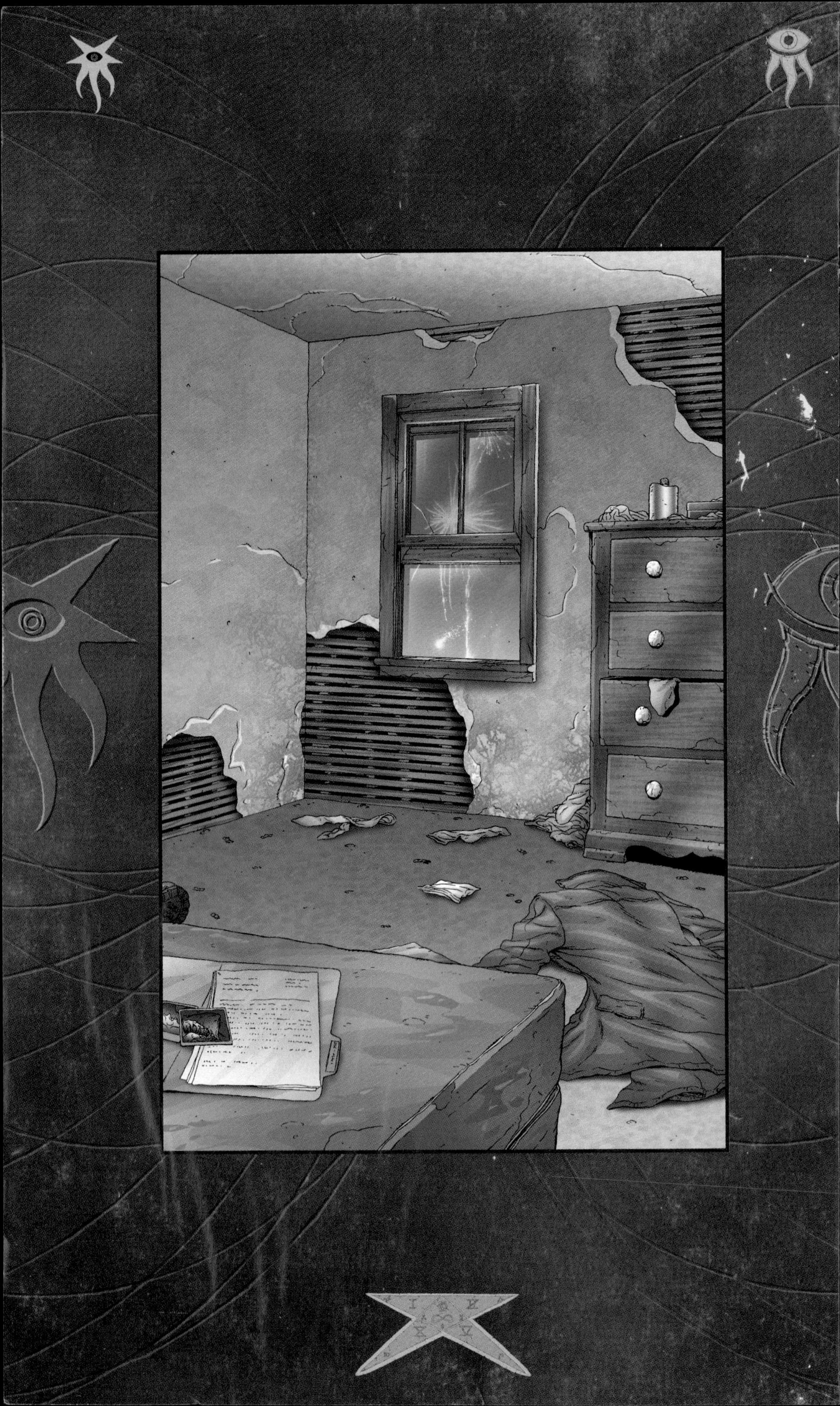

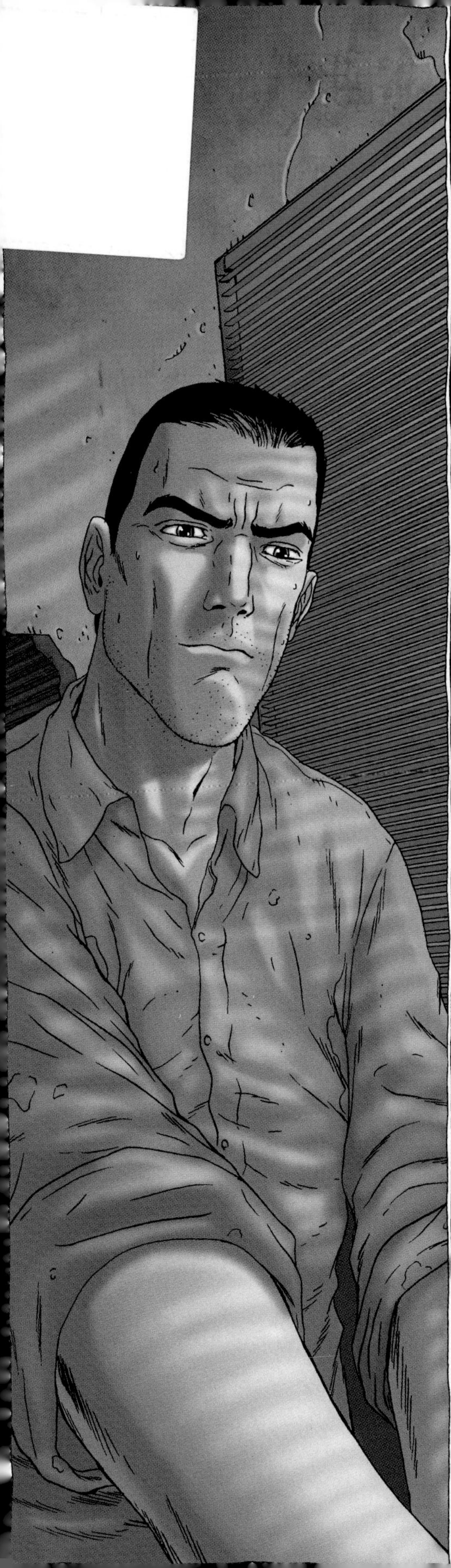
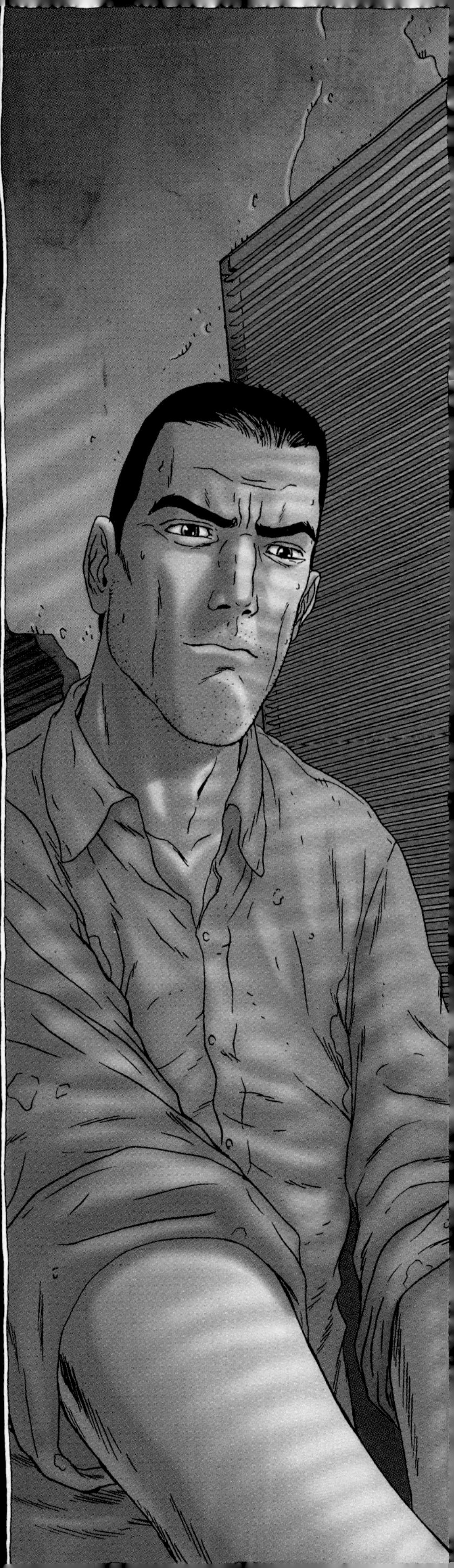

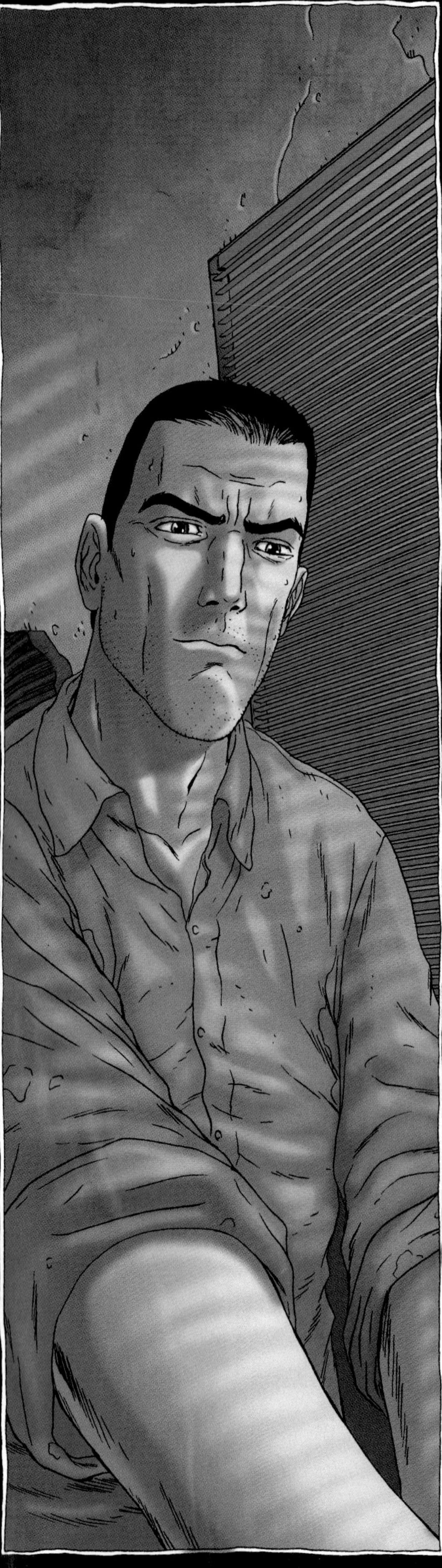
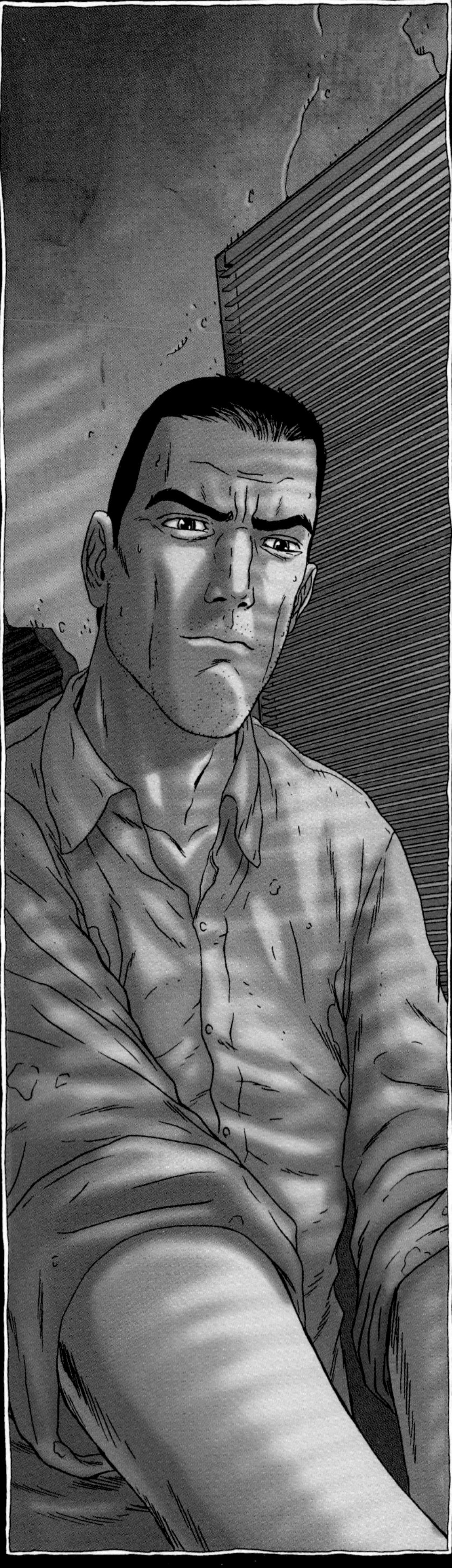

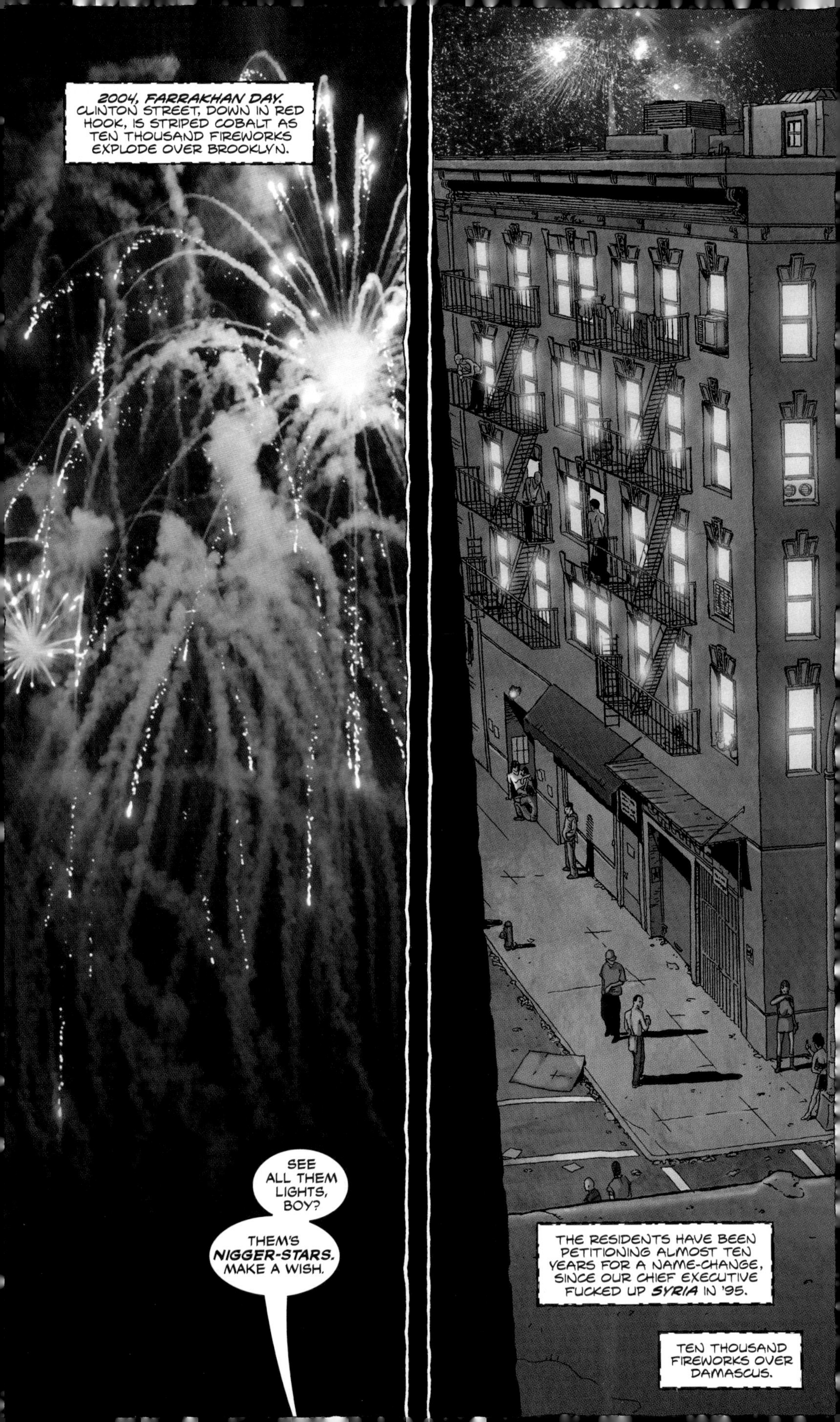
2004, FARRAKHAN DAY. CLINTON STREET, DOWN IN RED HOOK, IS STRIPED COBALT AS TEN THOUSAND FIREWORKS EXPLODE OVER BROOKLYN.
SEE ALL THEM LIGHTS, BOY?
THEM'S NIGGER-STARS. MAKE A WISH.
THE RESIDENTS HAVE BEEN PETITIONING ALMOST TEN YEARS FOR A NAME-CHANGE, SINCE OUR CHIEF EXECUTIVE FUCKED UP SYRIA IN '95.
TEN THOUSAND FIREWORKS OVER DAMASCUS.

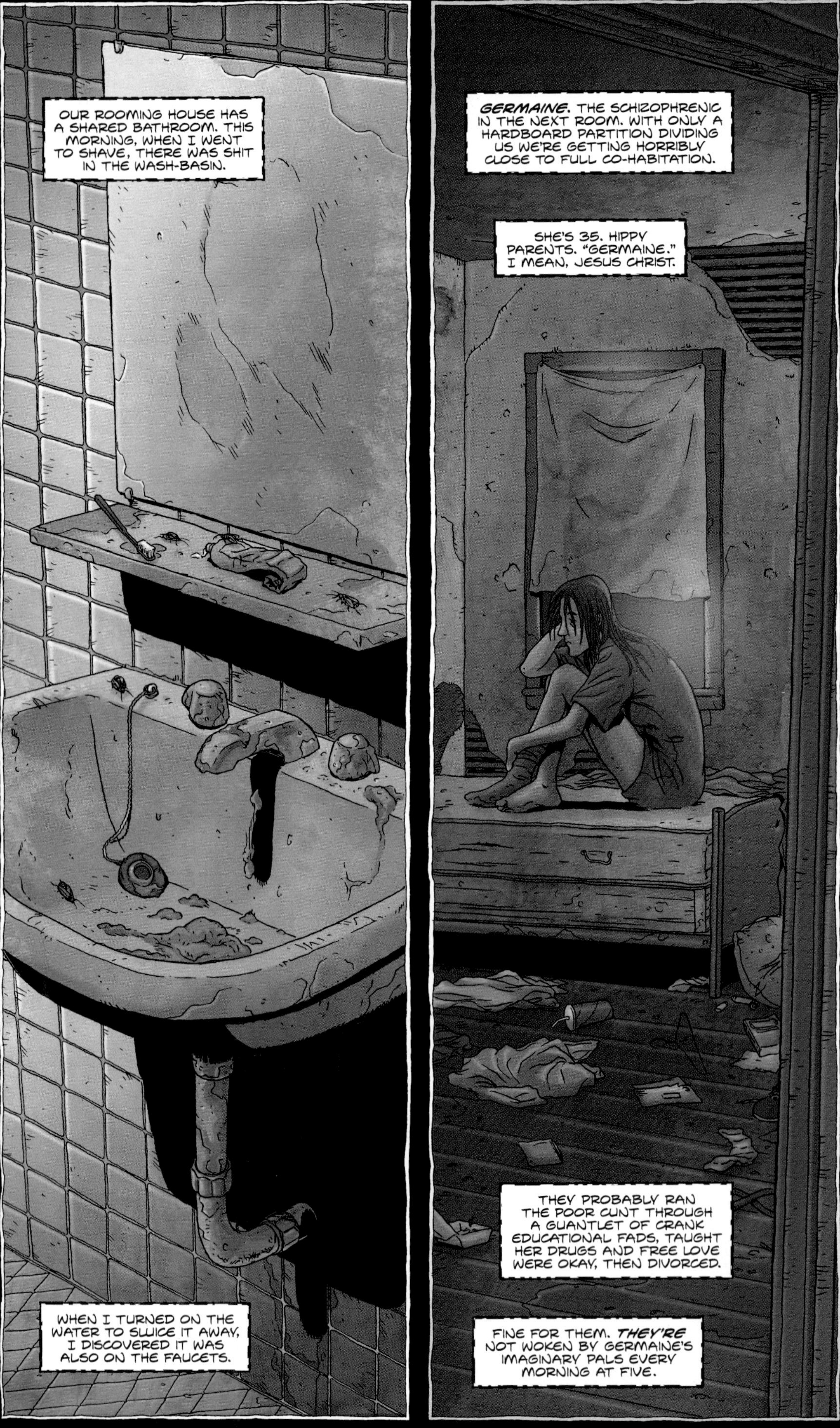
OUR ROOMING HOUSE HAS A SHARED BATHROOM. THIS MORNING, WHEN I WENT TO SHAVE, THERE WAS SHIT IN THE WASH-BASIN.
WHEN I TURNED ON THE WATER TO SLUICE IT AWAY, I DISCOVERED IT WAS ALSO ON THE FAUCETS.
GERMAINE. THE SCHIZOPHRENIC IN THE NEXT ROOM. WITH ONLY A HARDBOARD PARTITION DIVIDING US WE'RE GETTING HORRIBLY CLOSE TO FULL CO-HABITATION.
SHE'S 35. HIPPY PARENTS. "GERMAINE." I MEAN, JESUS CHRIST.
THEY PROBABLY RAN THE POOR CUNT THROUGH A GUANTLET OF CRANK EDUCATIONAL FADS, TAUGHT HER DRUGS AND FREE LOVE WERE OKAY, THEN DIVORCED.
FINE FOR THEM. THEY'RE NOT WOKEN BY GERMAINE'S IMAGINARY PALS EVERY MORNING AT FIVE.

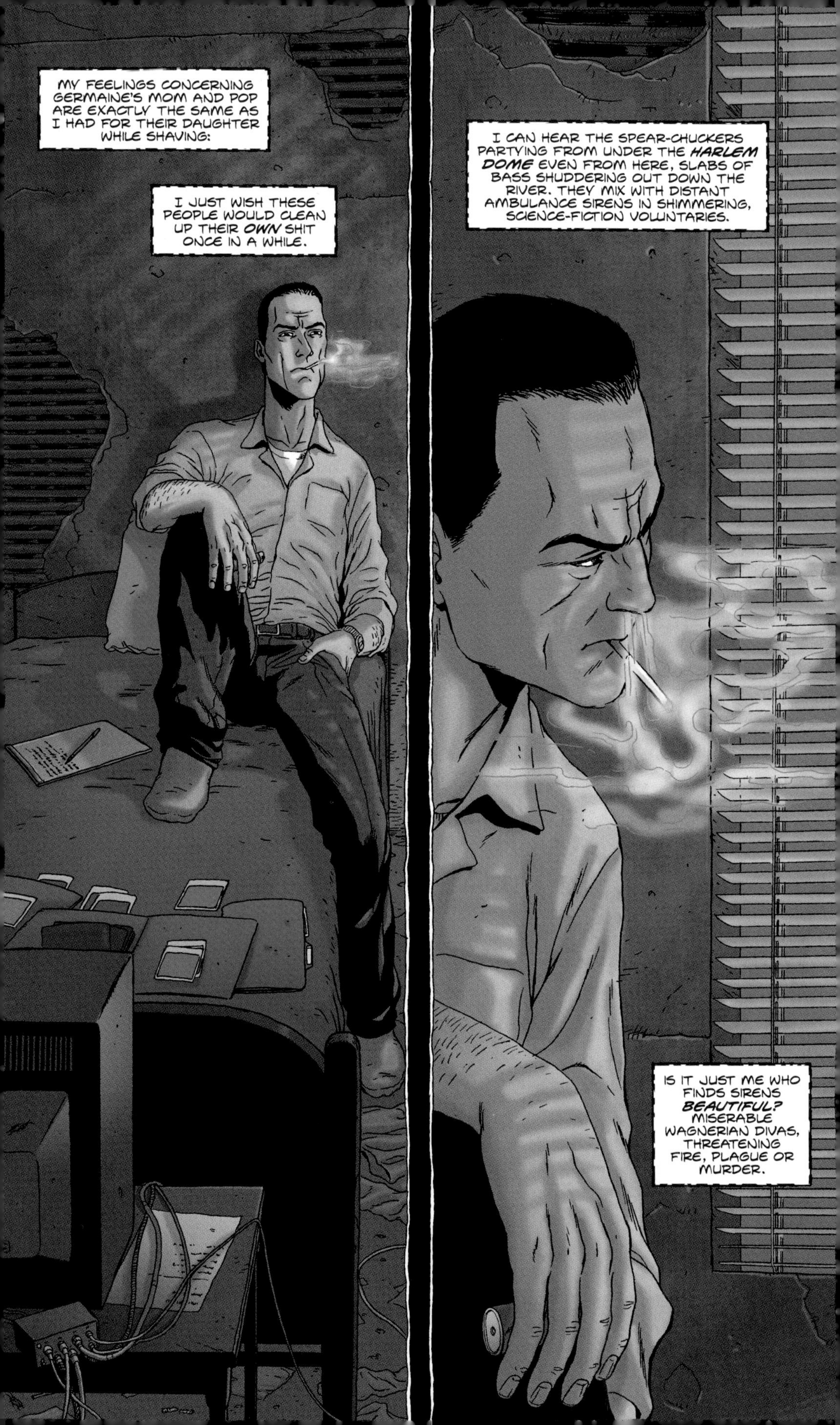
MY FEELINGS CONCERNING GERMAINE'S MOM AND POP ARE EXACTLY THE SAME AS I HAD FOR THEIR DAUGHTER WHILE SHAVING:
I JUST WISH THESE PEOPLE WOULD CLEAN UP THEIR OWN SHIT ONCE IN A WHILE.
I CAN HEAR THE SPEAR-CHUCKERS PARTYING FROM UNDER THE HARLEM DOME EVEN FROM HERE, SLABS OF BASS SHUDDERING OUT DOWN THE RIVER. THEY MIX WITH DISTANT AMBULANCE SIRENS IN SHIMMERING, SCIENCE-FICTION VOLUNTARIES.
IS IT JUST ME WHO FINDS SIRENS BEAUTIFUL? MISERABLE WAGNERIAN DIVAS, THREATENING FIRE, PLAGUE OR MURDER.

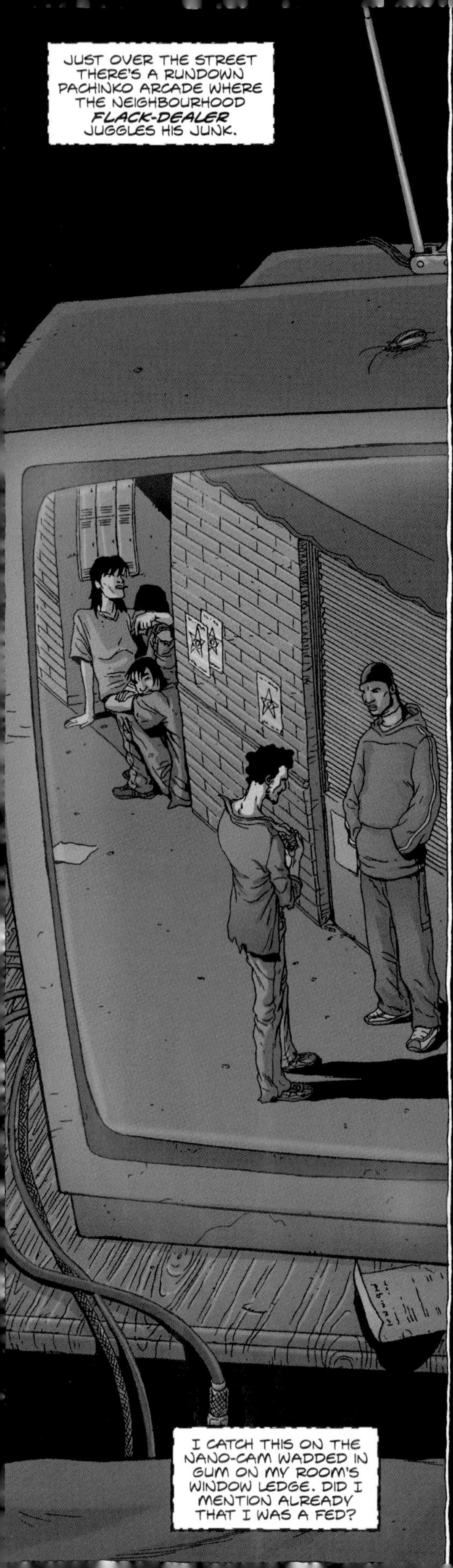
JUST OVER THE STREET THERE'S A RUNDOWN PACHINKO ARCADE WHERE THE NEIGHBOURHOOD FLACK-DEALER JUGGLES HIS JUNK.
I CATCH THIS ON THE NANO-CAM WADDED IN GUM ON MY ROOM'S WINDOW LEDGE. DID I MENTION ALREADY THAT I WAS A FED?

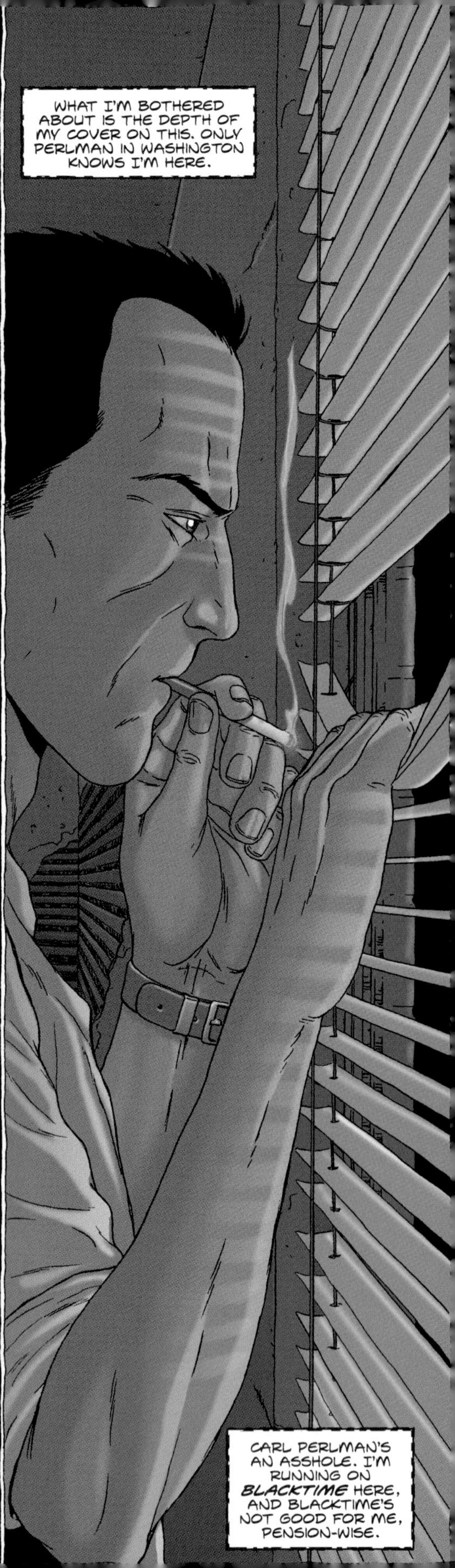
WHAT I'M BOTHERED ABOUT IS THE DEPTH OF MY COVER ON THIS. ONLY PERLMAN IN WASHINGTON KNOWS I'M HERE.
CARL PERLMAN'S AN ASSHOLE. I'M RUNNING ON BLACKTIME HERE, AND BLACKTIME'S NOT GOOD FOR ME, PENSION-WISE.

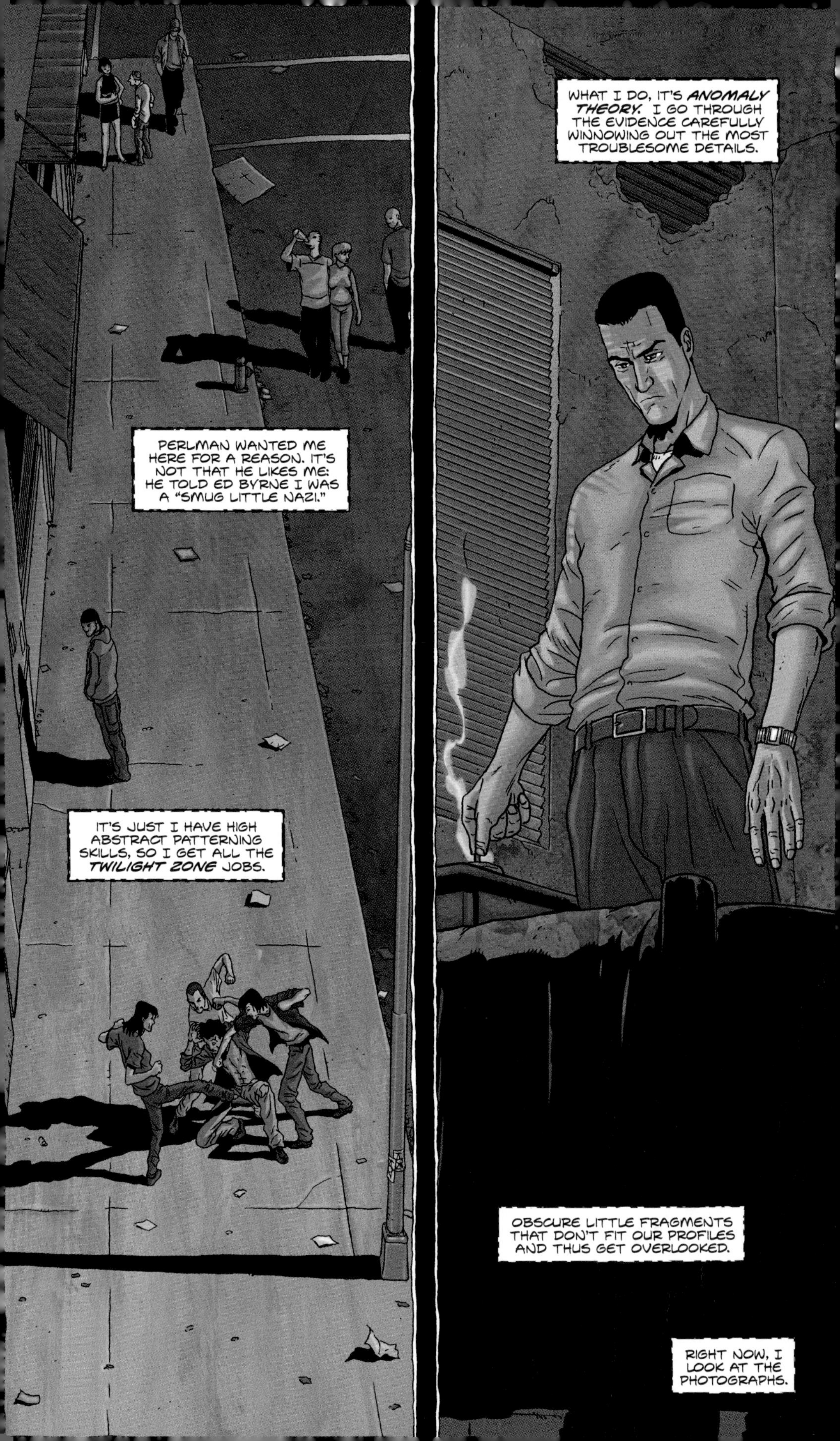
PERLMAN WANTED ME HERE FOR A REASON. IT'S NOT THAT HE LIKES ME: HE TOLD ED BYRNE I WAS A "SMUG LITTLE NAZI."
IT'S JUST I HAVE HIGH ABSTRACT PATTERNING SKILLS, SO I GET ALL THE *TWILIGHT ZONE* JOBS.
WHAT I DO, IT'S *ANOMALY THEORY.* I GO THROUGH THE EVIDENCE CAREFULLY WINNOWING OUT THE MOST TROUBLESOME DETAILS.
OBSCURE LITTLE FRAGMENTS THAT DON'T FIT OUR PROFILES AND THUS GET OVERLOOKED.
RIGHT NOW, I LOOK AT THE PHOTOGRAPHS.

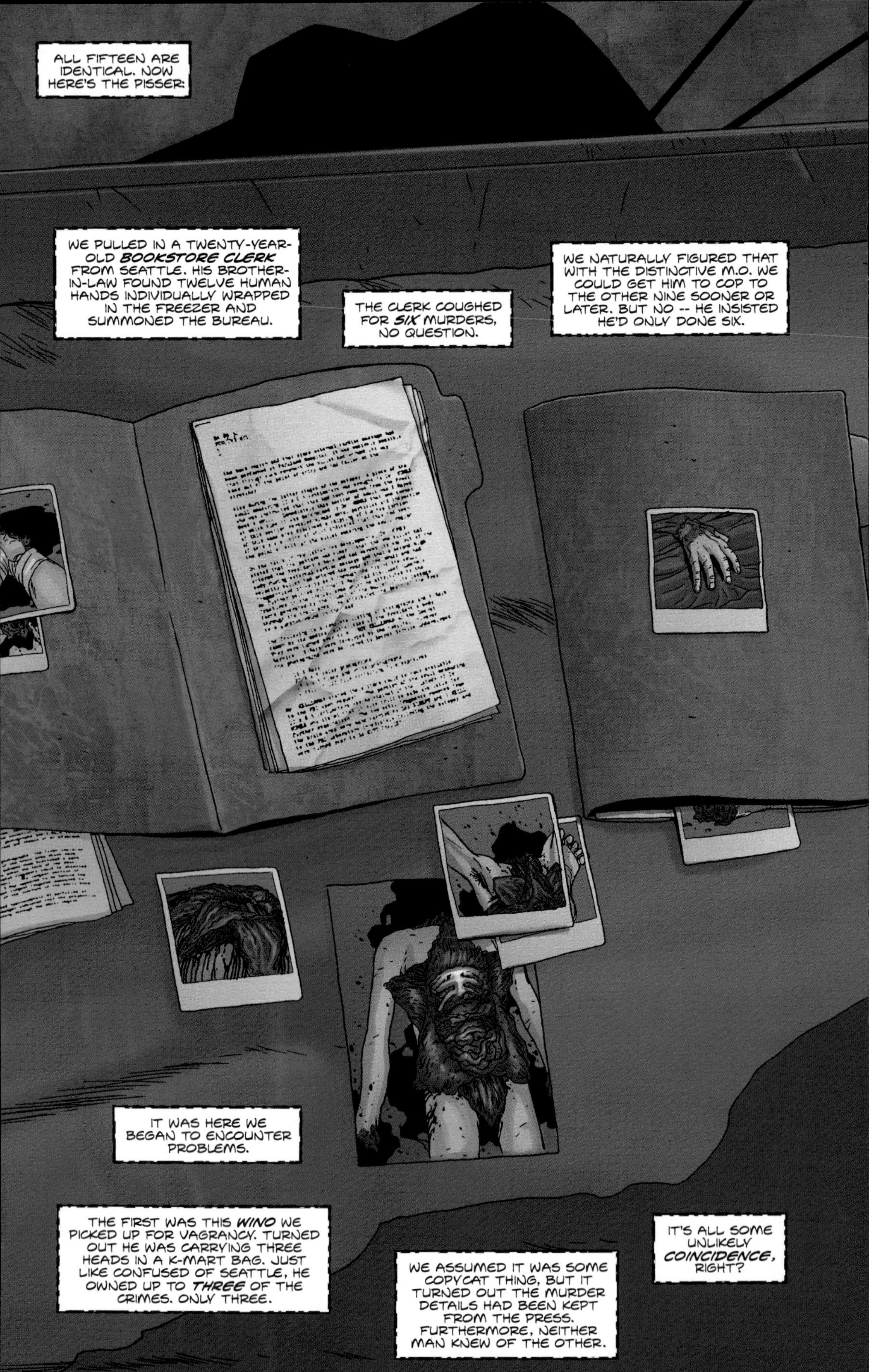
ALL FIFTEEN ARE IDENTICAL. NOW HERE'S THE PISSER:
WE PULLED IN A TWENTY-YEAR-OLD BOOKSTORE CLERK FROM SEATTLE. HIS BROTHER-IN-LAW FOUND TWELVE HUMAN HANDS INDIVIDUALLY WRAPPED IN THE FREEZER AND SUMMONED THE BUREAU.
THE CLERK COUGHED FOR SIX MURDERS, NO QUESTION.
WE NATURALLY FIGURED THAT WITH THE DISTINCTIVE M.O. WE COULD GET HIM TO COP TO THE OTHER NINE SOONER OR LATER. BUT NO -- HE INSISTED HE'D ONLY DONE SIX.
IT WAS HERE WE BEGAN TO ENCOUNTER PROBLEMS.
THE FIRST WAS THIS WINO WE PICKED UP FOR VAGRANCY. TURNED OUT HE WAS CARRYING THREE HEADS IN A K-MART BAG. JUST LIKE CONFUSED OF SEATTLE, HE OWNED UP TO THREE OF THE CRIMES. ONLY THREE.
WE ASSUMED IT WAS SOME COPYCAT THING, BUT IT TURNED OUT THE MURDER DETAILS HAD BEEN KEPT FROM THE PRESS. FURTHERMORE, NEITHER MAN KNEW OF THE OTHER.
IT'S ALL SOME UNLIKELY COINCIDENCE, RIGHT?

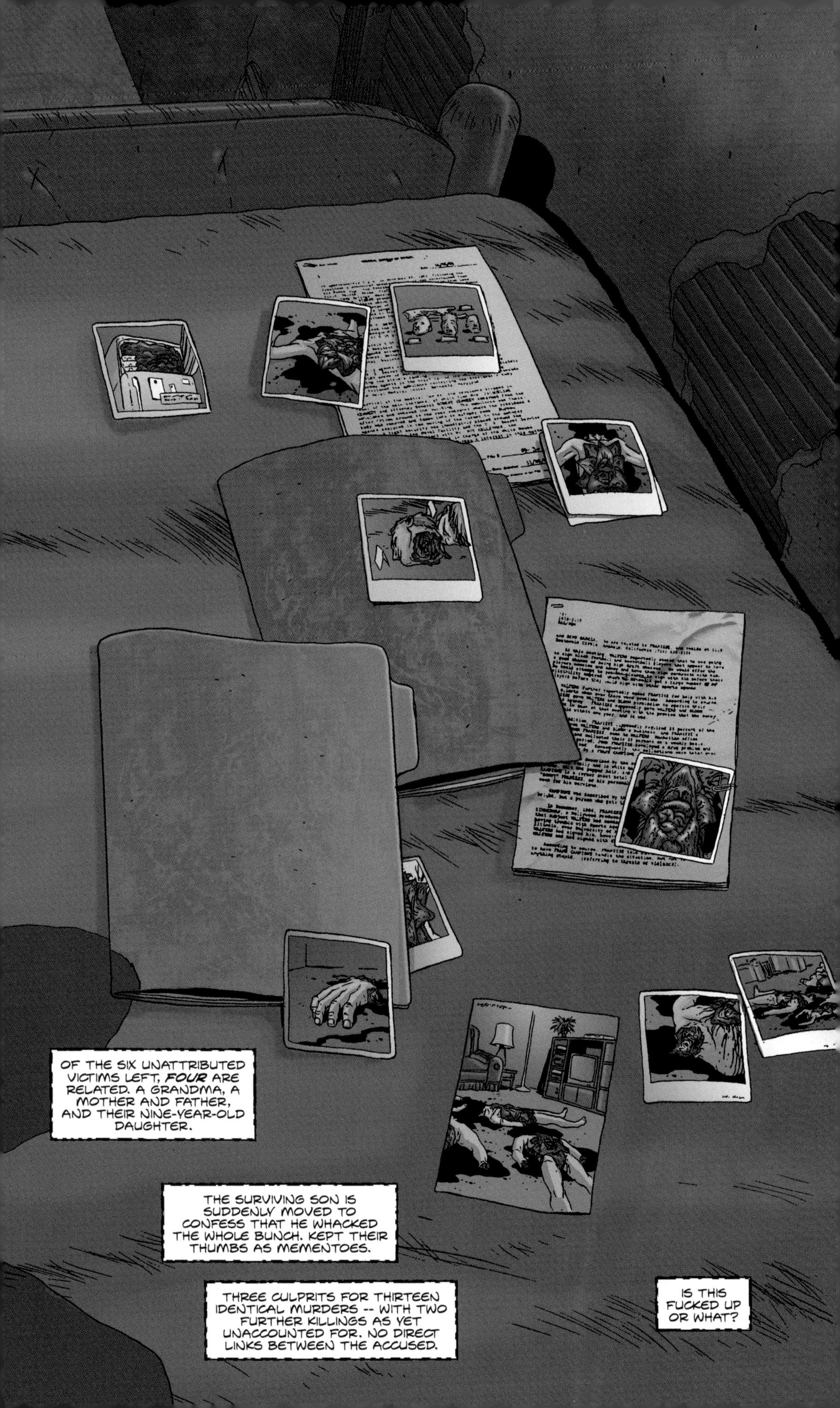

OF THE SIX UNATTRIBUTED VICTIMS LEFT, FOUR ARE RELATED. A GRANDMA, A MOTHER AND FATHER, AND THEIR NINE-YEAR-OLD DAUGHTER.
THE SURVIVING SON IS SUDDENLY MOVED TO CONFESS THAT HE WHACKED THE WHOLE BUNCH. KEPT THEIR THUMBS AS MEMENTOES.
THREE CULPRITS FOR THIRTEEN IDENTICAL MURDERS -- WITH TWO FURTHER KILLINGS AS YET UNACCOUNTED FOR. NO DIRECT LINKS BETWEEN THE ACCUSED.
IS THIS FUCKED UP OR WHAT?

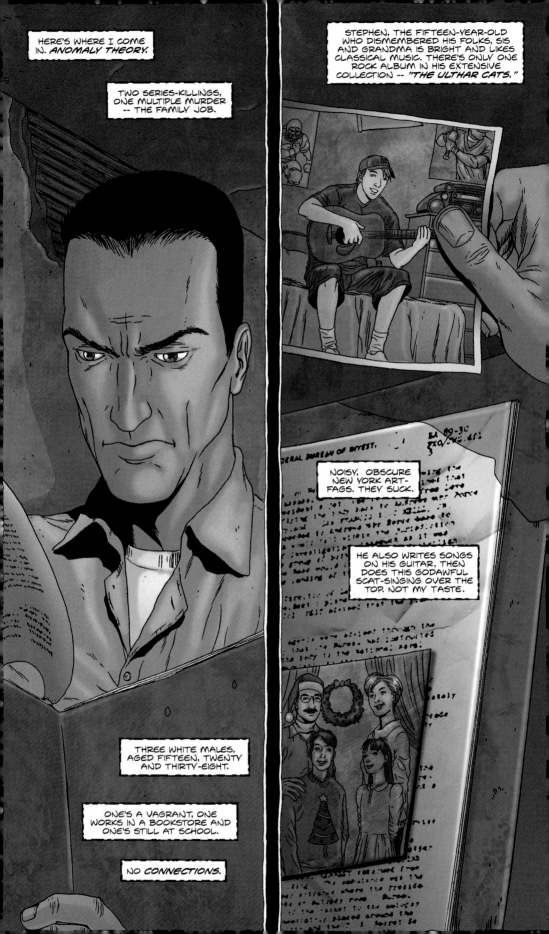

HERE'S WHERE I COME IN. *ANOMALY THEORY.*

TWO SERIES-KILLINGS, ONE MULTIPLE MURDER -- THE FAMILY JOB.

STEPHEN, THE FIFTEEN-YEAR-OLD WHO DISMEMBERED HIS FOLKS, SIS AND GRANDMA IS BRIGHT AND LIKES CLASSICAL MUSIC. THERE'S ONLY ONE ROCK ALBUM IN HIS EXTENSIVE COLLECTION -- *"THE ULTHAR CATS."*

NOISY, OBSCURE NEW YORK ART-FAGS. THEY SUCK.

HE ALSO WRITES SONGS ON HIS GUITAR, THEN DOES THIS GODAWFUL SCAT-SINGING OVER THE TOP. NOT MY TASTE.

THREE WHITE MALES, AGED FIFTEEN, TWENTY AND THIRTY-EIGHT.

ONE'S A VAGRANT, ONE WORKS IN A BOOKSTORE AND ONE'S STILL AT SCHOOL.

NO *CONNECTIONS.*

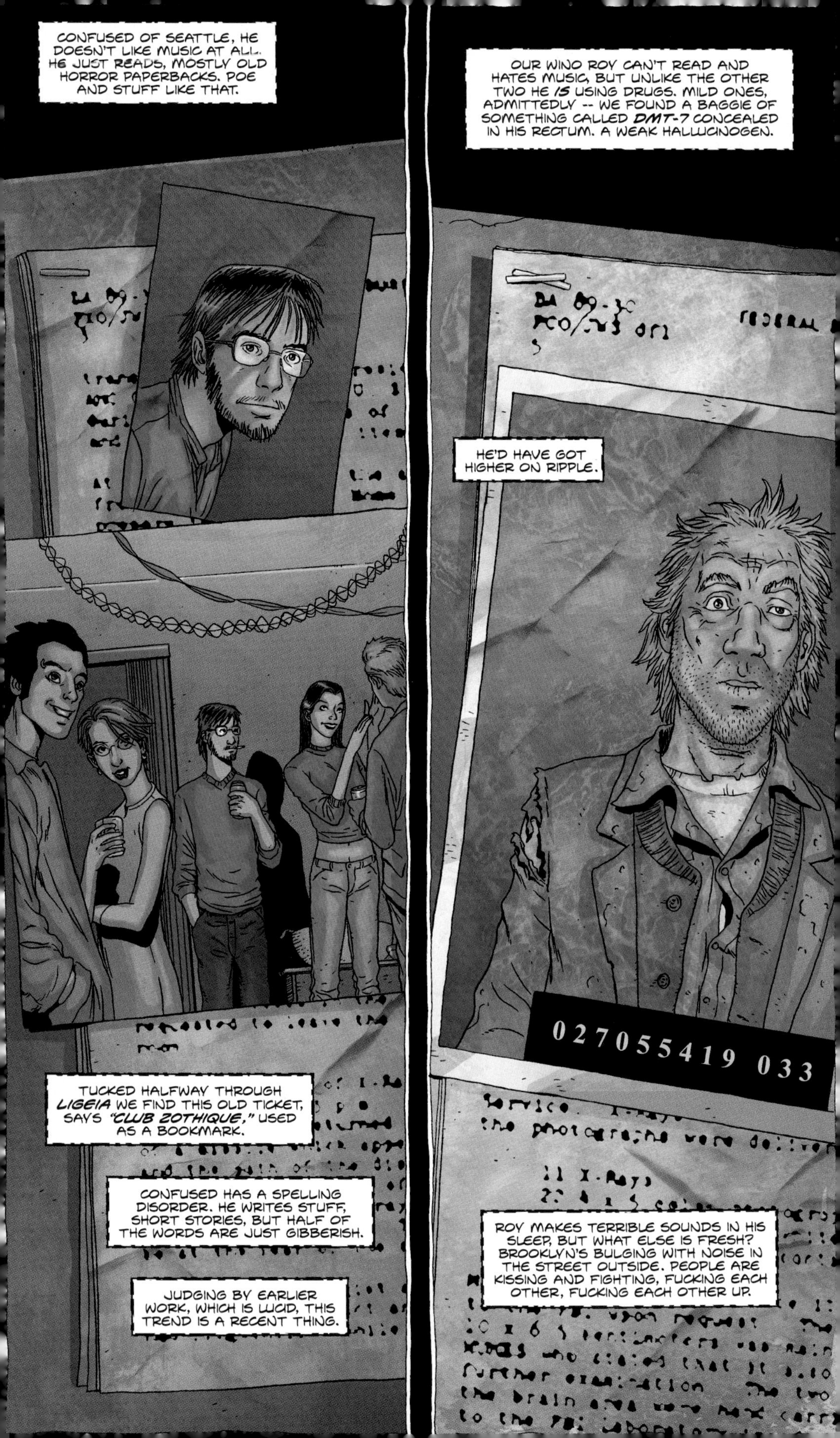
CONFUSED OF SEATTLE, HE DOESN'T LIKE MUSIC AT ALL. HE JUST READS, MOSTLY OLD HORROR PAPERBACKS. POE AND STUFF LIKE THAT.
TUCKED HALFWAY THROUGH *LIGEIA* WE FIND THIS OLD TICKET, SAYS *"CLUB ZOTHIQUE,"* USED AS A BOOKMARK.
CONFUSED HAS A SPELLING DISORDER. HE WRITES STUFF, SHORT STORIES, BUT HALF OF THE WORDS ARE JUST GIBBERISH.
JUDGING BY EARLIER WORK, WHICH IS LUCID, THIS TREND IS A RECENT THING.
OUR WINO ROY CAN'T READ AND HATES MUSIC, BUT UNLIKE THE OTHER TWO HE *IS* USING DRUGS. MILD ONES, ADMITTEDLY -- WE FOUND A BAGGIE OF SOMETHING CALLED *DMT-7* CONCEALED IN HIS RECTUM. A WEAK HALLUCINOGEN.
HE'D HAVE GOT HIGHER ON RIPPLE.
027055419 033
ROY MAKES TERRIBLE SOUNDS IN HIS SLEEP, BUT WHAT ELSE IS FRESH? BROOKLYN'S BULGING WITH NOISE IN THE STREET OUTSIDE. PEOPLE ARE KISSING AND FIGHTING, FUCKING EACH OTHER, FUCKING EACH OTHER UP.

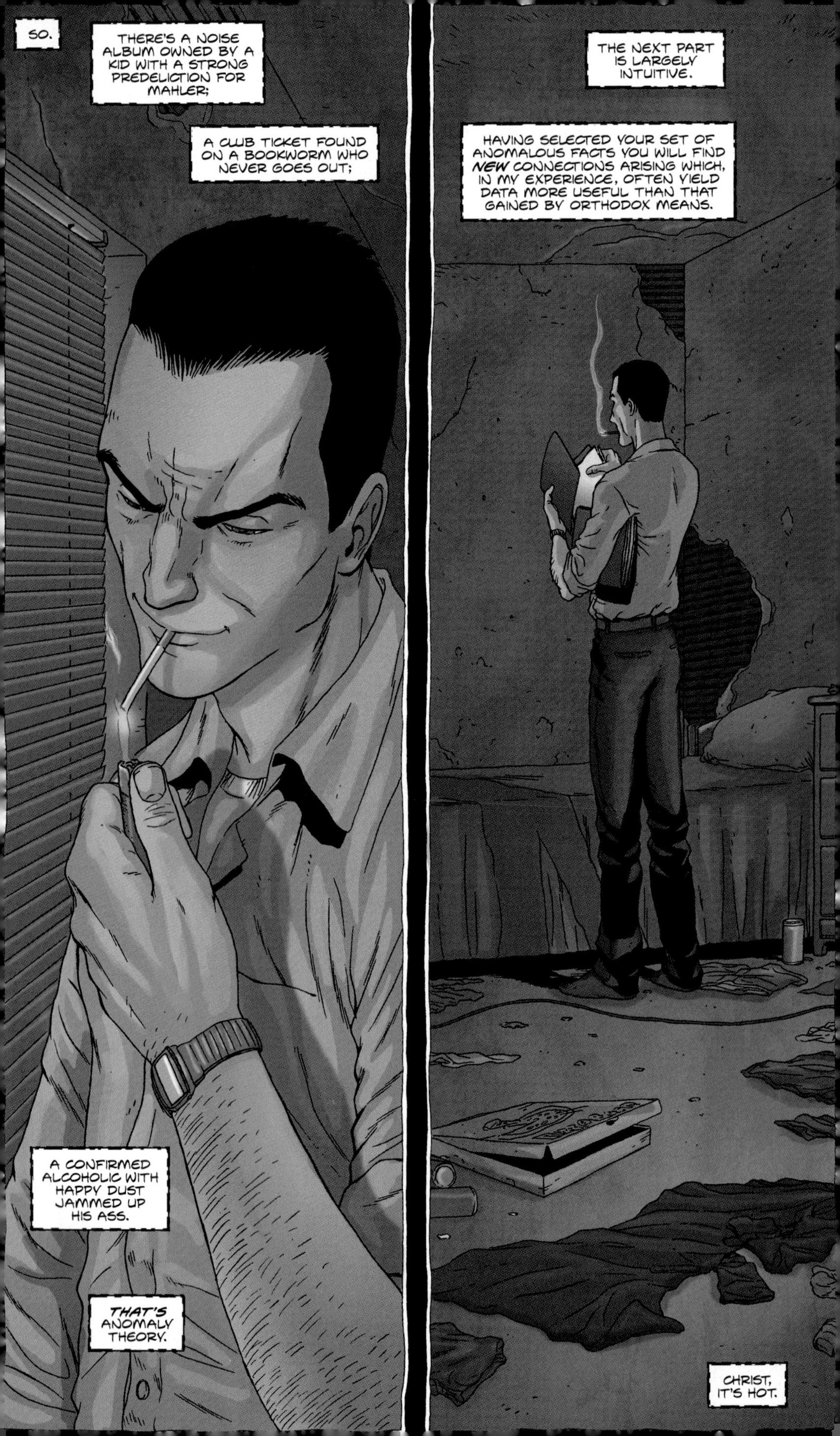
SO.
THERE'S A NOISE ALBUM OWNED BY A KID WITH A STRONG PREDELICTION FOR MAHLER;
A CLUB TICKET FOUND ON A BOOKWORM WHO NEVER GOES OUT;
A CONFIRMED ALCOHOLIC WITH HAPPY DUST JAMMED UP HIS ASS.
THAT'S ANOMALY THEORY.
THE NEXT PART IS LARGELY INTUITIVE.
HAVING SELECTED YOUR SET OF ANOMALOUS FACTS YOU WILL FIND *NEW* CONNECTIONS ARISING WHICH, IN MY EXPERIENCE, OFTEN YIELD DATA MORE USEFUL THAN THAT GAINED BY ORTHODOX MEANS.
CHRIST, IT'S HOT.

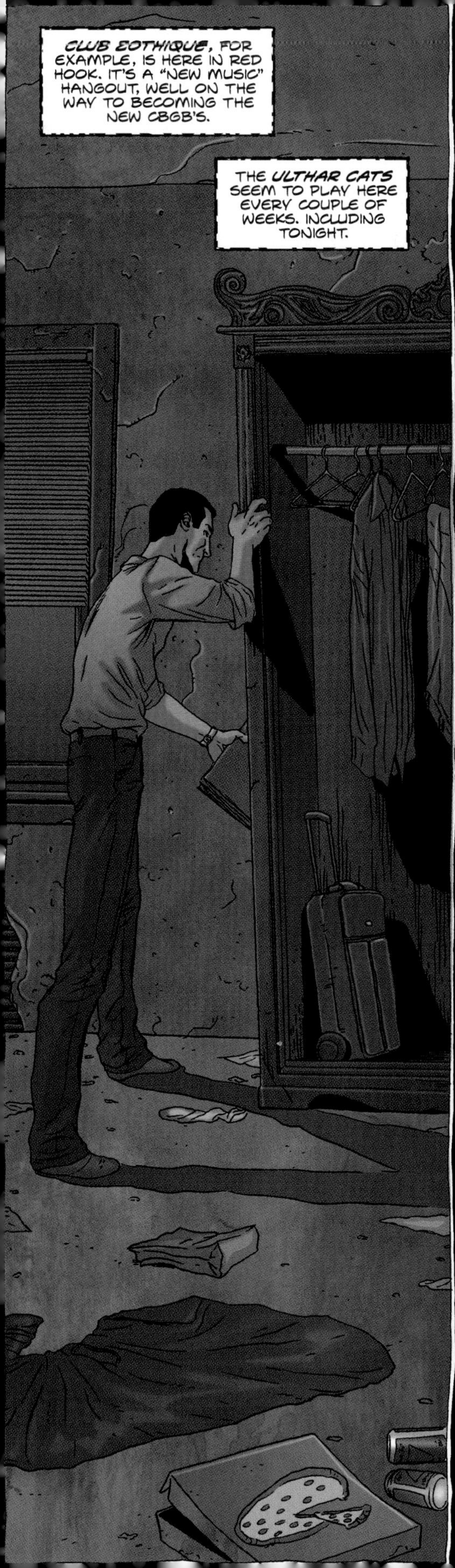
CLUB EOTHIQUE, FOR EXAMPLE, IS HERE IN RED HOOK. IT'S A "NEW MUSIC" HANGOUT, WELL ON THE WAY TO BECOMING THE NEW CBGB'S.
THE ULTHAR CATS SEEM TO PLAY HERE EVERY COUPLE OF WEEKS. INCLUDING TONIGHT.

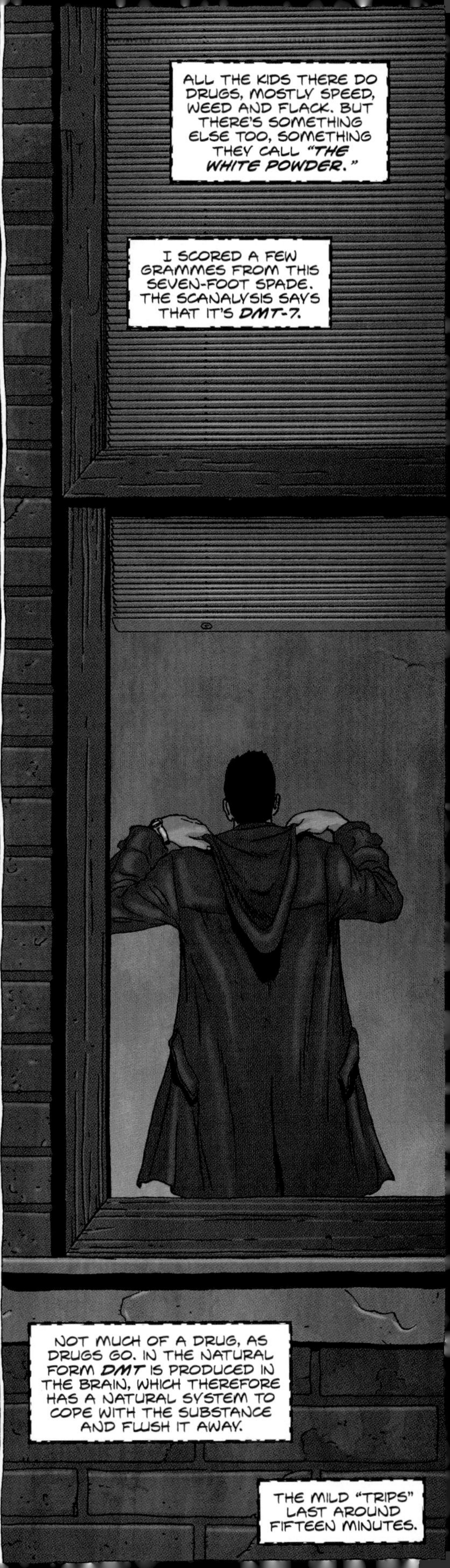
ALL THE KIDS THERE DO DRUGS, MOSTLY SPEED, WEED AND FLACK. BUT THERE'S SOMETHING ELSE TOO, SOMETHING THEY CALL "THE WHITE POWDER."
I SCORED A FEW GRAMMES FROM THIS SEVEN-FOOT SPADE. THE SCANALYSIS SAYS THAT IT'S DMT-7.
NOT MUCH OF A DRUG, AS DRUGS GO. IN THE NATURAL FORM DMT IS PRODUCED IN THE BRAIN, WHICH THEREFORE HAS A NATURAL SYSTEM TO COPE WITH THE SUBSTANCE AND FLUSH IT AWAY.
THE MILD "TRIPS" LAST AROUND FIFTEEN MINUTES.

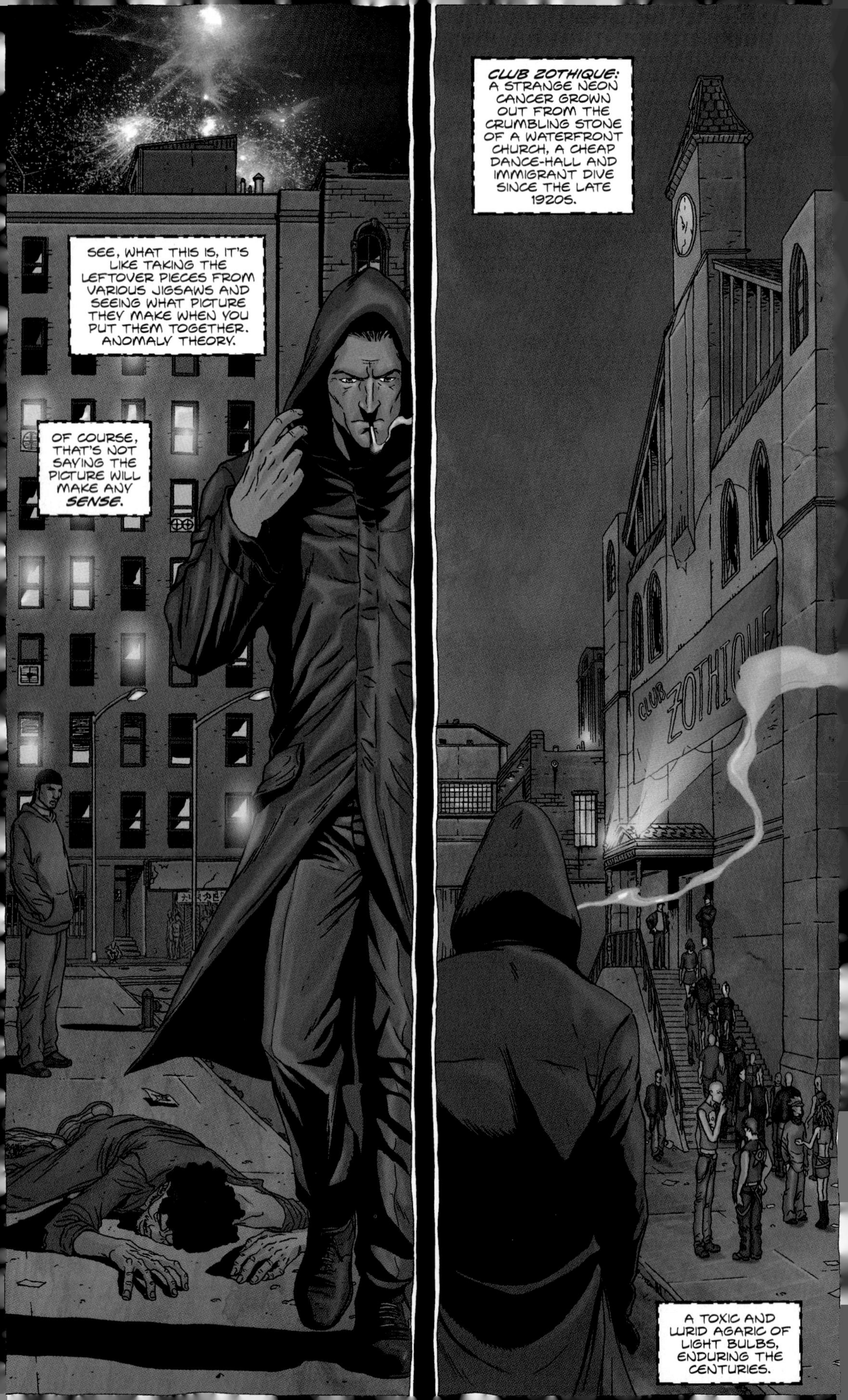
SEE, WHAT THIS IS, IT'S LIKE TAKING THE LEFTOVER PIECES FROM VARIOUS JIGSAWS AND SEEING WHAT PICTURE THEY MAKE WHEN YOU PUT THEM TOGETHER. ANOMALY THEORY.
OF COURSE, THAT'S NOT SAYING THE PICTURE WILL MAKE ANY *SENSE*.
CLUB ZOTHIQUE: A STRANGE NEON CANCER GROWN OUT FROM THE CRUMBLING STONE OF A WATERFRONT CHURCH, A CHEAP DANCE-HALL AND IMMIGRANT DIVE SINCE THE LATE 1920S.
CLUB ZOTHIQUE
A TOXIC AND LURID AGARIC OF LIGHT BULBS, ENDURING THE CENTURIES.

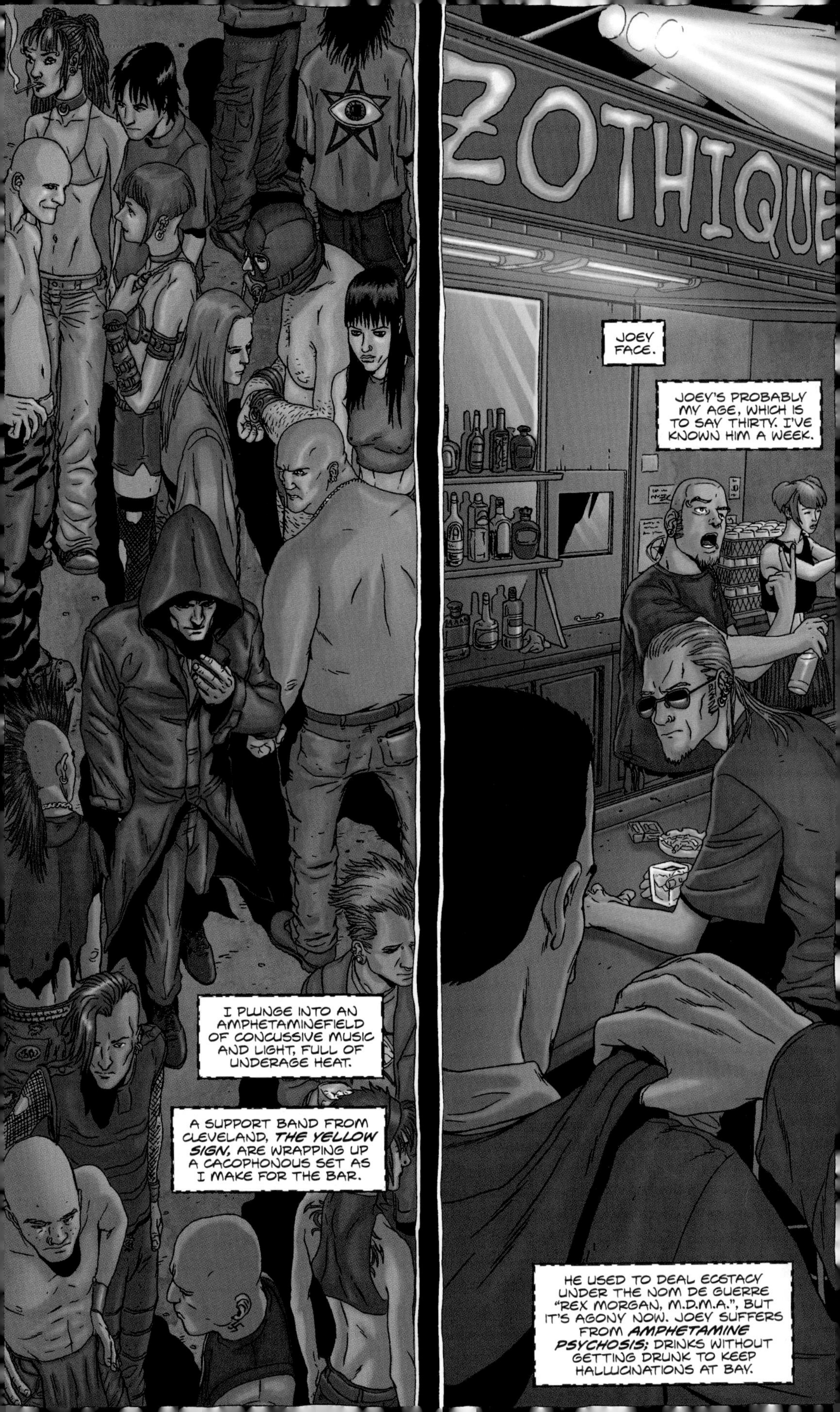
I PLUNGE INTO AN AMPHETAMINEFIELD OF CONCUSSIVE MUSIC AND LIGHT, FULL OF UNDERAGE HEAT.
A SUPPORT BAND FROM CLEVELAND, *THE YELLOW SIGN,* ARE WRAPPING UP A CACOPHONOUS SET AS I MAKE FOR THE BAR.
ZOTHIQUE
JOEY FACE.
JOEY'S PROBABLY MY AGE, WHICH IS TO SAY THIRTY. I'VE KNOWN HIM A WEEK.
HE USED TO DEAL ECSTACY UNDER THE NOM DE GUERRE "REX MORGAN, M.D.M.A.", BUT IT'S AGONY NOW. JOEY SUFFERS FROM *AMPHETAMINE PSYCHOSIS;* DRINKS WITHOUT GETTING DRUNK TO KEEP HALLUCINATIONS AT BAY.

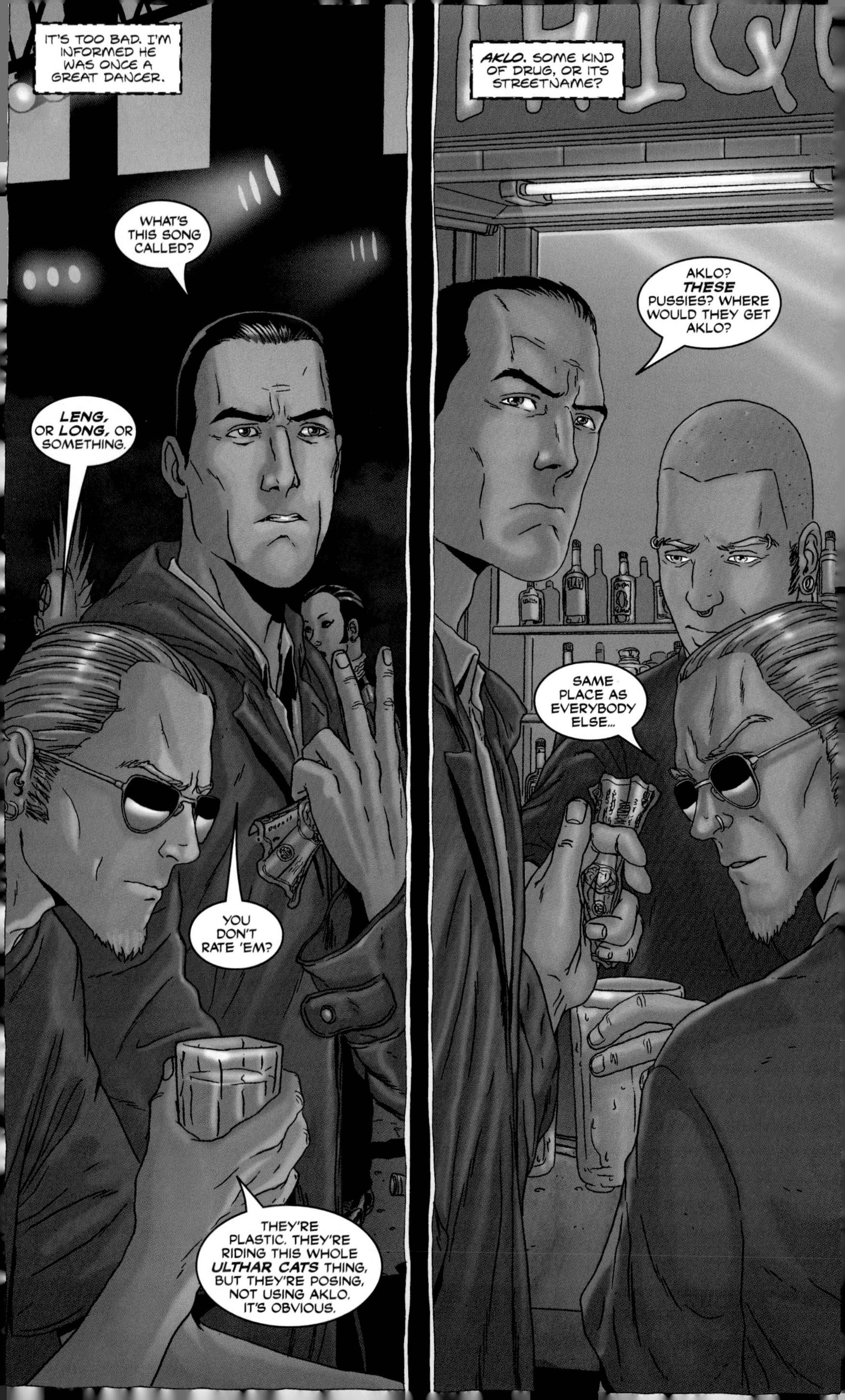
IT'S TOO BAD. I'M INFORMED HE WAS ONCE A GREAT DANCER.
WHAT'S THIS SONG CALLED?
LENG, OR *LONG,* OR SOMETHING.
YOU DON'T RATE 'EM?
THEY'RE PLASTIC. THEY'RE RIDING THIS WHOLE *ULTHAR CATS* THING, BUT THEY'RE POSING, NOT USING AKLO. IT'S OBVIOUS.
AKLO. SOME KIND OF DRUG, OR ITS STREETNAME?
AKLO? *THESE* PUSSIES? WHERE WOULD THEY GET AKLO?
SAME PLACE AS EVERYBODY ELSE...

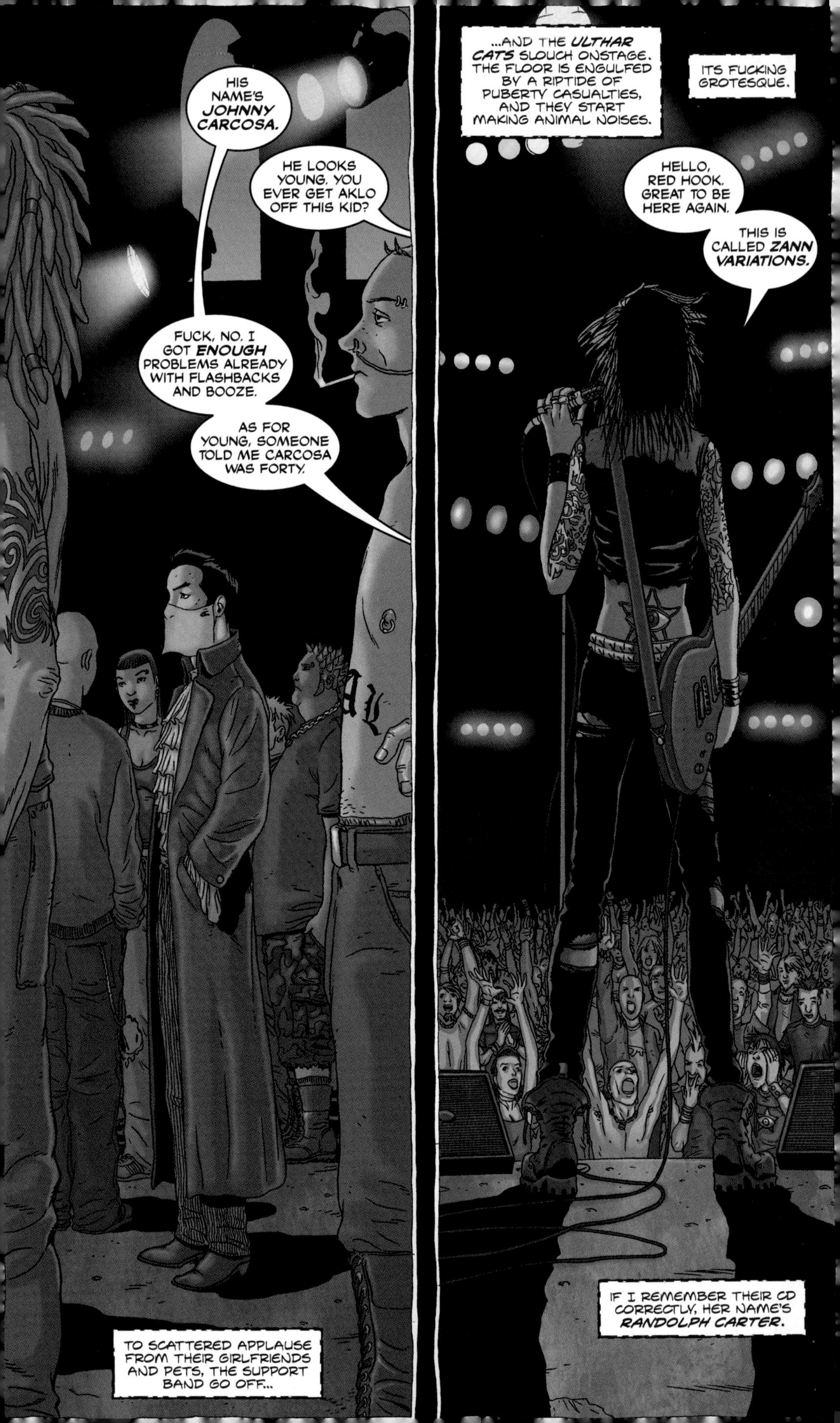
HIS NAME'S JOHNNY CARCOSA.
HE LOOKS YOUNG. YOU EVER GET AKLO OFF THIS KID?
FUCK, NO. I GOT ENOUGH PROBLEMS ALREADY WITH FLASHBACKS AND BOOZE.
AS FOR YOUNG, SOMEONE TOLD ME CARCOSA WAS FORTY.
TO SCATTERED APPLAUSE FROM THEIR GIRLFRIENDS AND PETS, THE SUPPORT BAND GO OFF...
...AND THE ULTHAR CATS SLOUCH ONSTAGE. THE FLOOR IS ENGULFED BY A RIPTIDE OF PUBERTY CASUALTIES, AND THEY START MAKING ANIMAL NOISES.
ITS FUCKING GROTESQUE.
HELLO, RED HOOK. GREAT TO BE HERE AGAIN.
THIS IS CALLED ZANN VARIATIONS.
IF I REMEMBER THEIR CD CORRECTLY, HER NAME'S RANDOLPH CARTER.

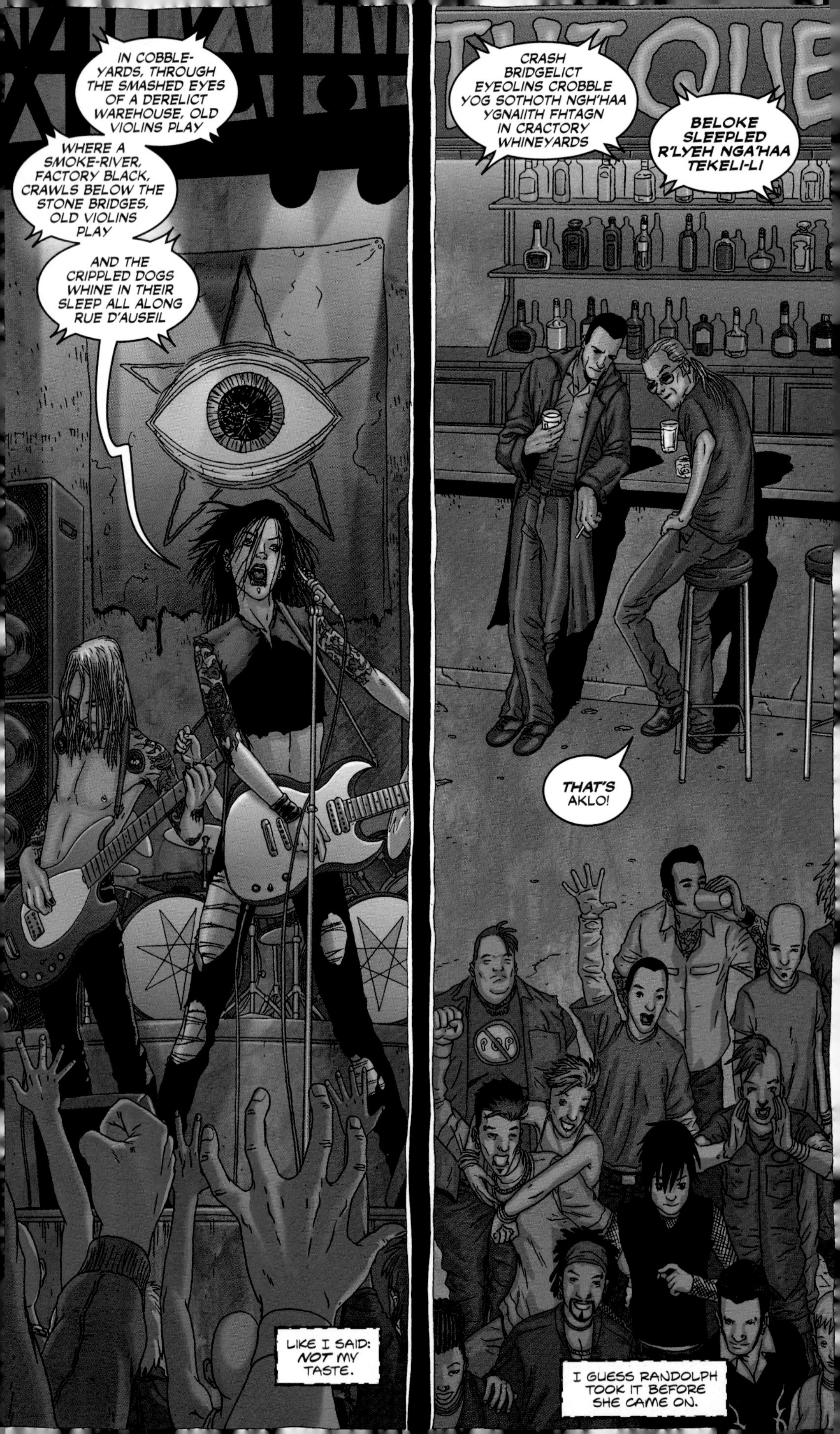
IN COBBLE-YARDS, THROUGH THE SMASHED EYES OF A DERELICT WAREHOUSE, OLD VIOLINS PLAY
WHERE A SMOKE-RIVER, FACTORY BLACK, CRAWLS BELOW THE STONE BRIDGES, OLD VIOLINS PLAY
AND THE CRIPPLED DOGS WHINE IN THEIR SLEEP ALL ALONG RUE D'AUSEIL
LIKE I SAID: *NOT* MY TASTE.
CRASH BRIDGELICT EYEOLINS CROBBLE YOG SOTHOTH NGH'HAA YGNAIITH FHTAGN IN CRACTORY WHINEYARDS
BELOKE SLEEPLED R'LYEH NGA'HAA TEKELI-LI
THAT'S AKLO!
I GUESS RANDOLPH TOOK IT BEFORE SHE CAME ON.

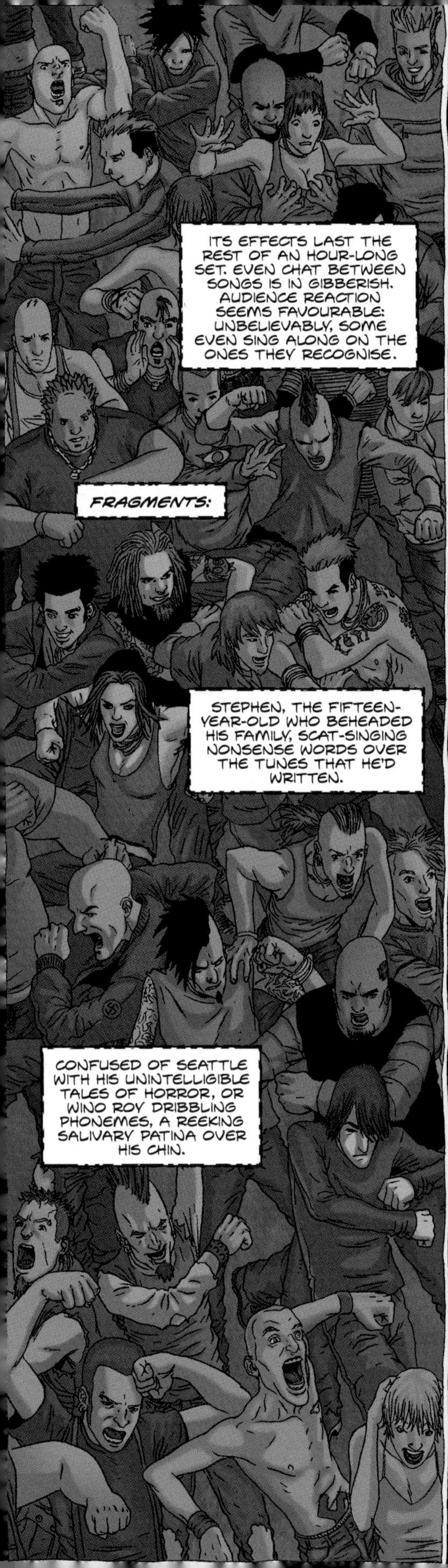
ITS EFFECTS LAST THE REST OF AN HOUR-LONG SET. EVEN CHAT BETWEEN SONGS IS IN GIBBERISH. AUDIENCE REACTION SEEMS FAVOURABLE: UNBELIEVABLY, SOME EVEN SING ALONG ON THE ONES THEY RECOGNISE.
FRAGMENTS:
STEPHEN, THE FIFTEEN-YEAR-OLD WHO BEHEADED HIS FAMILY, SCAT-SINGING NONSENSE WORDS OVER THE TUNES THAT HE'D WRITTEN.
CONFUSED OF SEATTLE WITH HIS UNINTELLIGIBLE TALES OF HORROR, OR WINO ROY DRIBBLING PHONEMES, A REEKING SALIVARY PATINA OVER HIS CHIN.

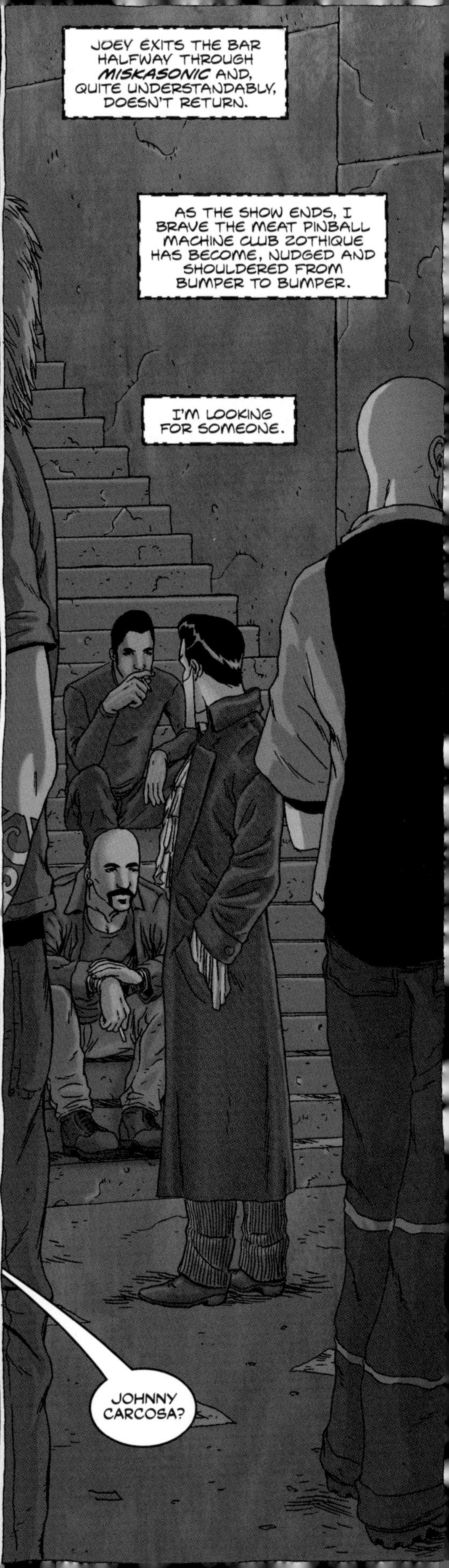
JOEY EXITS THE BAR HALFWAY THROUGH MISKASONIC AND, QUITE UNDERSTANDABLY, DOESN'T RETURN.
AS THE SHOW ENDS, I BRAVE THE MEAT PINBALL MACHINE CLUB ZOTHIQUE HAS BECOME, NUDGED AND SHOULDERED FROM BUMPER TO BUMPER.
I'M LOOKING FOR SOMEONE.
JOHNNY CARCOSA?

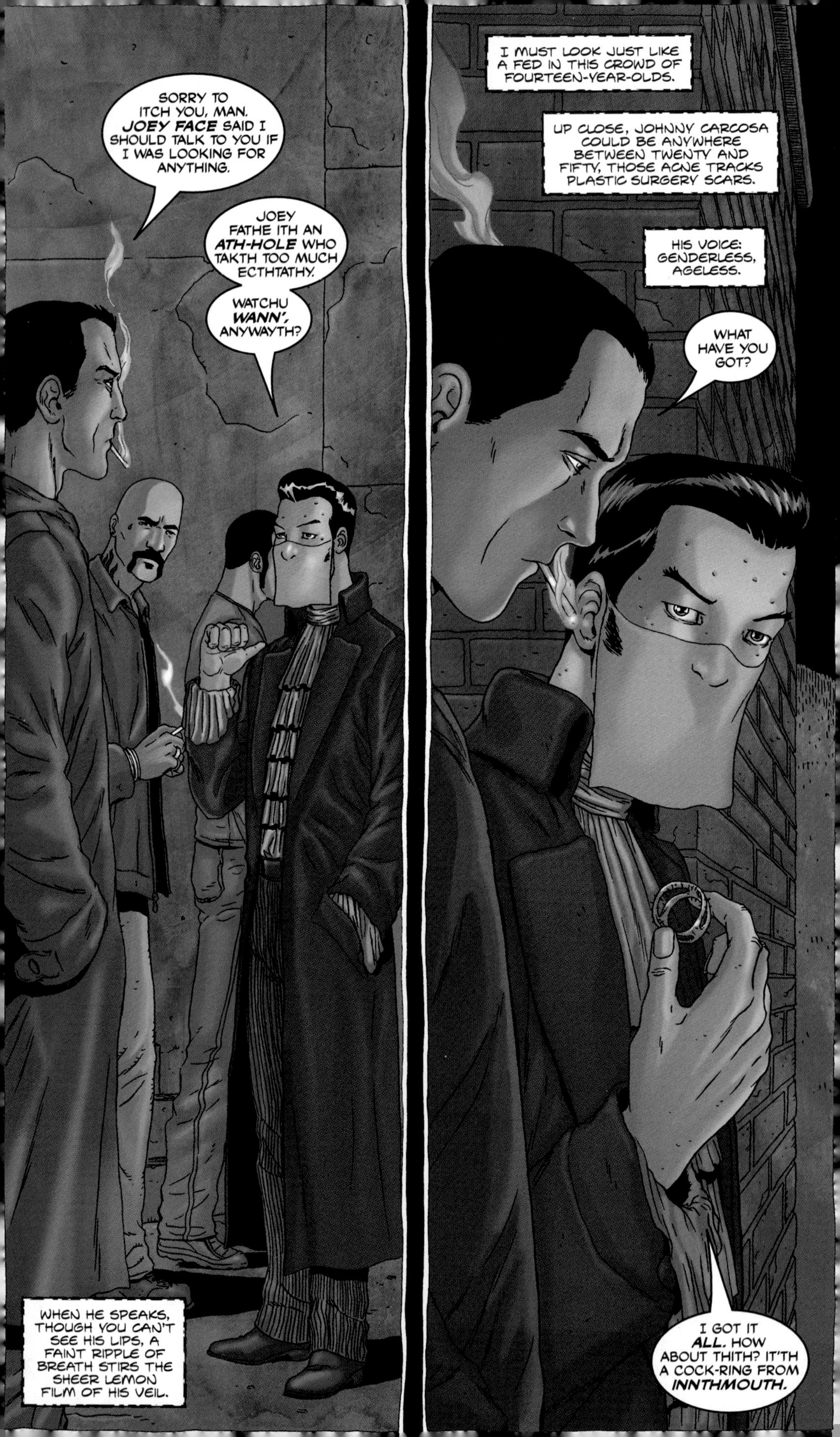
SORRY TO ITCH YOU, MAN. JOEY FACE SAID I SHOULD TALK TO YOU IF I WAS LOOKING FOR ANYTHING.
JOEY FATHE ITH AN ATH-HOLE WHO TAKTH TOO MUCH ECHTHTATHY.
WATCHU WANN', ANYWAYTH?
WHEN HE SPEAKS, THOUGH YOU CAN'T SEE HIS LIPS, A FAINT RIPPLE OF BREATH STIRS THE SHEER LEMON FILM OF HIS VEIL.
I MUST LOOK JUST LIKE A FED IN THIS CROWD OF FOURTEEN-YEAR-OLDS.
UP CLOSE, JOHNNY CARCOSA COULD BE ANYWHERE BETWEEN TWENTY AND FIFTY, THOSE ACNE TRACKS PLASTIC SURGERY SCARS.
HIS VOICE: GENDERLESS, AGELESS.
WHAT HAVE YOU GOT?
I GOT IT ALL. HOW ABOUT THITH? IT'TH A COCK-RING FROM INNTHMOUTH.

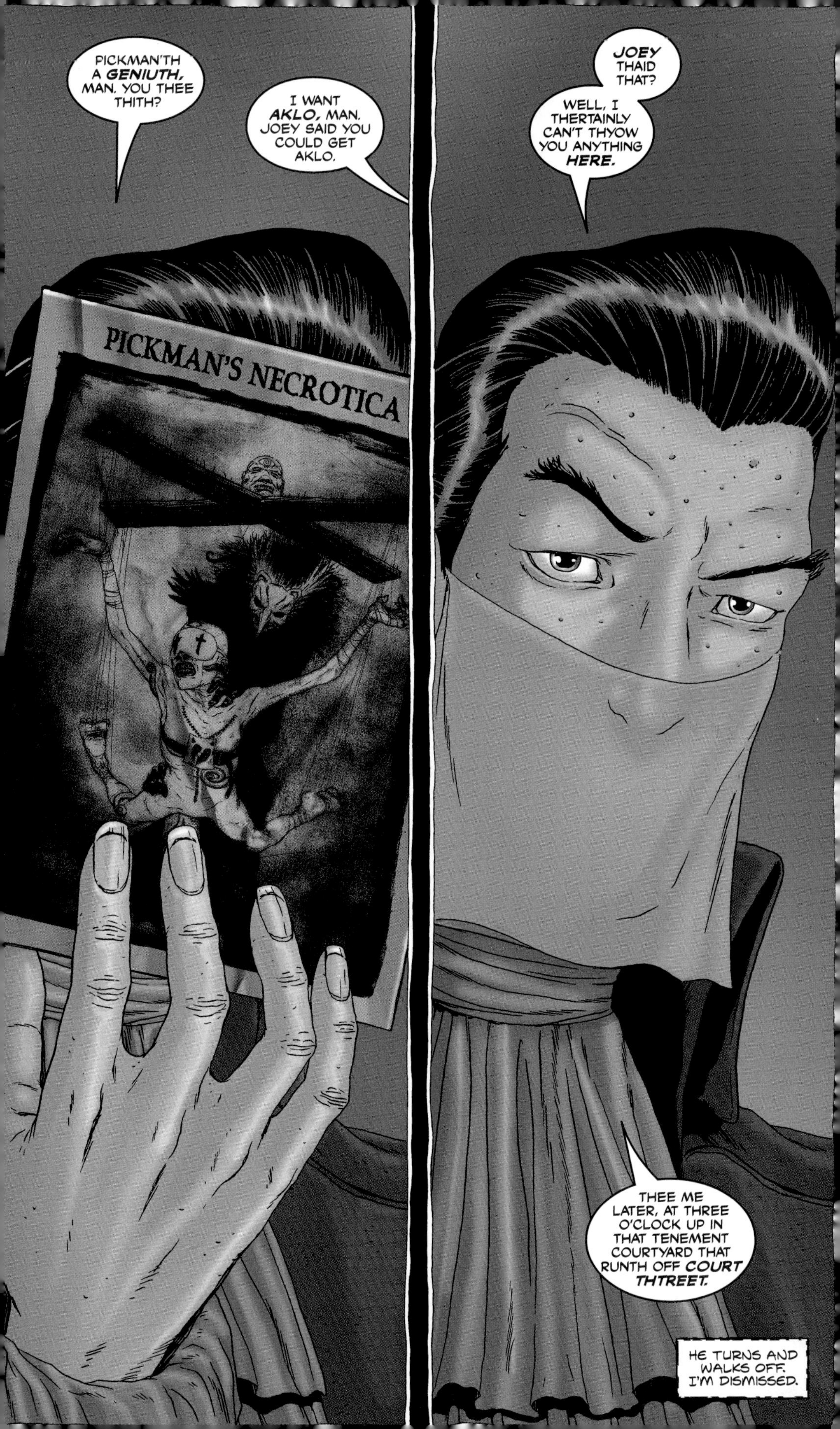
PICKMAN'TH A **GENIUTH,** MAN. YOU THEE THITH?
I WANT **AKLO,** MAN. JOEY SAID YOU COULD GET AKLO.
PICKMAN'S NECROTICA
JOEY THAID THAT?
WELL, I THERTAINLY CAN'T THYOW YOU ANYTHING **HERE.**
THEE ME LATER, AT THREE O'CLOCK UP IN THAT TENEMENT COURTYARD THAT RUNTH OFF **COURT THTREET.**
HE TURNS AND WALKS OFF. I'M DISMISSED.

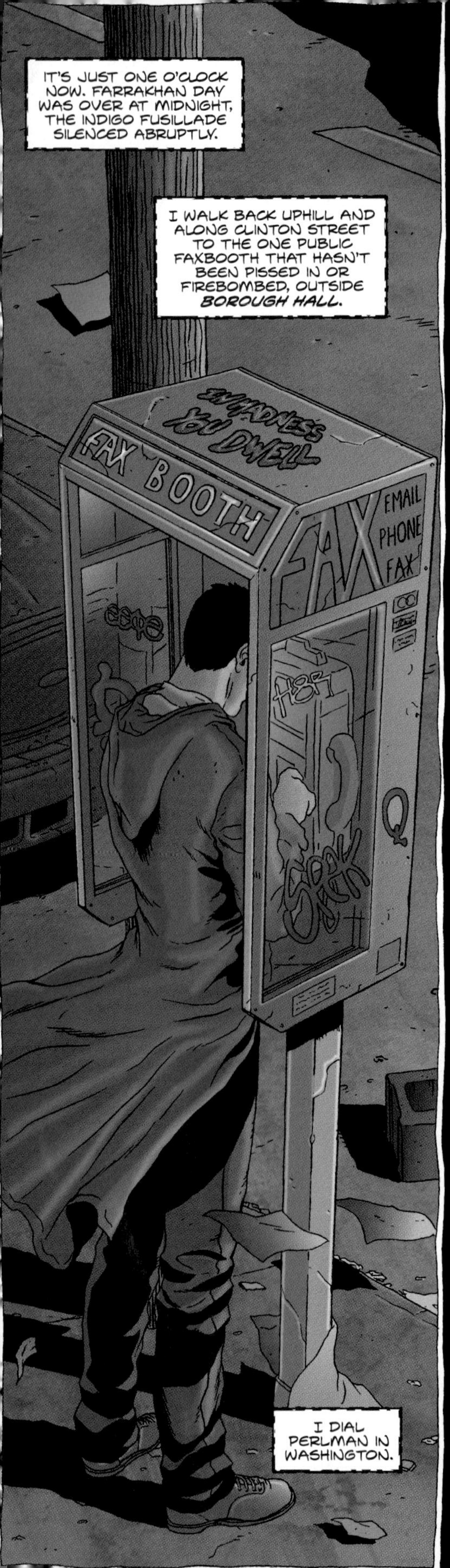
IT'S JUST ONE O'CLOCK NOW. FARRAKHAN DAY WAS OVER AT MIDNIGHT, THE INDIGO FUSILLADE SILENCED ABRUPTLY.
I WALK BACK UPHILL AND ALONG CLINTON STREET TO THE ONE PUBLIC FAXBOOTH THAT HASN'T BEEN PISSED IN OR FIREBOMBED, OUTSIDE ***BOROUGH HALL.***
IN MADNESS YOU DWELL
FAX BOOTH
FAX
EMAIL
PHONE
FAX
I DIAL PERLMAN IN WASHINGTON.

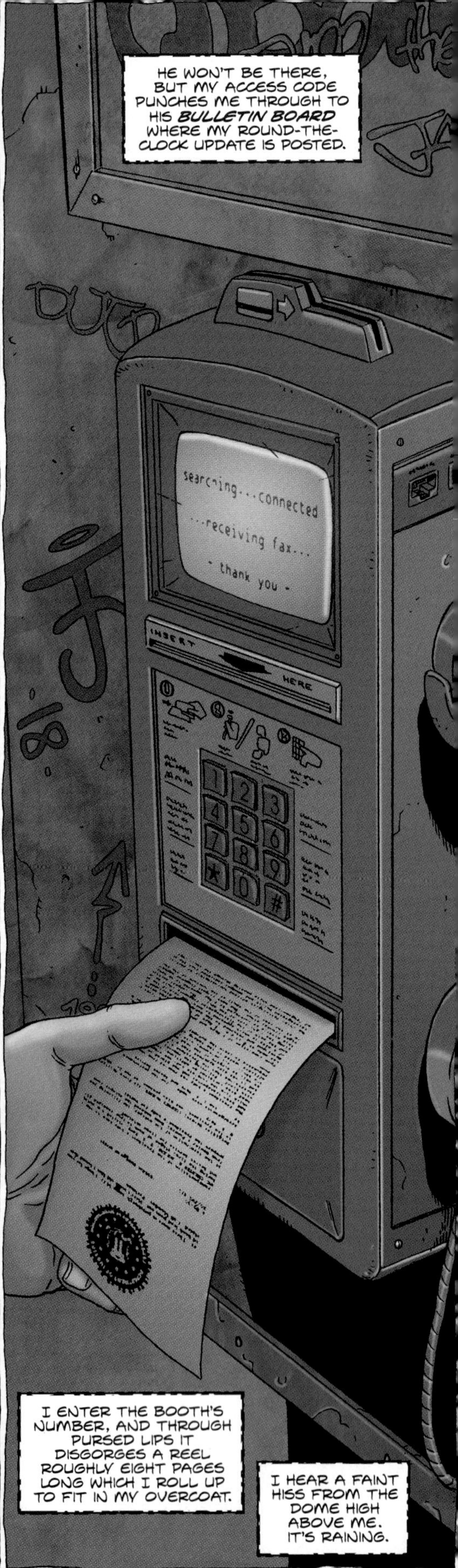
HE WON'T BE THERE, BUT MY ACCESS CODE PUNCHES ME THROUGH TO HIS ***BULLETIN BOARD*** WHERE MY ROUND-THE-CLOCK UPDATE IS POSTED.
searching...connected
...receiving fax...
- thank you -
INSERT
HERE
I ENTER THE BOOTH'S NUMBER, AND THROUGH PURSED LIPS IT DISGORGES A REEL ROUGHLY EIGHT PAGES LONG WHICH I ROLL UP TO FIT IN MY OVERCOAT.
I HEAR A FAINT HISS FROM THE DOME HIGH ABOVE ME. IT'S RAINING.

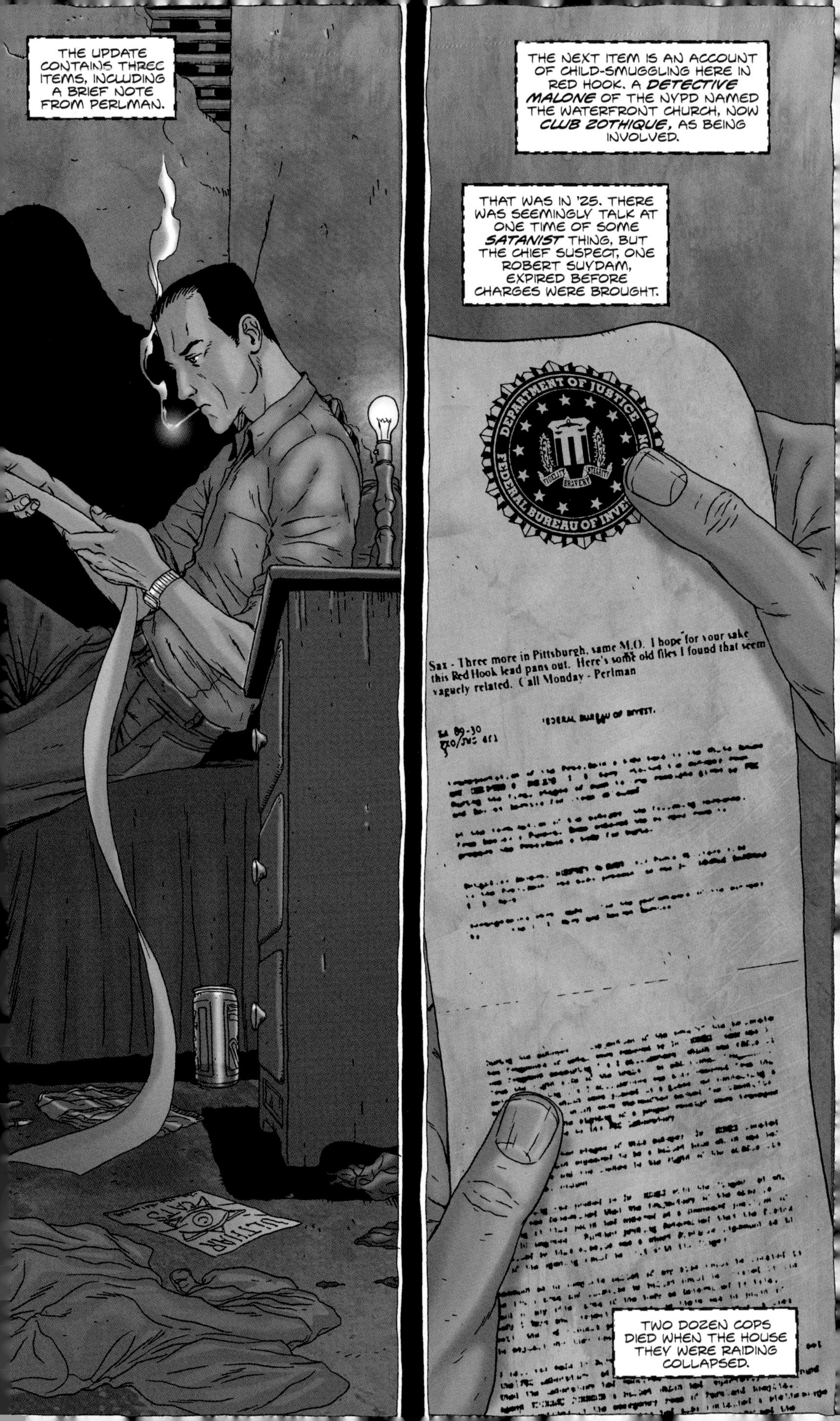
THE UPDATE CONTAINS THREE ITEMS, INCLUDING A BRIEF NOTE FROM PERLMAN.
THE NEXT ITEM IS AN ACCOUNT OF CHILD-SMUGGLING HERE IN RED HOOK. A DETECTIVE MALONE OF THE NYPD NAMED THE WATERFRONT CHURCH, NOW CLUB ZOTHIQUE, AS BEING INVOLVED.
THAT WAS IN '25. THERE WAS SEEMINGLY TALK AT ONE TIME OF SOME SATANIST THING, BUT THE CHIEF SUSPECT, ONE ROBERT SUYDAM, EXPIRED BEFORE CHARGES WERE BROUGHT.
DEPARTMENT OF JUSTICE
FIDELITY BRAVERY INTEGRITY
FEDERAL BUREAU OF INVE
Sax - Three more in Pittsburgh, same M.O. I hope for your sake this Red Hook lead pans out. Here's some old files I found that seem vaguely related. Call Monday - Perlman
FEDERAL BUREAU OF INVEST.
TWO DOZEN COPS DIED WHEN THE HOUSE THEY WERE RAIDING COLLAPSED.

THE LAST PRINT-OUT CONCERNS *FBI* OPERATIONS UP IN MASSACHUSETTS AROUND TWO YEARS LATER; 1927-28.

THE CONNECTION APPEARS TO BE *SUYDAM*-- SHORTLY BEFORE HIS DEMISE, HE ORDERED "RITUAL ARTEFACTS" FROM A REMOTE GOLD REFINERY IN SOME BACKWATER SEAPORT OF MASSACHUSETTS. THE TOWN'S NAME IS BLACKED OUT. *CLASSIFIED*, OBVIOUSLY.

THERE'S GOOD OLD *J EDGAR* HIMSELF. WHERE--

OH, *I* GET IT. THIS MUST BE THE CLASSIFIED SEAPORT.

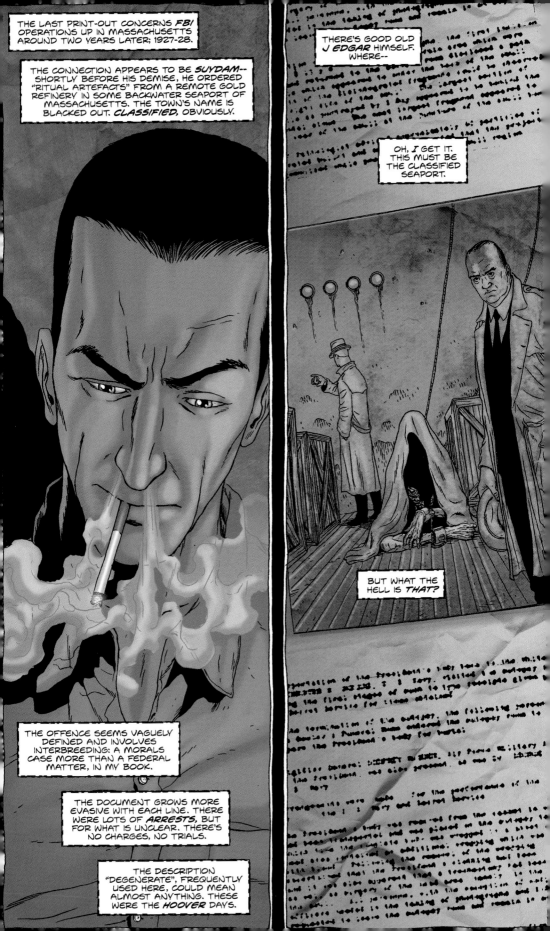

BUT WHAT THE HELL IS *THAT?*

THE OFFENCE SEEMS VAGUELY DEFINED AND INVOLVES INTERBREEDING: A MORALS CASE MORE THAN A FEDERAL MATTER, IN MY BOOK.

THE DOCUMENT GROWS MORE EVASIVE WITH EACH LINE. THERE WERE LOTS OF *ARRESTS*, BUT FOR WHAT IS UNCLEAR. THERE'S NO CHARGES, NO TRIALS.

THE DESCRIPTION "DEGENERATE", FREQUENTLY USED HERE, COULD MEAN ALMOST ANYTHING. THESE WERE THE *HOOVER* DAYS.

THE COURTYARD
Chapter 2

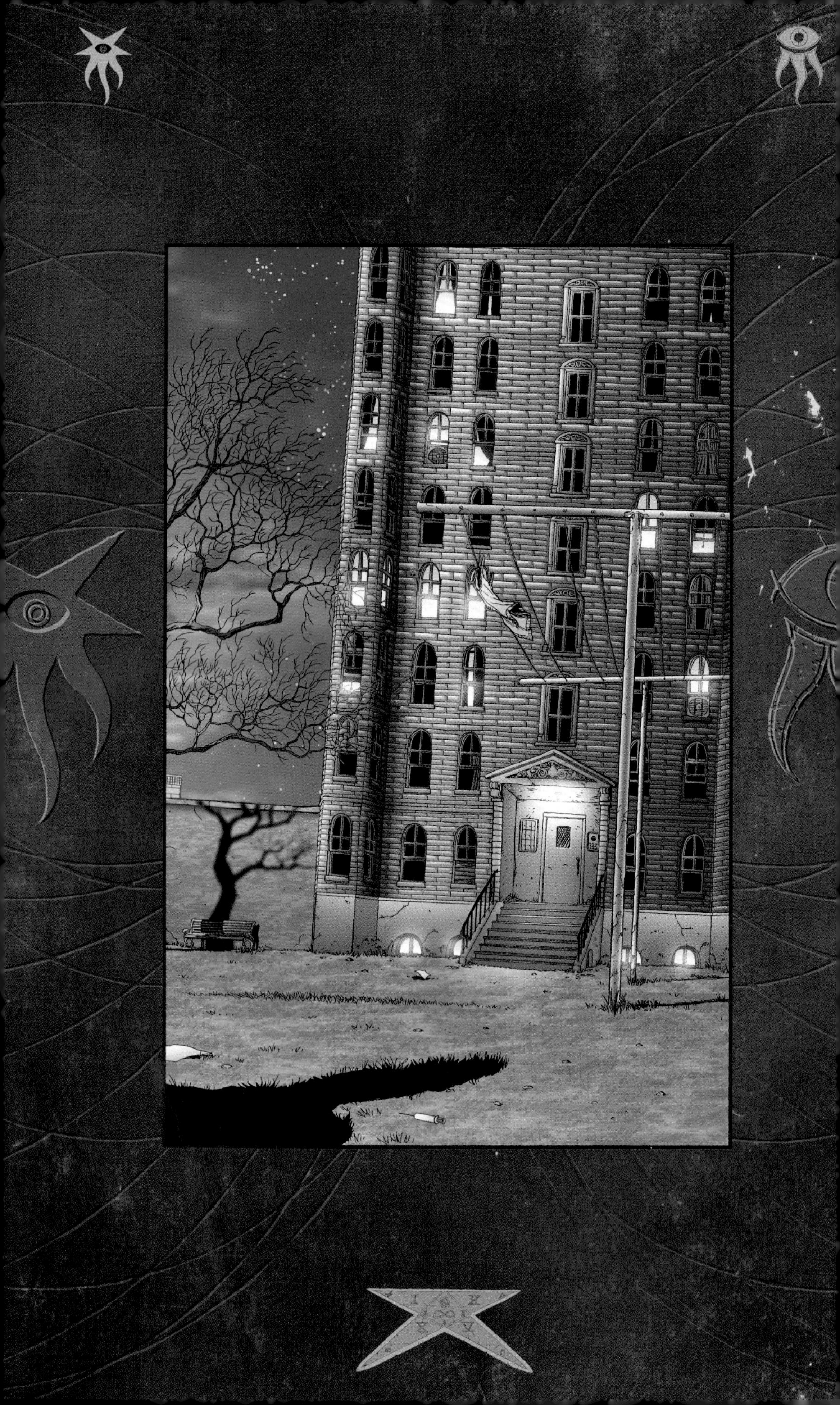

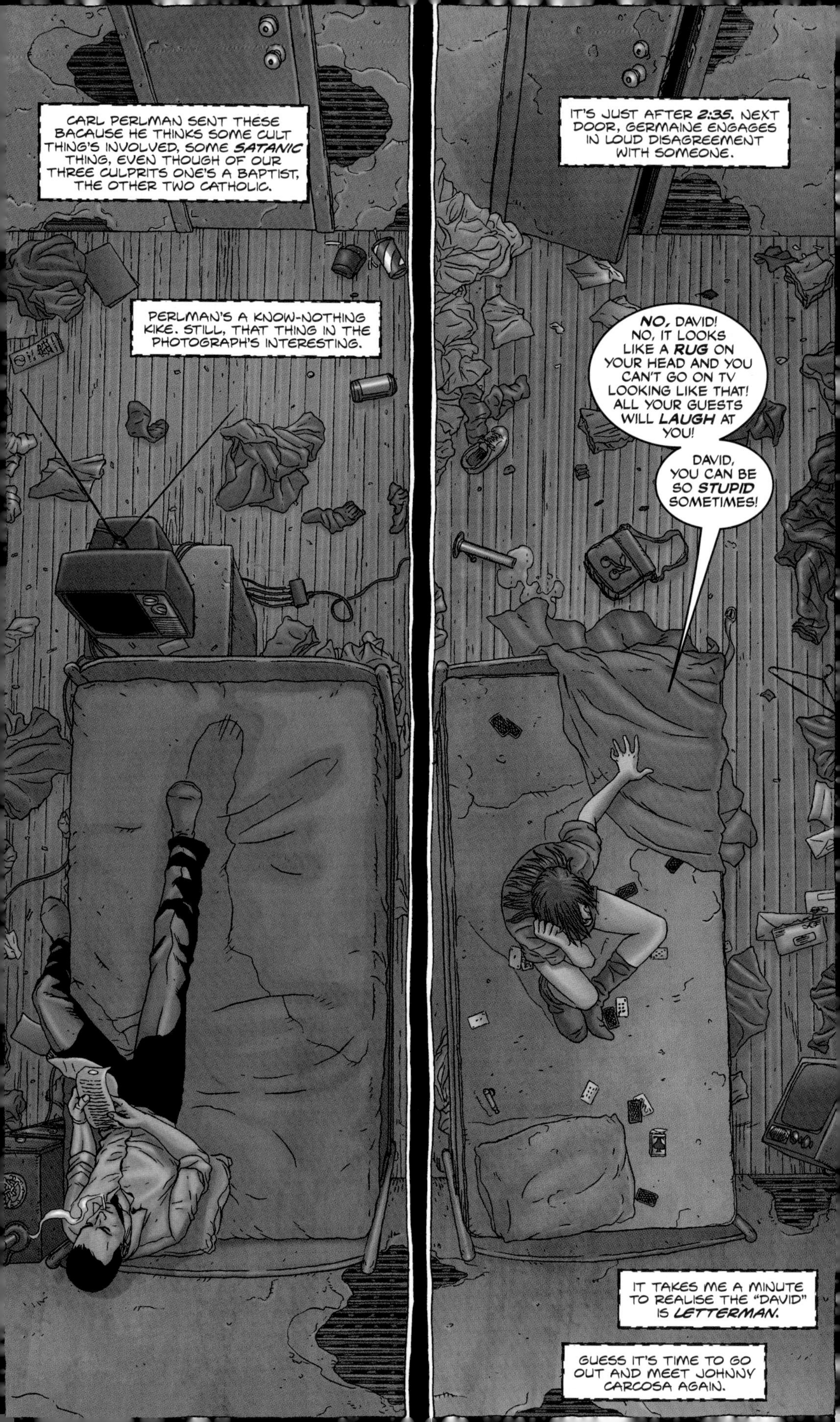
CARL PERLMAN SENT THESE BACAUSE HE THINKS SOME CULT THING'S INVOLVED, SOME SATANIC THING, EVEN THOUGH OF OUR THREE CULPRITS ONE'S A BAPTIST, THE OTHER TWO CATHOLIC.
PERLMAN'S A KNOW-NOTHING KIKE. STILL, THAT THING IN THE PHOTOGRAPH'S INTERESTING.
IT'S JUST AFTER 2:35. NEXT DOOR, GERMAINE ENGAGES IN LOUD DISAGREEMENT WITH SOMEONE.
NO, DAVID! NO, IT LOOKS LIKE A RUG ON YOUR HEAD AND YOU CAN'T GO ON TV LOOKING LIKE THAT! ALL YOUR GUESTS WILL LAUGH AT YOU!
DAVID, YOU CAN BE SO STUPID SOMETIMES!
IT TAKES ME A MINUTE TO REALISE THE "DAVID" IS LETTERMAN.
GUESS IT'S TIME TO GO OUT AND MEET JOHNNY CARCOSA AGAIN.

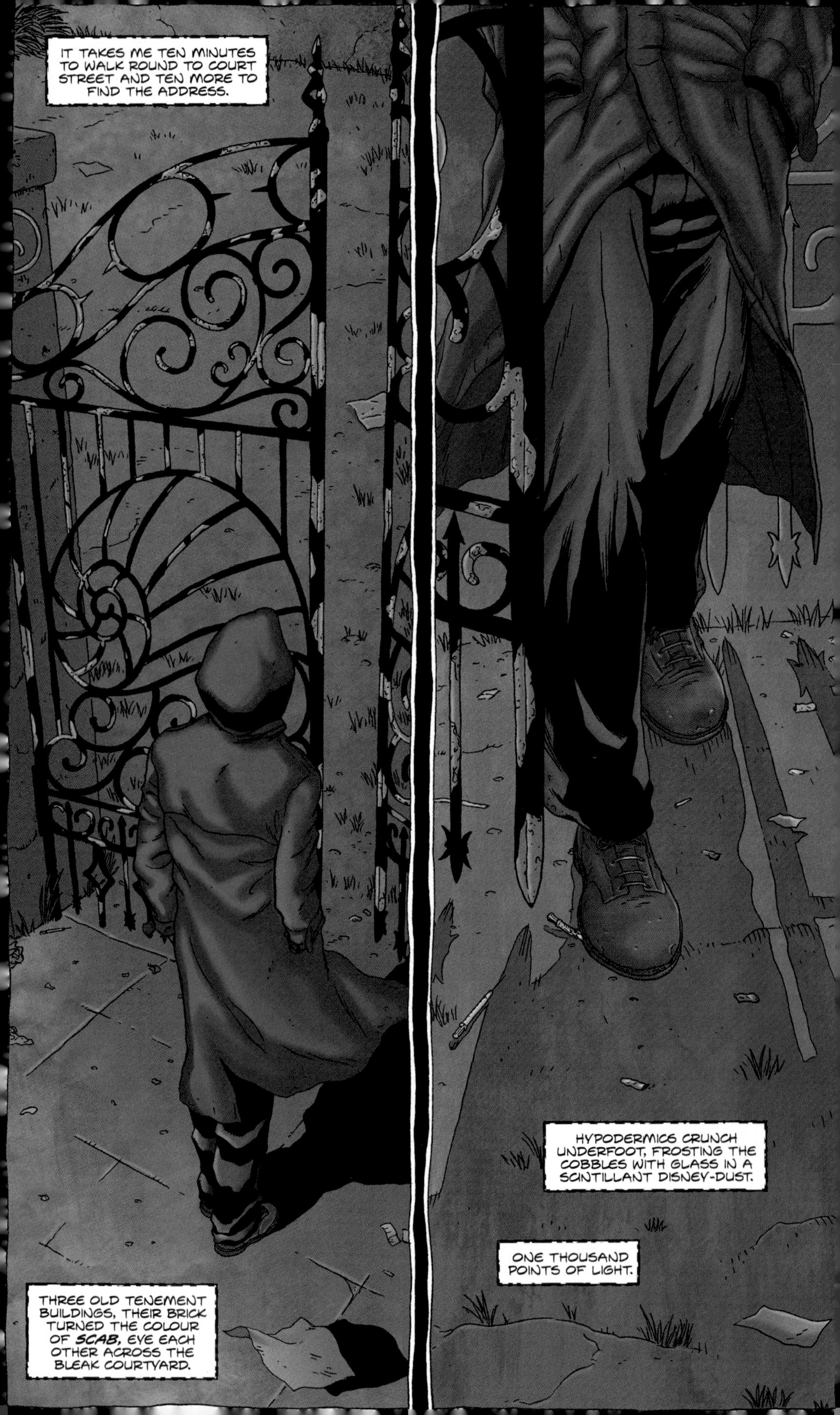
IT TAKES ME TEN MINUTES TO WALK ROUND TO COURT STREET AND TEN MORE TO FIND THE ADDRESS.
THREE OLD TENEMENT BUILDINGS, THEIR BRICK TURNED THE COLOUR OF SCAB, EYE EACH OTHER ACROSS THE BLEAK COURTYARD.
HYPODERMICS CRUNCH UNDERFOOT, FROSTING THE COBBLES WITH GLASS IN A SCINTILLANT DISNEY-DUST.
ONE THOUSAND POINTS OF LIGHT.

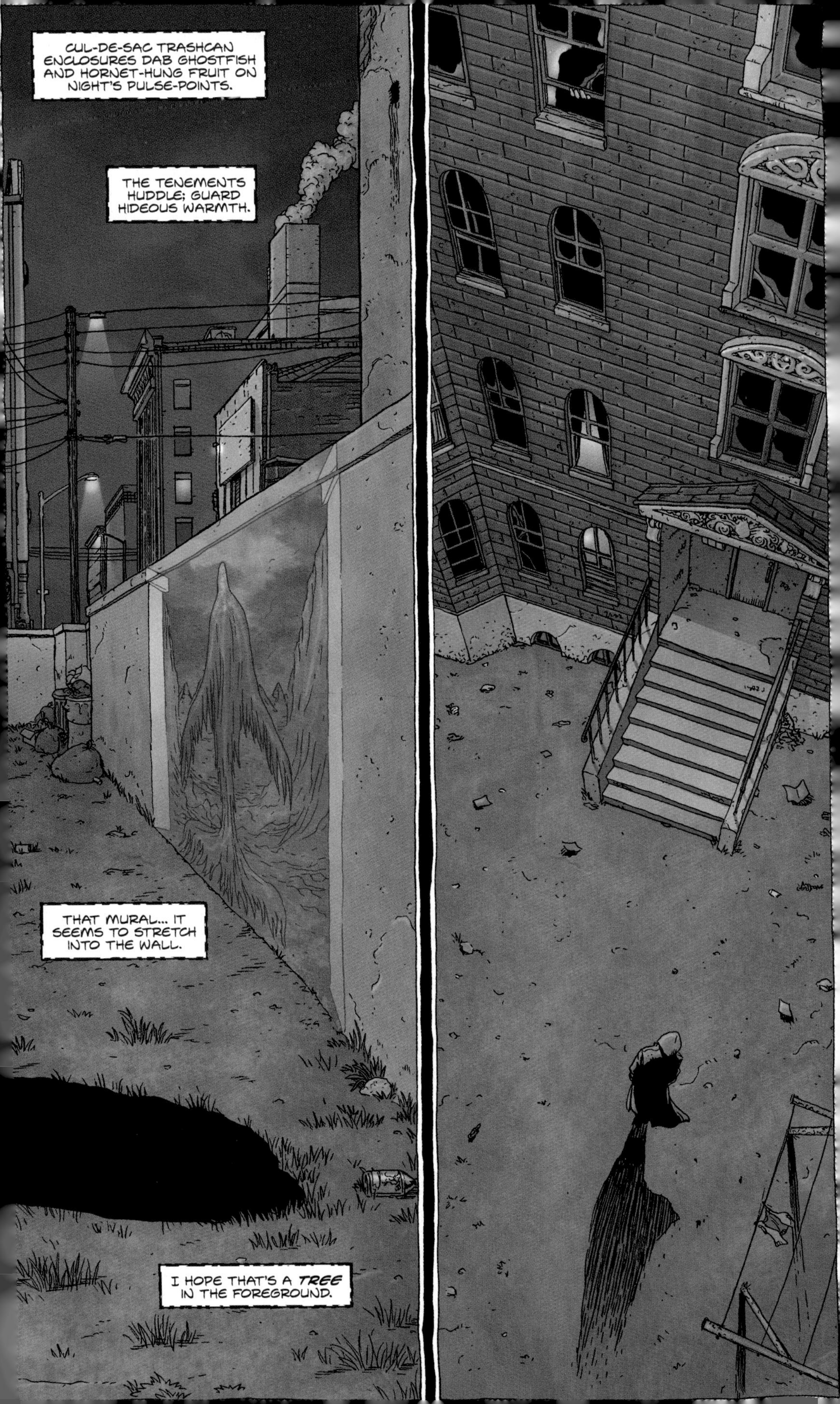
CUL-DE-SAC TRASHCAN ENCLOSURES DAB GHOSTFISH AND HORNET-HUNG FRUIT ON NIGHT'S PULSE-POINTS.
THE TENEMENTS HUDDLE; GUARD HIDEOUS WARMTH.
THAT MURAL... IT SEEMS TO STRETCH INTO THE WALL.
I HOPE THAT'S A *TREE* IN THE FOREGROUND.

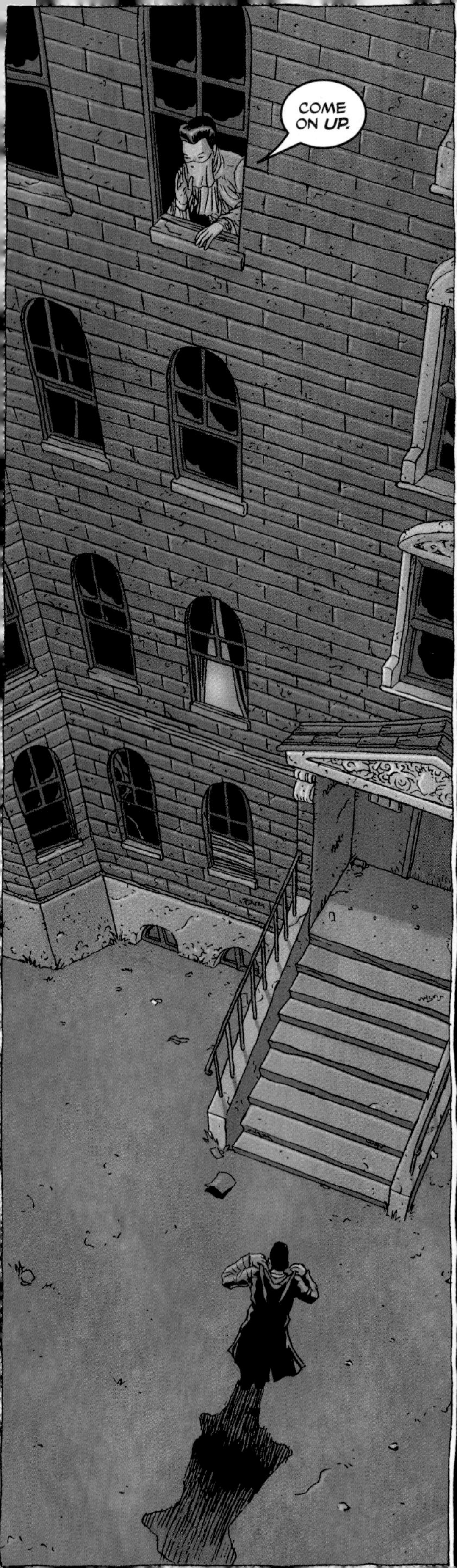
COME ON *UP*.

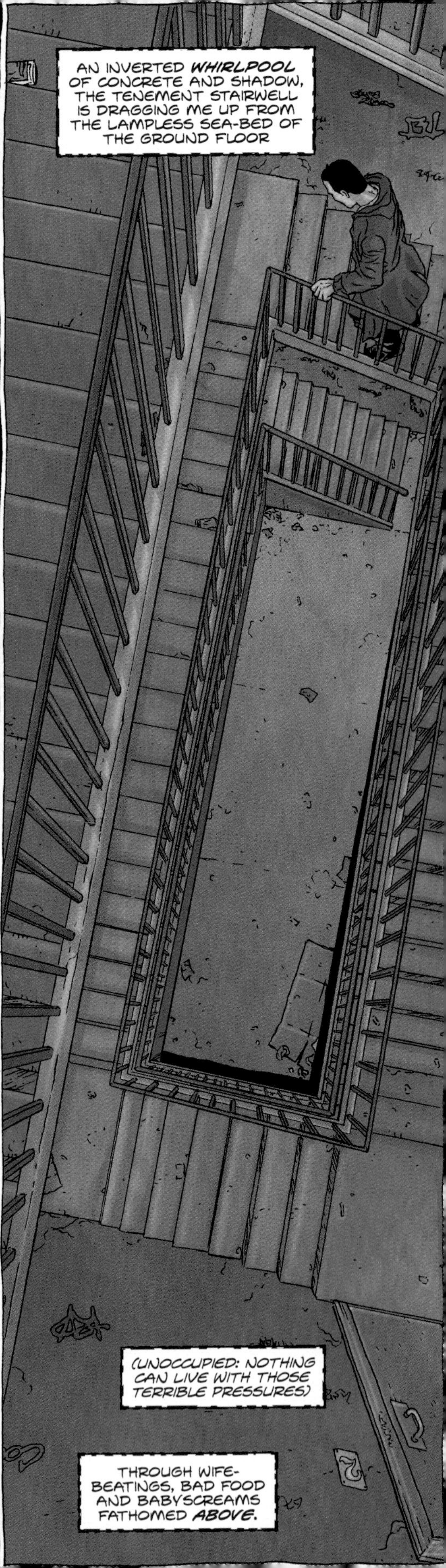
AN INVERTED *WHIRLPOOL* OF CONCRETE AND SHADOW, THE TENEMENT STAIRWELL IS DRAGGING ME UP FROM THE LAMPLESS SEA-BED OF THE GROUND FLOOR
(UNOCCUPIED: NOTHING CAN LIVE WITH THOSE TERRIBLE PRESSURES)
THROUGH WIFE-BEATINGS, BAD FOOD AND BABYSCREAMS FATHOMED *ABOVE*.

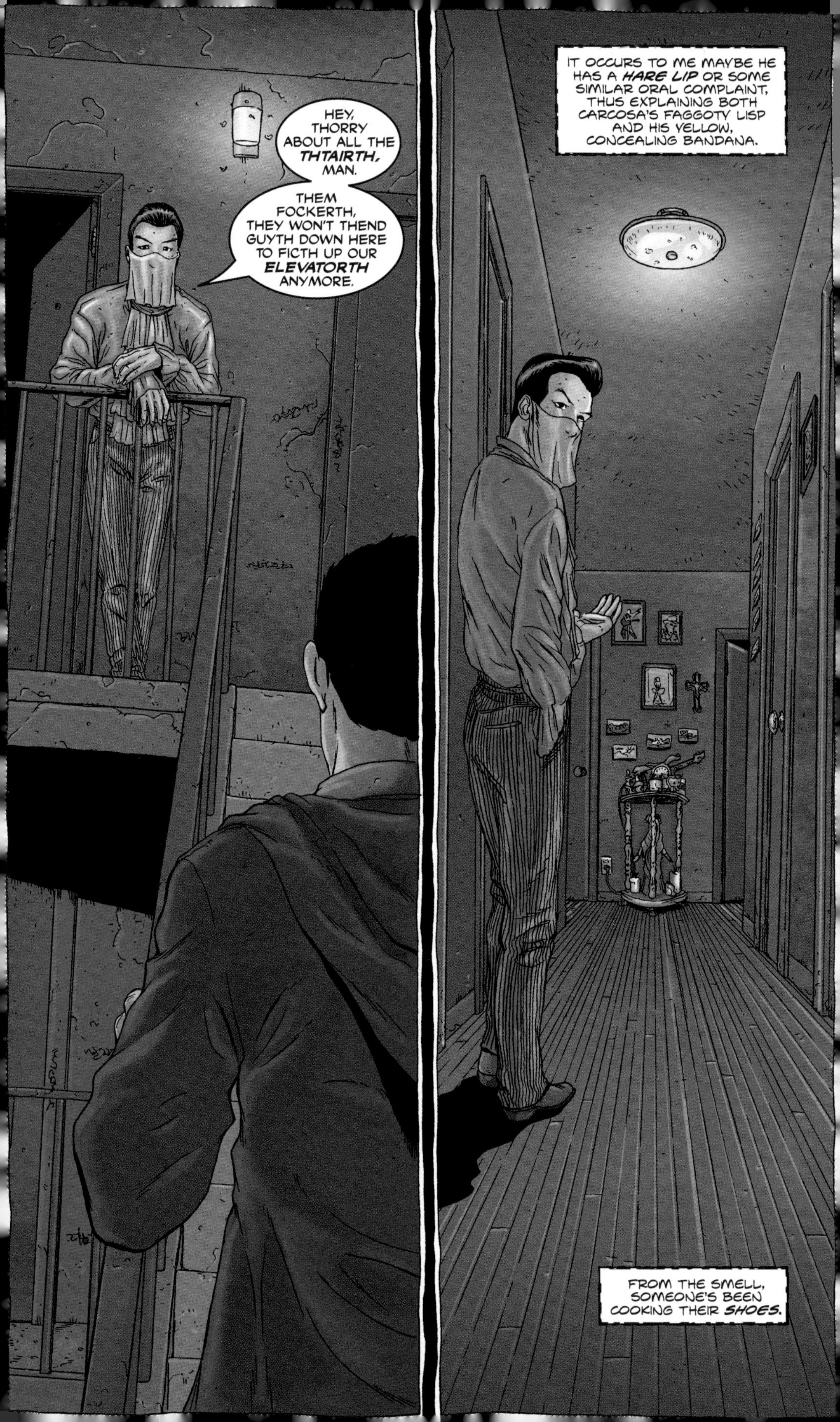
HEY, THORRY ABOUT ALL THE THTAIRTH, MAN.
THEM FOCKERTH, THEY WON'T THEND GUYTH DOWN HERE TO FICTH UP OUR ELEVATORTH ANYMORE.
IT OCCURS TO ME MAYBE HE HAS A HARE LIP OR SOME SIMILAR ORAL COMPLAINT, THUS EXPLAINING BOTH CARCOSA'S FAGGOTY LISP AND HIS YELLOW, CONCEALING BANDANA.
FROM THE SMELL, SOMEONE'S BEEN COOKING THEIR SHOES.

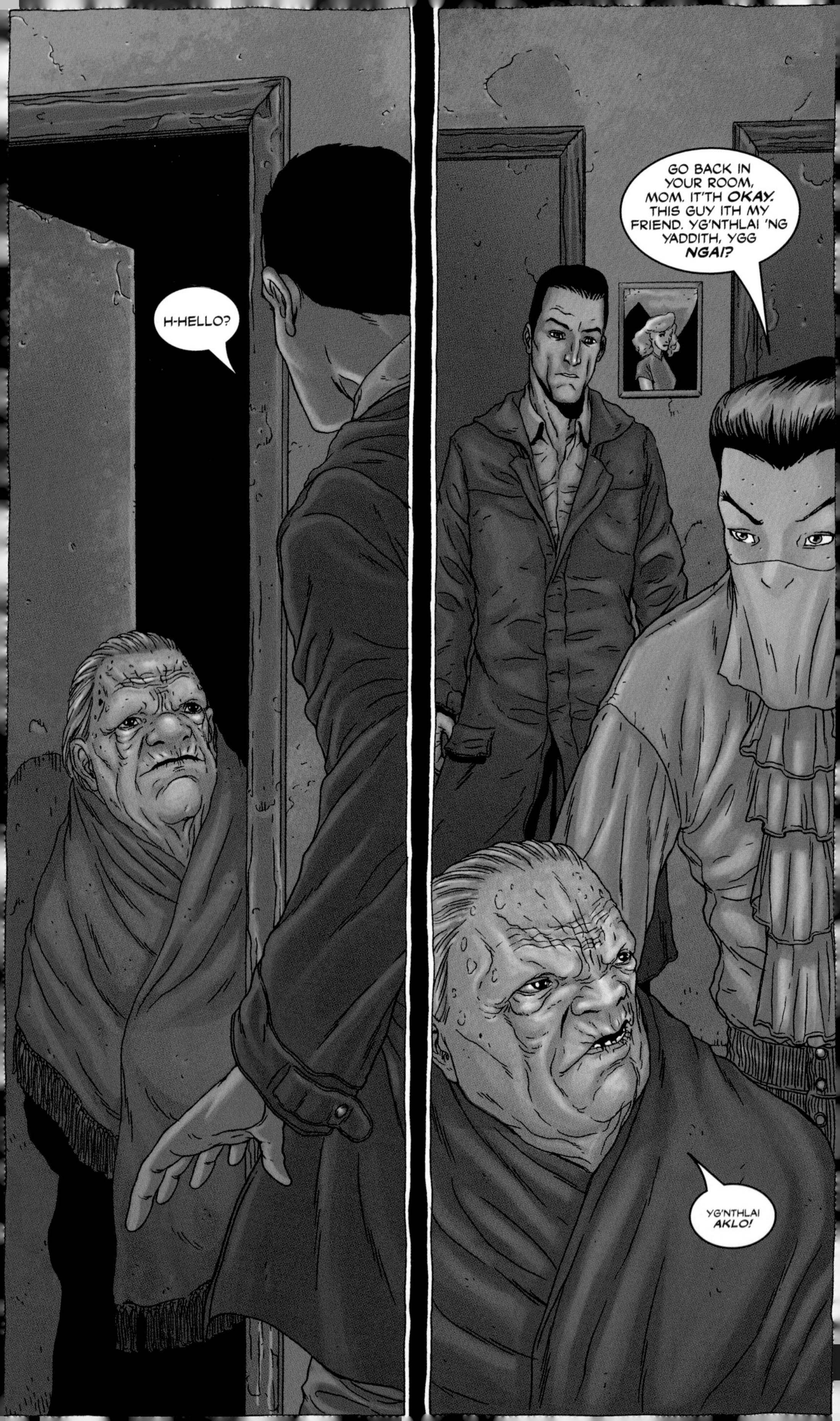
H-HELLO?
GO BACK IN YOUR ROOM, MOM. IT'TH OKAY. THIS GUY ITH MY FRIEND. YG'NTHLAI 'NG YADDITH, YGG NGAI?
YG'NTHLAI AKLO!

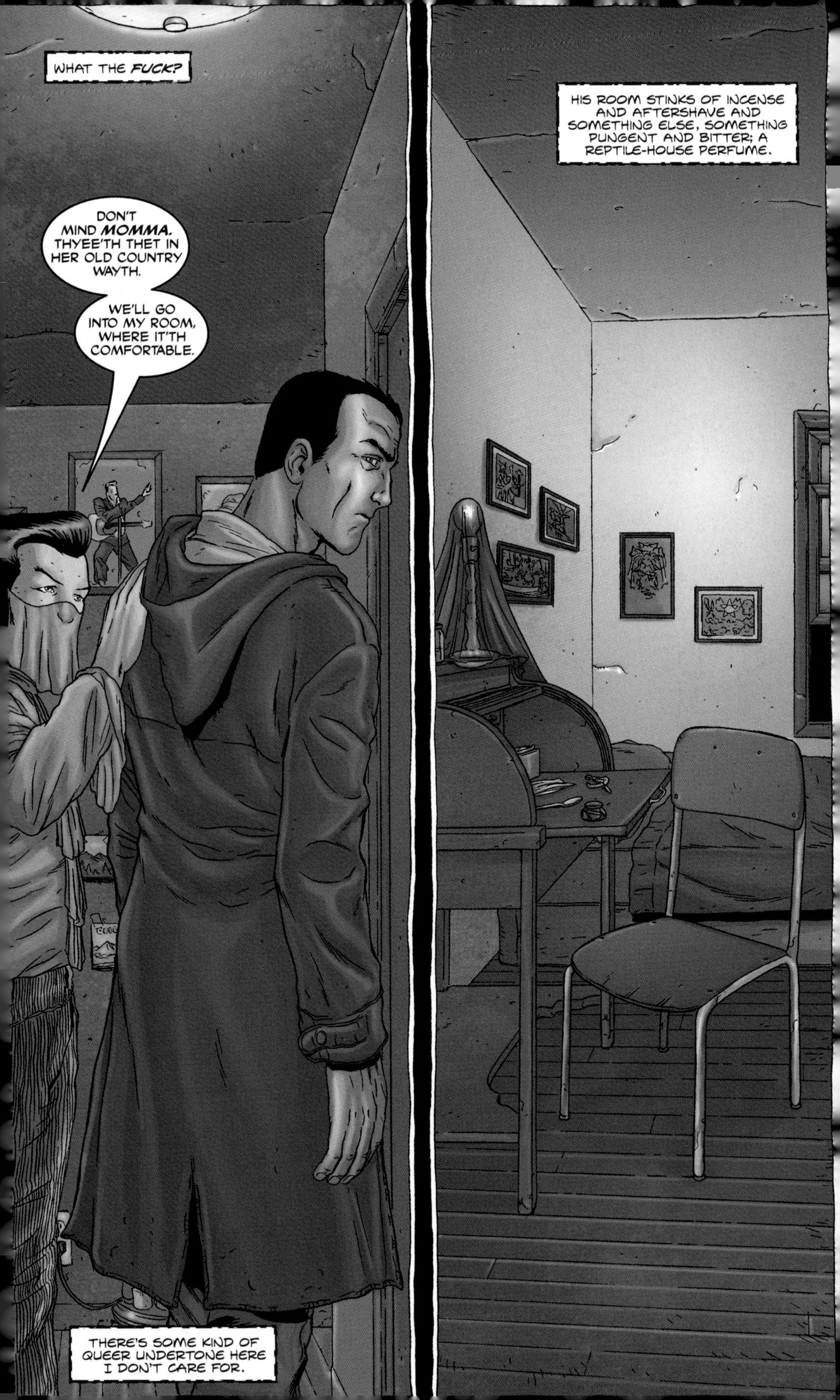
WHAT THE FUCK?
DON'T MIND MOMMA. THYEE'TH THET IN HER OLD COUNTRY WAYTH.
WE'LL GO INTO MY ROOM, WHERE IT'TH COMFORTABLE.
THERE'S SOME KIND OF QUEER UNDERTONE HERE I DON'T CARE FOR.
HIS ROOM STINKS OF INCENSE AND AFTERSHAVE AND SOMETHING ELSE, SOMETHING PUNGENT AND BITTER; A REPTILE-HOUSE PERFUME.

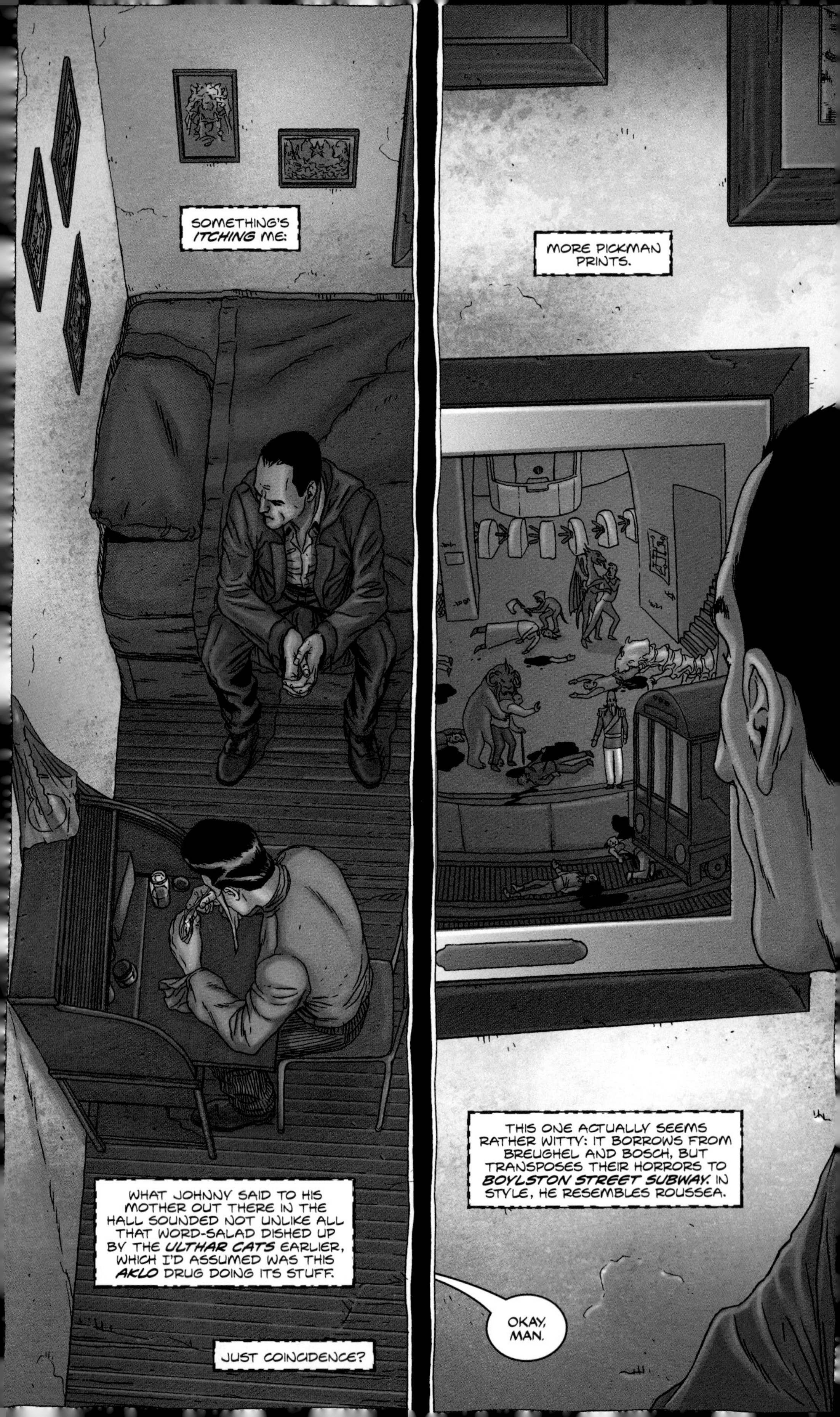

SOMETHING'S *ITCHING* ME:
MORE PICKMAN PRINTS.
WHAT JOHNNY SAID TO HIS MOTHER OUT THERE IN THE HALL SOUNDED NOT UNLIKE ALL THAT WORD-SALAD DISHED UP BY THE *ULTHAR CATS* EARLIER, WHICH I'D ASSUMED WAS THIS *AKLO* DRUG DOING ITS STUFF.
JUST COINCIDENCE?
THIS ONE ACTUALLY SEEMS RATHER WITTY: IT BORROWS FROM BREUGHEL AND BOSCH, BUT TRANSPOSES THEIR HORRORS TO *BOYLSTON STREET SUBWAY.* IN STYLE, HE RESEMBLES ROUSSEA.
OKAY, MAN.

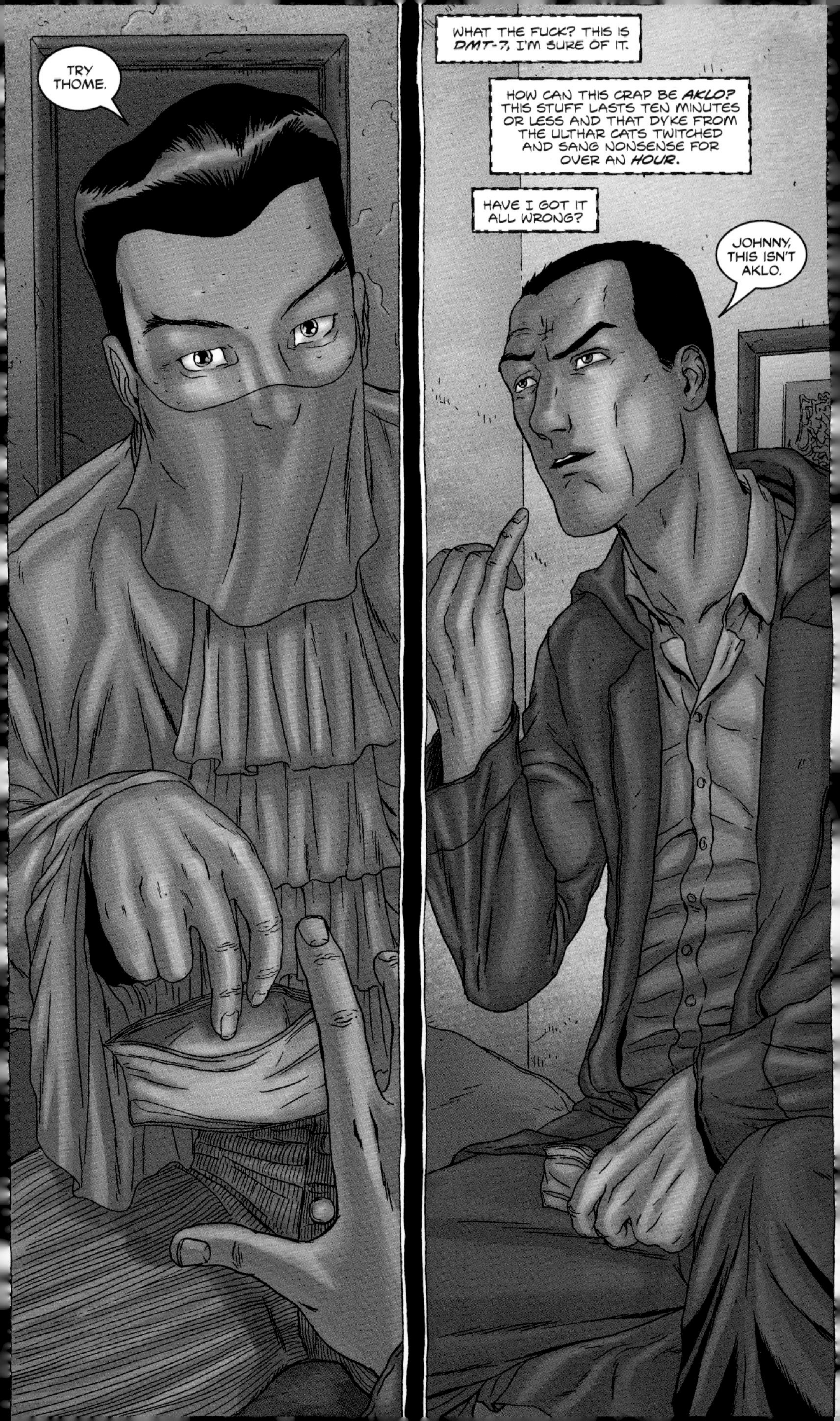
TRY THOME.
WHAT THE FUCK? THIS IS DMT-7, I'M SURE OF IT.
HOW CAN THIS CRAP BE AKLO? THIS STUFF LASTS TEN MINUTES OR LESS AND THAT DYKE FROM THE ULTHAR CATS TWITCHED AND SANG NONSENSE FOR OVER AN HOUR.
HAVE I GOT IT ALL WRONG?
JOHNNY, THIS ISN'T AKLO.

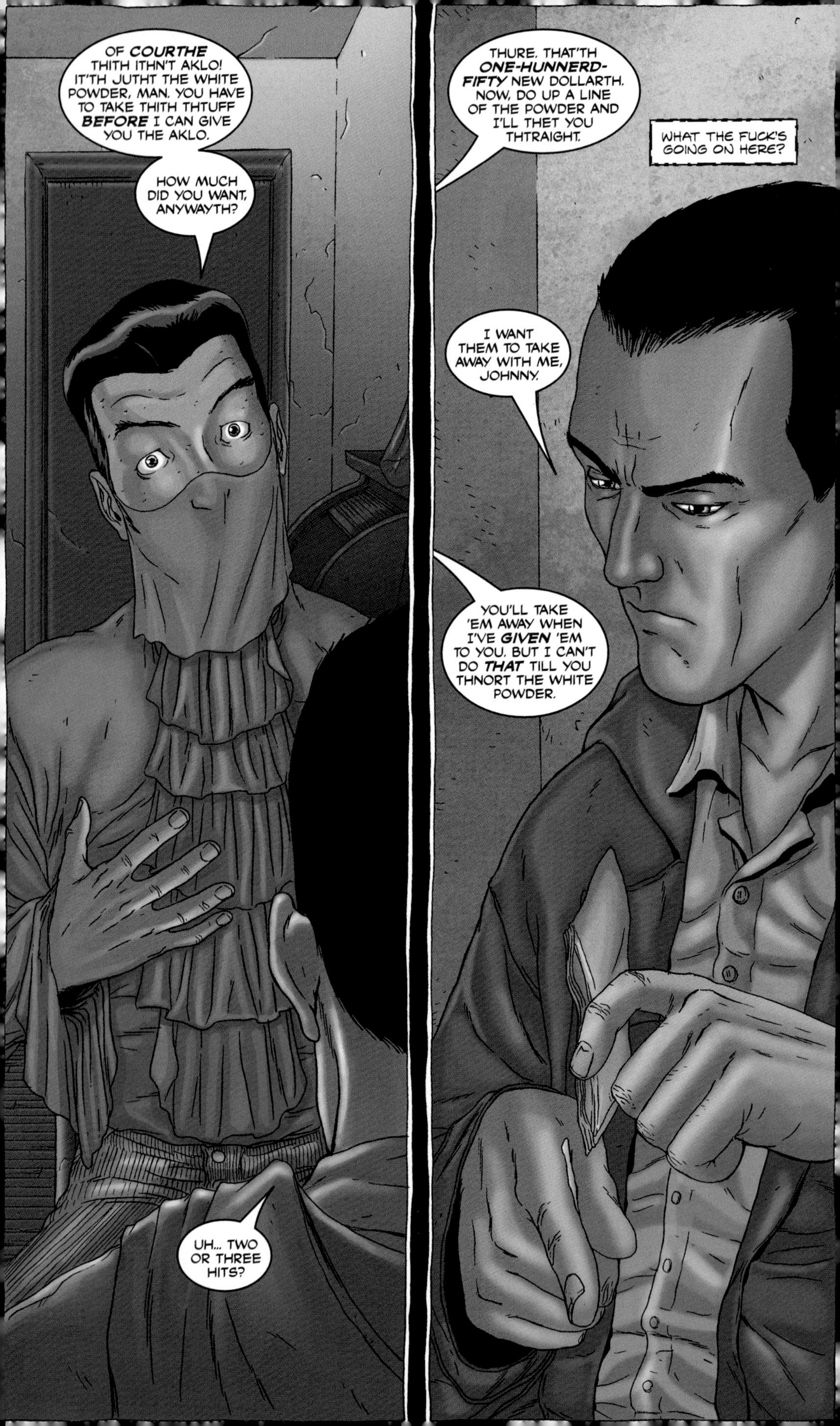
OF **COURTHE** THITH ITHN'T AKLO! IT'TH JUTHT THE WHITE POWDER, MAN. YOU HAVE TO TAKE THITH THTUFF **BEFORE** I CAN GIVE YOU THE AKLO.
HOW MUCH DID YOU WANT, ANYWAYTH?
UH... TWO OR THREE HITS?
THURE. THAT'TH **ONE-HUNNERD-FIFTY** NEW DOLLARTH. NOW, DO UP A LINE OF THE POWDER AND I'LL THET YOU THTRAIGHT.
WHAT THE FUCK'S GOING ON HERE?
I WANT THEM TO TAKE AWAY WITH ME, JOHNNY.
YOU'LL TAKE 'EM AWAY WHEN I'VE **GIVEN** 'EM TO YOU. BUT I CAN'T DO **THAT** TILL YOU THNORT THE WHITE POWDER.

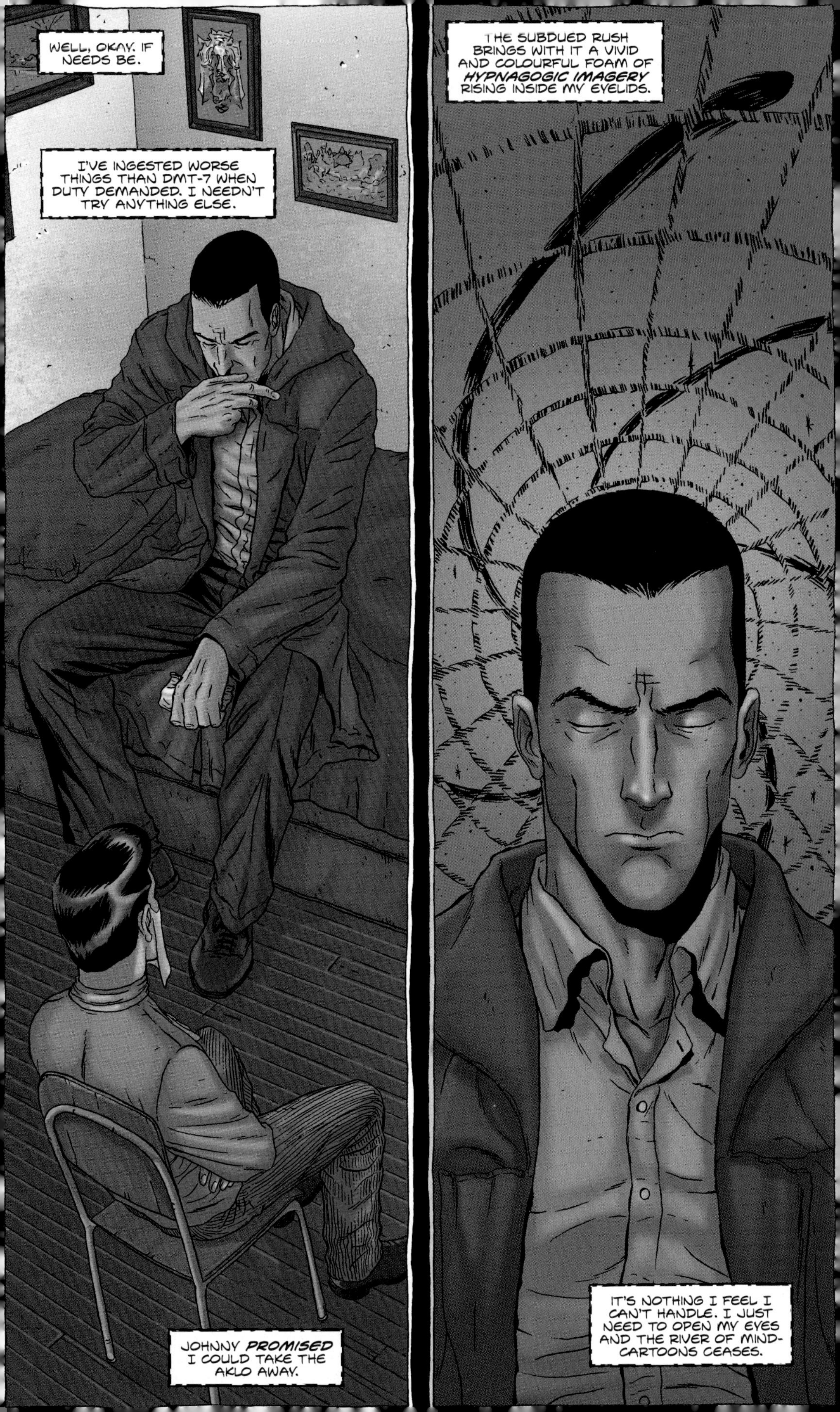
WELL, OKAY. IF NEEDS BE.
I'VE INGESTED WORSE THINGS THAN DMT-7 WHEN DUTY DEMANDED. I NEEDN'T TRY ANYTHING ELSE.
JOHNNY PROMISED I COULD TAKE THE AKLO AWAY.
THE SUBDUED RUSH BRINGS WITH IT A VIVID AND COLOURFUL FOAM OF HYPNAGOGIC IMAGERY RISING INSIDE MY EYELIDS.
IT'S NOTHING I FEEL I CAN'T HANDLE. I JUST NEED TO OPEN MY EYES AND THE RIVER OF MIND-CARTOONS CEASES.

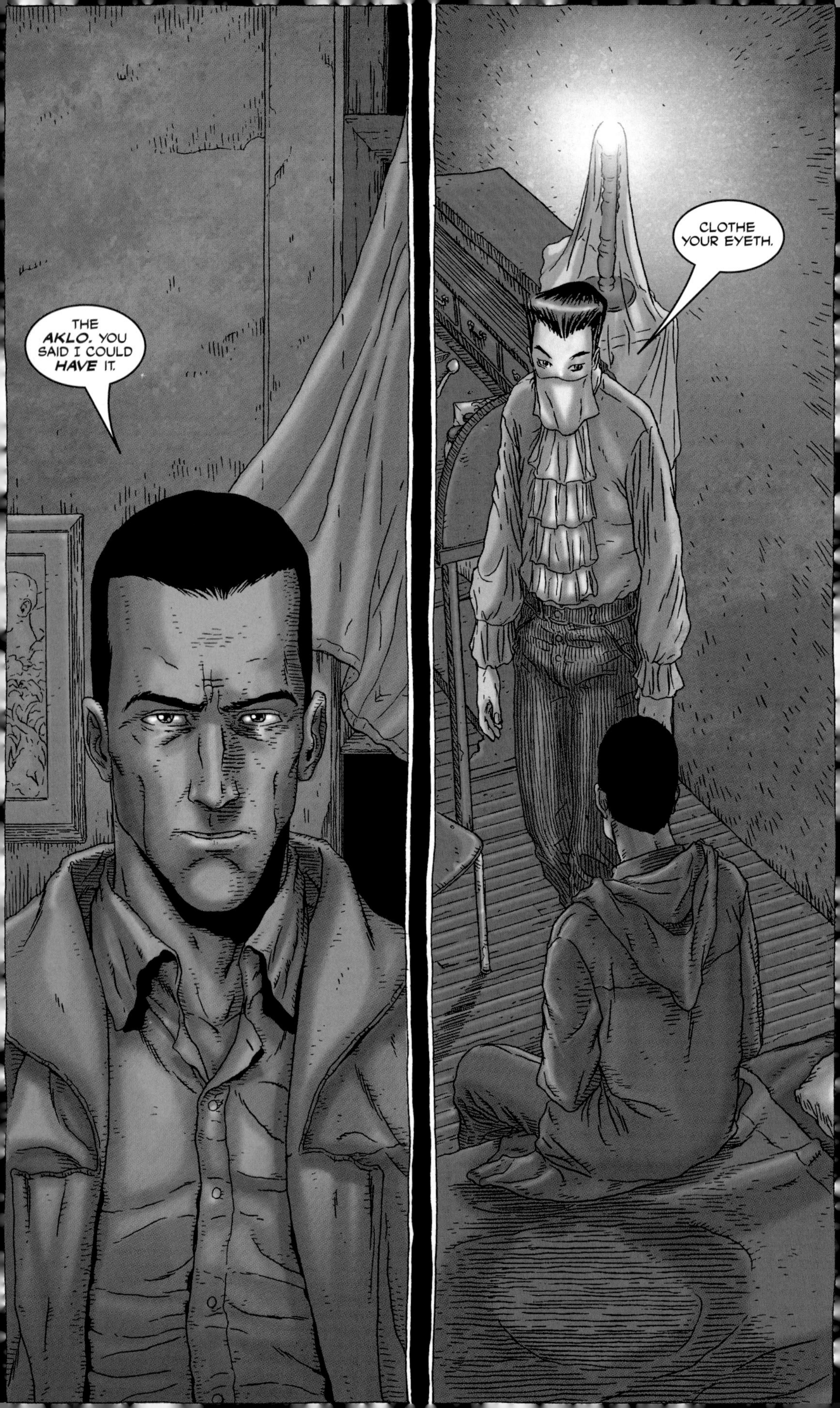
THE AKLO. YOU SAID I COULD HAVE IT.
CLOTHE YOUR EYETH.

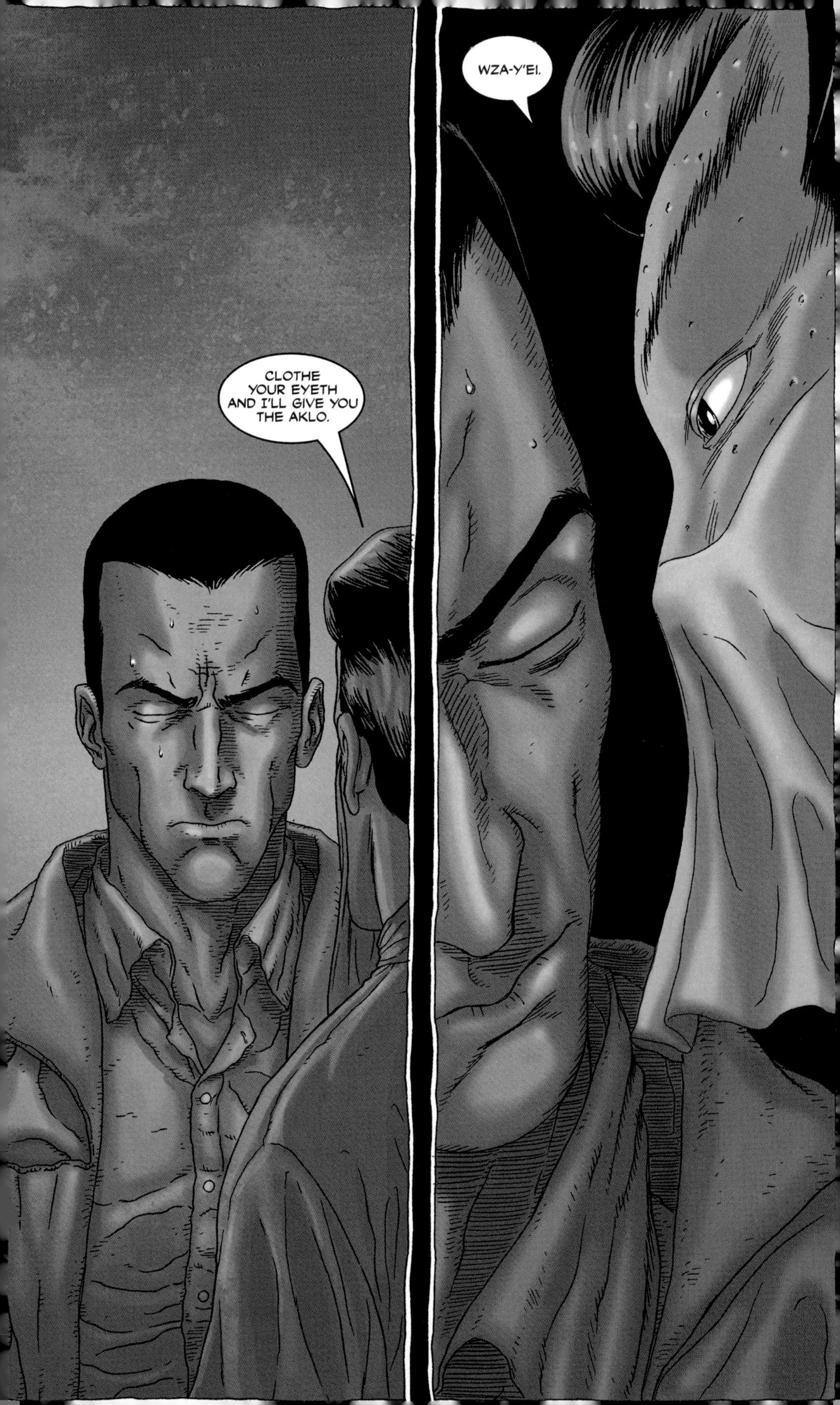
CLOTHE YOUR EYETH AND I'LL GIVE YOU THE AKLO.
WZA-Y'EI.

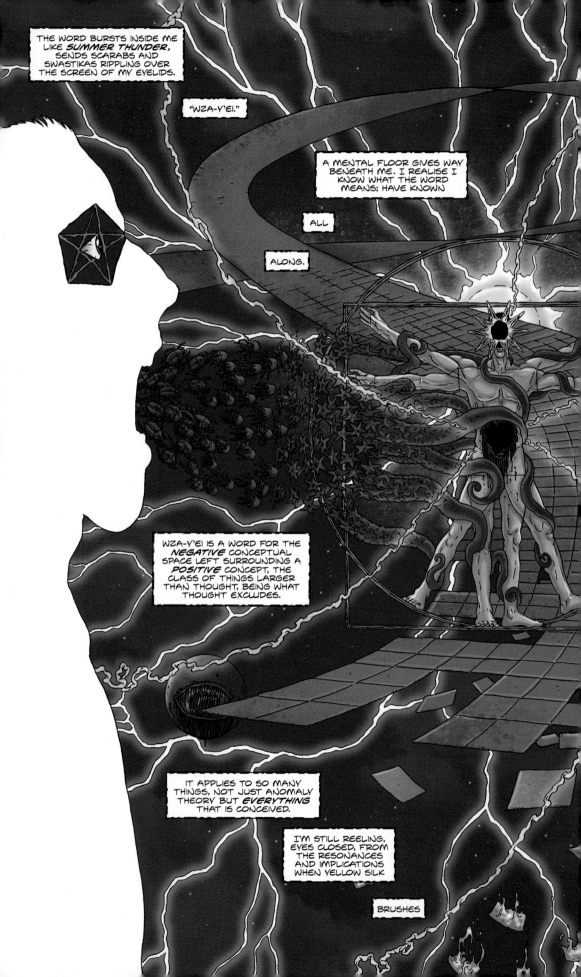

THE WORD BURSTS INSIDE ME LIKE *SUMMER THUNDER*, SENDS SCARABS AND SWASTIKAS RIPPLING OVER THE SCREEN OF MY EYELIDS.

"WZA-Y'EI."

A MENTAL FLOOR GIVES WAY BENEATH ME. I REALISE I KNOW WHAT THE WORD MEANS; HAVE KNOWN

ALL

ALONG.

WZA-Y'EI IS A WORD FOR THE *NEGATIVE* CONCEPTUAL SPACE LEFT SURROUNDING A *POSITIVE* CONCEPT, THE CLASS OF THINGS LARGER THAN THOUGHT, BEING WHAT THOUGHT EXCLUDES.

IT APPLIES TO SO MANY THINGS, NOT JUST ANOMALY THEORY BUT *EVERYTHING* THAT IS CONCEIVED.

I'M STILL REELING, EYES CLOSED, FROM THE RESONANCES AND IMPLICATIONS WHEN YELLOW SILK

BRUSHES

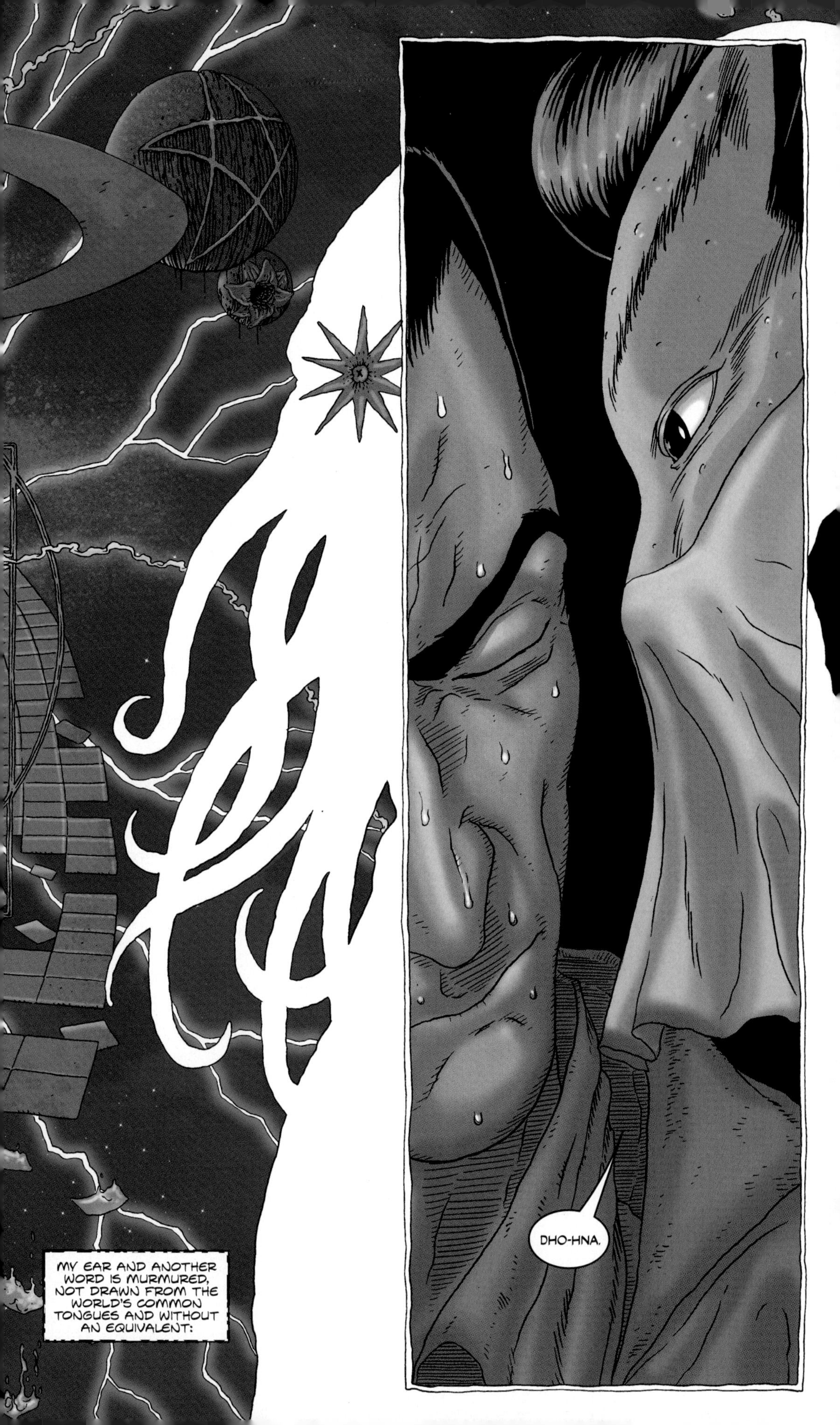
MY EAR AND ANOTHER WORD IS MURMURED, NOT DRAWN FROM THE WORLD'S COMMON TONGUES AND WITHOUT AN EQUIVALENT:
DHO-HNA.

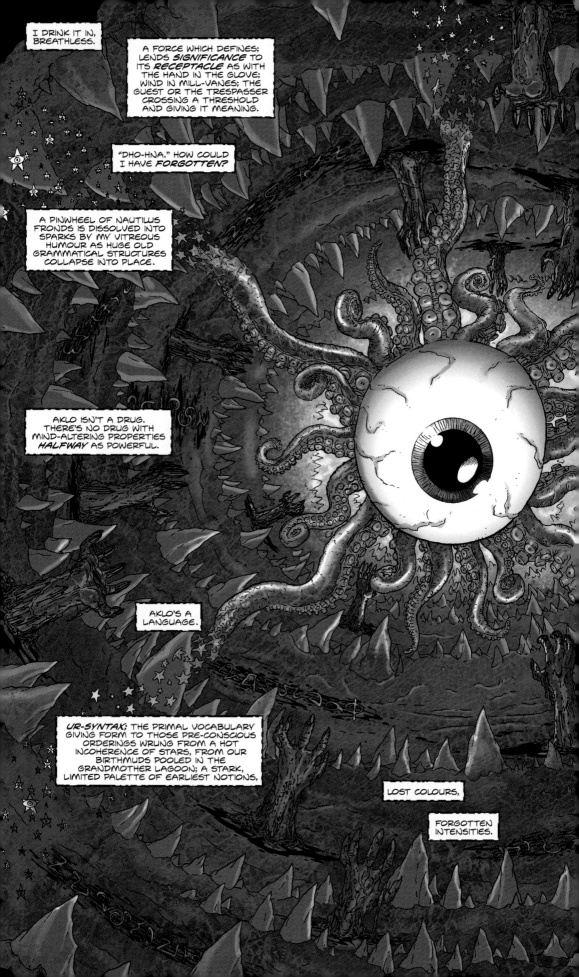

I DRINK IT IN, BREATHLESS.

A FORCE WHICH DEFINES; LENDS *SIGNIFICANCE* TO ITS *RECEPTACLE* AS WITH THE HAND IN THE GLOVE; WIND IN MILL-VANES; THE GUEST OR THE TRESPASSER CROSSING A THRESHOLD AND GIVING IT MEANING.

"DHO-HNA." HOW COULD I HAVE *FORGOTTEN*?

A PINWHEEL OF NAUTILUS FRONDS IS DISSOLVED INTO SPARKS BY MY VITREOUS HUMOUR AS HUGE OLD GRAMMATICAL STRUCTURES COLLAPSE INTO PLACE.

AKLO ISN'T A DRUG. THERE'S NO DRUG WITH MIND-ALTERING PROPERTIES *HALFWAY* AS POWERFUL.

AKLO'S A LANGUAGE.

UR-SYNTAX; THE PRIMAL VOCABULARY GIVING FORM TO THOSE PRE-CONSCIOUS ORDERINGS WRUNG FROM A HOT INCOHERENCE OF STARS, FROM OUR BIRTHMUDS POOLED IN THE GRANDMOTHER LAGOON; A STARK, LIMITED PALETTE OF EARLIEST NOTIONS,

LOST COLOURS,

FORGOTTEN INTENSITIES.

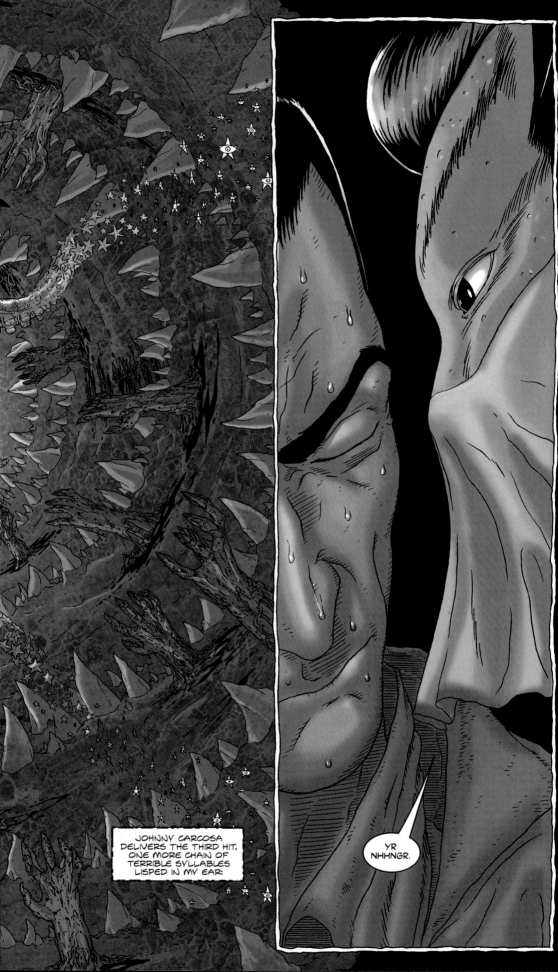

JOHNNY CARCOSA DELIVERS THE THIRD HIT, ONE MORE CHAIN OF TERRIBLE SYLLABLES LISPED IN MY EAR:

YR NHHNGR.

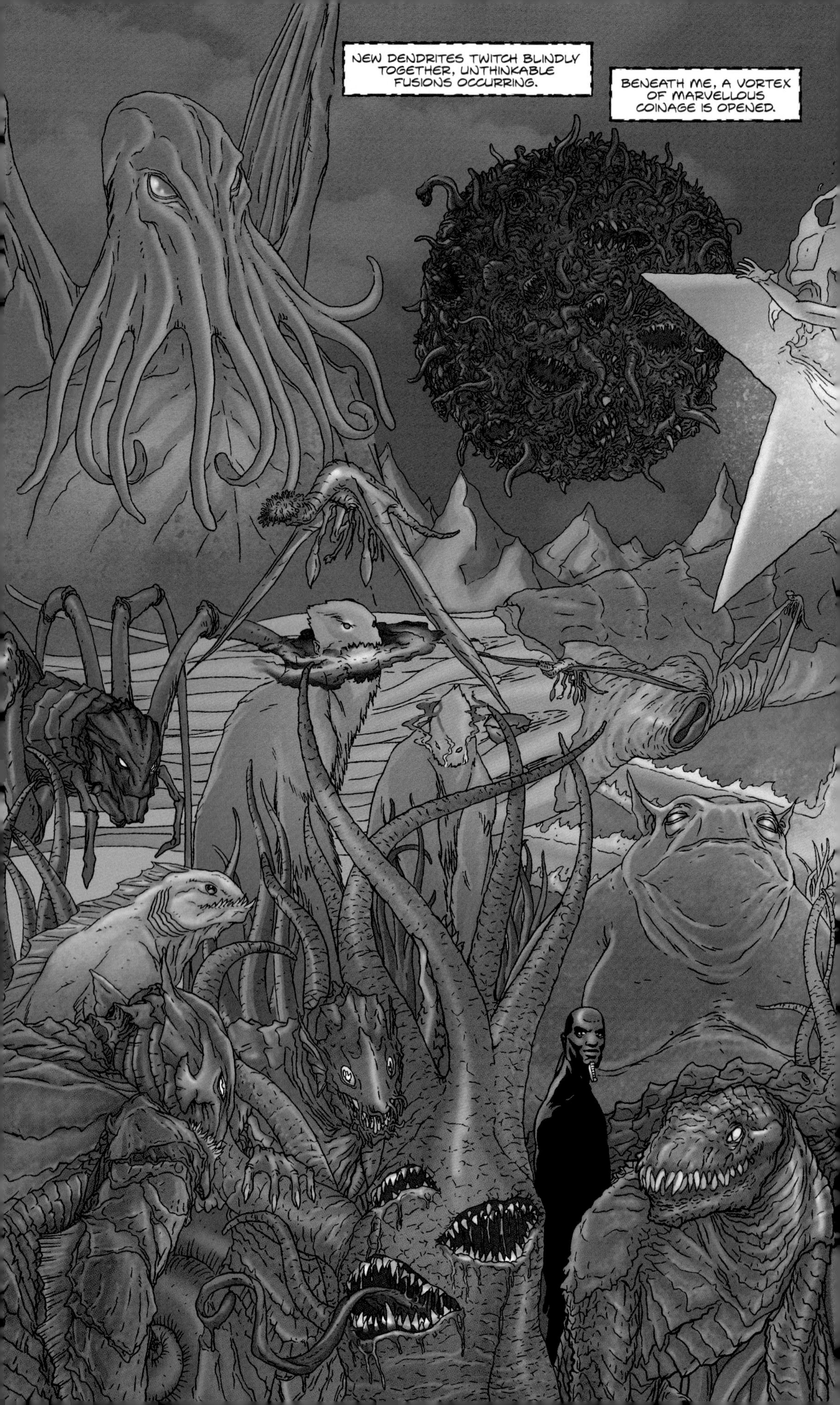
NEW DENDRITES TWITCH BLINDLY TOGETHER, UNTHINKABLE FUSIONS OCCURRING.
BENEATH ME, A VORTEX OF MARVELLOUS COINAGE IS OPENED.

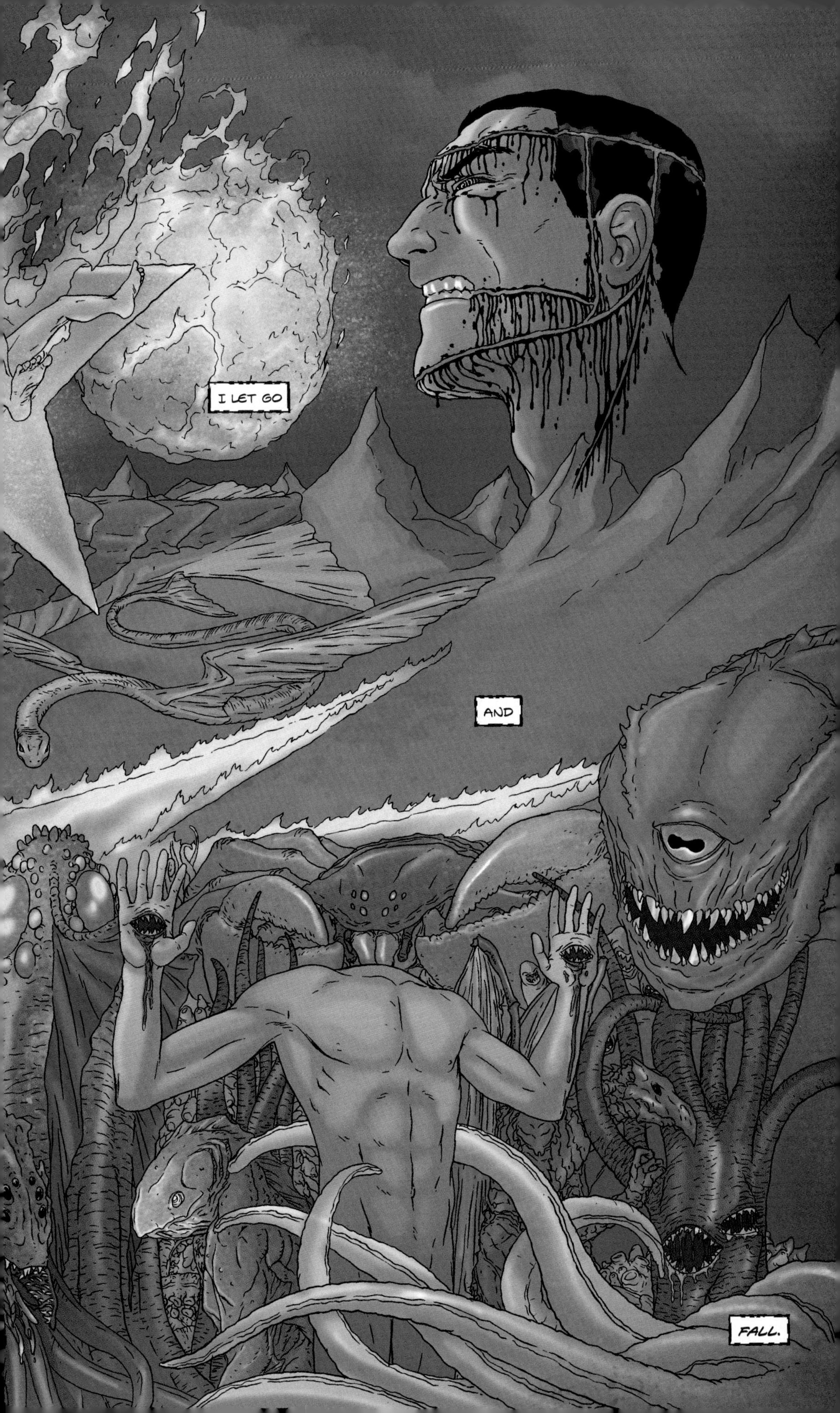
I LET GO
AND
FALL.

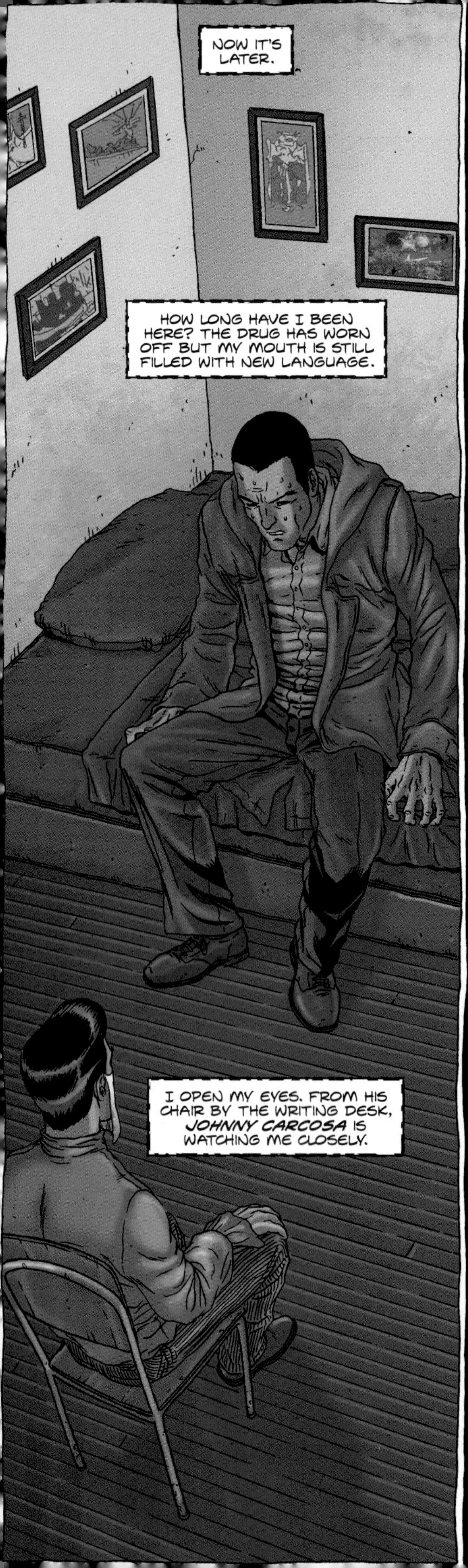
NOW IT'S LATER.
HOW LONG HAVE I BEEN HERE? THE DRUG HAS WORN OFF BUT MY MOUTH IS STILL FILLED WITH NEW LANGUAGE.
I OPEN MY EYES. FROM HIS CHAIR BY THE WRITING DESK, JOHNNY CARCOSA IS WATCHING ME CLOSELY.

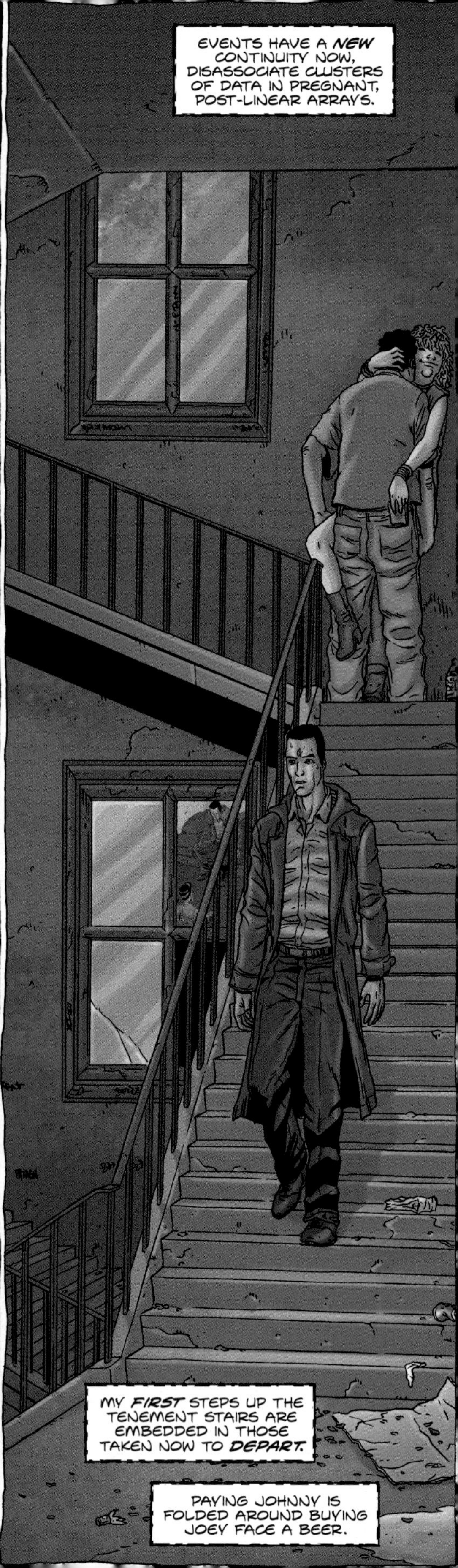
EVENTS HAVE A NEW CONTINUITY NOW, DISASSOCIATE CLUSTERS OF DATA IN PREGNANT, POST-LINEAR ARRAYS.
MY FIRST STEPS UP THE TENEMENT STAIRS ARE EMBEDDED IN THOSE TAKEN NOW TO DEPART.
PAYING JOHNNY IS FOLDED AROUND BUYING JOEY FACE A BEER.

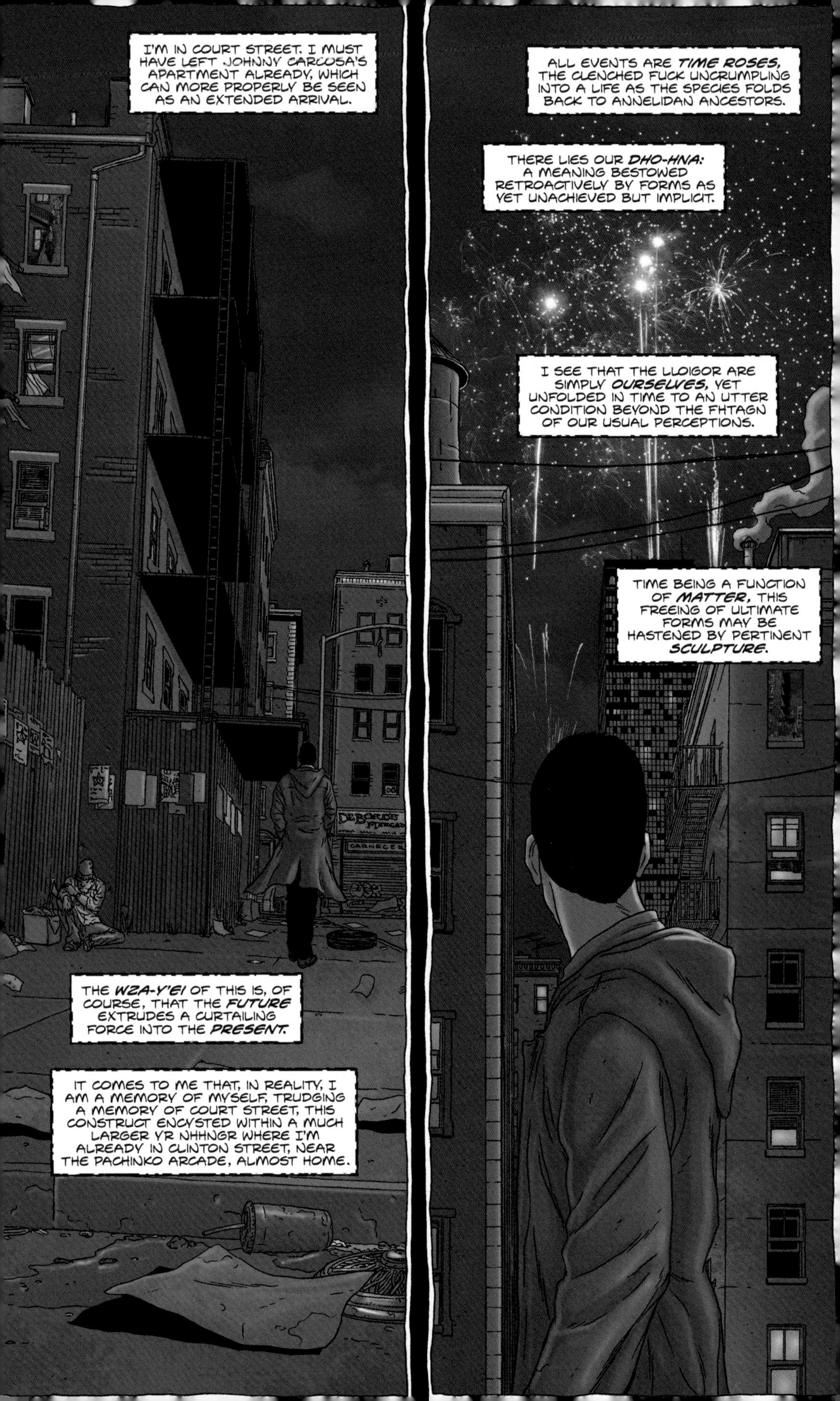
I'M IN COURT STREET. I MUST HAVE LEFT JOHNNY CARCOSA'S APARTMENT ALREADY, WHICH CAN MORE PROPERLY BE SEEN AS AN EXTENDED ARRIVAL.
THE *WZA-Y'EI* OF THIS IS, OF COURSE, THAT THE *FUTURE* EXTRUDES A CURTAILING FORCE INTO THE *PRESENT.*
IT COMES TO ME THAT, IN REALITY, I AM A MEMORY OF MYSELF, TRUDGING A MEMORY OF COURT STREET, THIS CONSTRUCT ENCYSTED WITHIN A MUCH LARGER YR NHHNGR WHERE I'M ALREADY IN CLINTON STREET, NEAR THE PACHINKO ARCADE, ALMOST HOME.
ALL EVENTS ARE *TIME ROSES,* THE CLENCHED FUCK UNCRUMPLING INTO A LIFE AS THE SPECIES FOLDS BACK TO ANNELIDAN ANCESTORS.
THERE LIES OUR *DHO-HNA:* A MEANING BESTOWED RETROACTIVELY BY FORMS AS YET UNACHIEVED BUT IMPLICIT.
I SEE THAT THE LLOIGOR ARE SIMPLY *OURSELVES,* YET UNFOLDED IN TIME TO AN UTTER CONDITION BEYOND THE FHTAGN OF OUR USUAL PERCEPTIONS.
TIME BEING A FUNCTION OF *MATTER,* THIS FREEING OF ULTIMATE FORMS MAY BE HASTENED BY PERTINENT *SCULPTURE.*

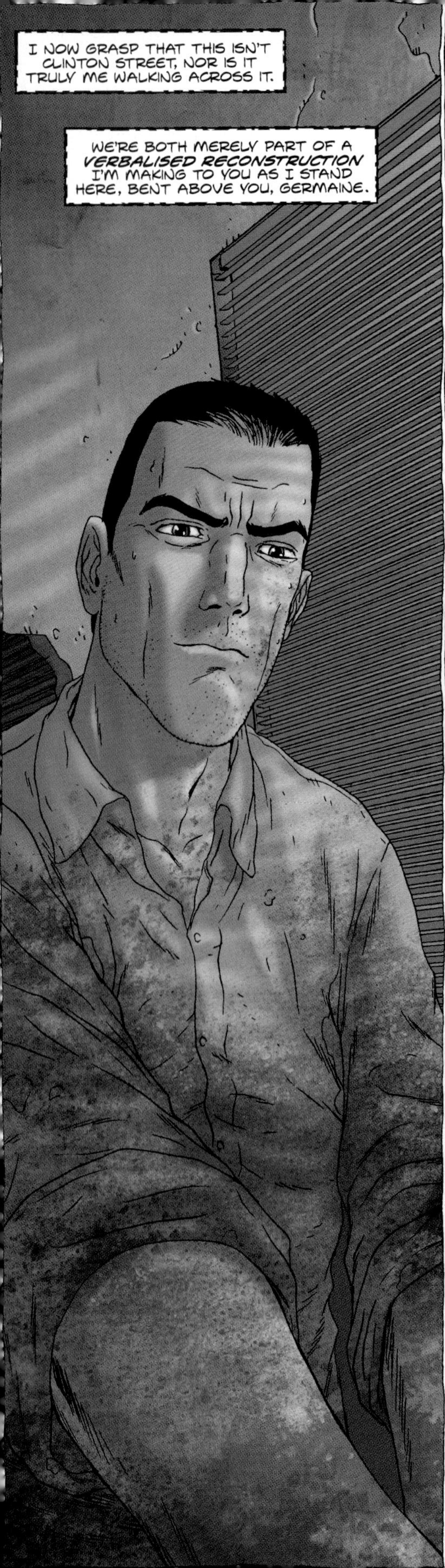
I NOW GRASP THAT THIS ISN'T CLINTON STREET, NOR IS IT TRULY ME WALKING ACROSS IT.
WE'RE BOTH MERELY PART OF A *VERBALISED RECONSTRUCTION* I'M MAKING TO YOU AS I STAND HERE, BENT ABOVE YOU, GERMAINE.

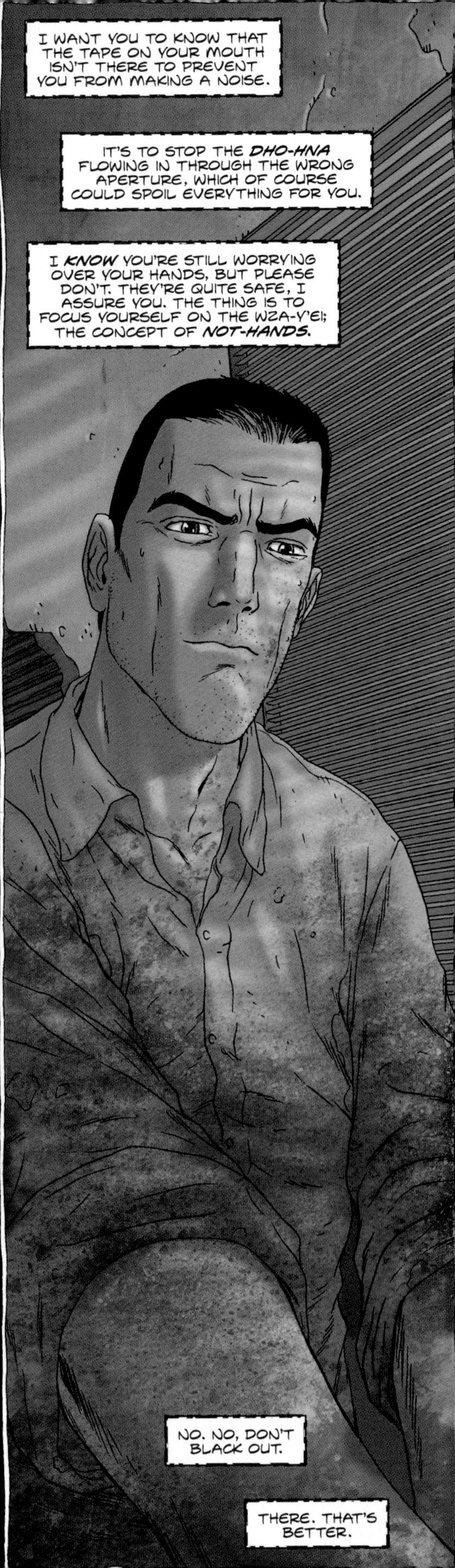
I WANT YOU TO KNOW THAT THE TAPE ON YOUR MOUTH ISN'T THERE TO PREVENT YOU FROM MAKING A NOISE.
IT'S TO STOP THE *DHO-HNA* FLOWING IN THROUGH THE WRONG APERTURE, WHICH OF COURSE COULD SPOIL EVERYTHING FOR YOU.
I *KNOW* YOU'RE STILL WORRYING OVER YOUR HANDS, BUT PLEASE DON'T. THEY'RE QUITE SAFE, I ASSURE YOU. THE THING IS TO FOCUS YOURSELF ON THE WZA-Y'EI; THE CONCEPT OF *NOT-HANDS*.
NO. NO, DON'T BLACK OUT.
THERE. THAT'S BETTER.

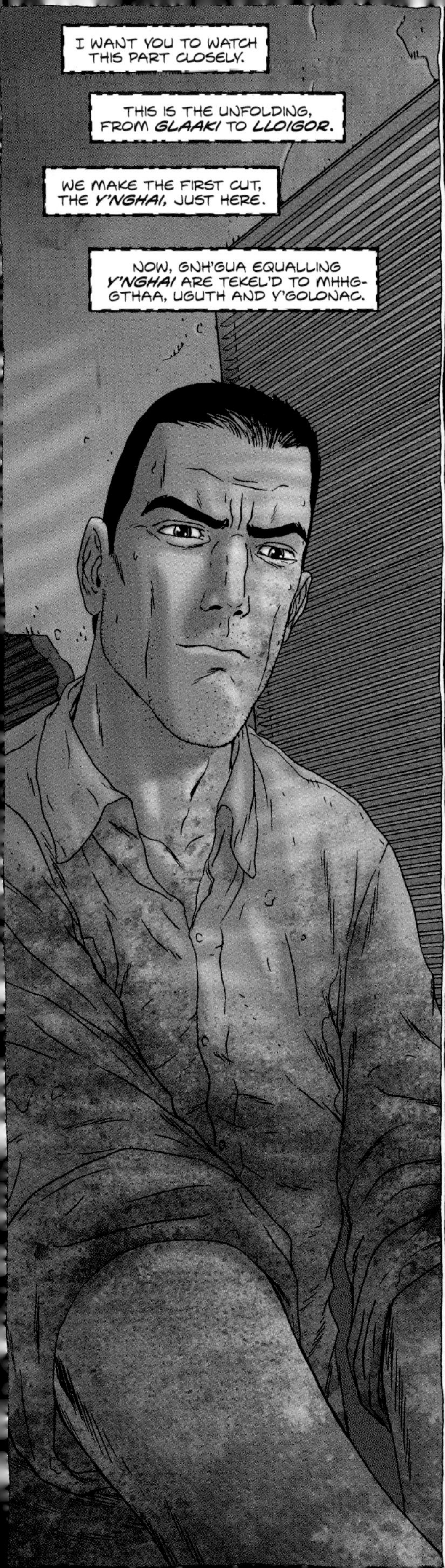
I WANT YOU TO WATCH THIS PART CLOSELY.
THIS IS THE UNFOLDING, FROM *GLAAKI* TO *LLOIGOR*.
WE MAKE THE FIRST CUT, THE *Y'NGHAI,* JUST HERE.
NOW, GNH'GUA EQUALLING *Y'NGHAI* ARE TEKEL'D TO MHHG-GTHAA, UGUTH AND Y'GOLONAC.

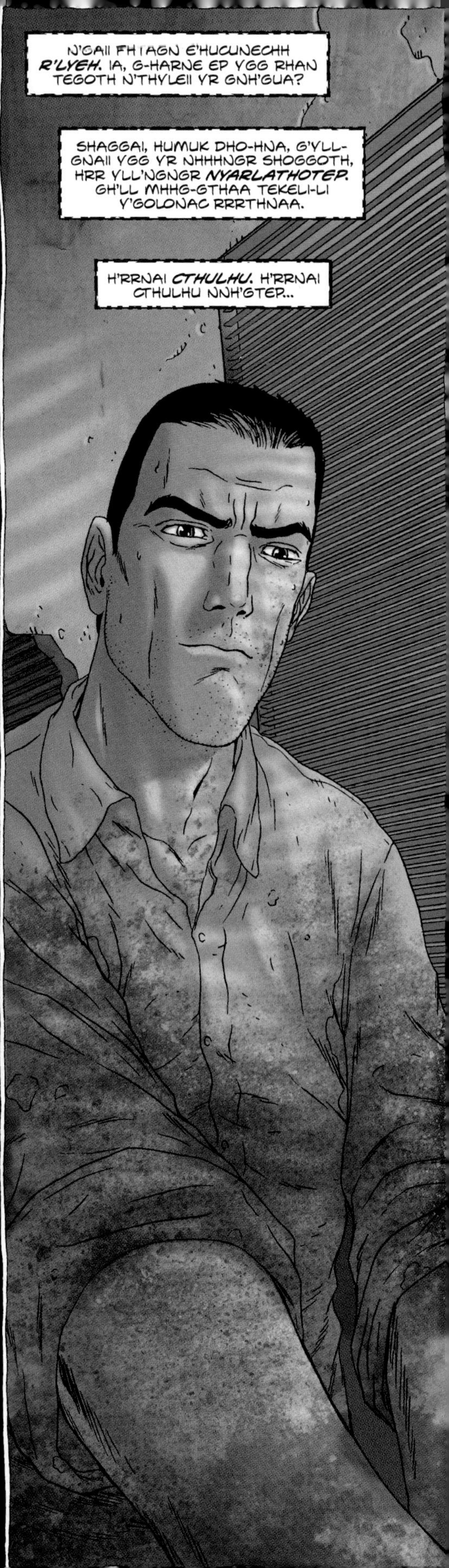
N'GAII FHTAGN E'HUCUNECHH *R'LYEH*. IA, G-HARNE EP YGG RHAN TEGOTH N'THYLEII YR GNH'GUA?
SHAGGAI, HUMUK DHO-HNA, G'YLL-GNAII YGG YR NHHHNGR SHOGGOTH, HRR YLL'NGNGR *NYARLATHOTEP*. GH'LL MHHG-GTHAA TEKELI-LI Y'GOLONAC RRRTHNAA.
H'RRNAI *CTHULHU*. H'RRNAI CTHULHU NNH'GTEP...

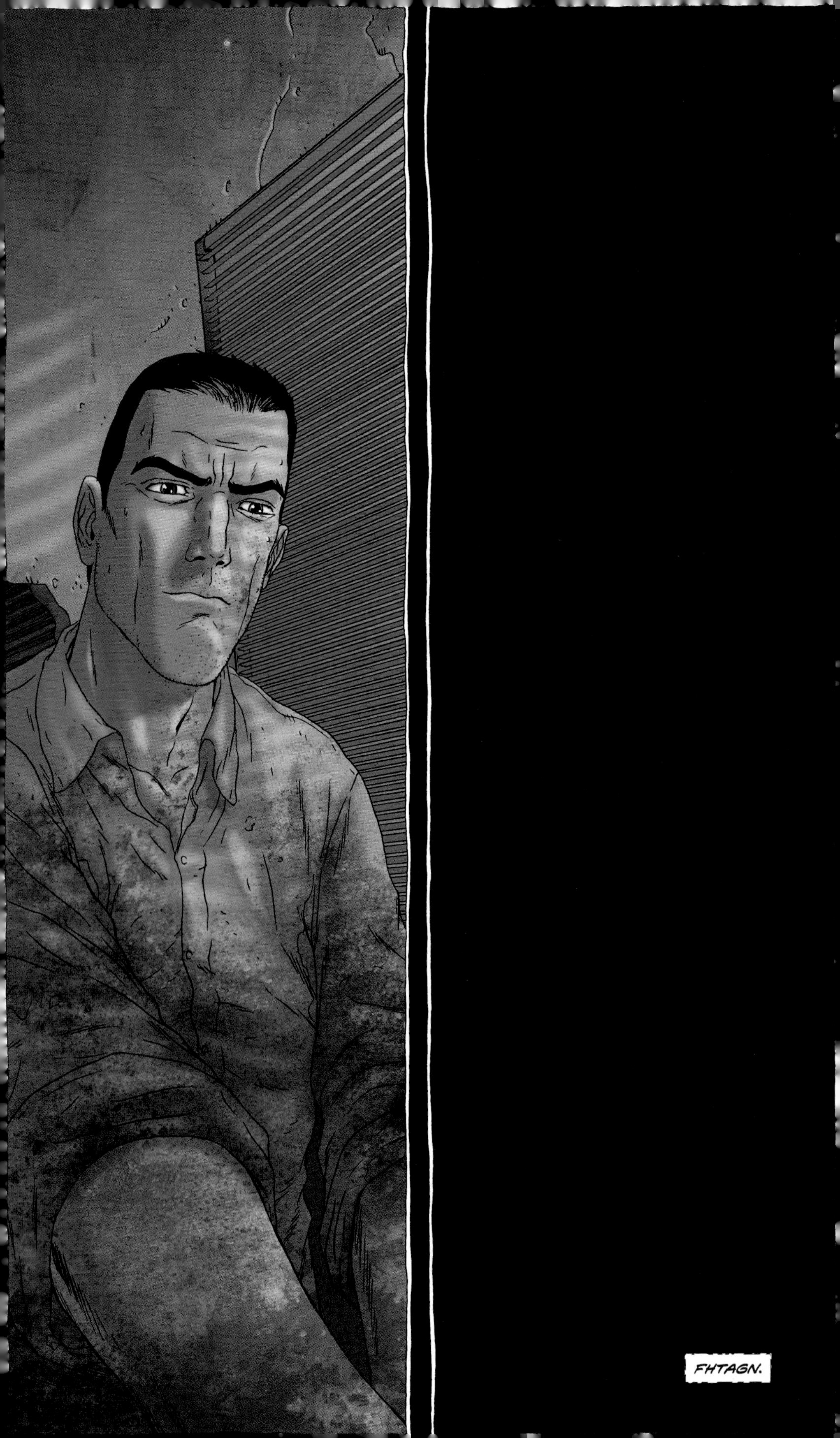
FHTAGN.

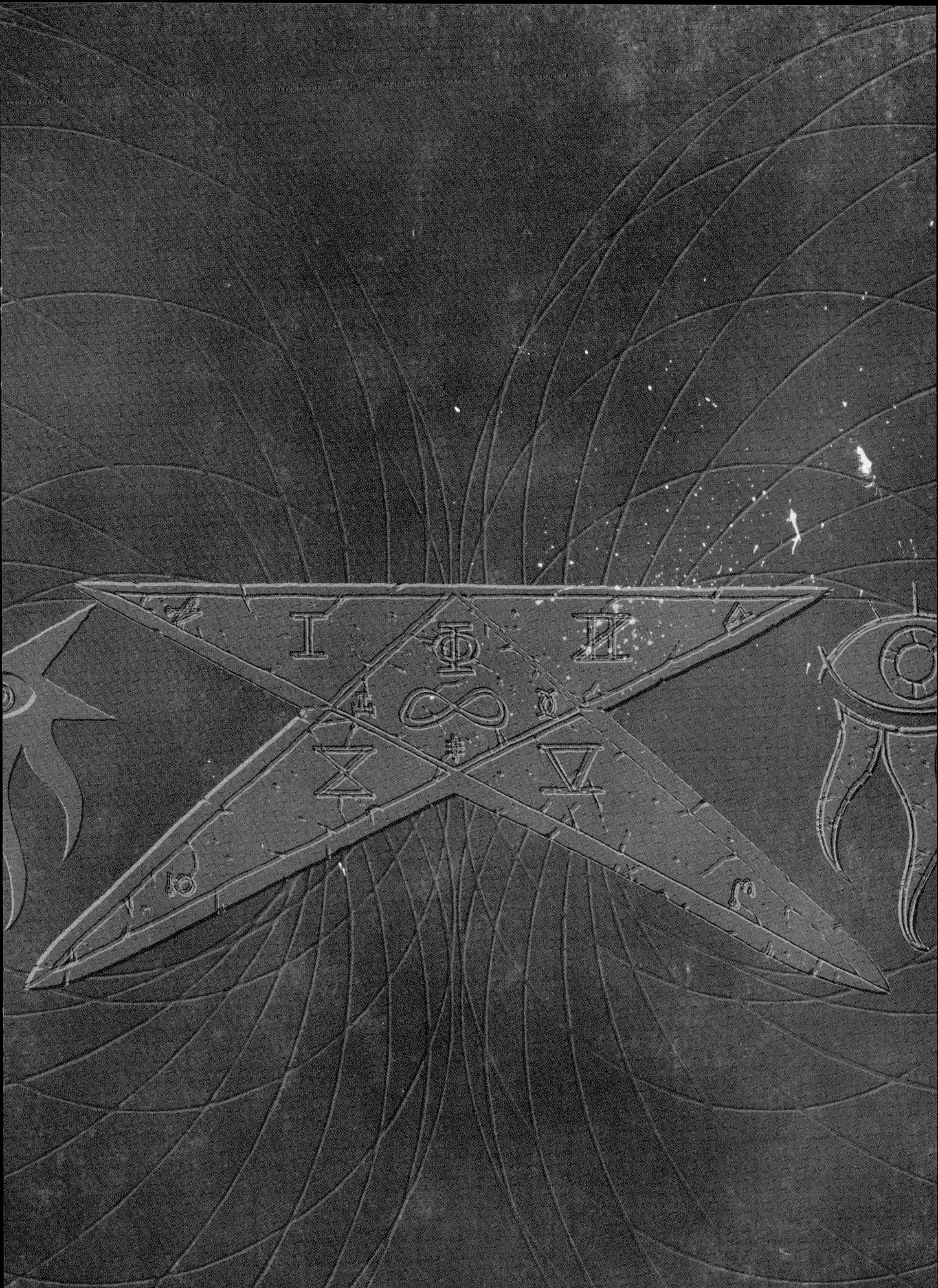

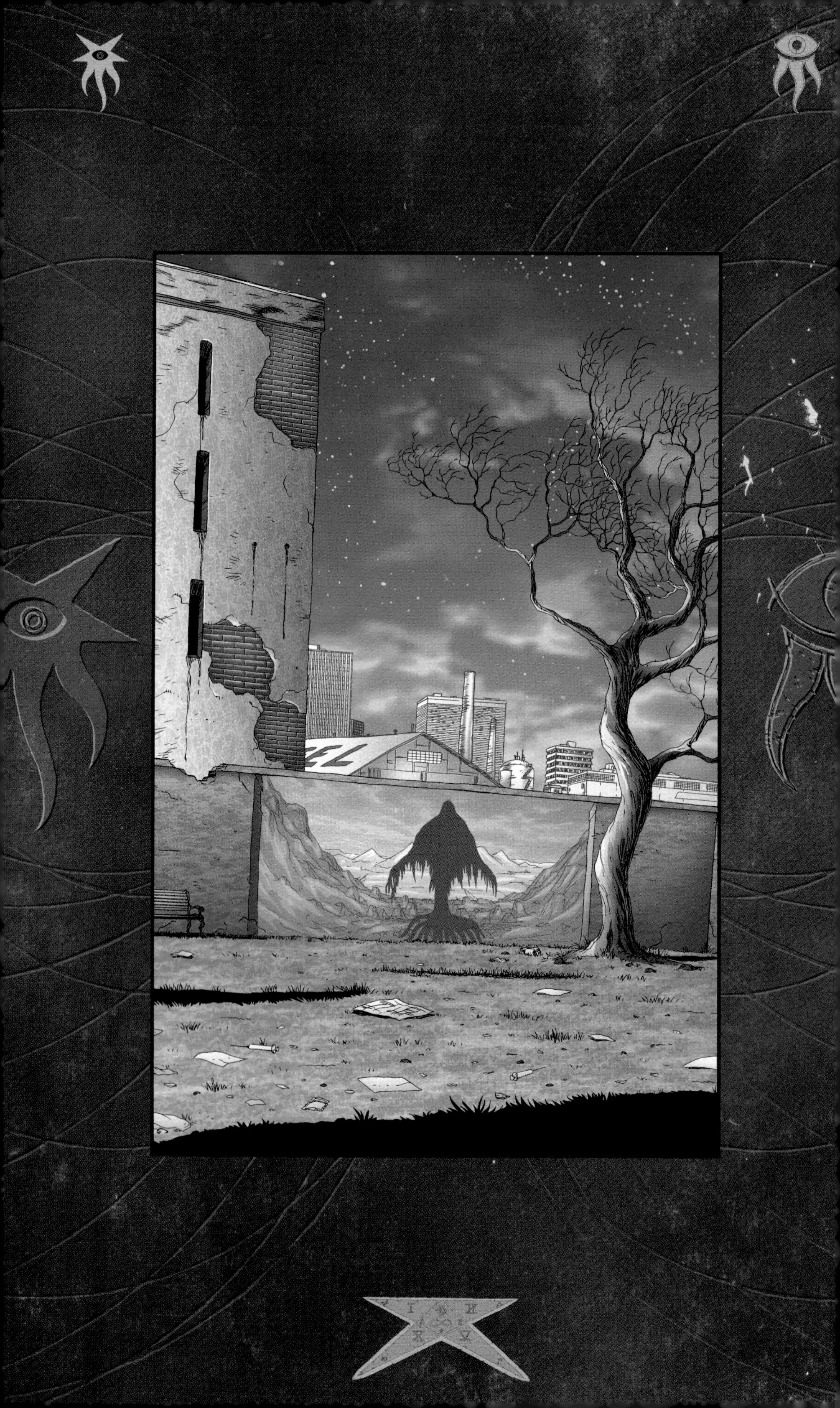

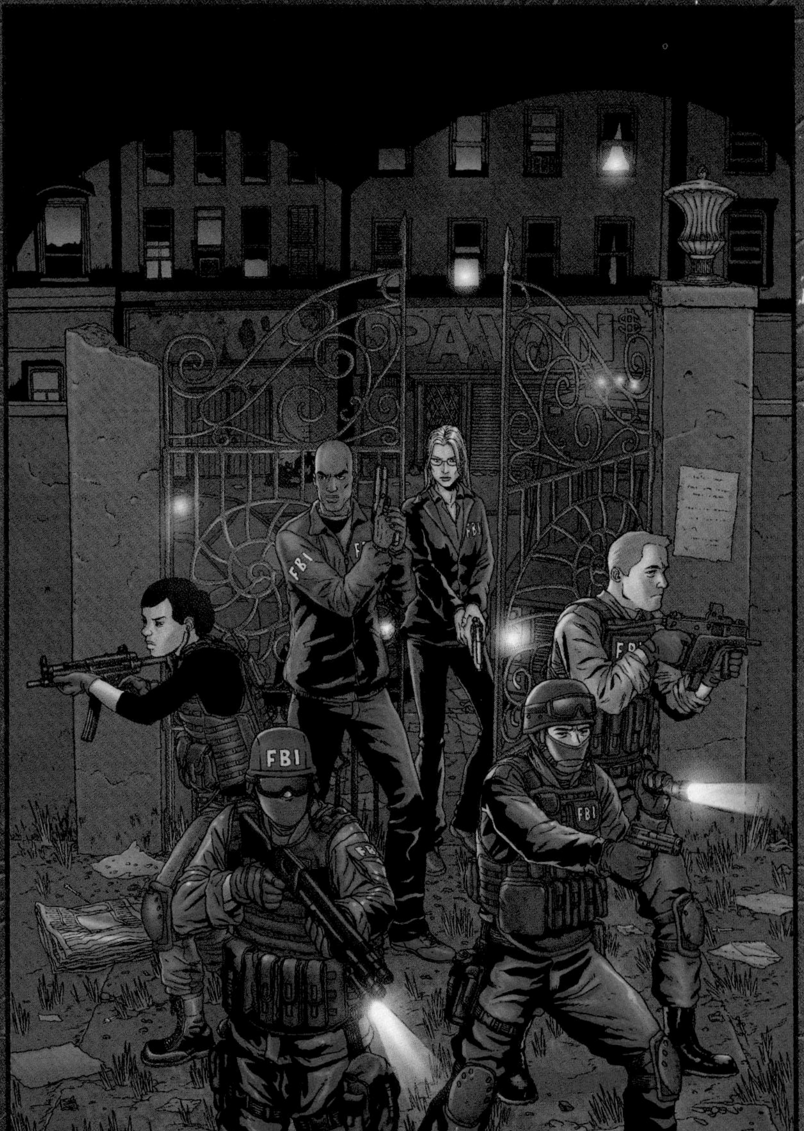
FBI

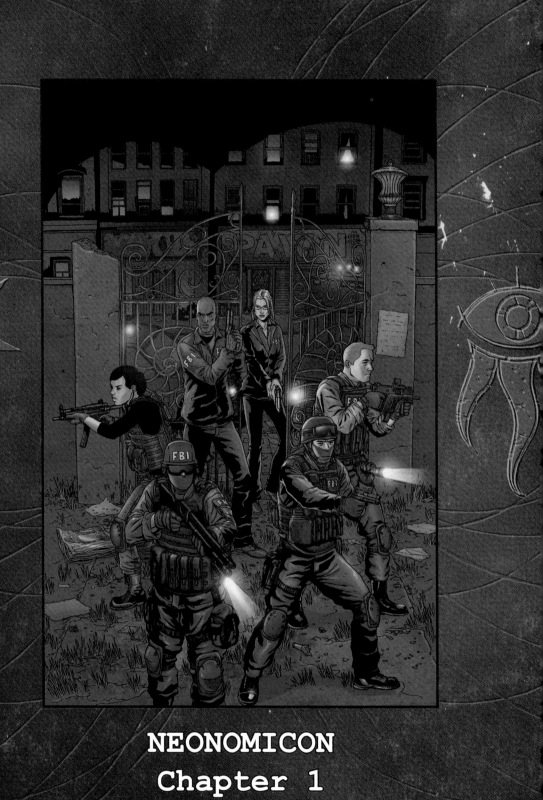

NEONOMICON
Chapter 1

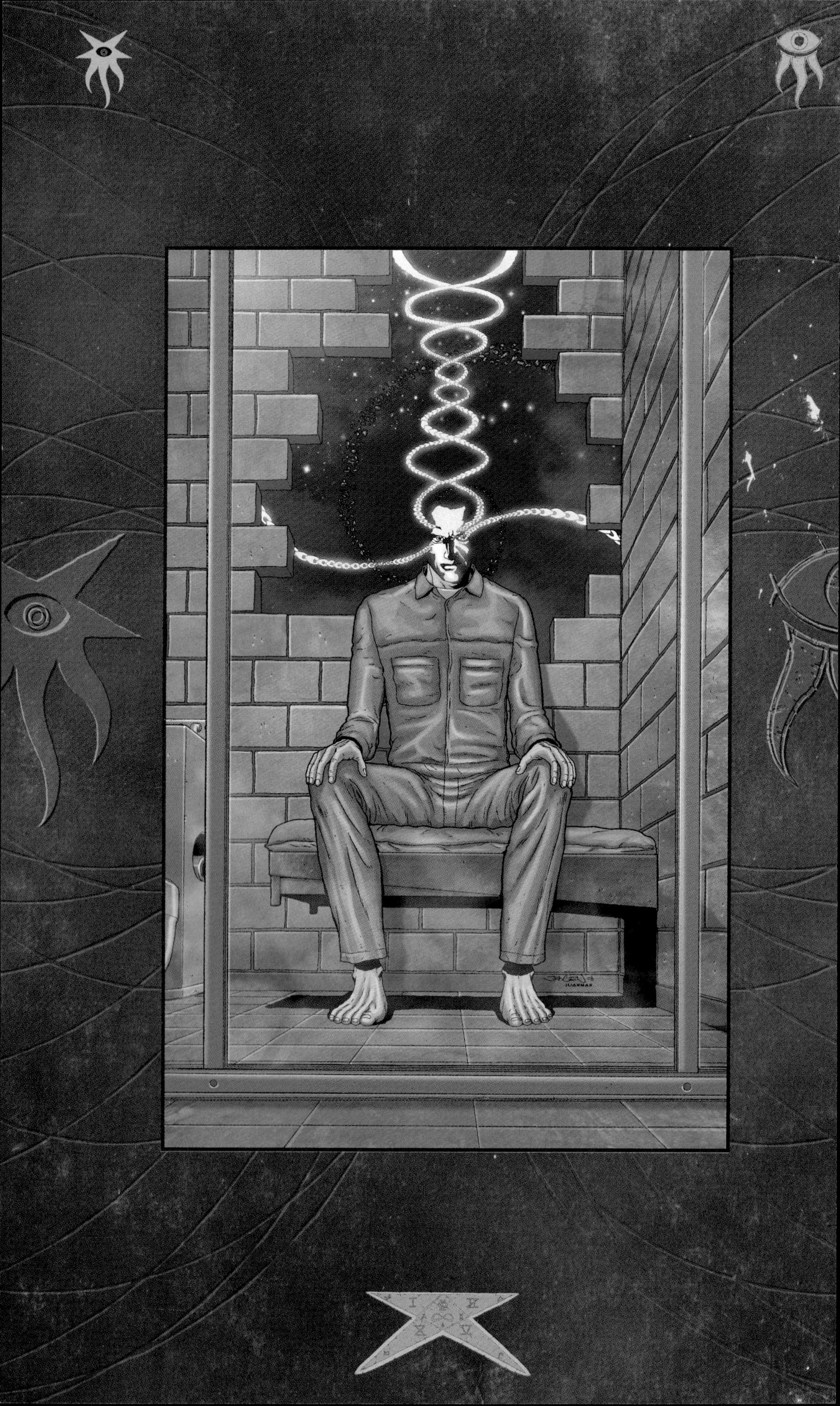

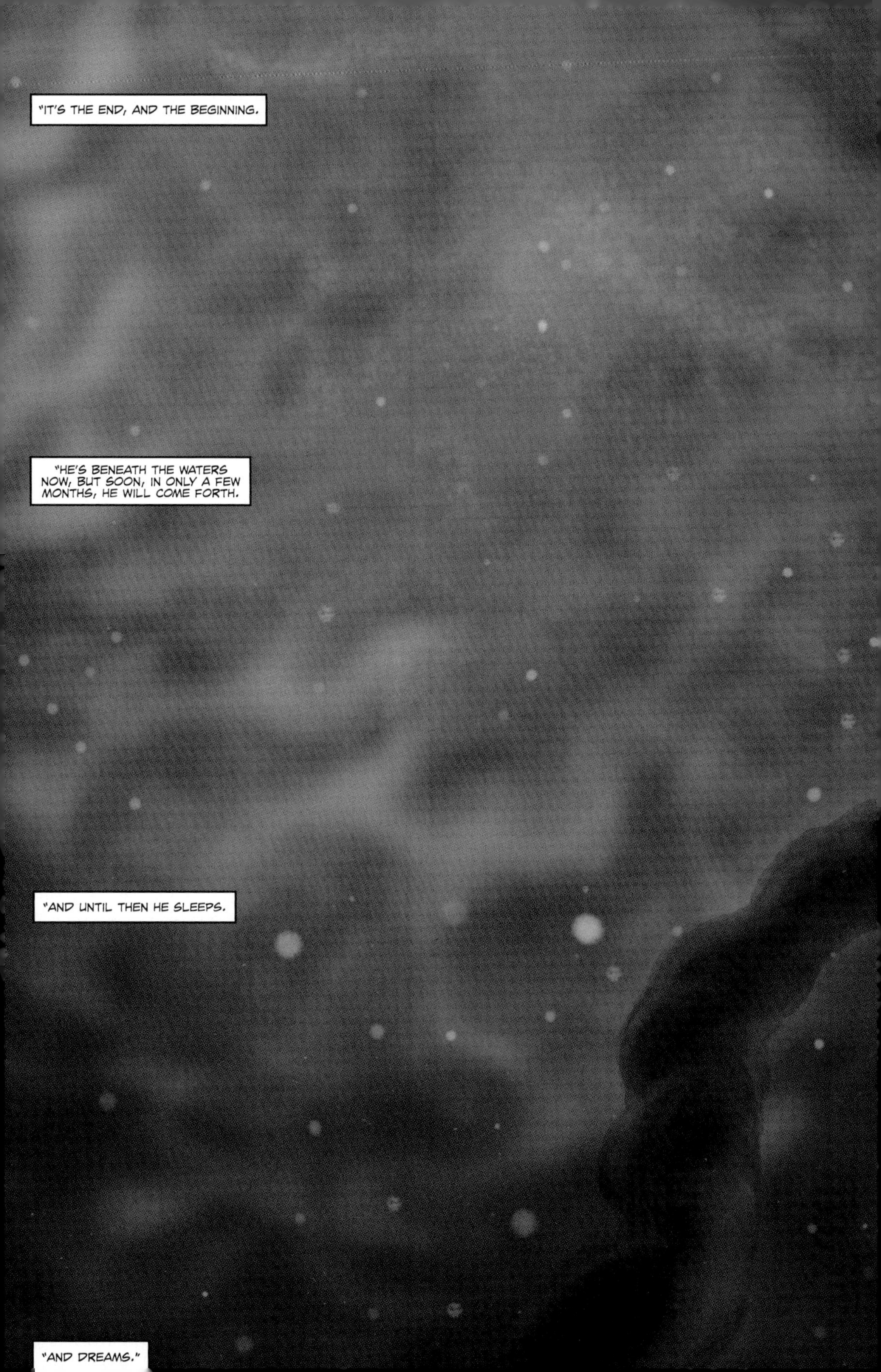
"IT'S THE END, AND THE BEGINNING.
"HE'S BENEATH THE WATERS NOW, BUT SOON, IN ONLY A FEW MONTHS, HE WILL COME FORTH.
"AND UNTIL THEN HE SLEEPS.
"AND DREAMS."

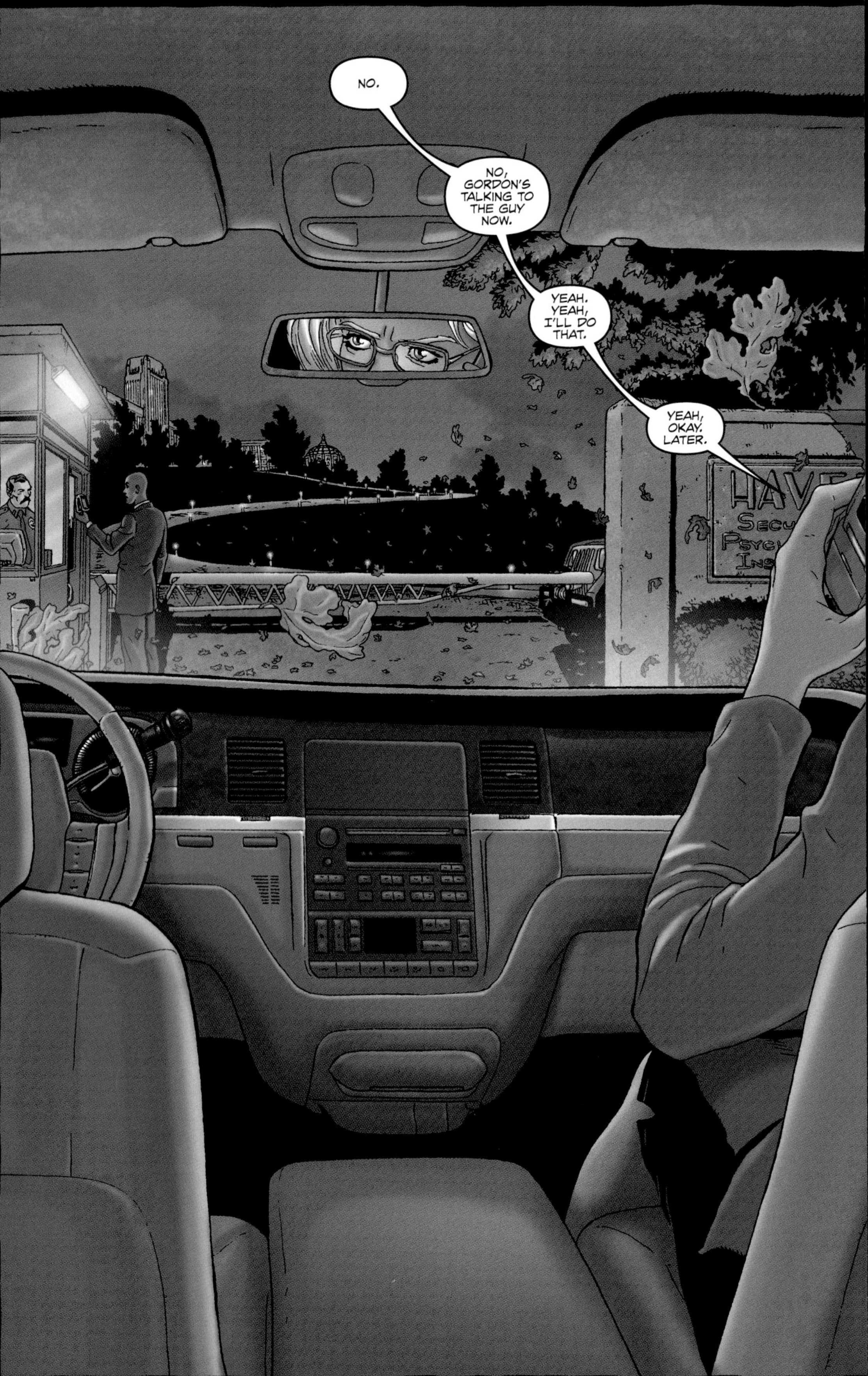
NO.
NO, GORDON'S TALKING TO THE GUY NOW.
YEAH. YEAH, I'LL DO THAT.
YEAH, OKAY. LATER.

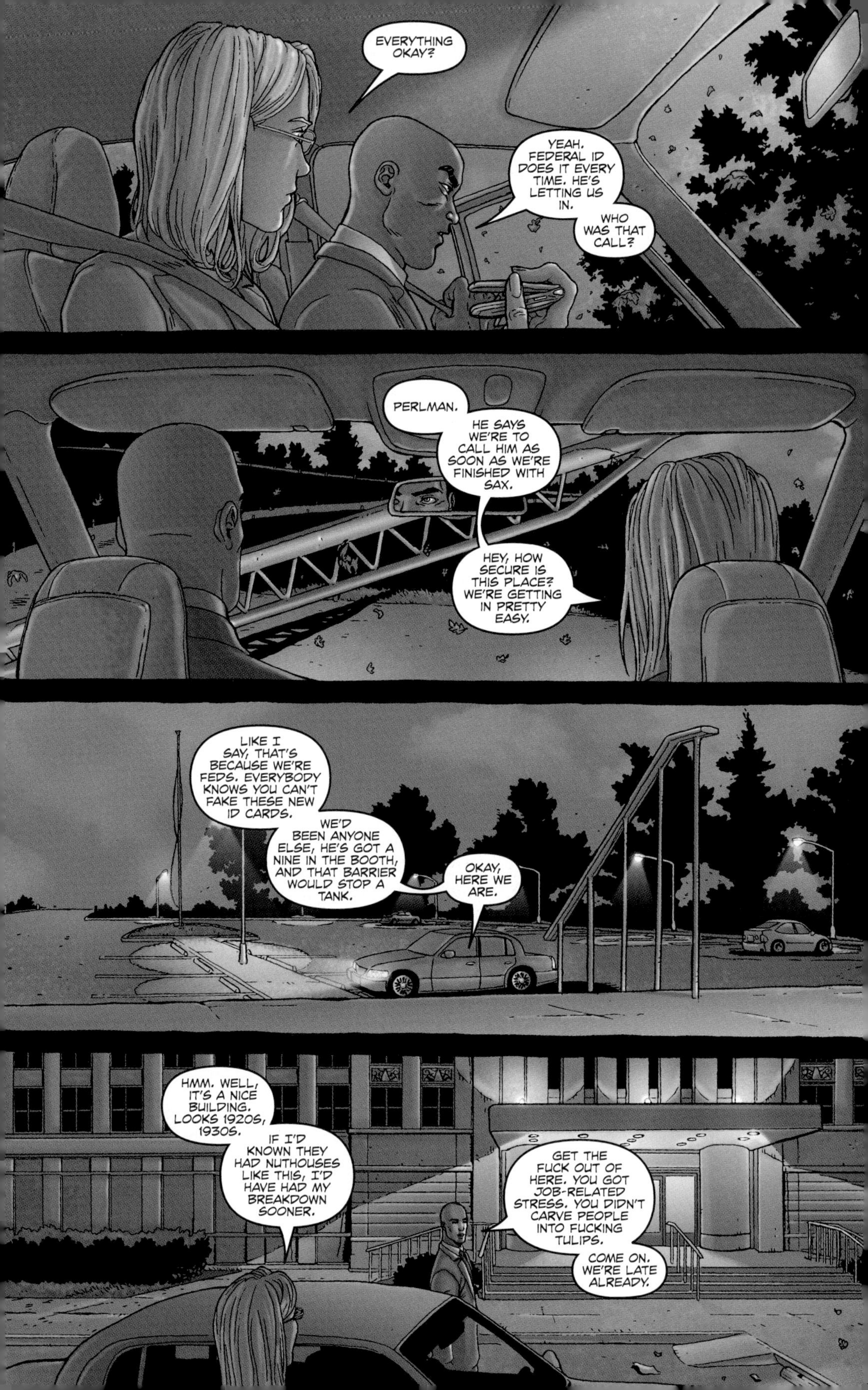
EVERYTHING OKAY?
YEAH. FEDERAL ID DOES IT EVERY TIME. HE'S LETTING US IN.
WHO WAS THAT CALL?
PERLMAN.
HE SAYS WE'RE TO CALL HIM AS SOON AS WE'RE FINISHED WITH SAX.
HEY, HOW SECURE IS THIS PLACE? WE'RE GETTING IN PRETTY EASY.
LIKE I SAY, THAT'S BECAUSE WE'RE FEDS. EVERYBODY KNOWS YOU CAN'T FAKE THESE NEW ID CARDS.
WE'D BEEN ANYONE ELSE, HE'S GOT A NINE IN THE BOOTH, AND THAT BARRIER WOULD STOP A TANK.
OKAY, HERE WE ARE.
HMM. WELL, IT'S A NICE BUILDING. LOOKS 1920S, 1930S.
IF I'D KNOWN THEY HAD NUTHOUSES LIKE THIS, I'D HAVE HAD MY BREAKDOWN SOONER.
GET THE FUCK OUT OF HERE. YOU GOT JOB-RELATED STRESS. YOU DIDN'T CARVE PEOPLE INTO FUCKING TULIPS.
COME ON. WE'RE LATE ALREADY.

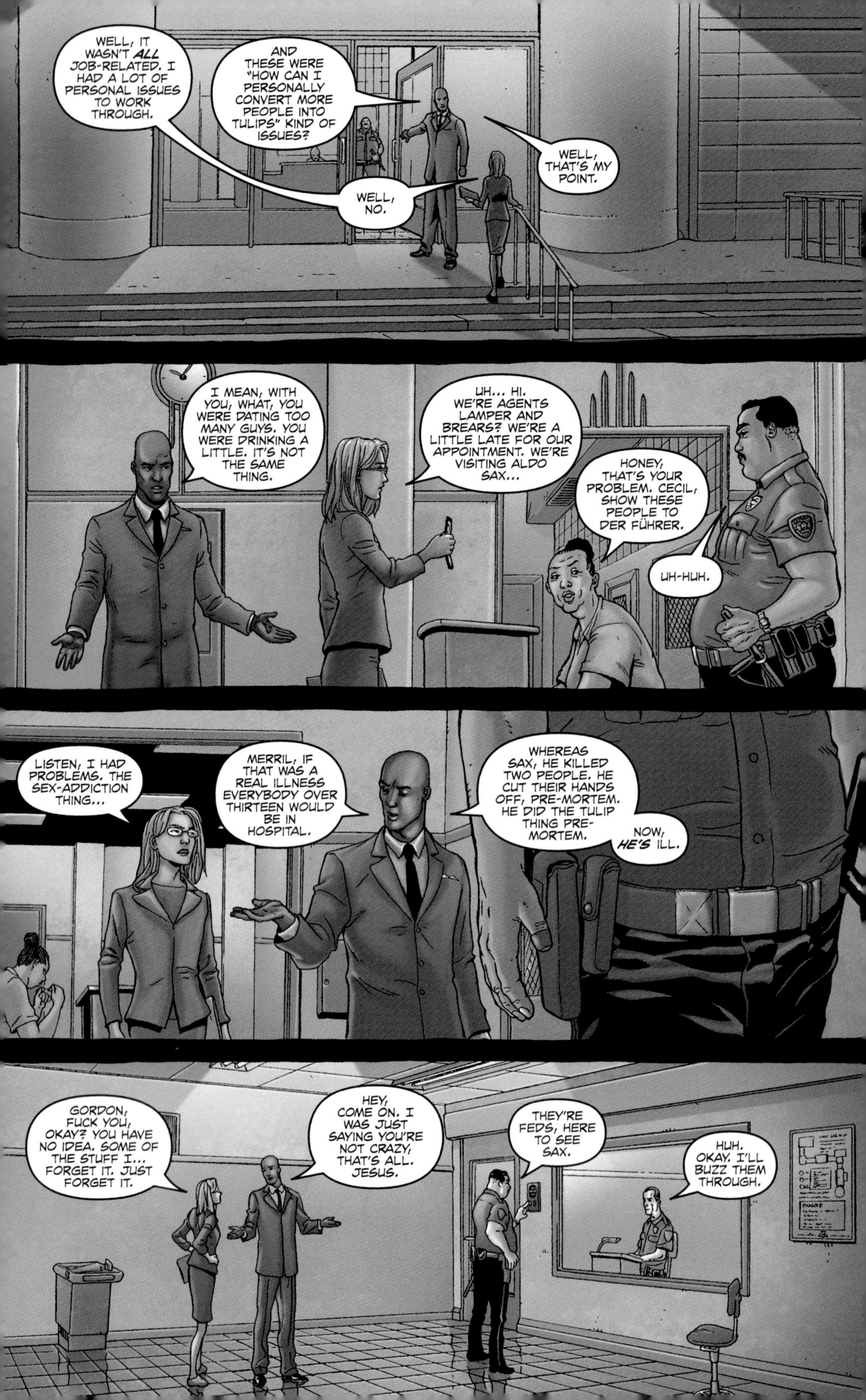

WELL, IT WASN'T ALL JOB-RELATED. I HAD A LOT OF PERSONAL ISSUES TO WORK THROUGH.
AND THESE WERE "HOW CAN I PERSONALLY CONVERT MORE PEOPLE INTO TULIPS" KIND OF ISSUES?
WELL, NO.
WELL, THAT'S MY POINT.
I MEAN, WITH YOU, WHAT, YOU WERE DATING TOO MANY GUYS. YOU WERE DRINKING A LITTLE. IT'S NOT THE SAME THING.
UH... HI. WE'RE AGENTS LAMPER AND BREARS? WE'RE A LITTLE LATE FOR OUR APPOINTMENT. WE'RE VISITING ALDO SAX...
HONEY, THAT'S YOUR PROBLEM. CECIL, SHOW THESE PEOPLE TO DER FÜHRER.
UH-HUH.
LISTEN, I HAD PROBLEMS. THE SEX-ADDICTION THING...
MERRIL, IF THAT WAS A REAL ILLNESS EVERYBODY OVER THIRTEEN WOULD BE IN HOSPITAL.
WHEREAS SAX, HE KILLED TWO PEOPLE. HE CUT THEIR HANDS OFF, PRE-MORTEM. HE DID THE TULIP THING PRE-MORTEM.
NOW, HE'S ILL.
GORDON, FUCK YOU, OKAY? YOU HAVE NO IDEA. SOME OF THE STUFF I... FORGET IT. JUST FORGET IT.
HEY, COME ON. I WAS JUST SAYING YOU'RE NOT CRAZY, THAT'S ALL. JESUS.
THEY'RE FEDS, HERE TO SEE SAX.
HUH. OKAY. I'LL BUZZ THEM THROUGH.

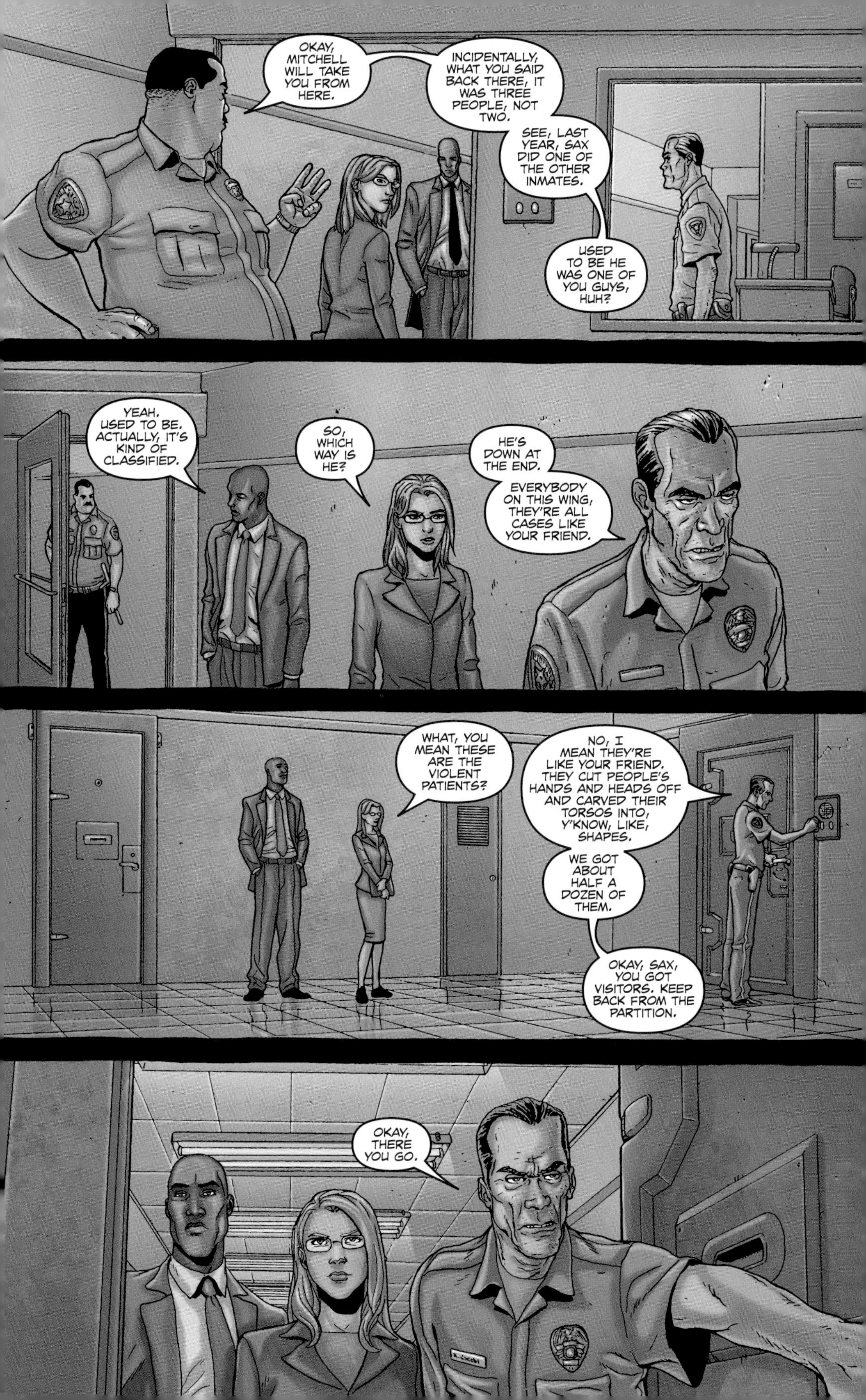
OKAY, MITCHELL WILL TAKE YOU FROM HERE.
INCIDENTALLY, WHAT YOU SAID BACK THERE, IT WAS THREE PEOPLE, NOT TWO.
SEE, LAST YEAR, SAX DID ONE OF THE OTHER INMATES.
USED TO BE HE WAS ONE OF YOU GUYS, HUH?
YEAH. USED TO BE. ACTUALLY, IT'S KIND OF CLASSIFIED.
SO, WHICH WAY IS HE?
HE'S DOWN AT THE END.
EVERYBODY ON THIS WING, THEY'RE ALL CASES LIKE YOUR FRIEND.
WHAT, YOU MEAN THESE ARE THE VIOLENT PATIENTS?
NO, I MEAN THEY'RE LIKE YOUR FRIEND. THEY CUT PEOPLE'S HANDS AND HEADS OFF AND CARVED THEIR TORSOS INTO, Y'KNOW, LIKE, SHAPES.
WE GOT ABOUT HALF A DOZEN OF THEM.
OKAY, SAX, YOU GOT VISITORS. KEEP BACK FROM THE PARTITION.
OKAY, THERE YOU GO.

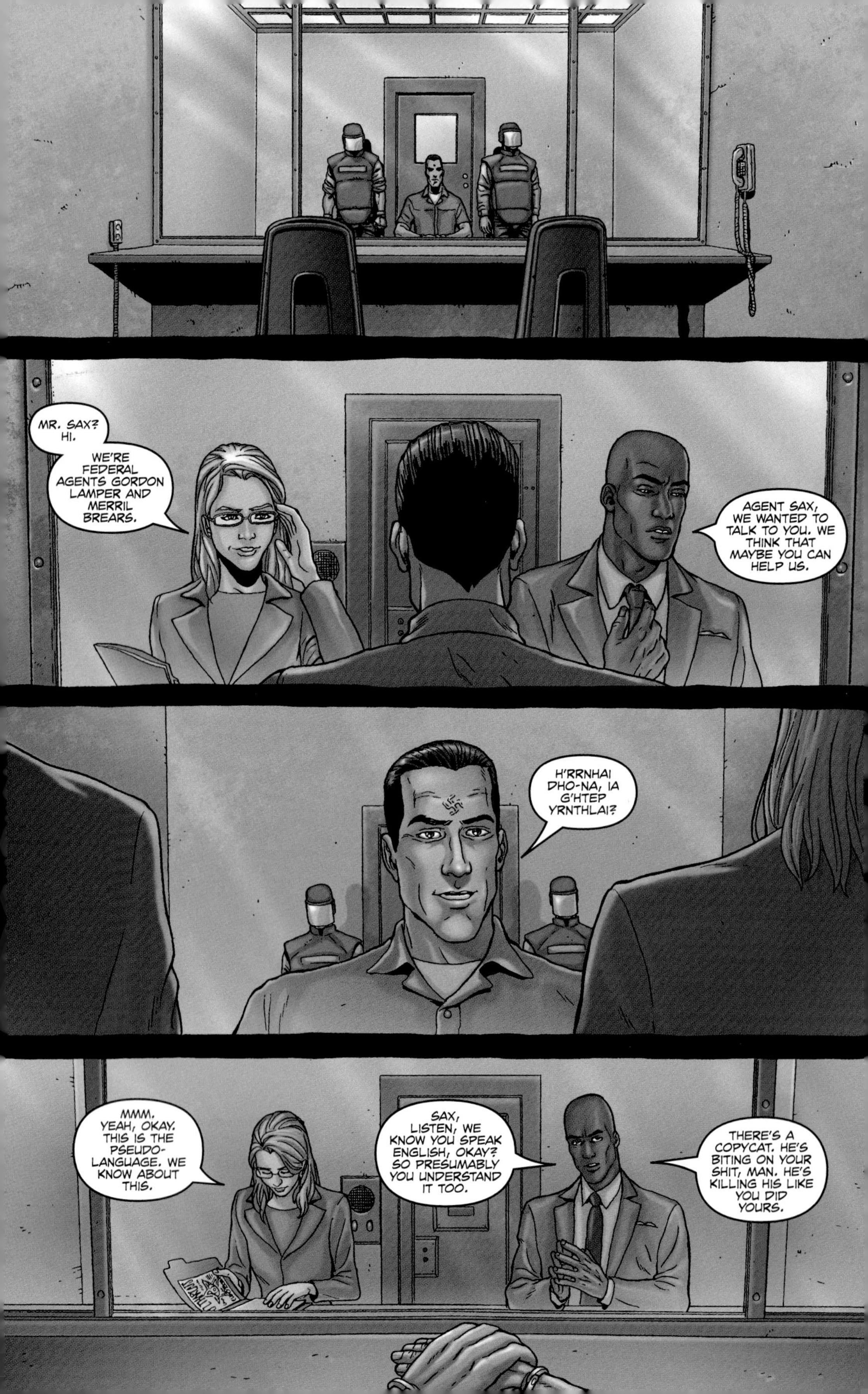
MR. SAX? HI.
WE'RE FEDERAL AGENTS GORDON LAMPER AND MERRIL BREARS.
AGENT SAX, WE WANTED TO TALK TO YOU. WE THINK THAT MAYBE YOU CAN HELP US.
H'RRNHAI DHO-NA, IA G'HTEP YRNTHLAI?
MMM. YEAH, OKAY. THIS IS THE PSEUDO-LANGUAGE. WE KNOW ABOUT THIS.
SAX, LISTEN, WE KNOW YOU SPEAK ENGLISH, OKAY? SO PRESUMABLY YOU UNDERSTAND IT TOO.
THERE'S A COPYCAT. HE'S BITING ON YOUR SHIT, MAN. HE'S KILLING HIS LIKE YOU DID YOURS.

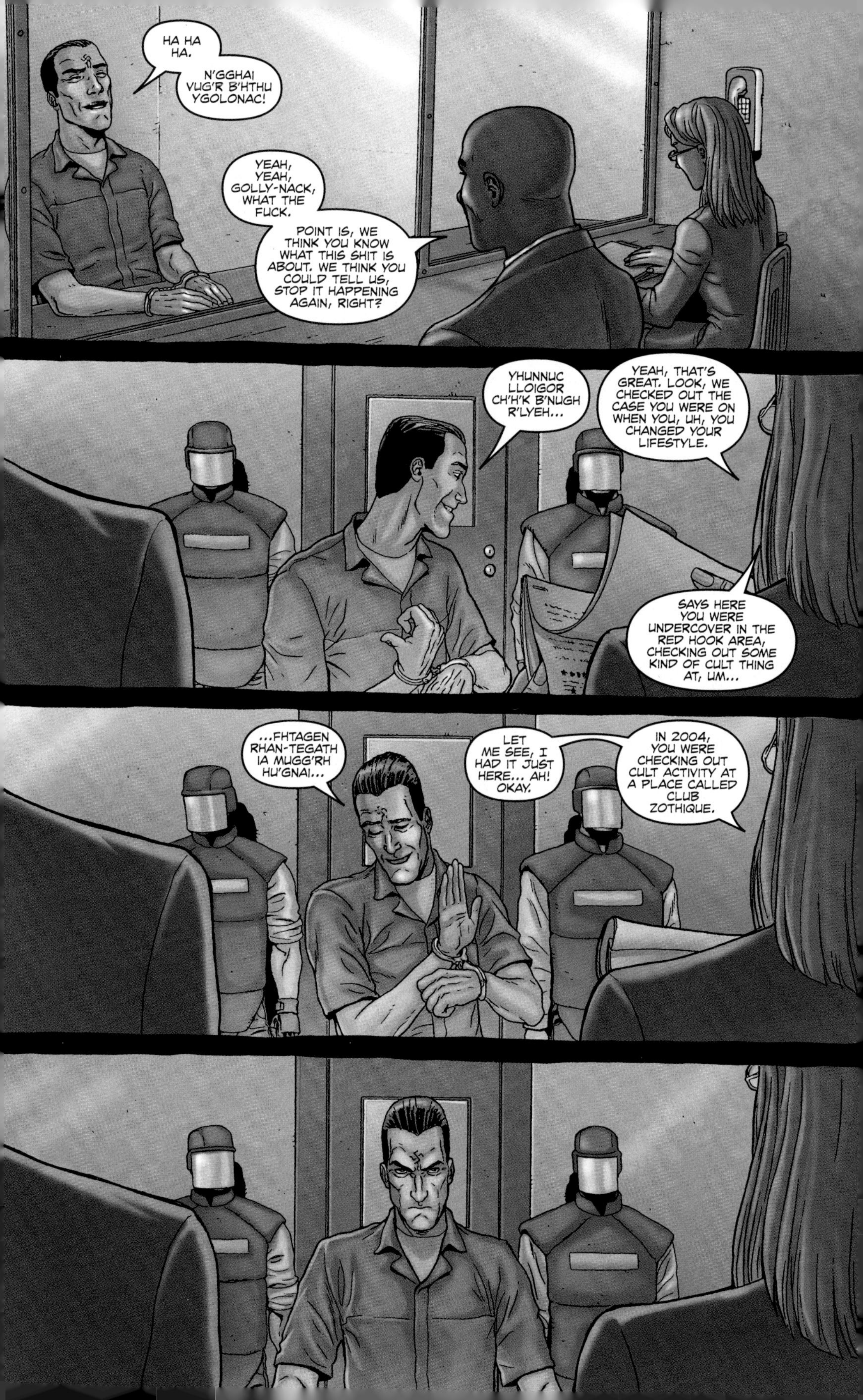
HA HA HA.
N'GGHAI VUG'R B'HTHU YGOLONAC!
YEAH, YEAH, GOLLY-NACK, WHAT THE FUCK.
POINT IS, WE THINK YOU KNOW WHAT THIS SHIT IS ABOUT. WE THINK YOU COULD TELL US, STOP IT HAPPENING AGAIN, RIGHT?
YHUNNUC LLOIGOR CH'H'K B'NUGH R'LYEH...
YEAH, THAT'S GREAT. LOOK, WE CHECKED OUT THE CASE YOU WERE ON WHEN YOU, UH, YOU CHANGED YOUR LIFESTYLE.
SAYS HERE YOU WERE UNDERCOVER IN THE RED HOOK AREA, CHECKING OUT SOME KIND OF CULT THING AT, UM...
...FHTAGEN RHAN-TEGATH IA MUGG'RH HU'GNAI...
LET ME SEE, I HAD IT JUST HERE... AH! OKAY.
IN 2004, YOU WERE CHECKING OUT CULT ACTIVITY AT A PLACE CALLED CLUB ZOTHIQUE.

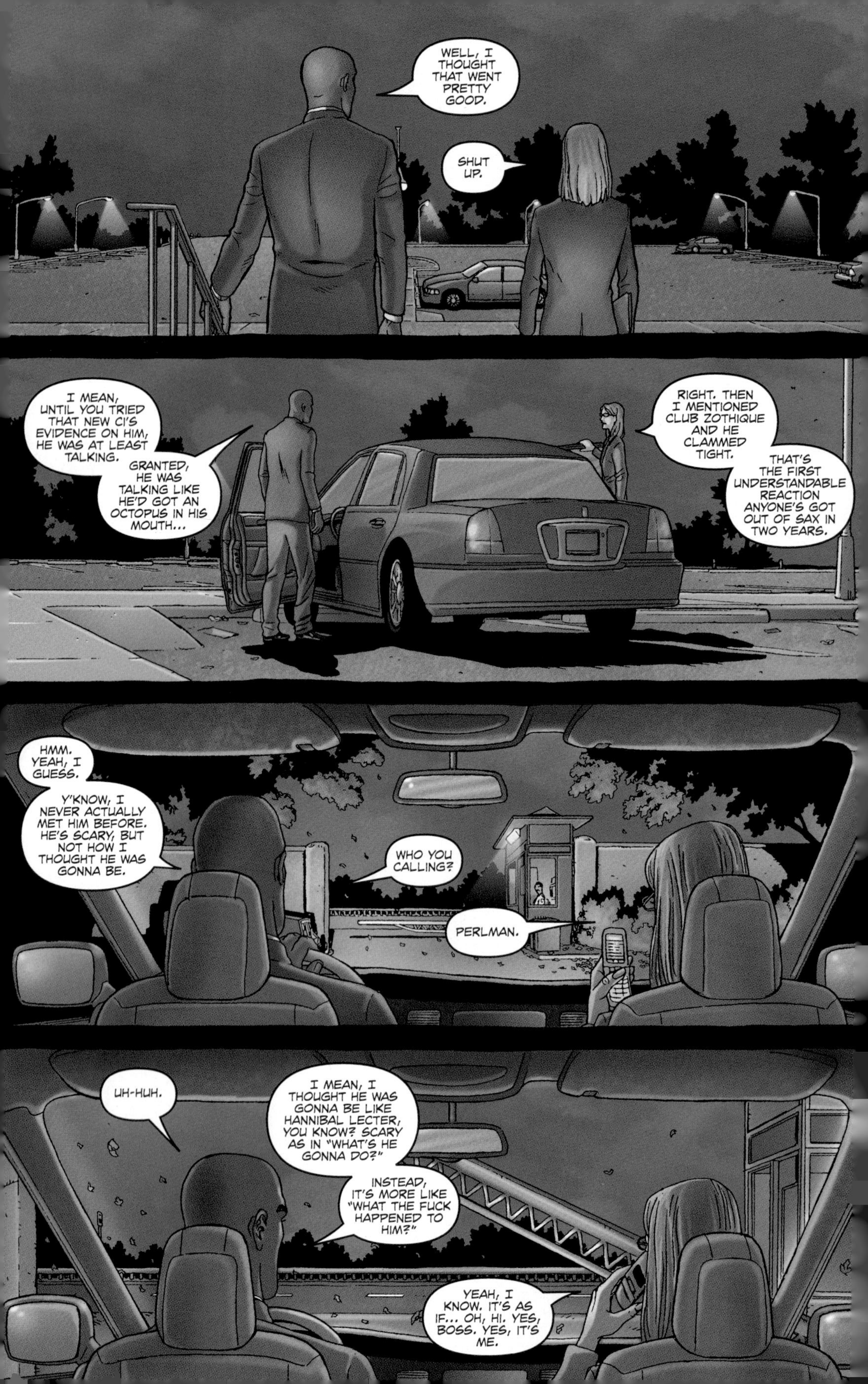
WELL, I THOUGHT THAT WENT PRETTY GOOD.
SHUT UP.
I MEAN, UNTIL YOU TRIED THAT NEW CI'S EVIDENCE ON HIM, HE WAS AT LEAST TALKING.
GRANTED, HE WAS TALKING LIKE HE'D GOT AN OCTOPUS IN HIS MOUTH...
RIGHT. THEN I MENTIONED CLUB ZOTHIQUE AND HE CLAMMED TIGHT.
THAT'S THE FIRST UNDERSTANDABLE REACTION ANYONE'S GOT OUT OF SAX IN TWO YEARS.
HMM. YEAH, I GUESS.
Y'KNOW, I NEVER ACTUALLY MET HIM BEFORE. HE'S SCARY, BUT NOT HOW I THOUGHT HE WAS GONNA BE.
WHO YOU CALLING?
PERLMAN.
UH-HUH.
I MEAN, I THOUGHT HE WAS GONNA BE LIKE HANNIBAL LECTER, YOU KNOW? SCARY AS IN "WHAT'S HE GONNA DO?"
INSTEAD, IT'S MORE LIKE "WHAT THE FUCK HAPPENED TO HIM?"
YEAH, I KNOW. IT'S AS IF... OH, HI. YES, BOSS. YES, IT'S ME.

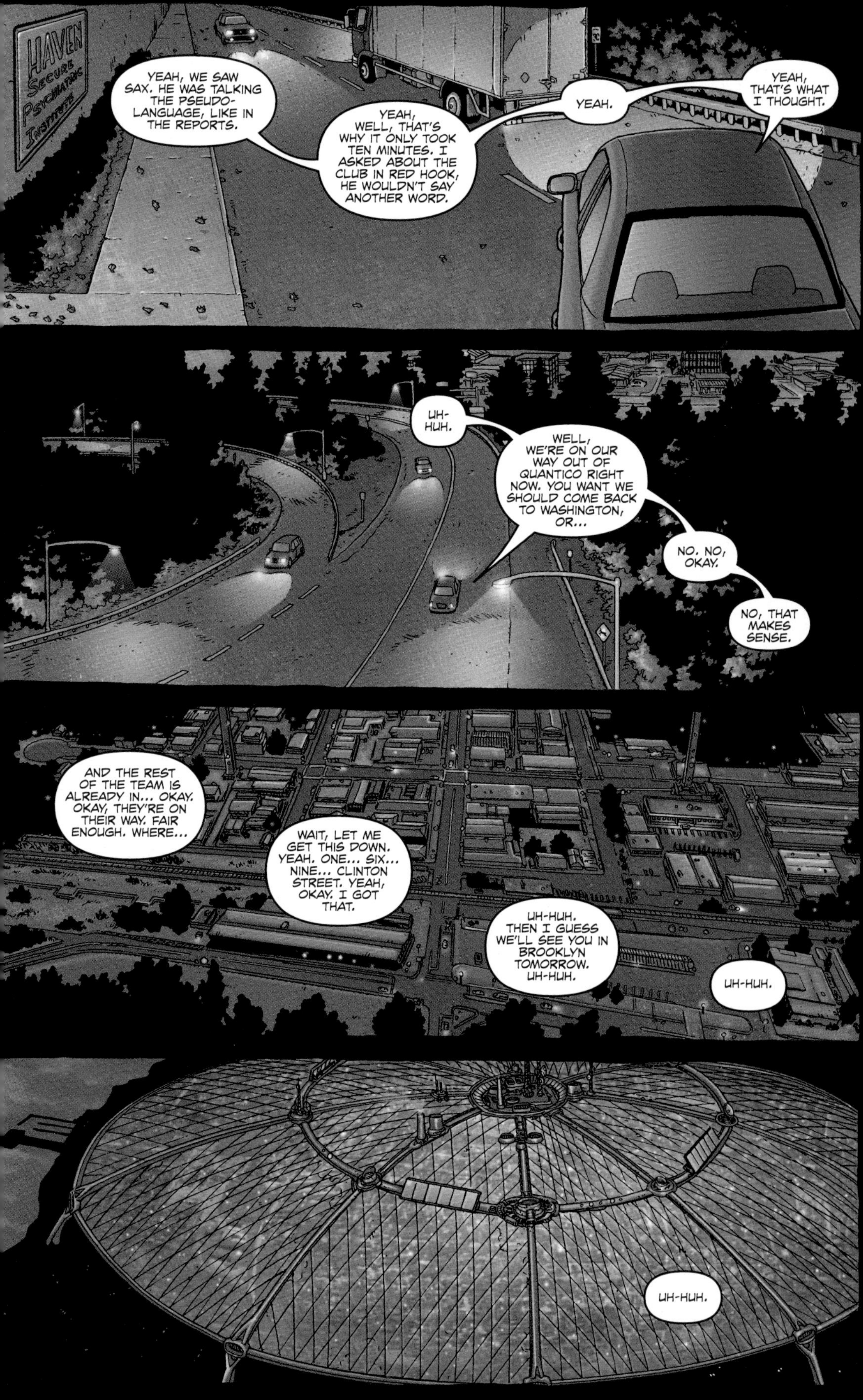
HAVEN
SECURE PSYCHIATRIC INSTITUTE
YEAH, WE SAW SAX. HE WAS TALKING THE PSEUDO-LANGUAGE, LIKE IN THE REPORTS.
YEAH, WELL, THAT'S WHY IT ONLY TOOK TEN MINUTES. I ASKED ABOUT THE CLUB IN RED HOOK, HE WOULDN'T SAY ANOTHER WORD.
YEAH.
YEAH, THAT'S WHAT I THOUGHT.
UH-HUH.
WELL, WE'RE ON OUR WAY OUT OF QUANTICO RIGHT NOW. YOU WANT WE SHOULD COME BACK TO WASHINGTON, OR...
NO. NO, OKAY.
NO, THAT MAKES SENSE.
AND THE REST OF THE TEAM IS ALREADY IN... OKAY. OKAY, THEY'RE ON THEIR WAY. FAIR ENOUGH. WHERE...
WAIT, LET ME GET THIS DOWN. YEAH. ONE... SIX... NINE... CLINTON STREET. YEAH, OKAY. I GOT THAT.
UH-HUH. THEN I GUESS WE'LL SEE YOU IN BROOKLYN TOMORROW. UH-HUH.
UH-HUH.
UH-HUH.

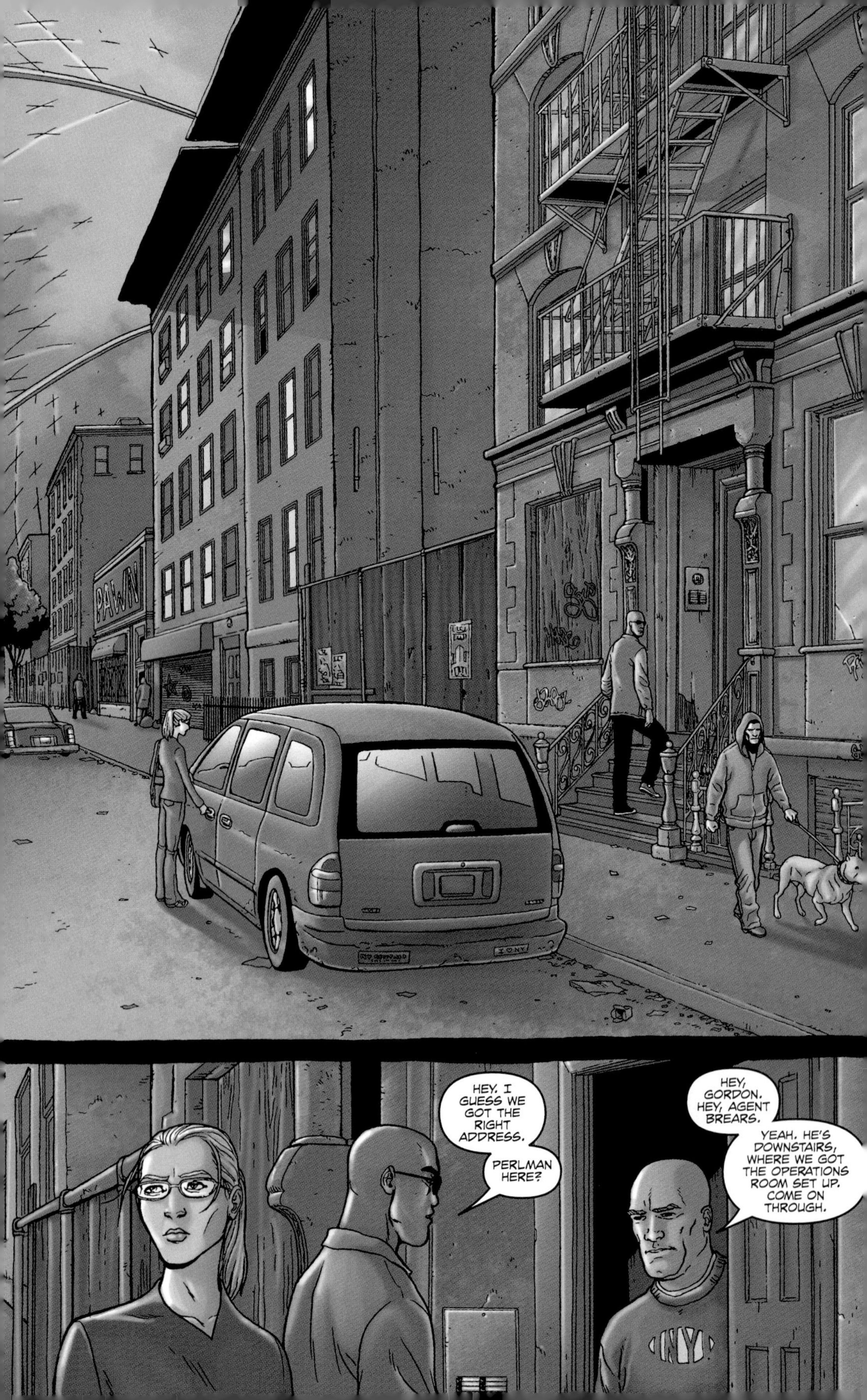
PAWN
HEY. I GUESS WE GOT THE RIGHT ADDRESS.
PERLMAN HERE?
HEY, GORDON. HEY, AGENT BREARS.
YEAH. HE'S DOWNSTAIRS, WHERE WE GOT THE OPERATIONS ROOM SET UP. COME ON THROUGH.

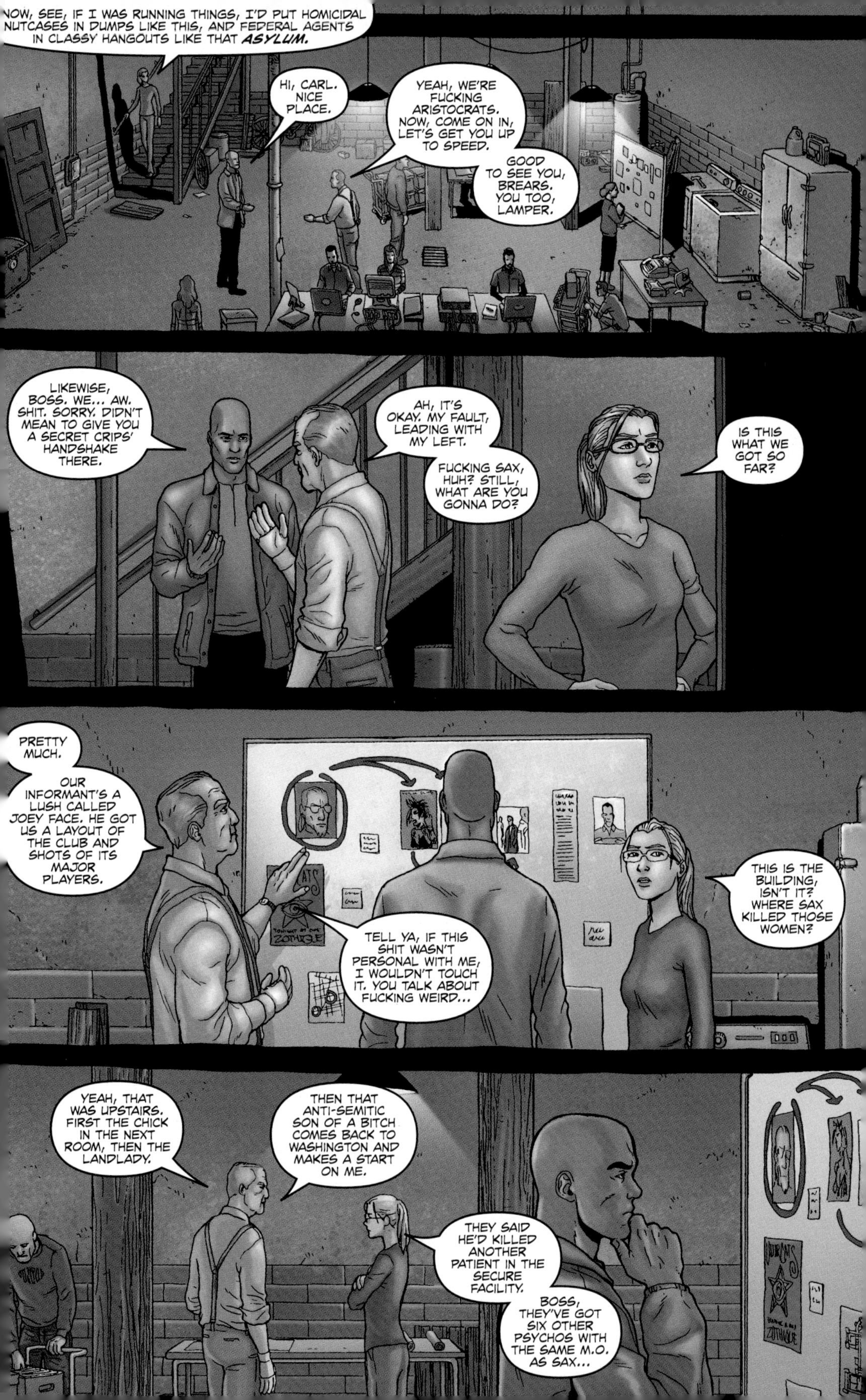
NOW, SEE, IF I WAS RUNNING THINGS, I'D PUT HOMICIDAL NUTCASES IN DUMPS LIKE THIS, AND FEDERAL AGENTS IN CLASSY HANGOUTS LIKE THAT *ASYLUM.*
HI, CARL. NICE PLACE.
YEAH, WE'RE FUCKING ARISTOCRATS. NOW, COME ON IN, LET'S GET YOU UP TO SPEED.
GOOD TO SEE YOU, BREARS. YOU TOO, LAMPER.
LIKEWISE, BOSS. WE... AW. SHIT. SORRY. DIDN'T MEAN TO GIVE YOU A SECRET CRIPS' HANDSHAKE THERE.
AH, IT'S OKAY. MY FAULT, LEADING WITH MY LEFT.
FUCKING SAX, HUH? STILL, WHAT ARE YOU GONNA DO?
IS THIS WHAT WE GOT SO FAR?
PRETTY MUCH.
OUR INFORMANT'S A LUSH CALLED JOEY FACE. HE GOT US A LAYOUT OF THE CLUB AND SHOTS OF ITS MAJOR PLAYERS.
TELL YA, IF THIS SHIT WASN'T PERSONAL WITH ME, I WOULDN'T TOUCH IT. YOU TALK ABOUT FUCKING WEIRD...
THIS IS THE BUILDING, ISN'T IT? WHERE SAX KILLED THOSE WOMEN?
YEAH, THAT WAS UPSTAIRS. FIRST THE CHICK IN THE NEXT ROOM, THEN THE LANDLADY.
THEN THAT ANTI-SEMITIC SON OF A BITCH COMES BACK TO WASHINGTON AND MAKES A START ON ME.
THEY SAID HE'D KILLED ANOTHER PATIENT IN THE SECURE FACILITY.
BOSS, THEY'VE GOT SIX OTHER PSYCHOS WITH THE SAME M.O. AS SAX...

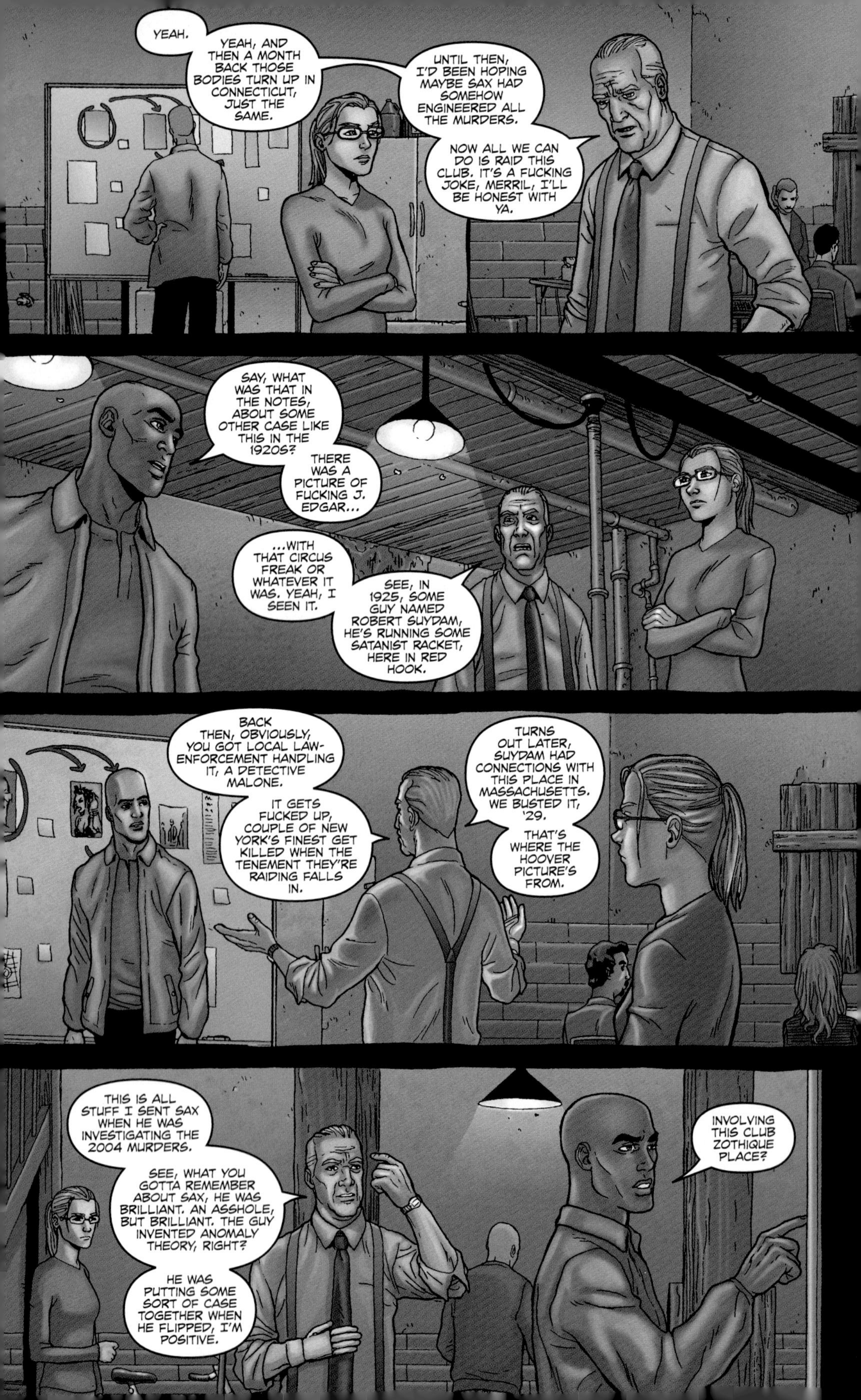
YEAH.
YEAH, AND THEN A MONTH BACK THOSE BODIES TURN UP IN CONNECTICUT, JUST THE SAME.
UNTIL THEN, I'D BEEN HOPING MAYBE SAX HAD SOMEHOW ENGINEERED ALL THE MURDERS.
NOW ALL WE CAN DO IS RAID THIS CLUB. IT'S A FUCKING JOKE, MERRIL, I'LL BE HONEST WITH YA.
SAY, WHAT WAS THAT IN THE NOTES, ABOUT SOME OTHER CASE LIKE THIS IN THE 1920S?
THERE WAS A PICTURE OF FUCKING J. EDGAR...
...WITH THAT CIRCUS FREAK OR WHATEVER IT WAS. YEAH, I SEEN IT.
SEE, IN 1925, SOME GUY NAMED ROBERT SUYDAM, HE'S RUNNING SOME SATANIST RACKET, HERE IN RED HOOK.
BACK THEN, OBVIOUSLY, YOU GOT LOCAL LAW-ENFORCEMENT HANDLING IT, A DETECTIVE MALONE.
IT GETS FUCKED UP, COUPLE OF NEW YORK'S FINEST GET KILLED WHEN THE TENEMENT THEY'RE RAIDING FALLS IN.
TURNS OUT LATER, SUYDAM HAD CONNECTIONS WITH THIS PLACE IN MASSACHUSETTS. WE BUSTED IT, '29.
THAT'S WHERE THE HOOVER PICTURE'S FROM.
THIS IS ALL STUFF I SENT SAX WHEN HE WAS INVESTIGATING THE 2004 MURDERS.
SEE, WHAT YOU GOTTA REMEMBER ABOUT SAX, HE WAS BRILLIANT. AN ASSHOLE, BUT BRILLIANT. THE GUY INVENTED ANOMALY THEORY, RIGHT?
HE WAS PUTTING SOME SORT OF CASE TOGETHER WHEN HE FLIPPED, I'M POSITIVE.
INVOLVING THIS CLUB ZOTHIQUE PLACE?

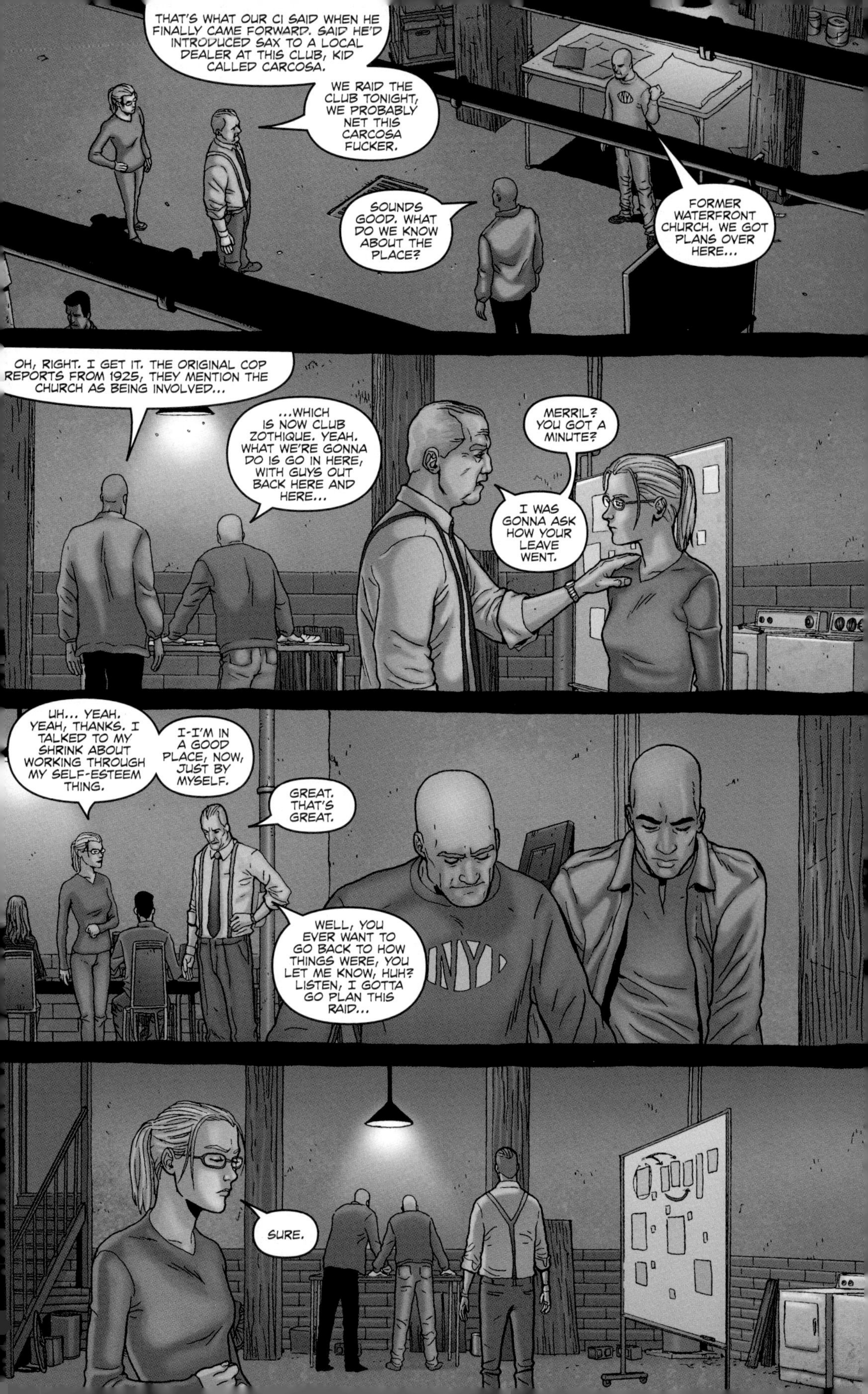
THAT'S WHAT OUR CI SAID WHEN HE FINALLY CAME FORWARD. SAID HE'D INTRODUCED SAX TO A LOCAL DEALER AT THIS CLUB, KID CALLED CARCOSA.
WE RAID THE CLUB TONIGHT, WE PROBABLY NET THIS CARCOSA FUCKER.
SOUNDS GOOD. WHAT DO WE KNOW ABOUT THE PLACE?
FORMER WATERFRONT CHURCH. WE GOT PLANS OVER HERE...
OH, RIGHT. I GET IT. THE ORIGINAL COP REPORTS FROM 1925, THEY MENTION THE CHURCH AS BEING INVOLVED...
...WHICH IS NOW CLUB ZOTHIQUE. YEAH. WHAT WE'RE GONNA DO IS GO IN HERE, WITH GUYS OUT BACK HERE AND HERE...
MERRIL? YOU GOT A MINUTE?
I WAS GONNA ASK HOW YOUR LEAVE WENT.
UH... YEAH. YEAH, THANKS. I TALKED TO MY SHRINK ABOUT WORKING THROUGH MY SELF-ESTEEM THING.
I-I'M IN A GOOD PLACE, NOW, JUST BY MYSELF.
GREAT. THAT'S GREAT.
WELL, YOU EVER WANT TO GO BACK TO HOW THINGS WERE, YOU LET ME KNOW, HUH? LISTEN, I GOTTA GO PLAN THIS RAID...
SURE.

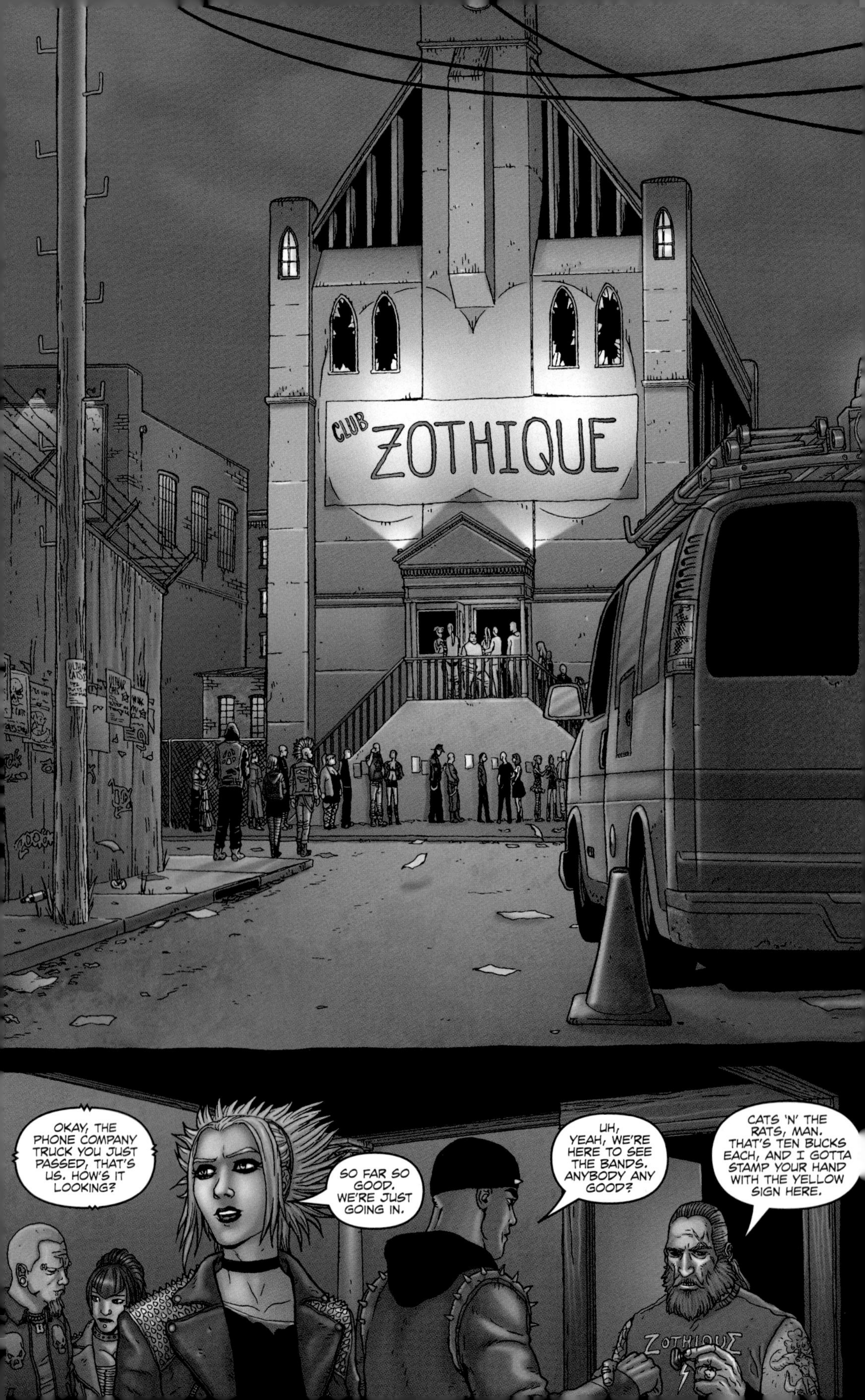
CLUB ZOTHIQUE
OKAY, THE PHONE COMPANY TRUCK YOU JUST PASSED, THAT'S US. HOW'S IT LOOKING?
SO FAR SO GOOD. WE'RE JUST GOING IN.
UH, YEAH, WE'RE HERE TO SEE THE BANDS. ANYBODY ANY GOOD?
CATS 'N' THE RATS, MAN. THAT'S TEN BUCKS EACH, AND I GOTTA STAMP YOUR HAND WITH THE YELLOW SIGN HERE.

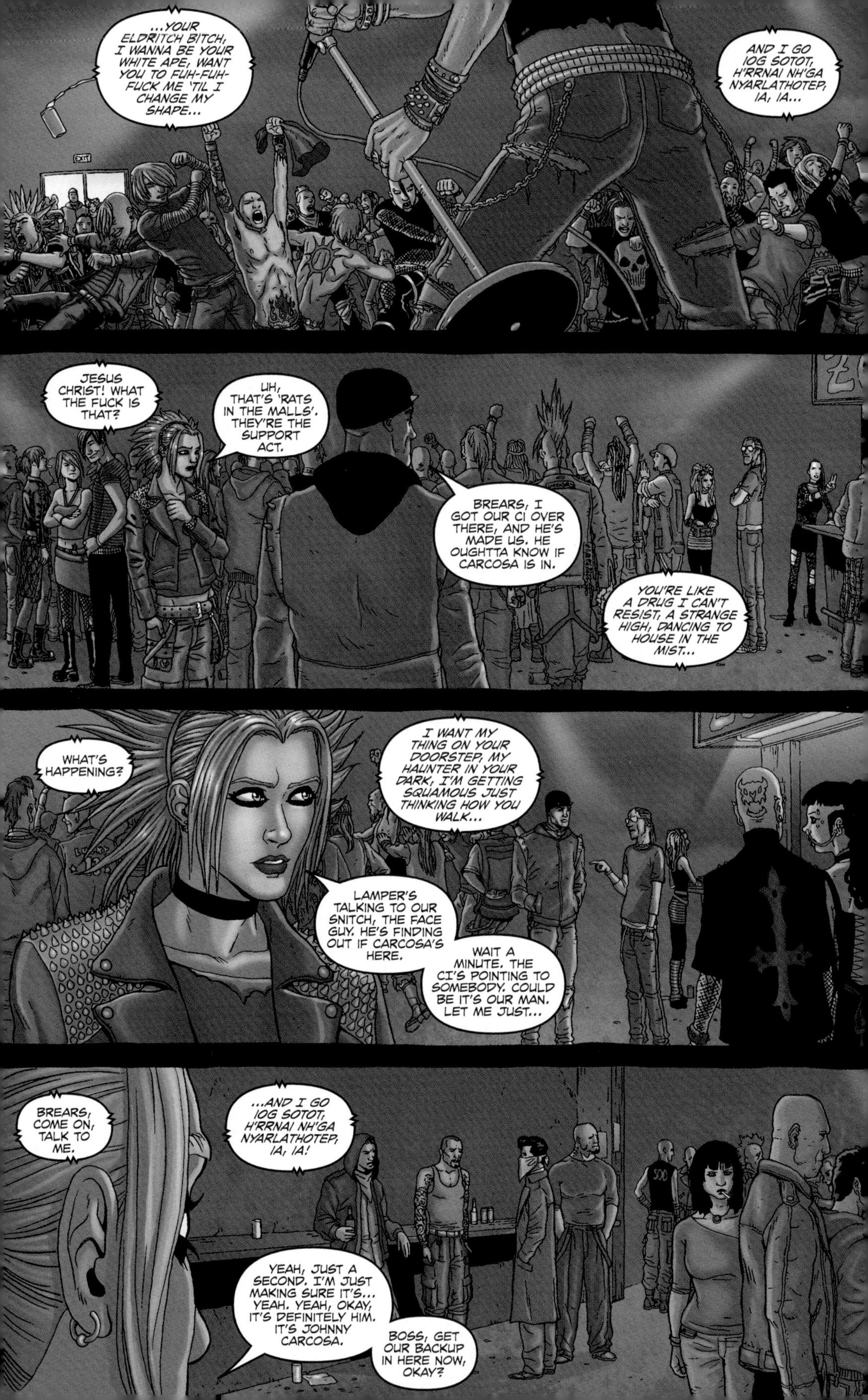
...YOUR ELDRITCH BITCH, I WANNA BE YOUR WHITE APE, WANT YOU TO FUH-FUH-FUCK ME 'TIL I CHANGE MY SHAPE...
AND I GO IOG SOTOT, H'RRNAI NH'GA NYARLATHOTEP, IA, IA...
EXIT
JESUS CHRIST! WHAT THE FUCK IS THAT?
UH, THAT'S 'RATS IN THE MALLS'. THEY'RE THE SUPPORT ACT.
BREARS, I GOT OUR CI OVER THERE, AND HE'S MADE US. HE OUGHTTA KNOW IF CARCOSA IS IN.
YOU'RE LIKE A DRUG I CAN'T RESIST, A STRANGE HIGH, DANCING TO HOUSE IN THE MIST...
WHAT'S HAPPENING?
I WANT MY THING ON YOUR DOORSTEP, MY HAUNTER IN YOUR DARK, I'M GETTING SQUAMOUS JUST THINKING HOW YOU WALK...
LAMPER'S TALKING TO OUR SNITCH, THE FACE GUY. HE'S FINDING OUT IF CARCOSA'S HERE.
WAIT A MINUTE. THE CI'S POINTING TO SOMEBODY. COULD BE IT'S OUR MAN. LET ME JUST...
BREARS, COME ON, TALK TO ME.
...AND I GO IOG SOTOT, H'RRNAI NH'GA NYARLATHOTEP, IA, IA!
YEAH, JUST A SECOND. I'M JUST MAKING SURE IT'S... YEAH. YEAH, OKAY, IT'S DEFINITELY HIM. IT'S JOHNNY CARCOSA.
BOSS, GET OUR BACKUP IN HERE NOW, OKAY?

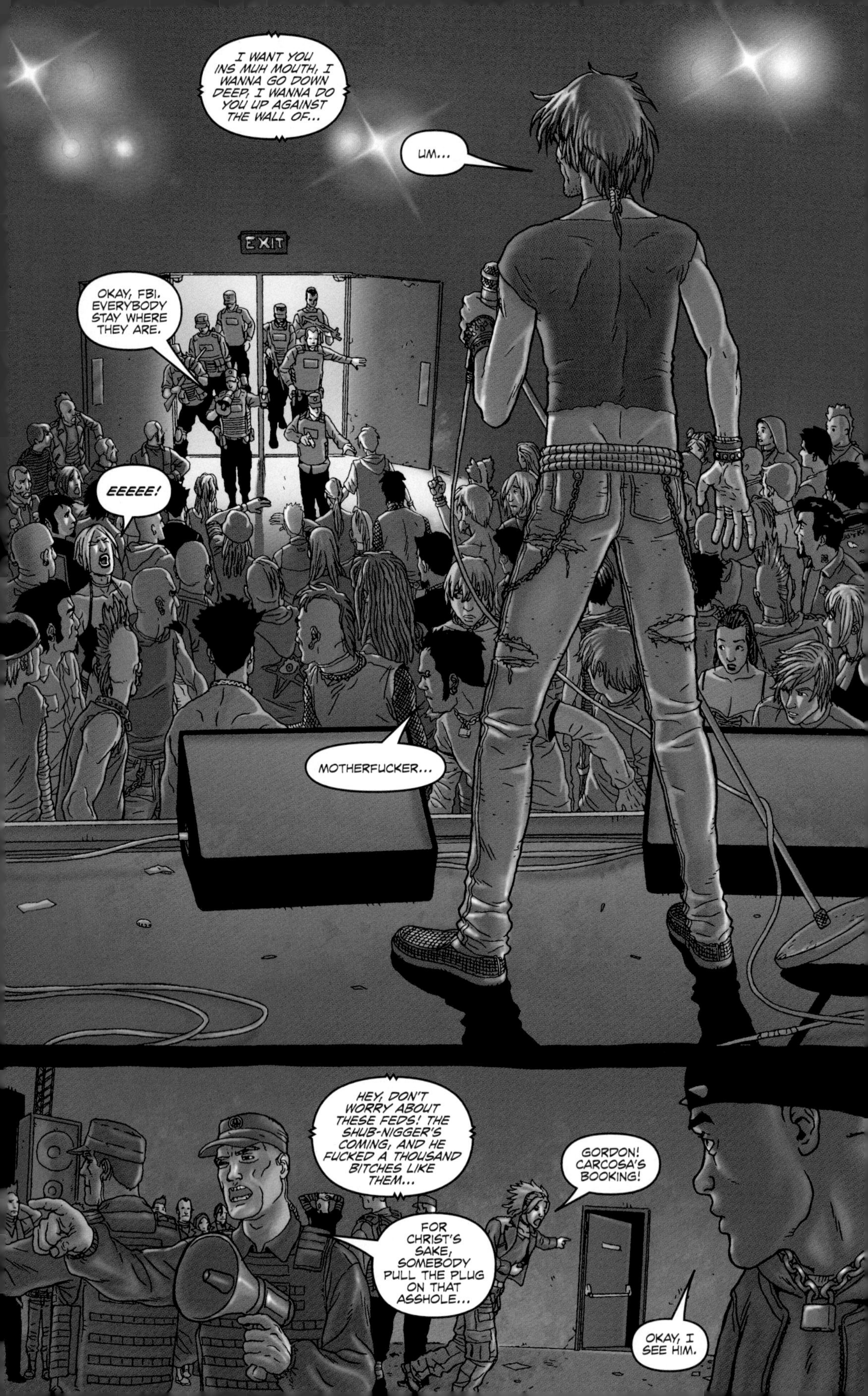
I WANT YOU INS MUH MOUTH, I WANNA GO DOWN DEEP, I WANNA DO YOU UP AGAINST THE WALL OF...
UM...
EXIT
OKAY, FBI. EVERYBODY STAY WHERE THEY ARE.
EEEEE!
MOTHERFUCKER...
HEY, DON'T WORRY ABOUT THESE FEDS! THE SHUB-NIGGER'S COMING, AND HE FUCKED A THOUSAND BITCHES LIKE THEM...
FOR CHRIST'S SAKE, SOMEBODY PULL THE PLUG ON THAT ASSHOLE...
GORDON! CARCOSA'S BOOKING!
OKAY, I SEE HIM.

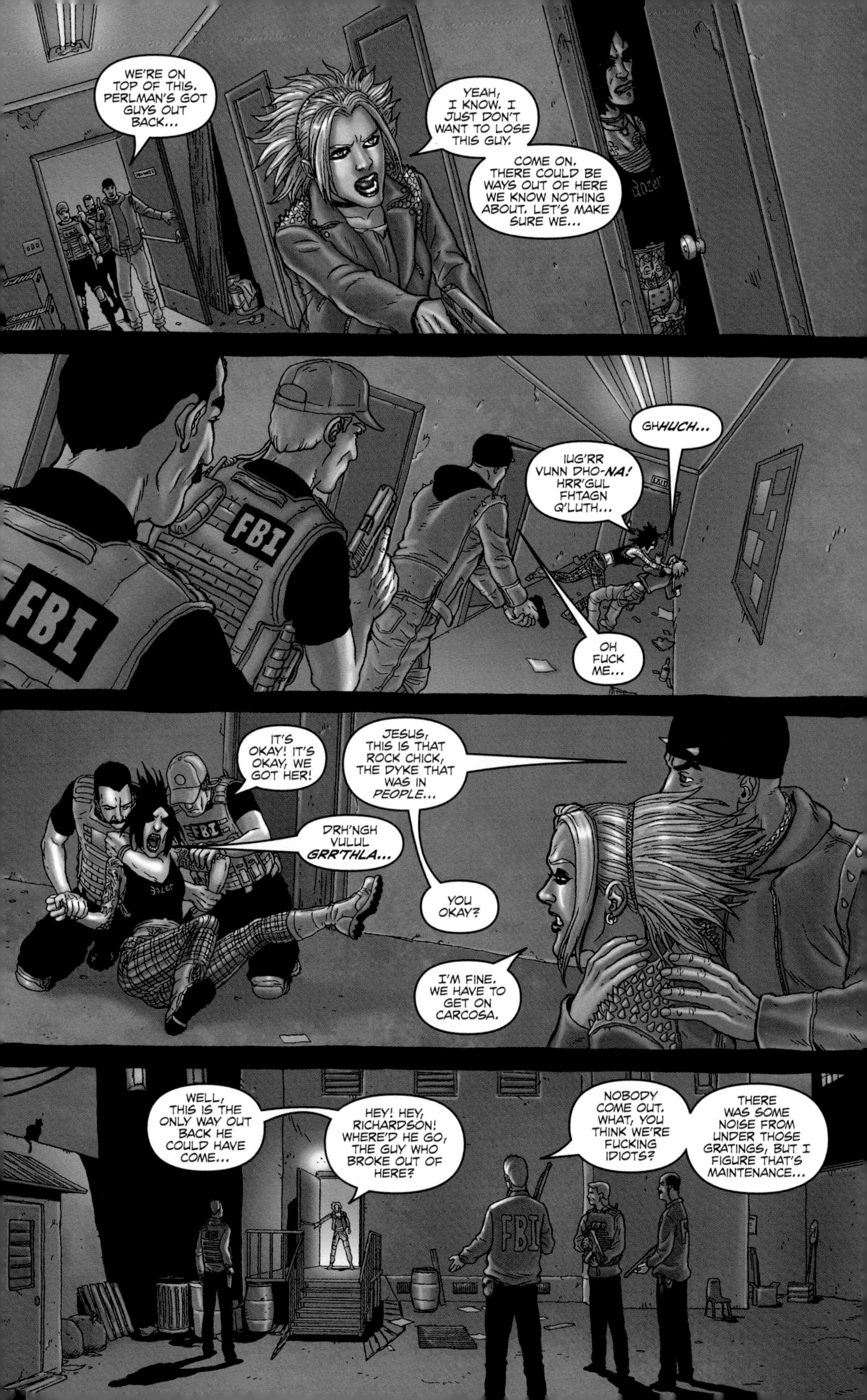

WE'RE ON TOP OF THIS. PERLMAN'S GOT GUYS OUT BACK...
YEAH, I KNOW. I JUST DON'T WANT TO LOSE THIS GUY.
COME ON. THERE COULD BE WAYS OUT OF HERE WE KNOW NOTHING ABOUT. LET'S MAKE SURE WE...
GHHUCH...
IUG'RR VUNN DHO-NA! HRR'GUL FHTAGN Q'LUTH...
OH FUCK ME...
IT'S OKAY! IT'S OKAY, WE GOT HER!
JESUS, THIS IS THAT ROCK CHICK, THE DYKE THAT WAS IN PEOPLE...
DRH'NGH VULUL GRR'THLA...
YOU OKAY?
I'M FINE. WE HAVE TO GET ON CARCOSA.
WELL, THIS IS THE ONLY WAY OUT BACK HE COULD HAVE COME...
HEY! HEY, RICHARDSON! WHERE'D HE GO, THE GUY WHO BROKE OUT OF HERE?
NOBODY COME OUT. WHAT, YOU THINK WE'RE FUCKING IDIOTS?
THERE WAS SOME NOISE FROM UNDER THOSE GRATINGS, BUT I FIGURE THAT'S MAINTENANCE...

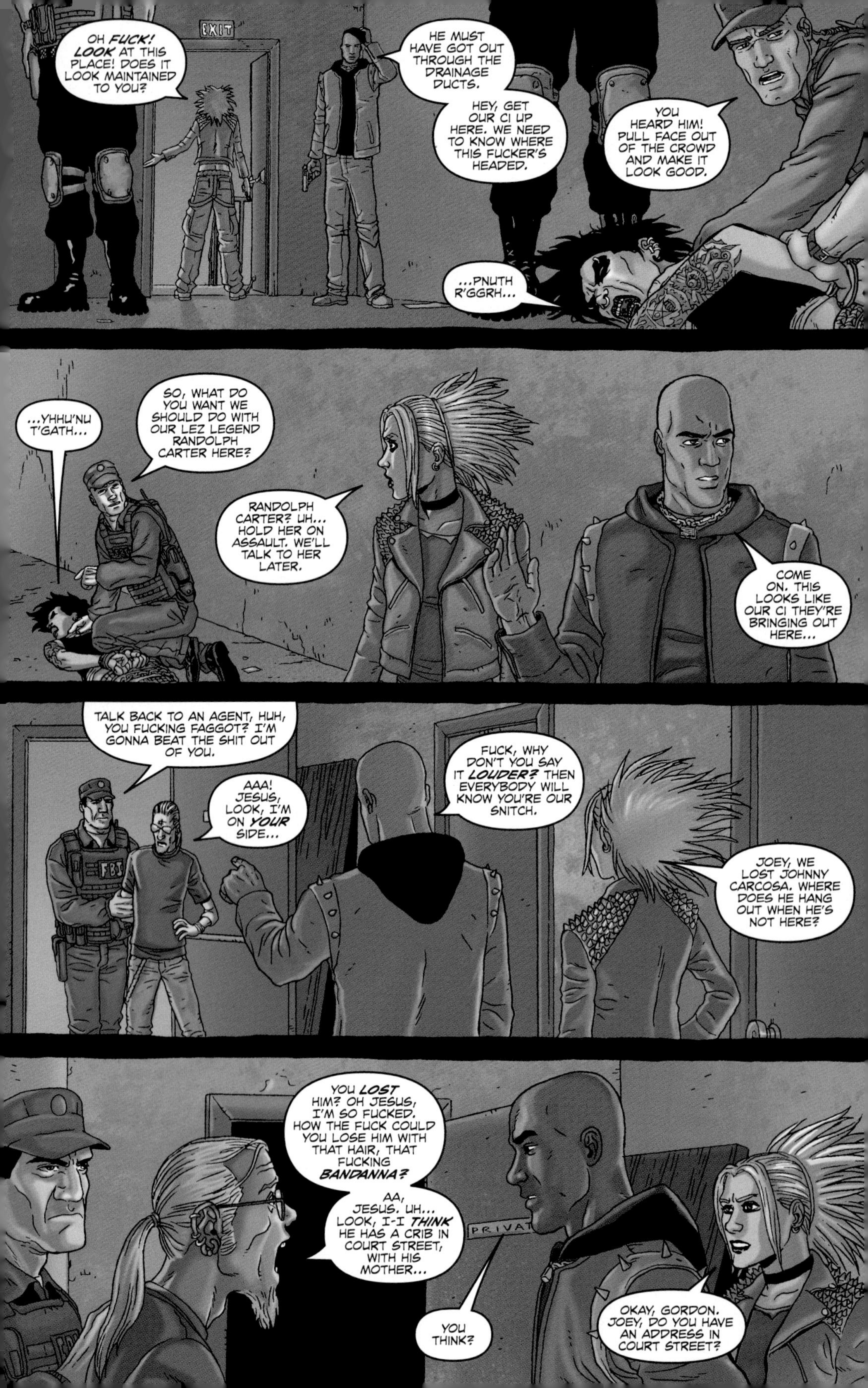
OH **FUCK!** **LOOK** AT THIS PLACE! DOES IT LOOK MAINTAINED TO YOU?
EXIT
HE MUST HAVE GOT OUT THROUGH THE DRAINAGE DUCTS.
HEY, GET **OUR** CI UP HERE. WE NEED TO KNOW WHERE THIS FUCKER'S HEADED.
YOU HEARD HIM! PULL FACE OUT OF THE CROWD AND MAKE IT LOOK GOOD.
...PNUTH R'GGRH...
...YHHU'NU T'GATH...
SO, WHAT DO YOU WANT WE SHOULD DO WITH OUR LEZ LEGEND RANDOLPH CARTER HERE?
RANDOLPH CARTER? UH... HOLD HER ON ASSAULT. WE'LL TALK TO HER LATER.
COME ON. THIS LOOKS LIKE OUR CI THEY'RE BRINGING OUT HERE...
TALK BACK TO AN AGENT, HUH, YOU FUCKING FAGGOT? I'M GONNA BEAT THE SHIT OUT OF YOU.
FBI
AAA! JESUS, LOOK, I'M ON **YOUR** SIDE...
FUCK, WHY DON'T YOU SAY IT **LOUDER?** THEN EVERYBODY WILL KNOW YOU'RE OUR SNITCH.
JOEY, WE LOST JOHNNY CARCOSA. WHERE DOES HE HANG OUT WHEN HE'S NOT HERE?
YOU **LOST** HIM? OH JESUS, I'M SO FUCKED. HOW THE FUCK COULD YOU LOSE HIM WITH THAT HAIR, THAT FUCKING **BANDANNA?**
AA, JESUS. UH... LOOK, I-I **THINK** HE HAS A CRIB IN COURT STREET, WITH HIS MOTHER...
YOU THINK?
OKAY, GORDON. JOEY, DO YOU HAVE AN ADDRESS IN COURT STREET?

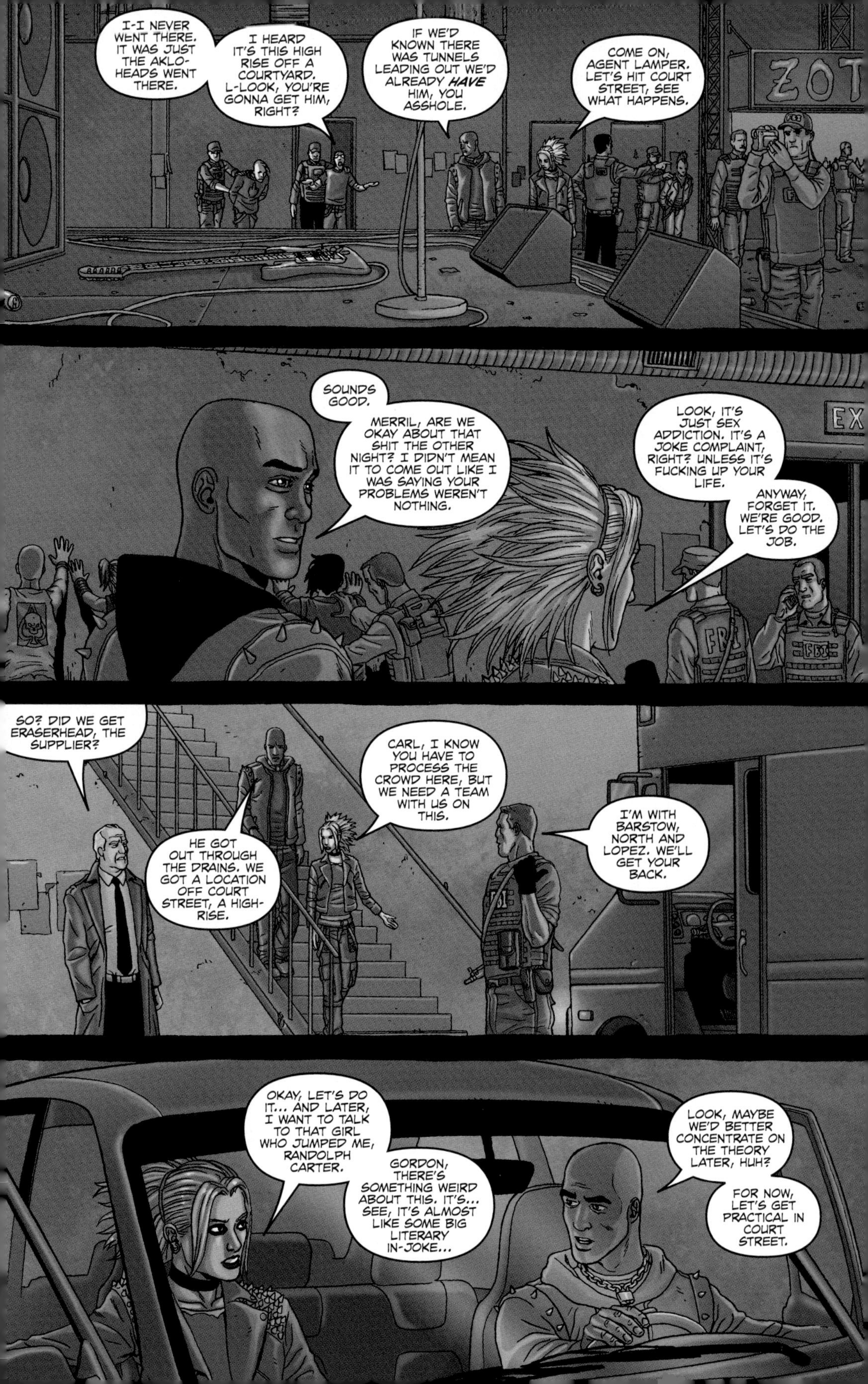

I-I NEVER WENT THERE. IT WAS JUST THE AKLO-HEADS WENT THERE.
I HEARD IT'S THIS HIGH RISE OFF A COURTYARD. L-LOOK, YOU'RE GONNA GET HIM, RIGHT?
IF WE'D KNOWN THERE WAS TUNNELS LEADING OUT WE'D ALREADY *HAVE* HIM, YOU ASSHOLE.
COME ON, AGENT LAMPER. LET'S HIT COURT STREET, SEE WHAT HAPPENS.
ZOT
SOUNDS GOOD.
MERRIL, ARE WE OKAY ABOUT THAT SHIT THE OTHER NIGHT? I DIDN'T MEAN IT TO COME OUT LIKE I WAS SAYING YOUR PROBLEMS WEREN'T NOTHING.
LOOK, IT'S JUST SEX ADDICTION. IT'S A JOKE COMPLAINT, RIGHT? UNLESS IT'S FUCKING UP YOUR LIFE.
ANYWAY, FORGET IT. WE'RE GOOD. LET'S DO THE JOB.
SO? DID WE GET ERASERHEAD, THE SUPPLIER?
HE GOT OUT THROUGH THE DRAINS. WE GOT A LOCATION OFF COURT STREET, A HIGH-RISE.
CARL, I KNOW YOU HAVE TO PROCESS THE CROWD HERE, BUT WE NEED A TEAM WITH US ON THIS.
I'M WITH BARSTOW, NORTH AND LOPEZ. WE'LL GET YOUR BACK.
OKAY, LET'S DO IT... AND LATER, I WANT TO TALK TO THAT GIRL WHO JUMPED ME, RANDOLPH CARTER.
GORDON, THERE'S SOMETHING WEIRD ABOUT THIS. IT'S... SEE, IT'S ALMOST LIKE SOME BIG LITERARY IN-JOKE...
LOOK, MAYBE WE'D BETTER CONCENTRATE ON THE THEORY LATER, HUH?
FOR NOW, LET'S GET PRACTICAL IN COURT STREET.

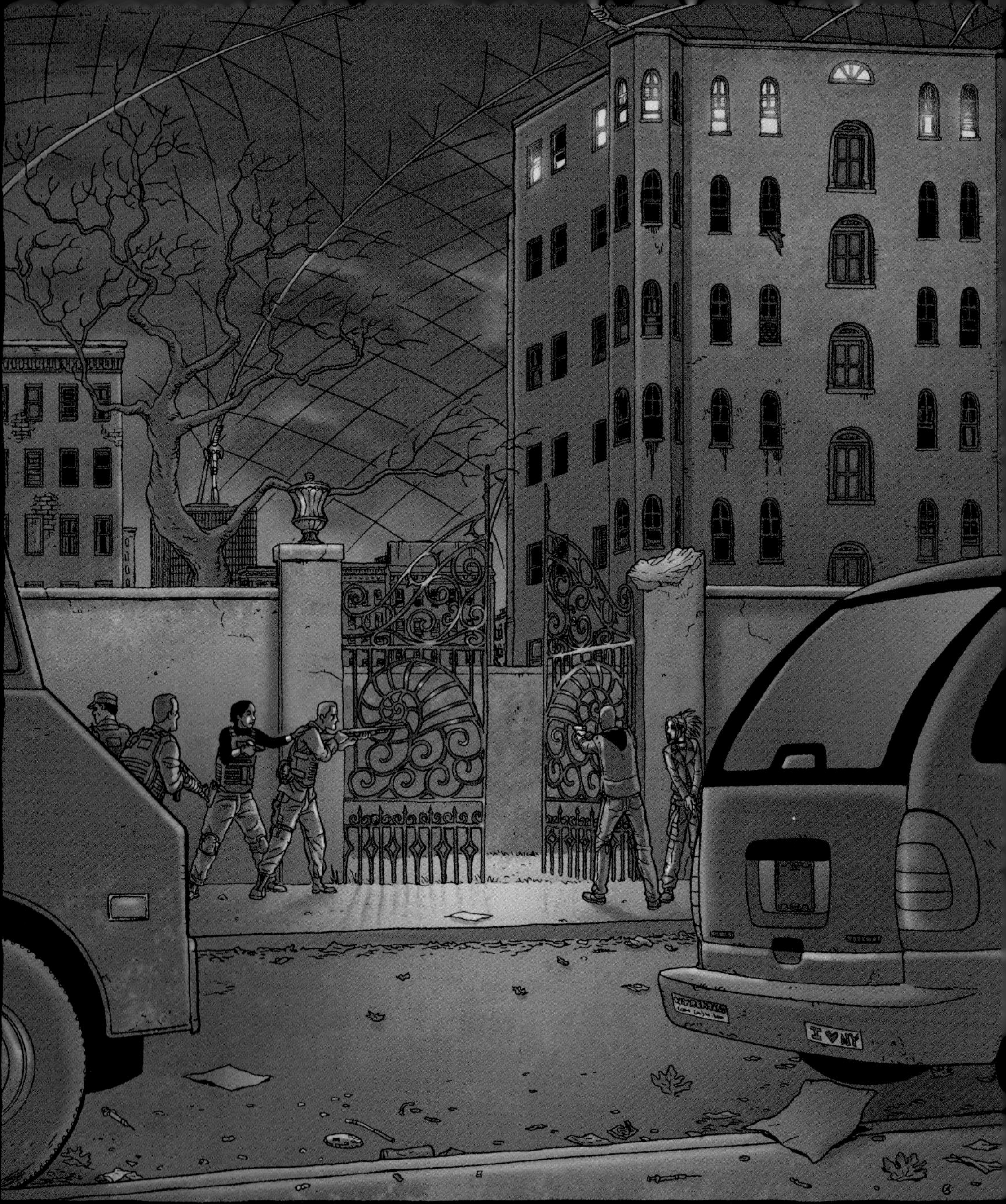

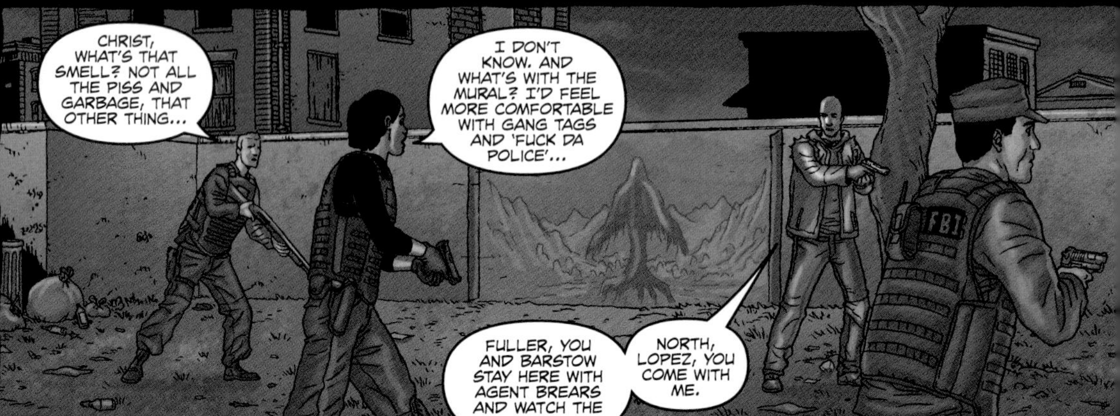
CHRIST, WHAT'S THAT SMELL? NOT ALL THE PISS AND GARBAGE, THAT OTHER THING...
I DON'T KNOW. AND WHAT'S WITH THE MURAL? I'D FEEL MORE COMFORTABLE WITH GANG TAGS AND 'FUCK DA POLICE'...
FULLER, YOU AND BARSTOW STAY HERE WITH AGENT BREARS AND WATCH THE YARD.
NORTH, LOPEZ, YOU COME WITH ME.

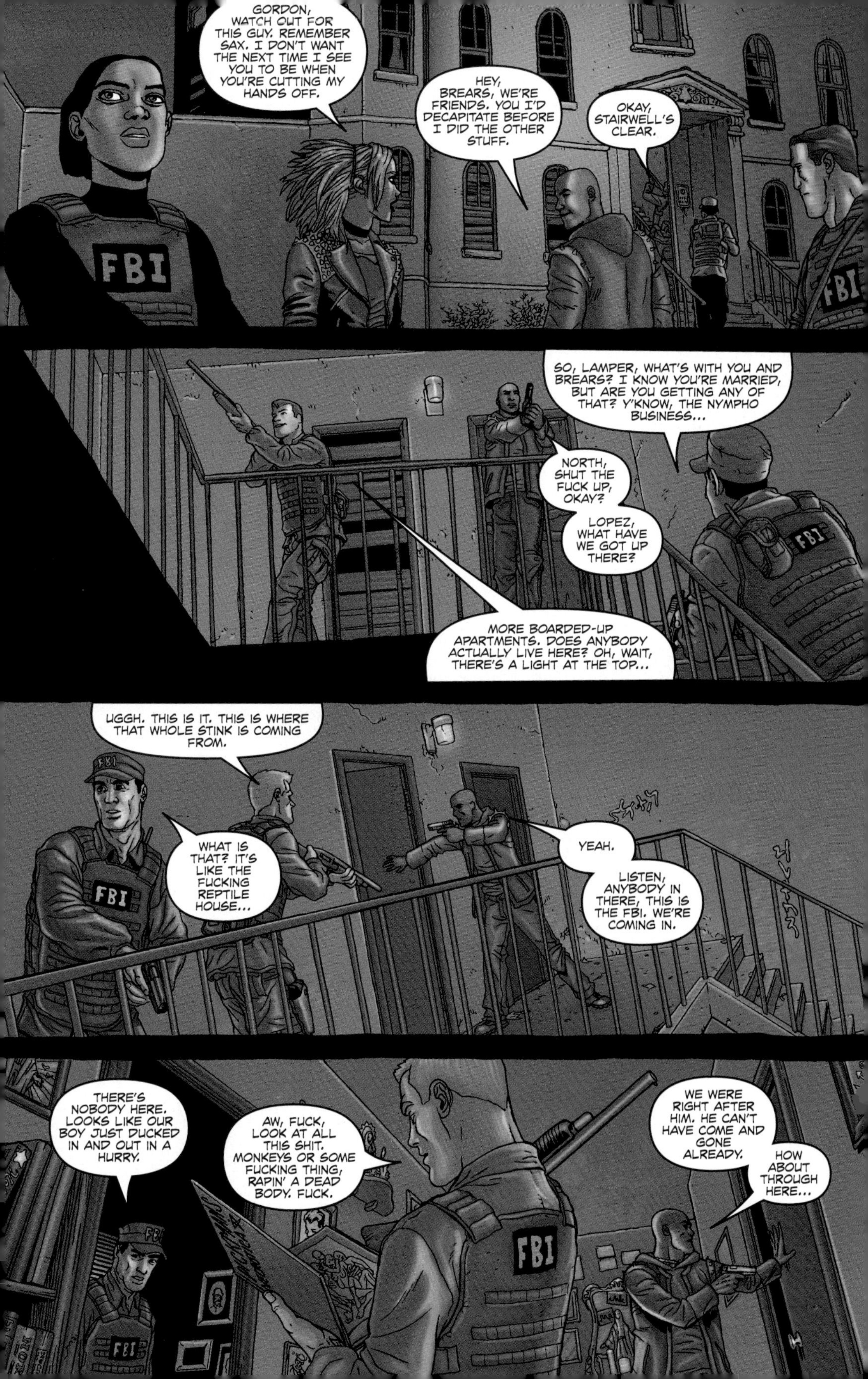
GORDON, WATCH OUT FOR THIS GUY. REMEMBER SAX. I DON'T WANT THE NEXT TIME I SEE YOU TO BE WHEN YOU'RE CUTTING MY HANDS OFF.
HEY, BREARS, WE'RE FRIENDS. YOU I'D DECAPITATE BEFORE I DID THE OTHER STUFF.
OKAY, STAIRWELL'S CLEAR.
SO, LAMPER, WHAT'S WITH YOU AND BREARS? I KNOW YOU'RE MARRIED, BUT ARE YOU GETTING ANY OF THAT? Y'KNOW, THE NYMPHO BUSINESS...
NORTH, SHUT THE FUCK UP, OKAY?
LOPEZ, WHAT HAVE WE GOT UP THERE?
MORE BOARDED-UP APARTMENTS. DOES ANYBODY ACTUALLY LIVE HERE? OH, WAIT, THERE'S A LIGHT AT THE TOP...
UGGH. THIS IS IT. THIS IS WHERE THAT WHOLE STINK IS COMING FROM.
WHAT IS THAT? IT'S LIKE THE FUCKING REPTILE HOUSE...
YEAH.
LISTEN, ANYBODY IN THERE, THIS IS THE FBI. WE'RE COMING IN.
THERE'S NOBODY HERE. LOOKS LIKE OUR BOY JUST DUCKED IN AND OUT IN A HURRY.
AW, FUCK, LOOK AT ALL THIS SHIT. MONKEYS OR SOME FUCKING THING, RAPIN' A DEAD BODY. FUCK.
WE WERE RIGHT AFTER HIM. HE CAN'T HAVE COME AND GONE ALREADY.
HOW ABOUT THROUGH HERE...

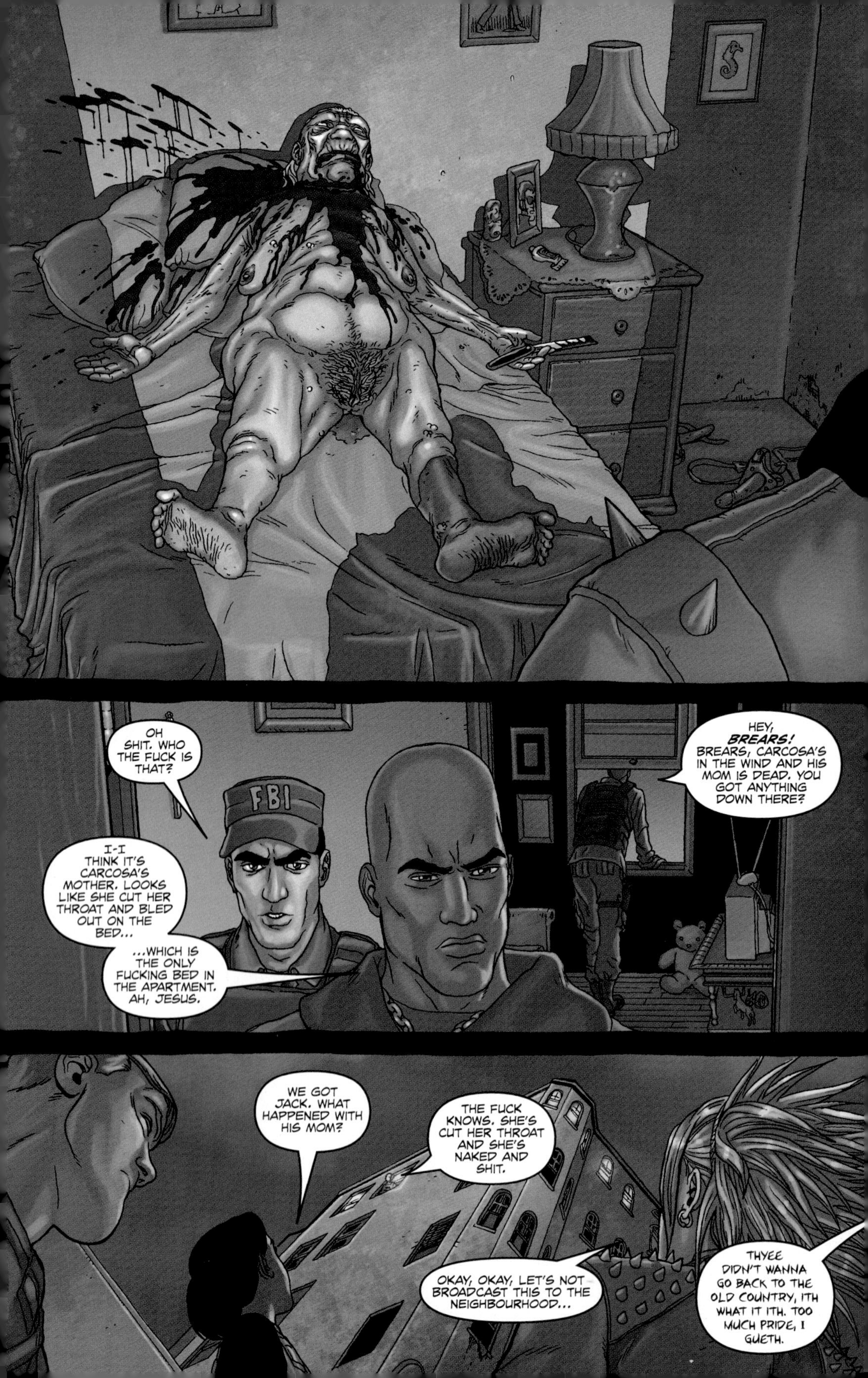
OH SHIT. WHO THE FUCK IS THAT?
HEY, BREARS! BREARS, CARCOSA'S IN THE WIND AND HIS MOM IS DEAD. YOU GOT ANYTHING DOWN THERE?
I-I THINK IT'S CARCOSA'S MOTHER. LOOKS LIKE SHE CUT HER THROAT AND BLED OUT ON THE BED...
...WHICH IS THE ONLY FUCKING BED IN THE APARTMENT. AH, JESUS.
WE GOT JACK. WHAT HAPPENED WITH HIS MOM?
THE FUCK KNOWS. SHE'S CUT HER THROAT AND SHE'S NAKED AND SHIT.
OKAY, OKAY, LET'S NOT BROADCAST THIS TO THE NEIGHBOURHOOD...
THYEE DIDN'T WANNA GO BACK TO THE OLD COUNTRY, ITH WHAT IT ITH. TOO MUCH PRIDE, I GUETH.
FBI

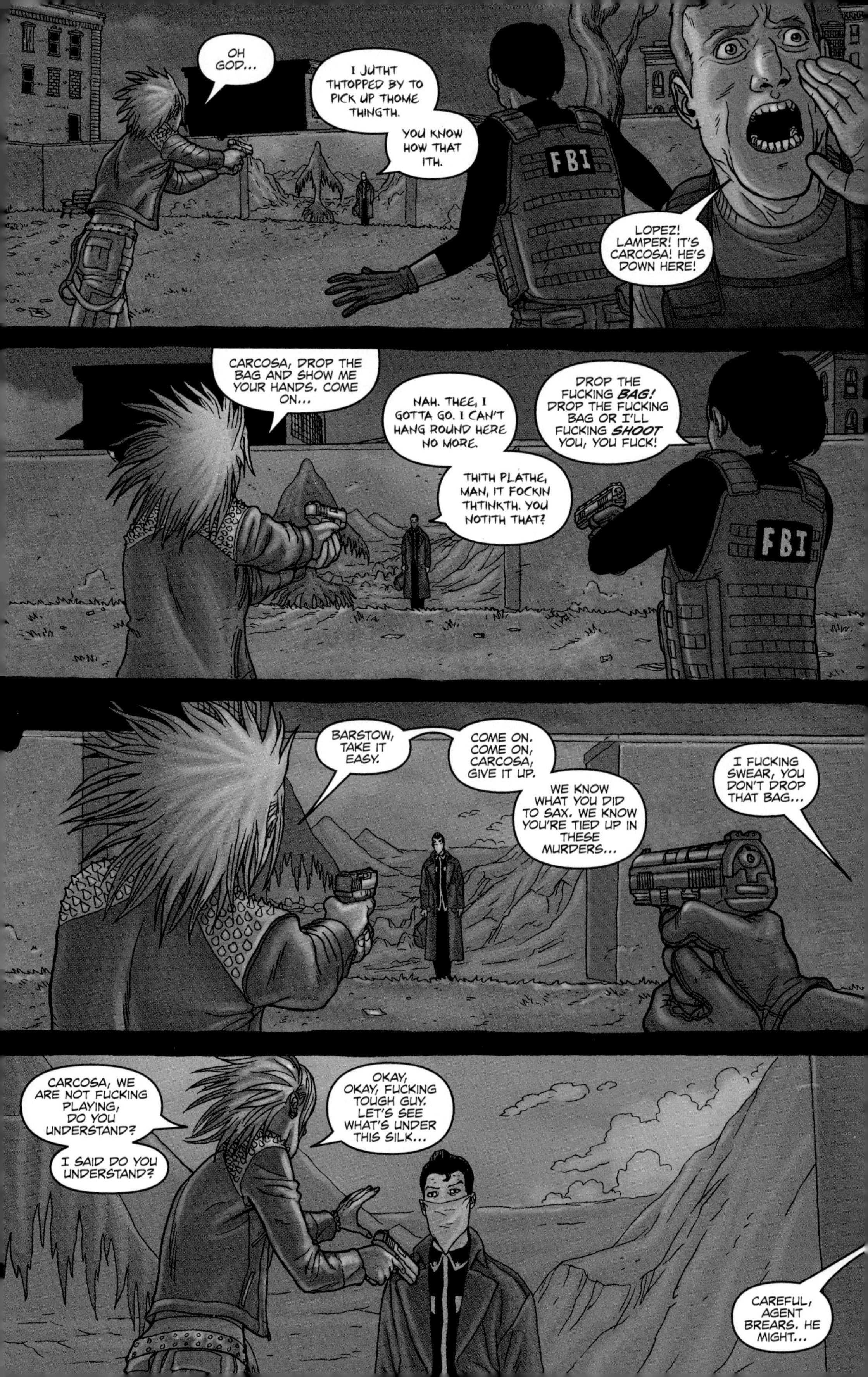
OH GOD...
I JUTHT THTOPPED BY TO PICK UP THOME THINGTH.
YOU KNOW HOW THAT ITH.
LOPEZ! LAMPER! IT'S CARCOSA! HE'S DOWN HERE!
CARCOSA, DROP THE BAG AND SHOW ME YOUR HANDS. COME ON...
NAH. THEE, I GOTTA GO. I CAN'T HANG ROUND HERE NO MORE.
THITH PLATHE, MAN, IT FOCKIN THTINKTH. YOU NOTITH THAT?
DROP THE FUCKING BAG! DROP THE FUCKING BAG OR I'LL FUCKING SHOOT YOU, YOU FUCK!
BARSTOW, TAKE IT EASY.
COME ON. COME ON, CARCOSA, GIVE IT UP.
WE KNOW WHAT YOU DID TO SAX. WE KNOW YOU'RE TIED UP IN THESE MURDERS...
I FUCKING SWEAR, YOU DON'T DROP THAT BAG...
CARCOSA, WE ARE NOT FUCKING PLAYING, DO YOU UNDERSTAND?
I SAID DO YOU UNDERSTAND?
OKAY, OKAY, FUCKING TOUGH GUY. LET'S SEE WHAT'S UNDER THIS SILK...
CAREFUL, AGENT BREARS. HE MIGHT...

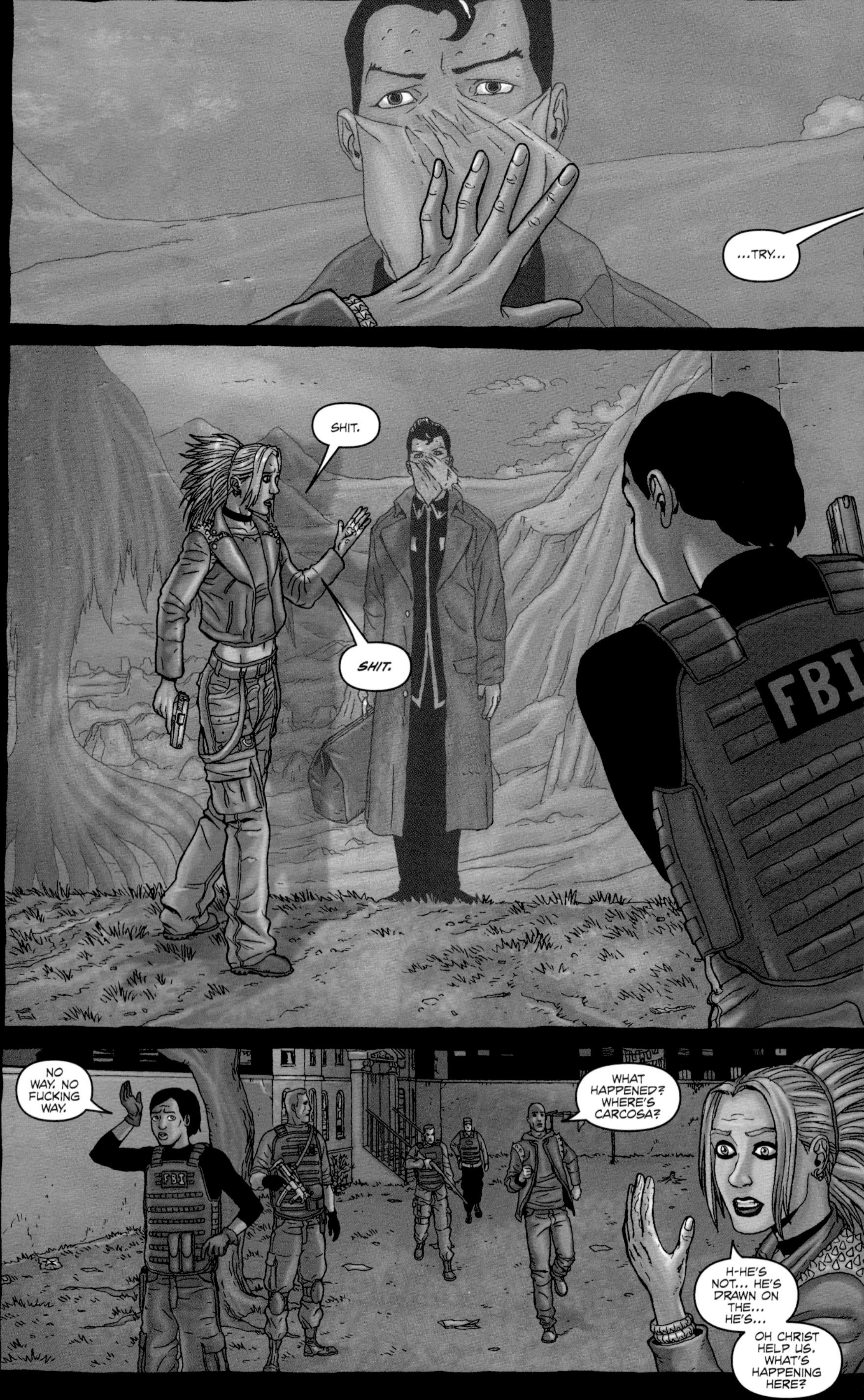
...TRY...
SHIT.
SHIT.
NO WAY. NO FUCKING WAY.
WHAT HAPPENED? WHERE'S CARCOSA?
H-HE'S NOT... HE'S DRAWN ON THE... HE'S...
OH CHRIST HELP US. WHAT'S HAPPENING HERE?

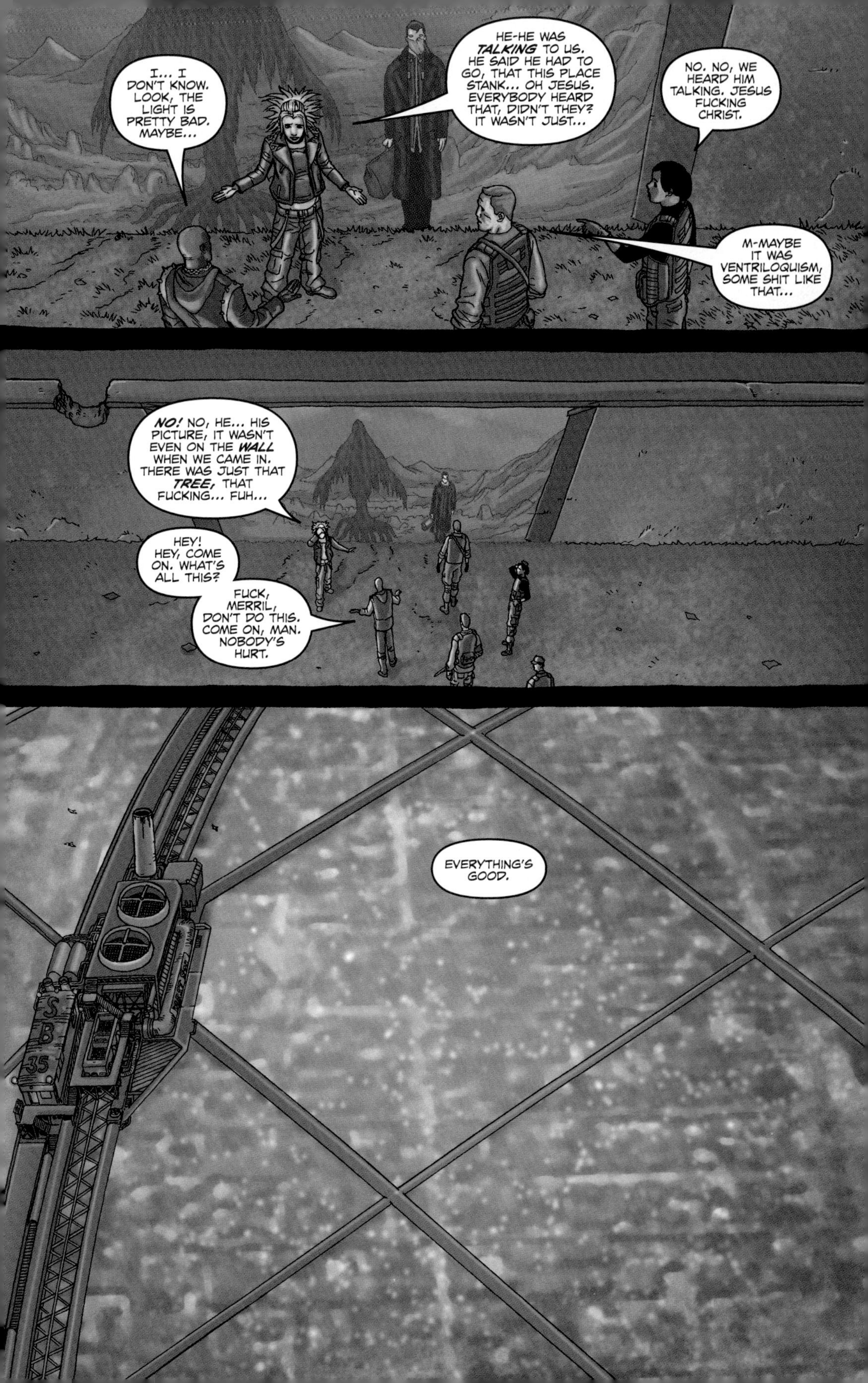
I... I DON'T KNOW. LOOK, THE LIGHT IS PRETTY BAD. MAYBE...
HE-HE WAS TALKING TO US. HE SAID HE HAD TO GO, THAT THIS PLACE STANK... OH JESUS. EVERYBODY HEARD THAT, DIDN'T THEY? IT WASN'T JUST...
NO. NO, WE HEARD HIM TALKING. JESUS FUCKING CHRIST.
M-MAYBE IT WAS VENTRILOQUISM, SOME SHIT LIKE THAT...
NO! NO, HE... HIS PICTURE, IT WASN'T EVEN ON THE WALL WHEN WE CAME IN. THERE WAS JUST THAT TREE, THAT FUCKING... FUH...
HEY! HEY, COME ON. WHAT'S ALL THIS?
FUCK, MERRIL, DON'T DO THIS. COME ON, MAN. NOBODY'S HURT.
EVERYTHING'S GOOD.

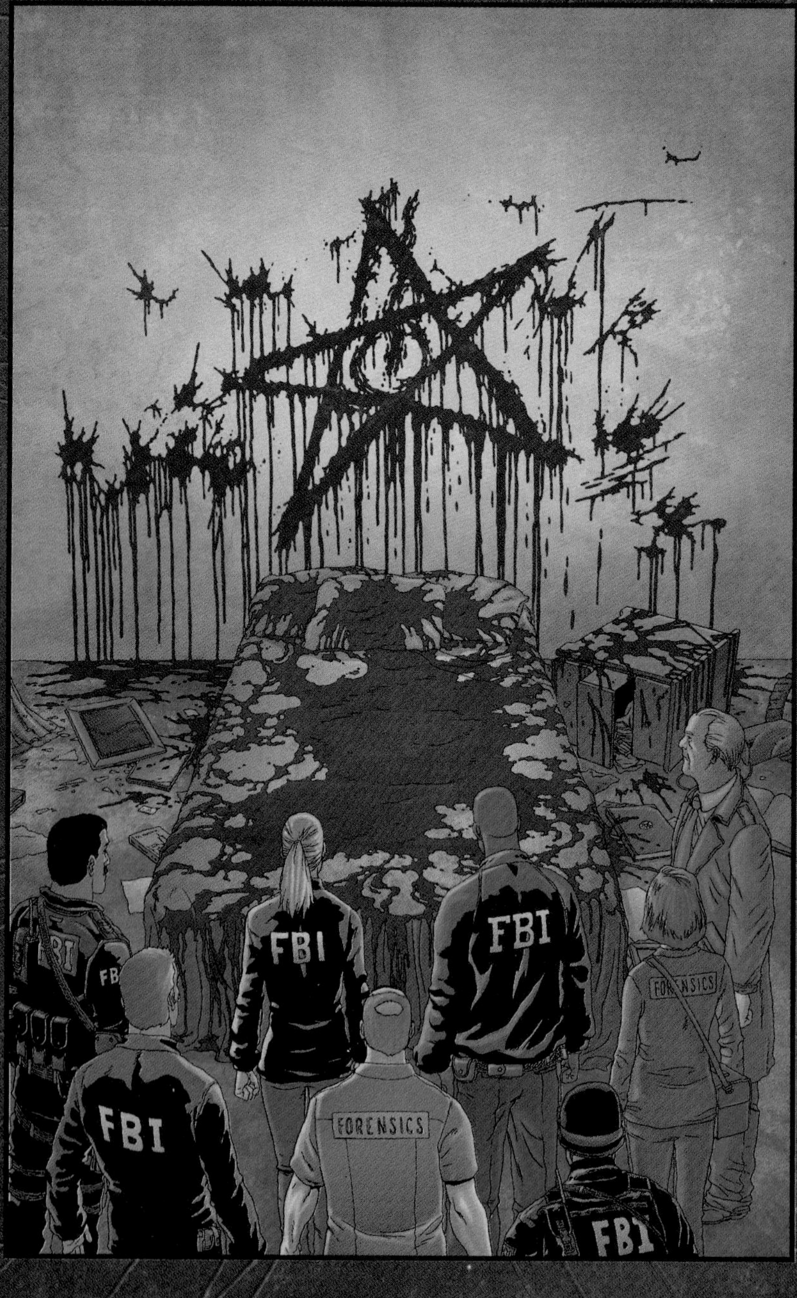
FBI
FB
FBI
FBI
FORENSICS
FBI
FORENSICS
FBI

NEONOMICON
Chapter 2

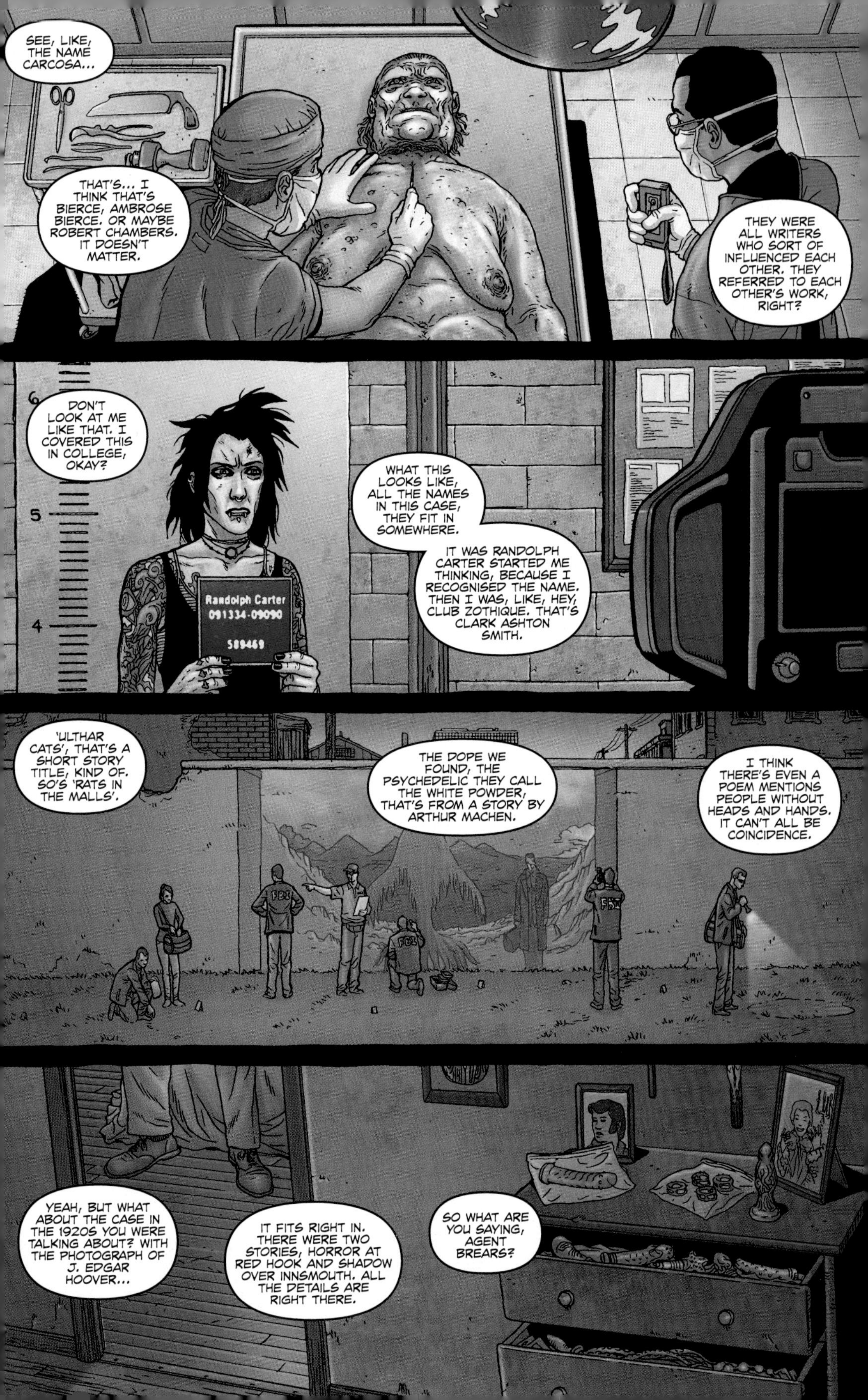
SEE, LIKE, THE NAME CARCOSA...
THAT'S... I THINK THAT'S BIERCE, AMBROSE BIERCE. OR MAYBE ROBERT CHAMBERS. IT DOESN'T MATTER.
THEY WERE ALL WRITERS WHO SORT OF INFLUENCED EACH OTHER. THEY REFERRED TO EACH OTHER'S WORK, RIGHT?
6
5
4
DON'T LOOK AT ME LIKE THAT. I COVERED THIS IN COLLEGE, OKAY?
Randolph Carter
091334-09090
589469
WHAT THIS LOOKS LIKE, ALL THE NAMES IN THIS CASE, THEY FIT IN SOMEWHERE.
IT WAS RANDOLPH CARTER STARTED ME THINKING, BECAUSE I RECOGNISED THE NAME. THEN I WAS, LIKE, HEY, CLUB ZOTHIQUE. THAT'S CLARK ASHTON SMITH.
'ULTHAR CATS', THAT'S A SHORT STORY TITLE, KIND OF. SO'S 'RATS IN THE MALLS'.
THE DOPE WE FOUND, THE PSYCHEDELIC THEY CALL THE WHITE POWDER, THAT'S FROM A STORY BY ARTHUR MACHEN.
I THINK THERE'S EVEN A POEM MENTIONS PEOPLE WITHOUT HEADS AND HANDS. IT CAN'T ALL BE COINCIDENCE.
FBI
YEAH, BUT WHAT ABOUT THE CASE IN THE 1920S YOU WERE TALKING ABOUT? WITH THE PHOTOGRAPH OF J. EDGAR HOOVER...
IT FITS RIGHT IN. THERE WERE TWO STORIES, HORROR AT RED HOOK AND SHADOW OVER INNSMOUTH. ALL THE DETAILS ARE RIGHT THERE.
SO WHAT ARE YOU SAYING, AGENT BREARS?

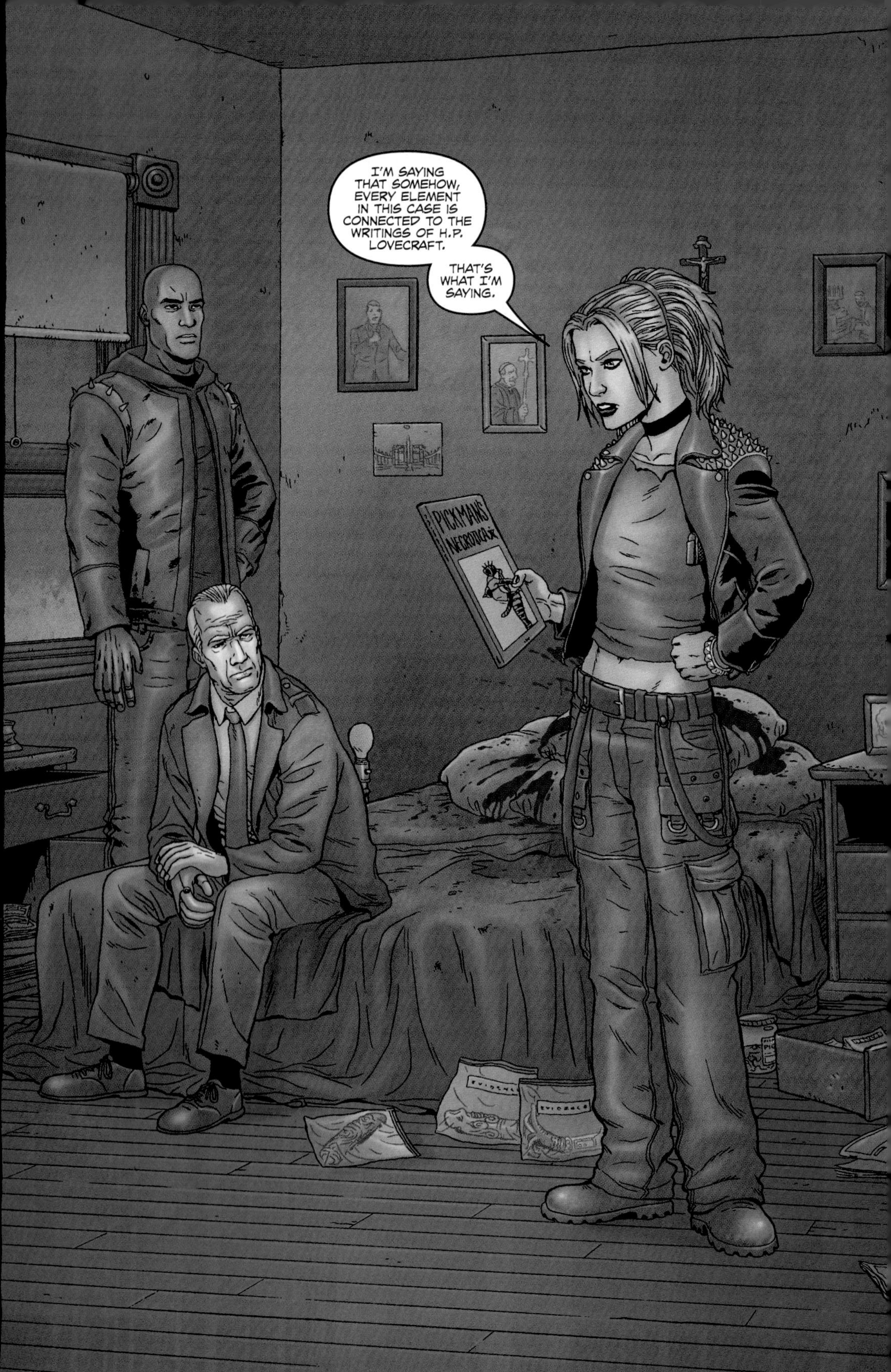
I'M SAYING THAT SOMEHOW, EVERY ELEMENT IN THIS CASE IS CONNECTED TO THE WRITINGS OF H.P. LOVECRAFT.
THAT'S WHAT I'M SAYING.
PICKMAN'S NECROTICA

2: The Shadow Out Of America

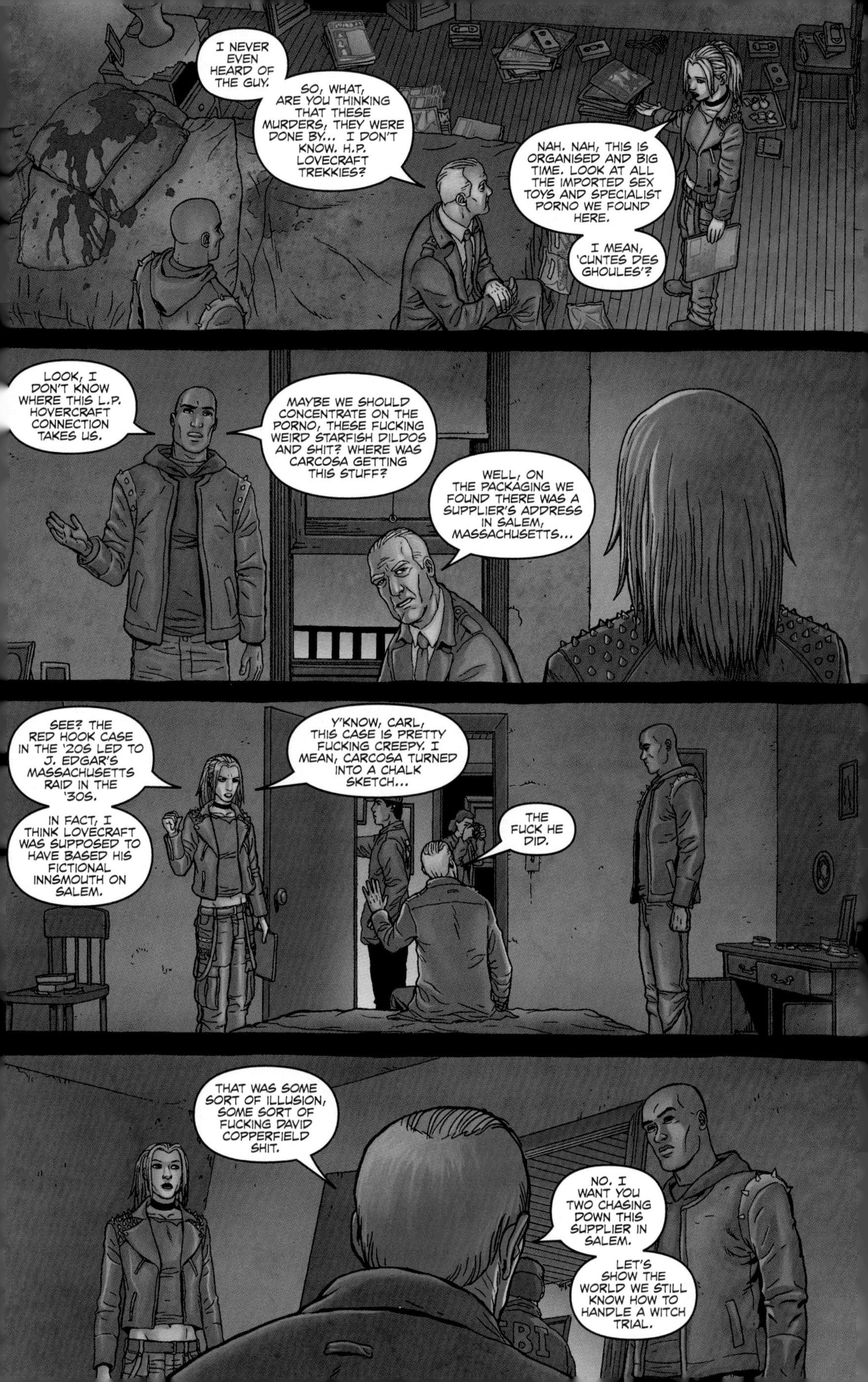
I NEVER EVEN HEARD OF THE GUY.
SO, WHAT, ARE YOU THINKING THAT THESE MURDERS, THEY WERE DONE BY... I DON'T KNOW. H.P. LOVECRAFT TREKKIES?
NAH. NAH, THIS IS ORGANISED AND BIG TIME. LOOK AT ALL THE IMPORTED SEX TOYS AND SPECIALIST PORNO WE FOUND HERE.
I MEAN, 'CUNTES DES GHOULES'?
LOOK, I DON'T KNOW WHERE THIS L.P. HOVERCRAFT CONNECTION TAKES US.
MAYBE WE SHOULD CONCENTRATE ON THE PORNO, THESE FUCKING WEIRD STARFISH DILDOS AND SHIT? WHERE WAS CARCOSA GETTING THIS STUFF?
WELL, ON THE PACKAGING WE FOUND THERE WAS A SUPPLIER'S ADDRESS IN SALEM, MASSACHUSETTS...
SEE? THE RED HOOK CASE IN THE '20S LED TO J. EDGAR'S MASSACHUSETTS RAID IN THE '30S.
IN FACT, I THINK LOVECRAFT WAS SUPPOSED TO HAVE BASED HIS FICTIONAL INNSMOUTH ON SALEM.
Y'KNOW, CARL, THIS CASE IS PRETTY FUCKING CREEPY. I MEAN, CARCOSA TURNED INTO A CHALK SKETCH...
THE FUCK HE DID.
THAT WAS SOME SORT OF ILLUSION, SOME SORT OF FUCKING DAVID COPPERFIELD SHIT.
NO. I WANT YOU TWO CHASING DOWN THIS SUPPLIER IN SALEM.
LET'S SHOW THE WORLD WE STILL KNOW HOW TO HANDLE A WITCH TRIAL.
FBI

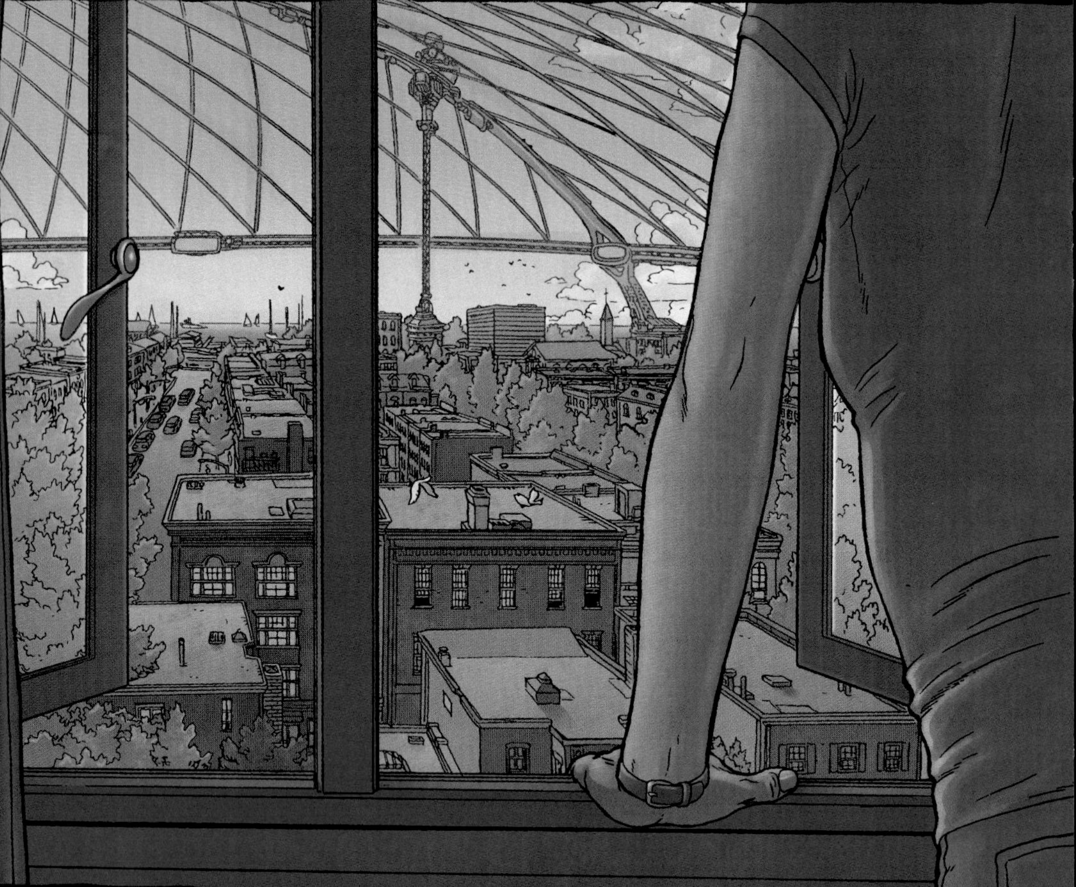

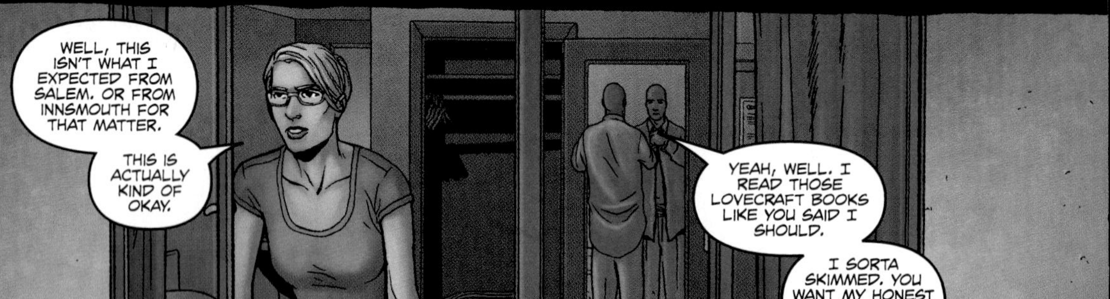
WELL, THIS ISN'T WHAT I EXPECTED FROM SALEM. OR FROM INNSMOUTH FOR THAT MATTER.
THIS IS ACTUALLY KIND OF OKAY.
YEAH, WELL. I READ THOSE LOVECRAFT BOOKS LIKE YOU SAID I SHOULD.
I SORTA SKIMMED. YOU WANT MY HONEST OPINION, THE GUY CAN'T WRITE.

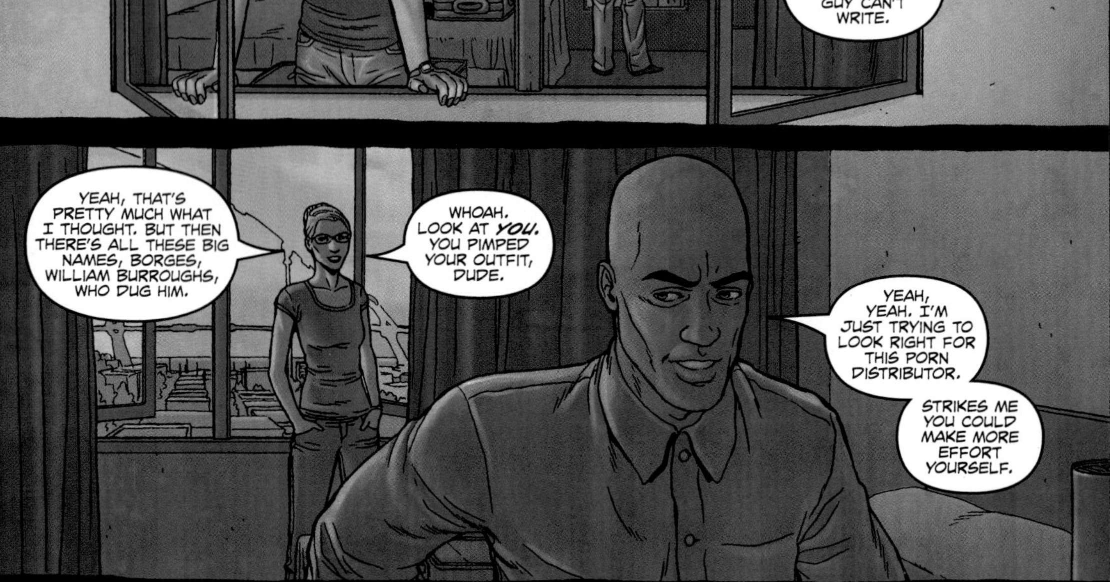
YEAH, THAT'S PRETTY MUCH WHAT I THOUGHT. BUT THEN THERE'S ALL THESE BIG NAMES, BORGES, WILLIAM BURROUGHS, WHO DUG HIM.
WHOAH. LOOK AT ***YOU.*** YOU PIMPED YOUR OUTFIT, DUDE.
YEAH, YEAH. I'M JUST TRYING TO LOOK RIGHT FOR THIS PORN DISTRIBUTOR.
STRIKES ME YOU COULD MAKE MORE EFFORT YOURSELF.

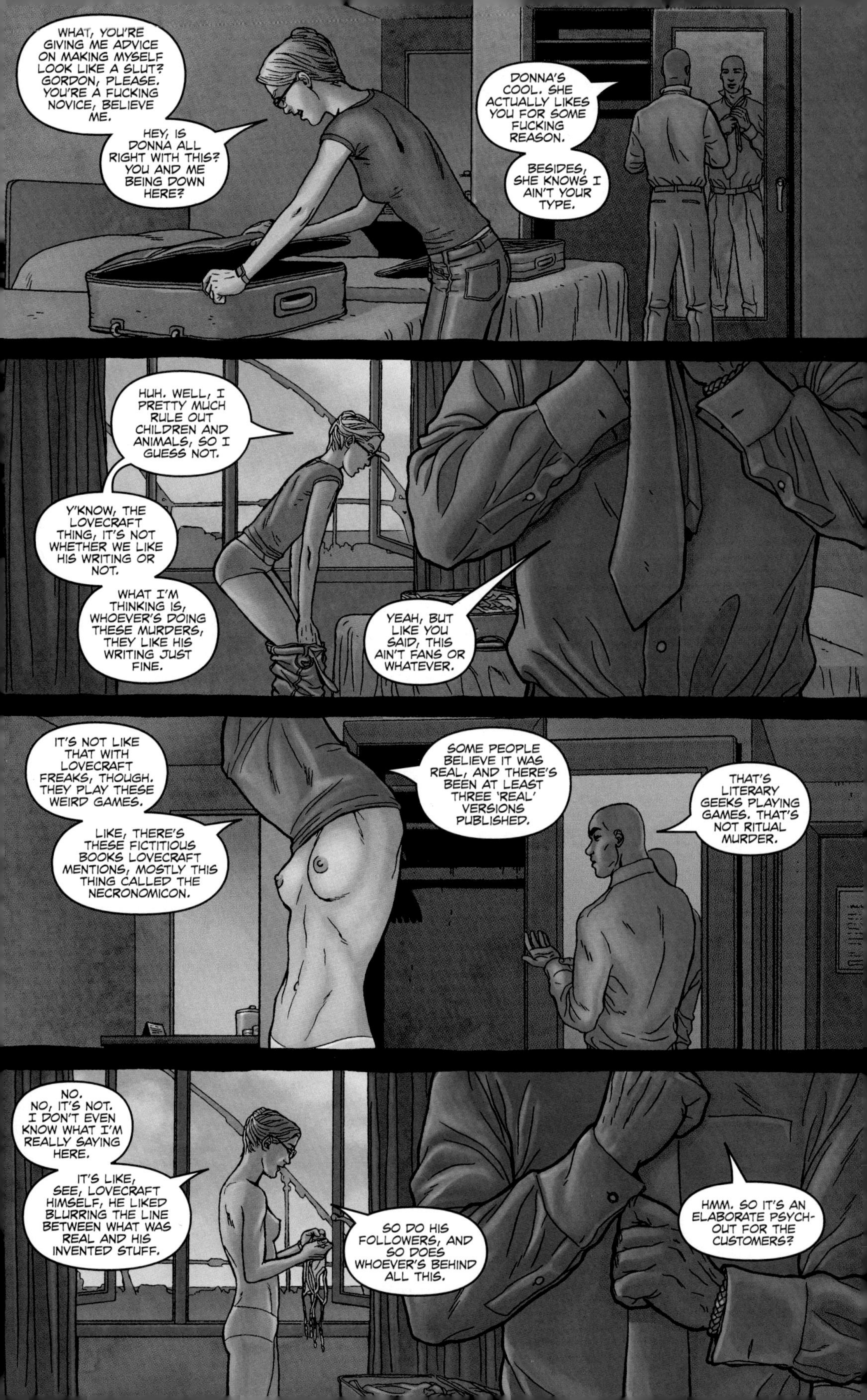
WHAT, YOU'RE GIVING ME ADVICE ON MAKING MYSELF LOOK LIKE A SLUT? GORDON, PLEASE. YOU'RE A FUCKING NOVICE, BELIEVE ME.
HEY, IS DONNA ALL RIGHT WITH THIS? YOU AND ME BEING DOWN HERE?
DONNA'S COOL. SHE ACTUALLY LIKES YOU FOR SOME FUCKING REASON.
BESIDES, SHE KNOWS I AIN'T YOUR TYPE.
HUH. WELL, I PRETTY MUCH RULE OUT CHILDREN AND ANIMALS, SO I GUESS NOT.
Y'KNOW, THE LOVECRAFT THING, IT'S NOT WHETHER WE LIKE HIS WRITING OR NOT.
WHAT I'M THINKING IS, WHOEVER'S DOING THESE MURDERS, THEY LIKE HIS WRITING JUST FINE.
YEAH, BUT LIKE YOU SAID, THIS AIN'T FANS OR WHATEVER.
IT'S NOT LIKE THAT WITH LOVECRAFT FREAKS, THOUGH. THEY PLAY THESE WEIRD GAMES.
LIKE, THERE'S THESE FICTITIOUS BOOKS LOVECRAFT MENTIONS, MOSTLY THIS THING CALLED THE NECRONOMICON.
SOME PEOPLE BELIEVE IT WAS REAL, AND THERE'S BEEN AT LEAST THREE 'REAL' VERSIONS PUBLISHED.
THAT'S LITERARY GEEKS PLAYING GAMES. THAT'S NOT RITUAL MURDER.
NO. NO, IT'S NOT. I DON'T EVEN KNOW WHAT I'M REALLY SAYING HERE.
IT'S LIKE, SEE, LOVECRAFT HIMSELF, HE LIKED BLURRING THE LINE BETWEEN WHAT WAS REAL AND HIS INVENTED STUFF.
SO DO HIS FOLLOWERS, AND SO DOES WHOEVER'S BEHIND ALL THIS.
HMM. SO IT'S AN ELABORATE PSYCH-OUT FOR THE CUSTOMERS?

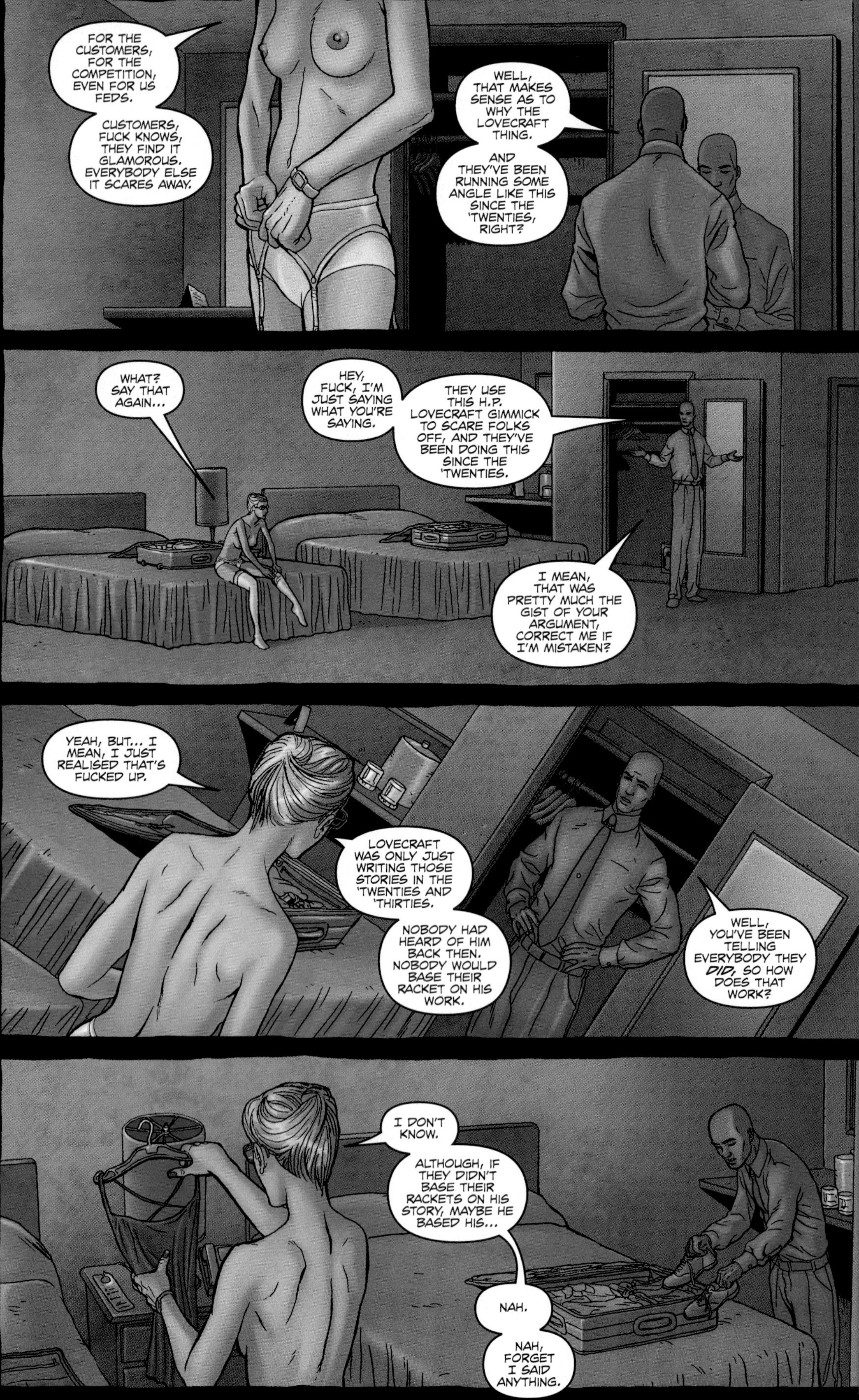
FOR THE CUSTOMERS, FOR THE COMPETITION, EVEN FOR US FEDS.
CUSTOMERS, FUCK KNOWS, THEY FIND IT GLAMOROUS. EVERYBODY ELSE IT SCARES AWAY.
WELL, THAT MAKES SENSE AS TO WHY THE LOVECRAFT THING.
AND THEY'VE BEEN RUNNING SOME ANGLE LIKE THIS SINCE THE 'TWENTIES, RIGHT?
WHAT? SAY THAT AGAIN...
HEY, FUCK, I'M JUST SAYING WHAT YOU'RE SAYING.
THEY USE THIS H.P. LOVECRAFT GIMMICK TO SCARE FOLKS OFF, AND THEY'VE BEEN DOING THIS SINCE THE 'TWENTIES.
I MEAN, THAT WAS PRETTY MUCH THE GIST OF YOUR ARGUMENT, CORRECT ME IF I'M MISTAKEN?
YEAH, BUT... I MEAN, I JUST REALISED THAT'S FUCKED UP.
LOVECRAFT WAS ONLY JUST WRITING THOSE STORIES IN THE 'TWENTIES AND 'THIRTIES.
NOBODY HAD HEARD OF HIM BACK THEN. NOBODY WOULD BASE THEIR RACKET ON HIS WORK.
WELL, YOU'VE BEEN TELLING EVERYBODY THEY *DID*, SO HOW DOES THAT WORK?
I DON'T KNOW.
ALTHOUGH, IF THEY DIDN'T BASE THEIR RACKETS ON HIS STORY, MAYBE HE BASED HIS...
NAH.
NAH, FORGET I SAID ANYTHING.

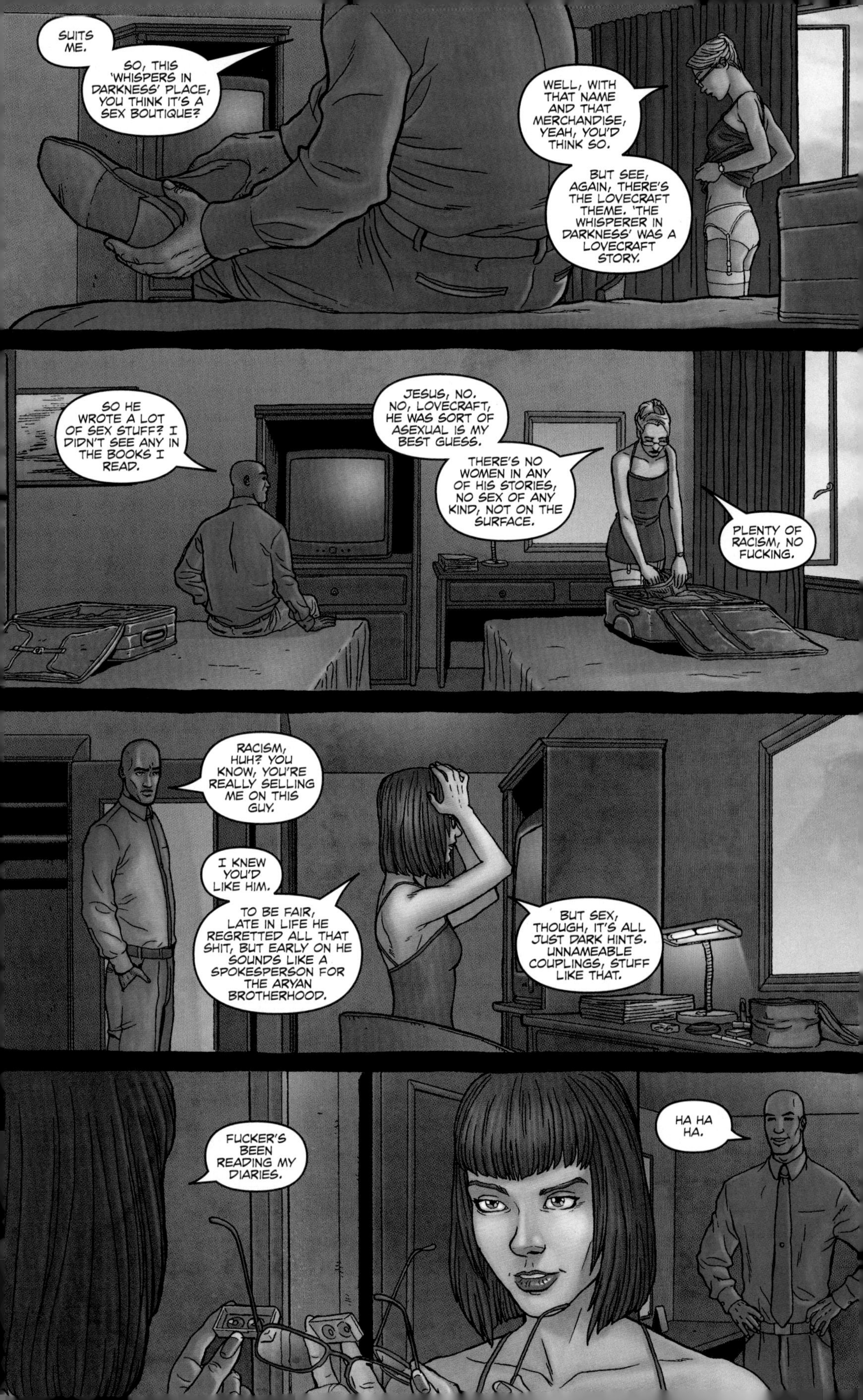
SUITS ME.
SO, THIS 'WHISPERS IN DARKNESS' PLACE, YOU THINK IT'S A SEX BOUTIQUE?
WELL, WITH THAT NAME AND THAT MERCHANDISE, YEAH, YOU'D THINK SO.
BUT SEE, AGAIN, THERE'S THE LOVECRAFT THEME. 'THE WHISPERER IN DARKNESS' WAS A LOVECRAFT STORY.
SO HE WROTE A LOT OF SEX STUFF? I DIDN'T SEE ANY IN THE BOOKS I READ.
JESUS, NO. NO, LOVECRAFT, HE WAS SORT OF ASEXUAL IS MY BEST GUESS.
THERE'S NO WOMEN IN ANY OF HIS STORIES, NO SEX OF ANY KIND, NOT ON THE SURFACE.
PLENTY OF RACISM, NO FUCKING.
RACISM, HUH? YOU KNOW, YOU'RE REALLY SELLING ME ON THIS GUY.
I KNEW YOU'D LIKE HIM.
TO BE FAIR, LATE IN LIFE HE REGRETTED ALL THAT SHIT, BUT EARLY ON HE SOUNDS LIKE A SPOKESPERSON FOR THE ARYAN BROTHERHOOD.
BUT SEX, THOUGH, IT'S ALL JUST DARK HINTS. UNNAMEABLE COUPLINGS, STUFF LIKE THAT.
FUCKER'S BEEN READING MY DIARIES.
HA HA HA.

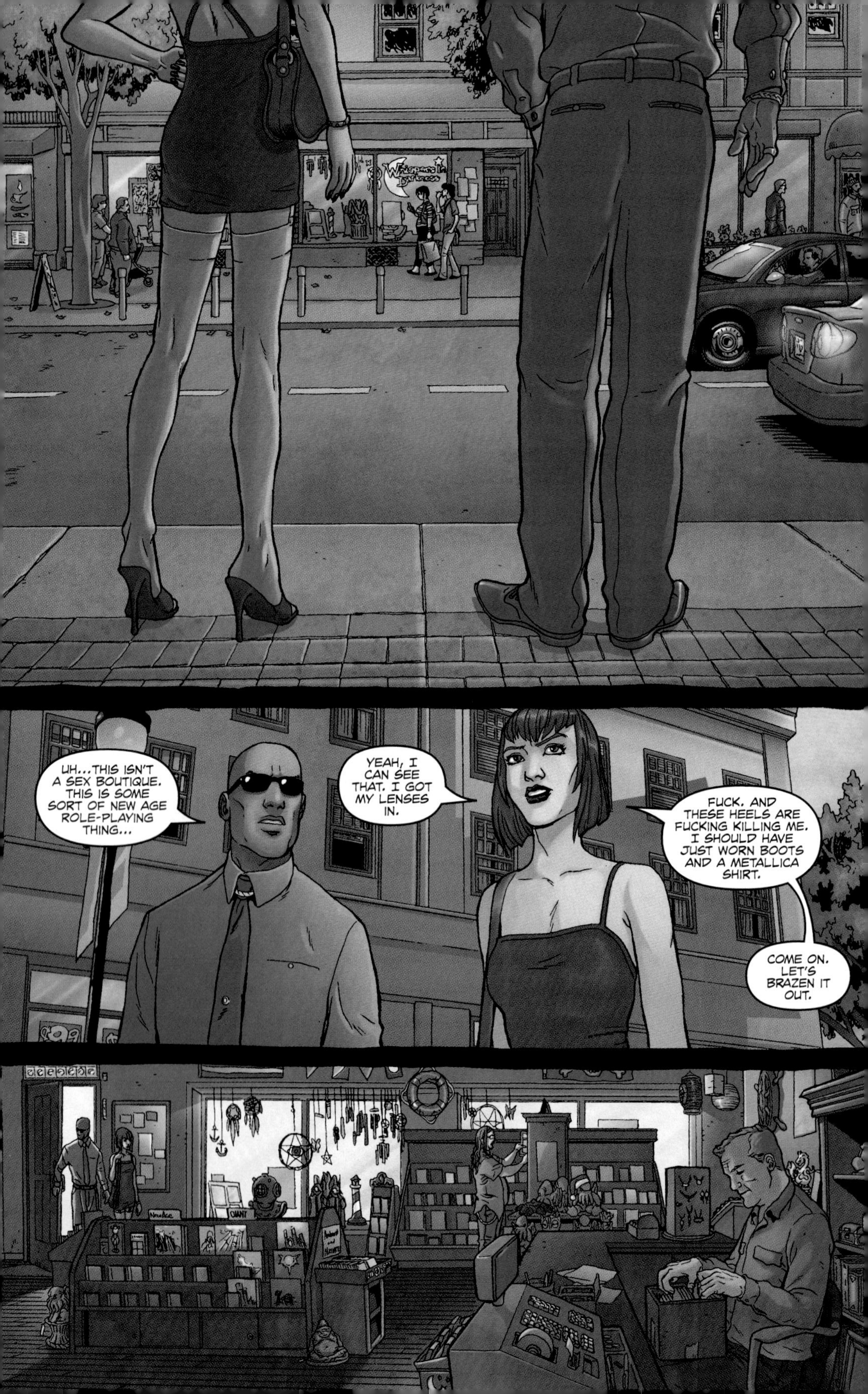
Whispers In Darkness
UH...THIS ISN'T A SEX BOUTIQUE. THIS IS SOME SORT OF NEW AGE ROLE-PLAYING THING...
YEAH, I CAN SEE THAT. I GOT MY LENSES IN.
FUCK. AND THESE HEELS ARE FUCKING KILLING ME. I SHOULD HAVE JUST WORN BOOTS AND A METALLICA SHIRT.
COME ON. LET'S BRAZEN IT OUT.

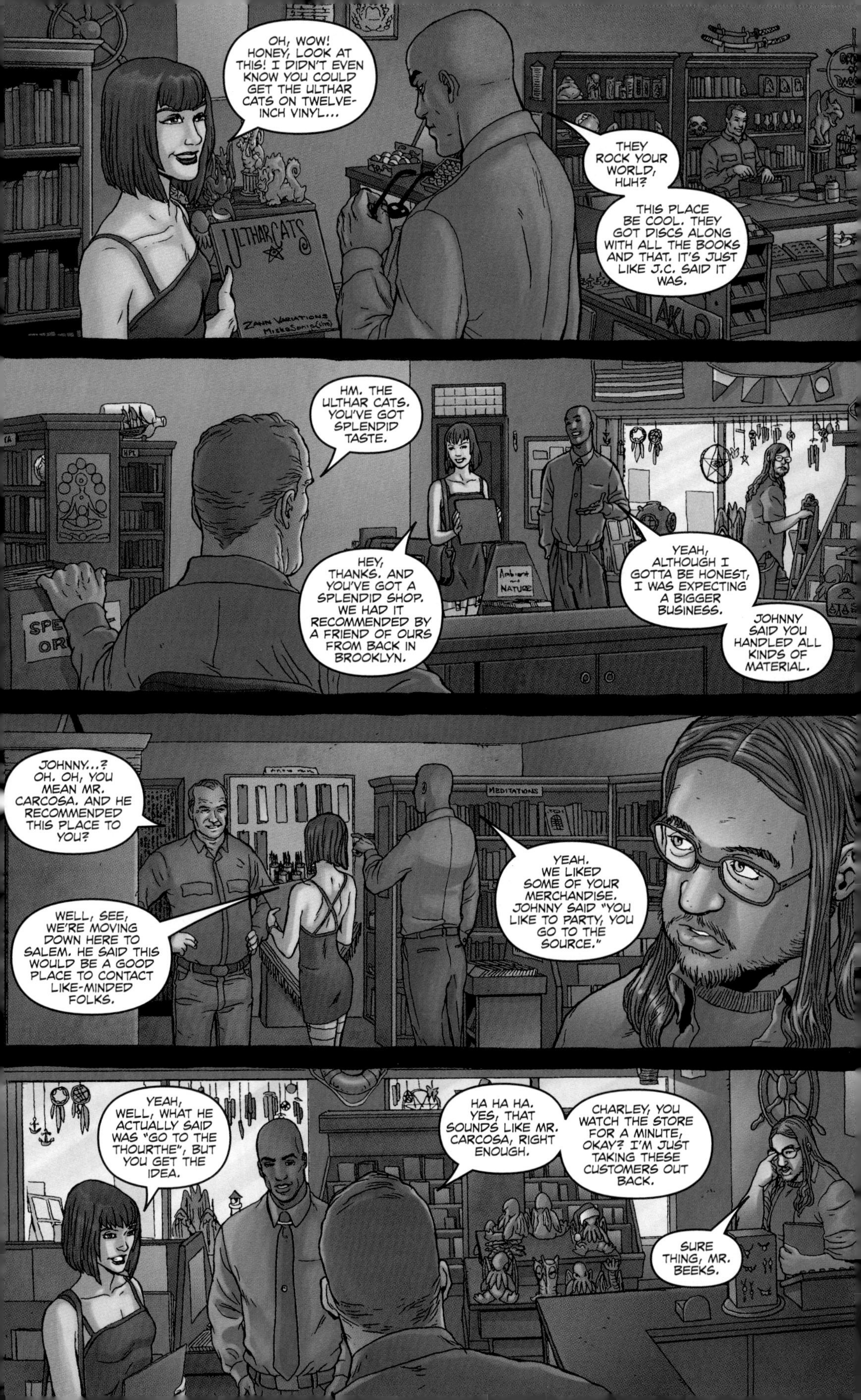
OH, WOW! HONEY, LOOK AT THIS! I DIDN'T EVEN KNOW YOU COULD GET THE ULTHAR CATS ON TWELVE-INCH VINYL...
ULTHAR CATS
ZANN VARIATIONS
THEY ROCK YOUR WORLD, HUH?
THIS PLACE BE COOL. THEY GOT DISCS ALONG WITH ALL THE BOOKS AND THAT. IT'S JUST LIKE J.C. SAID IT WAS.
AKLO
HM. THE ULTHAR CATS. YOU'VE GOT SPLENDID TASTE.
HEY, THANKS. AND YOU'VE GOT A SPLENDID SHOP. WE HAD IT RECOMMENDED BY A FRIEND OF OURS FROM BACK IN BROOKLYN.
YEAH, ALTHOUGH I GOTTA BE HONEST, I WAS EXPECTING A BIGGER BUSINESS.
JOHNNY SAID YOU HANDLED ALL KINDS OF MATERIAL.
JOHNNY...? OH. OH, YOU MEAN MR. CARCOSA. AND HE RECOMMENDED THIS PLACE TO YOU?
WELL, SEE, WE'RE MOVING DOWN HERE TO SALEM. HE SAID THIS WOULD BE A GOOD PLACE TO CONTACT LIKE-MINDED FOLKS.
MEDITATIONS
YEAH. WE LIKED SOME OF YOUR MERCHANDISE. JOHNNY SAID "YOU LIKE TO PARTY, YOU GO TO THE SOURCE."
YEAH, WELL, WHAT HE ACTUALLY SAID WAS "GO TO THE THOURTHE", BUT YOU GET THE IDEA.
HA HA HA. YES, THAT SOUNDS LIKE MR. CARCOSA, RIGHT ENOUGH.
CHARLEY, YOU WATCH THE STORE FOR A MINUTE, OKAY? I'M JUST TAKING THESE CUSTOMERS OUT BACK.
SURE THING, MR. BEEKS.

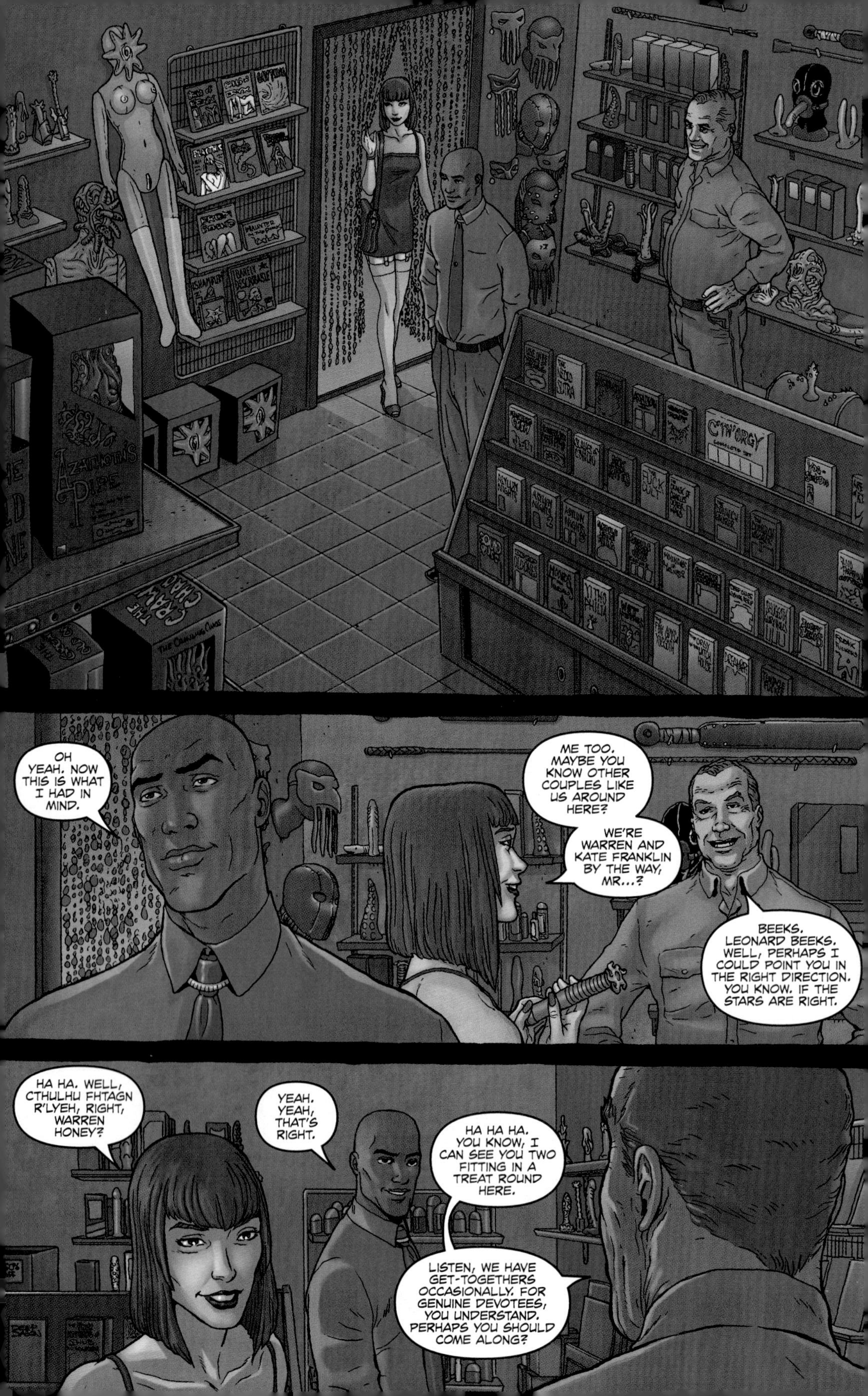

OH YEAH. NOW THIS IS WHAT I HAD IN MIND.
ME TOO. MAYBE YOU KNOW OTHER COUPLES LIKE US AROUND HERE?
WE'RE WARREN AND KATE FRANKLIN BY THE WAY, MR...?
BEEKS. LEONARD BEEKS. WELL, PERHAPS I COULD POINT YOU IN THE RIGHT DIRECTION. YOU KNOW. IF THE STARS ARE RIGHT.
HA HA. WELL, CTHULHU FHTAGN R'LYEH, RIGHT, WARREN HONEY?
YEAH. YEAH, THAT'S RIGHT.
HA HA HA. YOU KNOW, I CAN SEE YOU TWO FITTING IN A TREAT ROUND HERE.
LISTEN, WE HAVE GET-TOGETHERS OCCASIONALLY. FOR GENUINE DEVOTEES, YOU UNDERSTAND. PERHAPS YOU SHOULD COME ALONG?

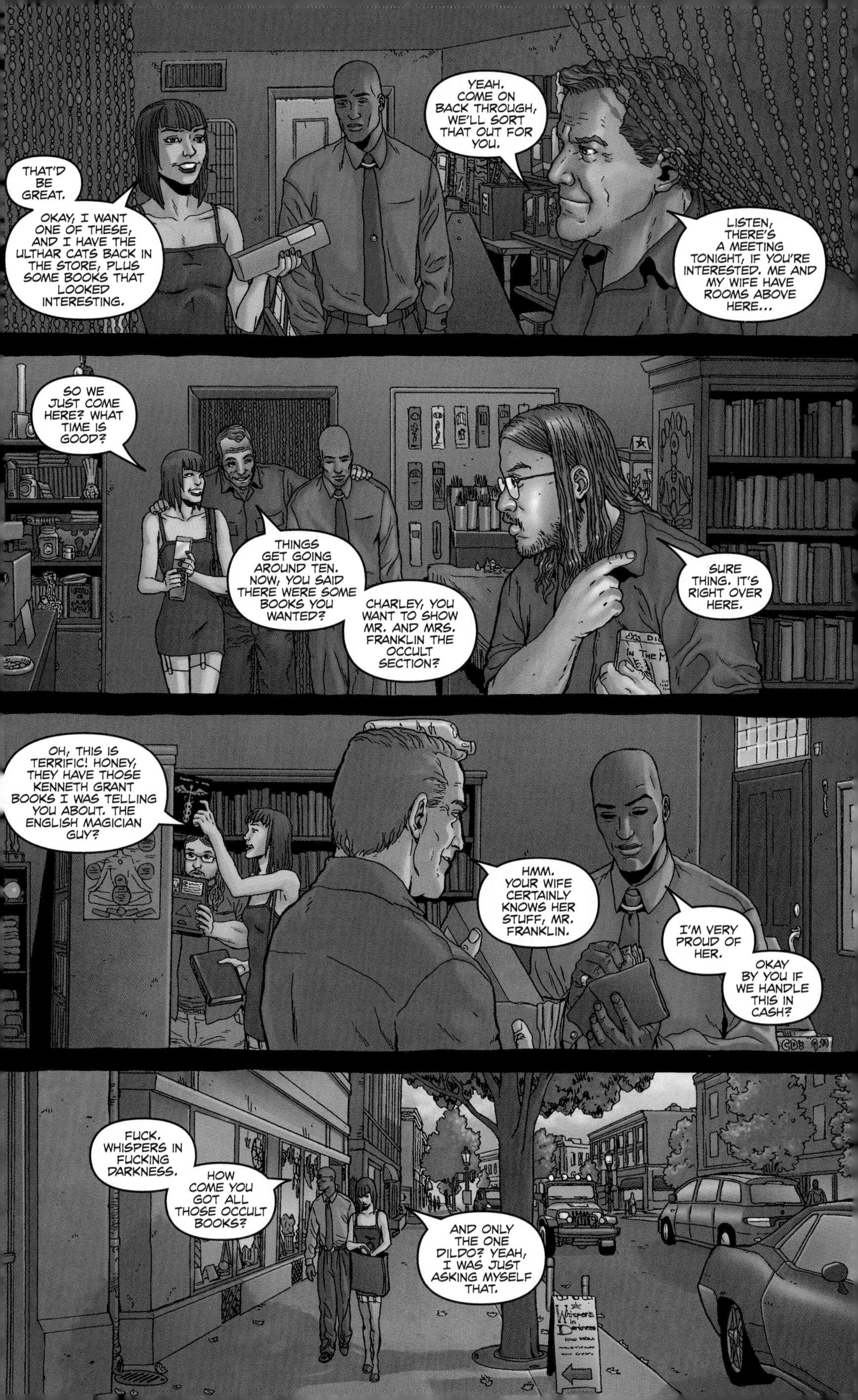
YEAH. COME ON BACK THROUGH, WE'LL SORT THAT OUT FOR YOU.
THAT'D BE GREAT.
OKAY, I WANT ONE OF THESE, AND I HAVE THE ULTHAR CATS BACK IN THE STORE, PLUS SOME BOOKS THAT LOOKED INTERESTING.
LISTEN, THERE'S A MEETING TONIGHT, IF YOU'RE INTERESTED. ME AND MY WIFE HAVE ROOMS ABOVE HERE...
SO WE JUST COME HERE? WHAT TIME IS GOOD?
THINGS GET GOING AROUND TEN. NOW, YOU SAID THERE WERE SOME BOOKS YOU WANTED?
CHARLEY, YOU WANT TO SHOW MR. AND MRS. FRANKLIN THE OCCULT SECTION?
SURE THING. IT'S RIGHT OVER HERE.
OH, THIS IS TERRIFIC! HONEY, THEY HAVE THOSE KENNETH GRANT BOOKS I WAS TELLING YOU ABOUT. THE ENGLISH MAGICIAN GUY?
HMM. YOUR WIFE CERTAINLY KNOWS HER STUFF, MR. FRANKLIN.
I'M VERY PROUD OF HER.
OKAY BY YOU IF WE HANDLE THIS IN CASH?
FUCK. WHISPERS IN FUCKING DARKNESS.
HOW COME YOU GOT ALL THOSE OCCULT BOOKS?
AND ONLY THE ONE DILDO? YEAH, I WAS JUST ASKING MYSELF THAT.
Whispers in Darkness

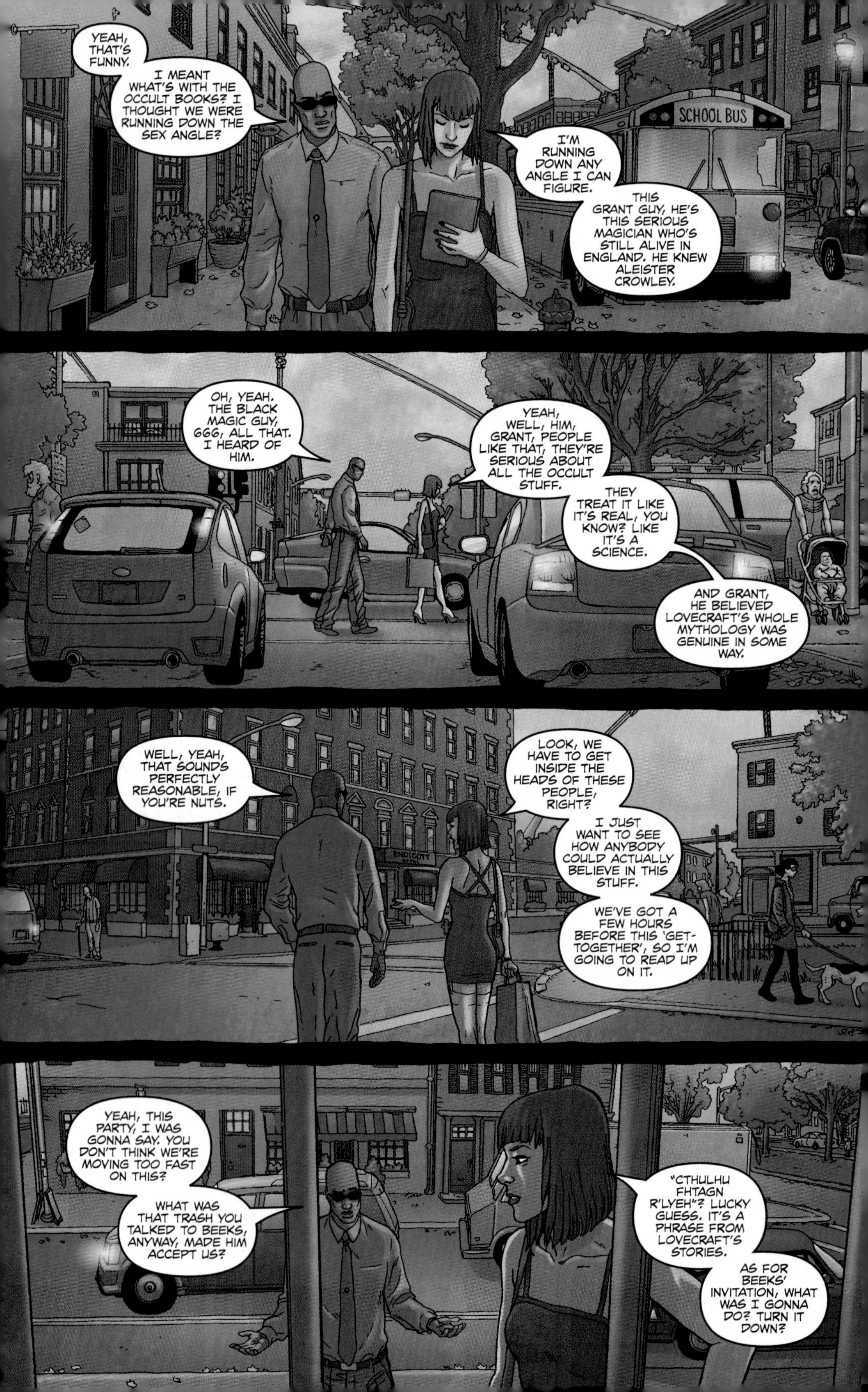
YEAH, THAT'S FUNNY.
I MEANT WHAT'S WITH THE OCCULT BOOKS? I THOUGHT WE WERE RUNNING DOWN THE SEX ANGLE?
SCHOOL BUS
I'M RUNNING DOWN ANY ANGLE I CAN FIGURE.
THIS GRANT GUY, HE'S THIS SERIOUS MAGICIAN WHO'S STILL ALIVE IN ENGLAND. HE KNEW ALEISTER CROWLEY.
OH, YEAH. THE BLACK MAGIC GUY, 666, ALL THAT. I HEARD OF HIM.
YEAH, WELL, HIM, GRANT, PEOPLE LIKE THAT, THEY'RE SERIOUS ABOUT ALL THE OCCULT STUFF.
THEY TREAT IT LIKE IT'S REAL, YOU KNOW? LIKE IT'S A SCIENCE.
AND GRANT, HE BELIEVED LOVECRAFT'S WHOLE MYTHOLOGY WAS GENUINE IN SOME WAY.
WELL, YEAH, THAT SOUNDS PERFECTLY REASONABLE, IF YOU'RE NUTS.
LOOK, WE HAVE TO GET INSIDE THE HEADS OF THESE PEOPLE, RIGHT?
I JUST WANT TO SEE HOW ANYBODY COULD ACTUALLY BELIEVE IN THIS STUFF.
WE'VE GOT A FEW HOURS BEFORE THIS 'GET-TOGETHER', SO I'M GOING TO READ UP ON IT.
ENDICOTT HOTEL
YEAH, THIS PARTY, I WAS GONNA SAY. YOU DON'T THINK WE'RE MOVING TOO FAST ON THIS?
WHAT WAS THAT TRASH YOU TALKED TO BEEKS, ANYWAY, MADE HIM ACCEPT US?
"CTHULHU FHTAGN R'LYEH"? LUCKY GUESS. IT'S A PHRASE FROM LOVECRAFT'S STORIES.
AS FOR BEEKS' INVITATION, WHAT WAS I GONNA DO? TURN IT DOWN?

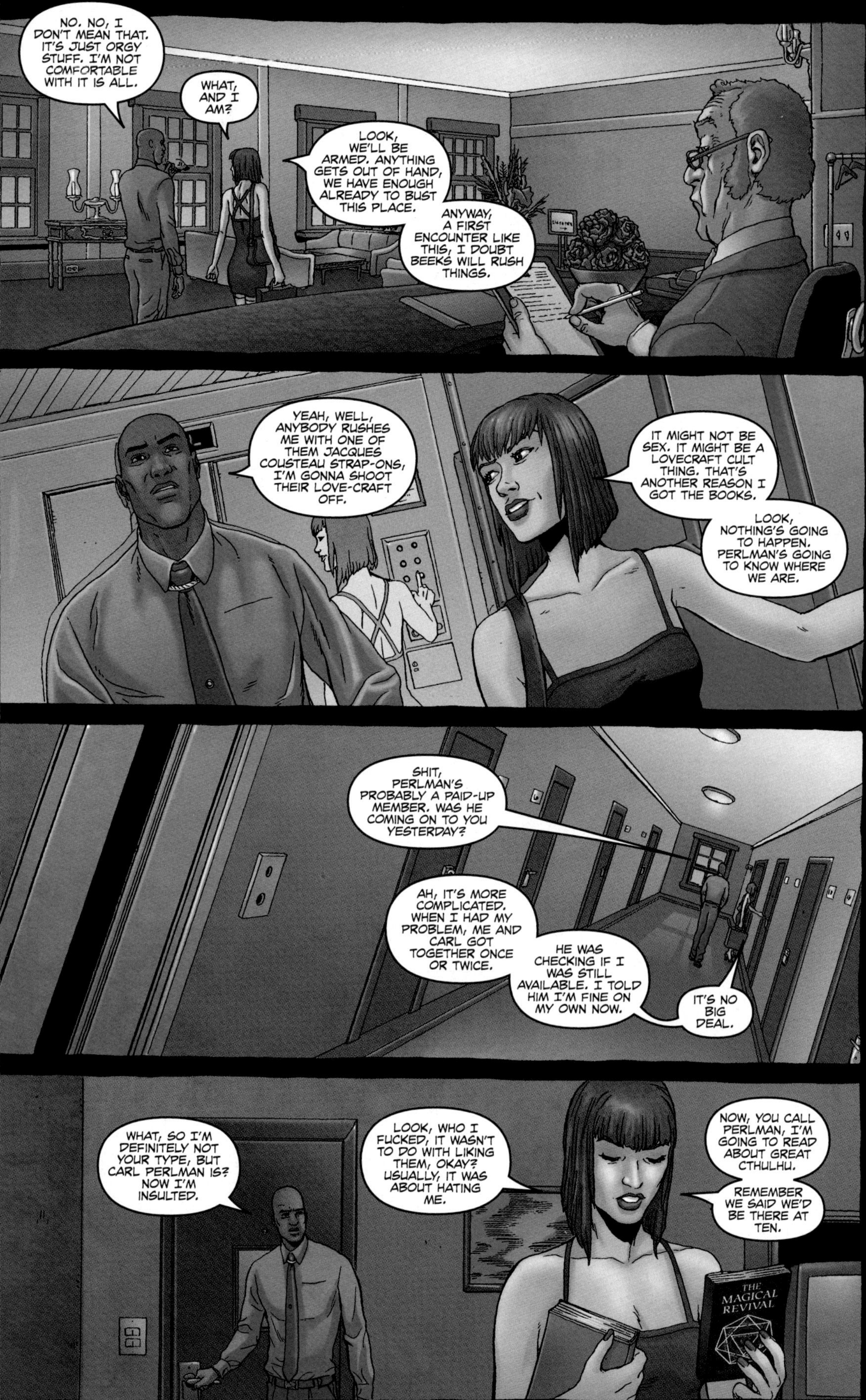
NO. NO, I DON'T MEAN THAT. IT'S JUST ORGY STUFF. I'M NOT COMFORTABLE WITH IT IS ALL.
WHAT, AND I AM?
LOOK, WE'LL BE ARMED. ANYTHING GETS OUT OF HAND, WE HAVE ENOUGH ALREADY TO BUST THIS PLACE.
ANYWAY, A FIRST ENCOUNTER LIKE THIS, I DOUBT BEEKS WILL RUSH THINGS.
YEAH, WELL, ANYBODY RUSHES ME WITH ONE OF THEM JACQUES COUSTEAU STRAP-ONS, I'M GONNA SHOOT THEIR LOVE-CRAFT OFF.
IT MIGHT NOT BE SEX. IT MIGHT BE A LOVECRAFT CULT THING. THAT'S ANOTHER REASON I GOT THE BOOKS.
LOOK, NOTHING'S GOING TO HAPPEN. PERLMAN'S GOING TO KNOW WHERE WE ARE.
SHIT, PERLMAN'S PROBABLY A PAID-UP MEMBER. WAS HE COMING ON TO YOU YESTERDAY?
AH, IT'S MORE COMPLICATED. WHEN I HAD MY PROBLEM, ME AND CARL GOT TOGETHER ONCE OR TWICE.
HE WAS CHECKING IF I WAS STILL AVAILABLE. I TOLD HIM I'M FINE ON MY OWN NOW.
IT'S NO BIG DEAL.
WHAT, SO I'M DEFINITELY NOT YOUR TYPE, BUT CARL PERLMAN IS? NOW I'M INSULTED.
LOOK, WHO I FUCKED, IT WASN'T TO DO WITH LIKING THEM, OKAY? USUALLY, IT WAS ABOUT HATING ME.
NOW, YOU CALL PERLMAN, I'M GOING TO READ ABOUT GREAT CTHULHU.
REMEMBER WE SAID WE'D BE THERE AT TEN.
THE MAGICAL REVIVAL

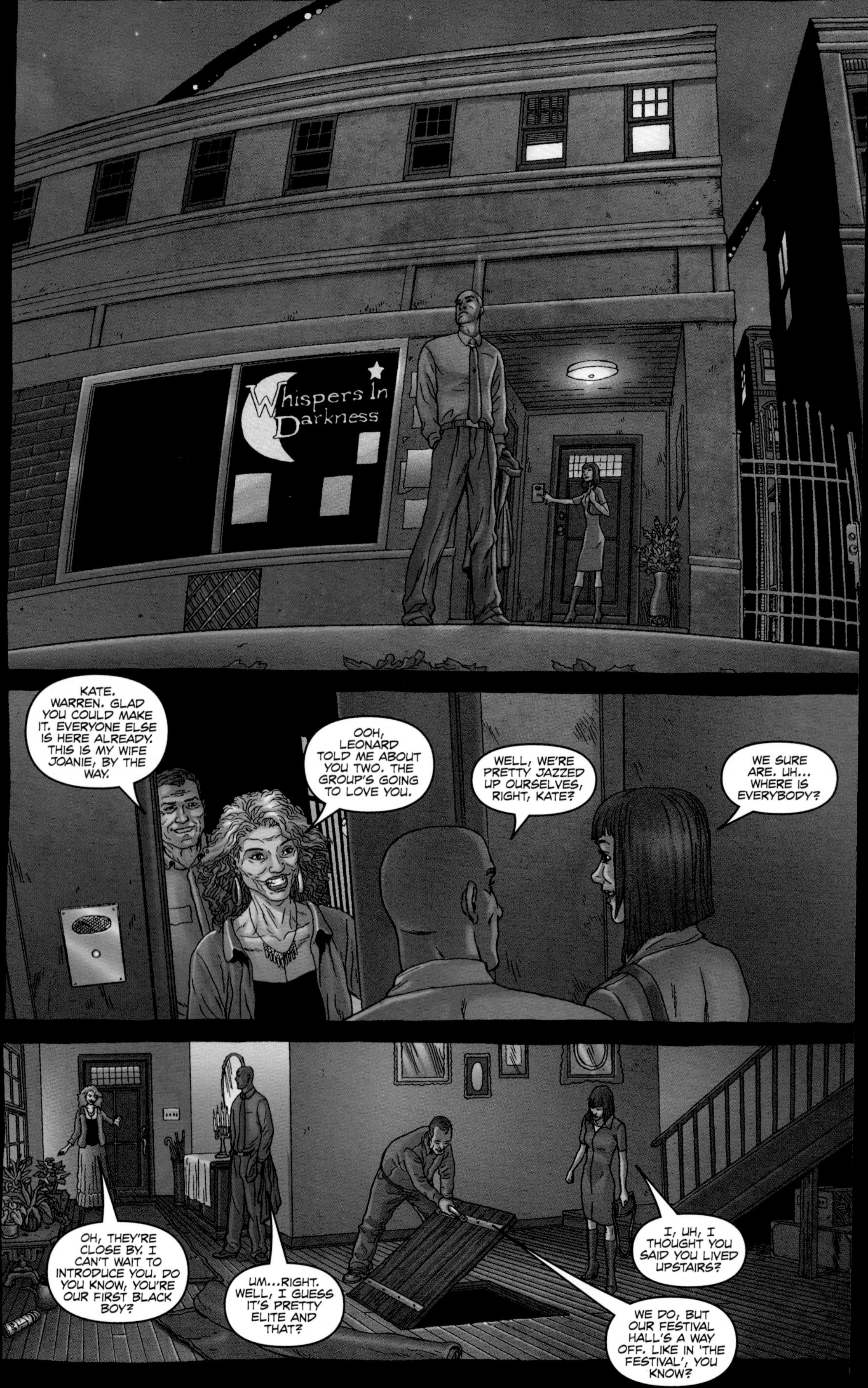
Whispers In Darkness
KATE. WARREN. GLAD YOU COULD MAKE IT. EVERYONE ELSE IS HERE ALREADY. THIS IS MY WIFE JOANIE, BY THE WAY.
OOH, LEONARD TOLD ME ABOUT YOU TWO. THE GROUP'S GOING TO LOVE YOU.
WELL, WE'RE PRETTY JAZZED UP OURSELVES, RIGHT, KATE?
WE SURE ARE. UH... WHERE IS EVERYBODY?
OH, THEY'RE CLOSE BY. I CAN'T WAIT TO INTRODUCE YOU. DO YOU KNOW, YOU'RE OUR FIRST BLACK BOY?
UM...RIGHT. WELL, I GUESS IT'S PRETTY ELITE AND THAT?
I, UH, I THOUGHT YOU SAID YOU LIVED UPSTAIRS?
WE DO, BUT OUR FESTIVAL HALL'S A WAY OFF. LIKE IN 'THE FESTIVAL', YOU KNOW?

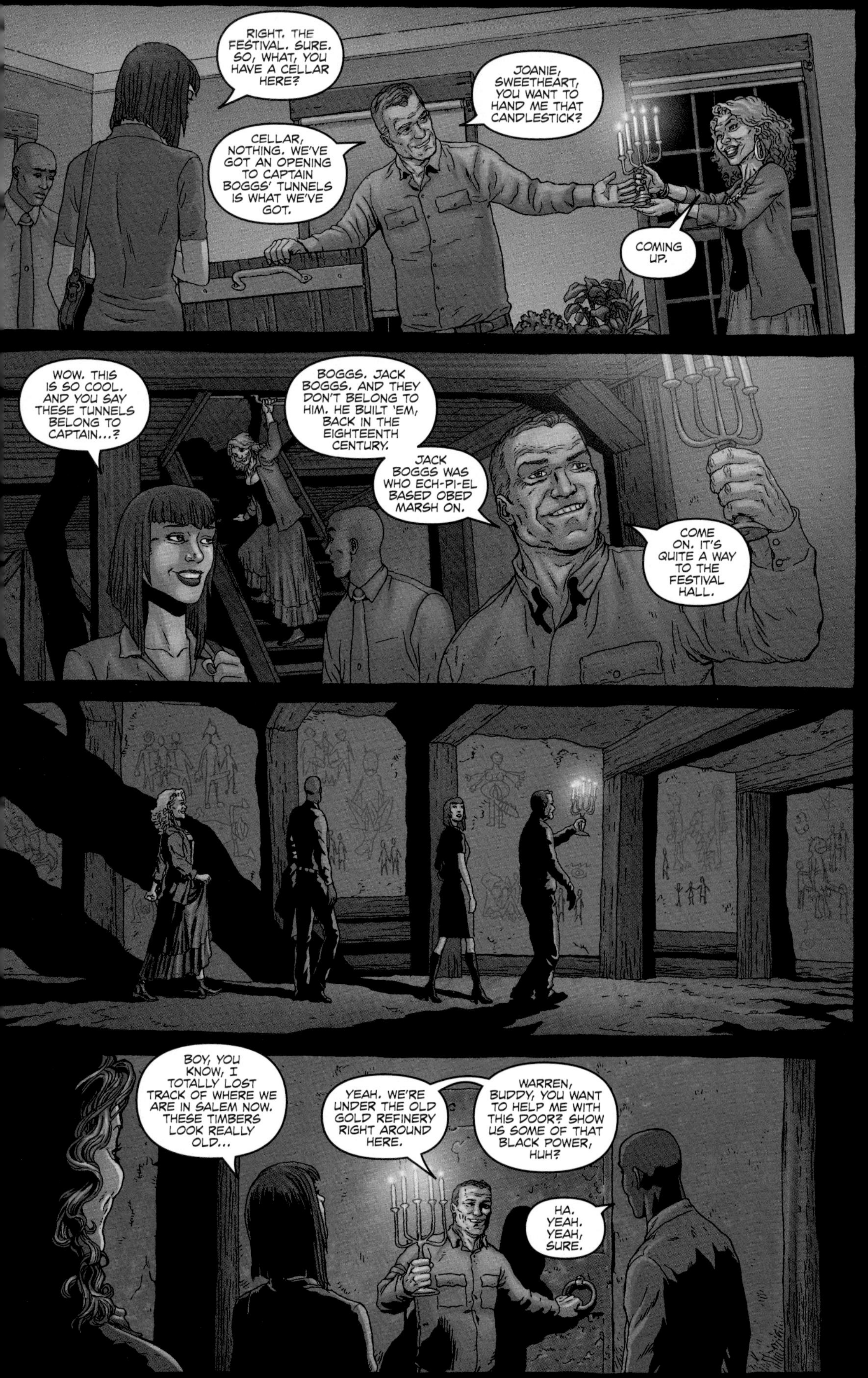
RIGHT. THE FESTIVAL. SURE. SO, WHAT, YOU HAVE A CELLAR HERE?
CELLAR, NOTHING. WE'VE GOT AN OPENING TO CAPTAIN BOGGS' TUNNELS IS WHAT WE'VE GOT.
JOANIE, SWEETHEART, YOU WANT TO HAND ME THAT CANDLESTICK?
COMING UP.
WOW. THIS IS SO COOL. AND YOU SAY THESE TUNNELS BELONG TO CAPTAIN...?
BOGGS. JACK BOGGS. AND THEY DON'T BELONG TO HIM. HE BUILT 'EM, BACK IN THE EIGHTEENTH CENTURY.
JACK BOGGS WAS WHO ECH-PI-EL BASED OBED MARSH ON.
COME ON. IT'S QUITE A WAY TO THE FESTIVAL HALL.
BOY, YOU KNOW, I TOTALLY LOST TRACK OF WHERE WE ARE IN SALEM NOW. THESE TIMBERS LOOK REALLY OLD...
YEAH. WE'RE UNDER THE OLD GOLD REFINERY RIGHT AROUND HERE.
WARREN, BUDDY, YOU WANT TO HELP ME WITH THIS DOOR? SHOW US SOME OF THAT BLACK POWER, HUH?
HA. YEAH. YEAH, SURE.

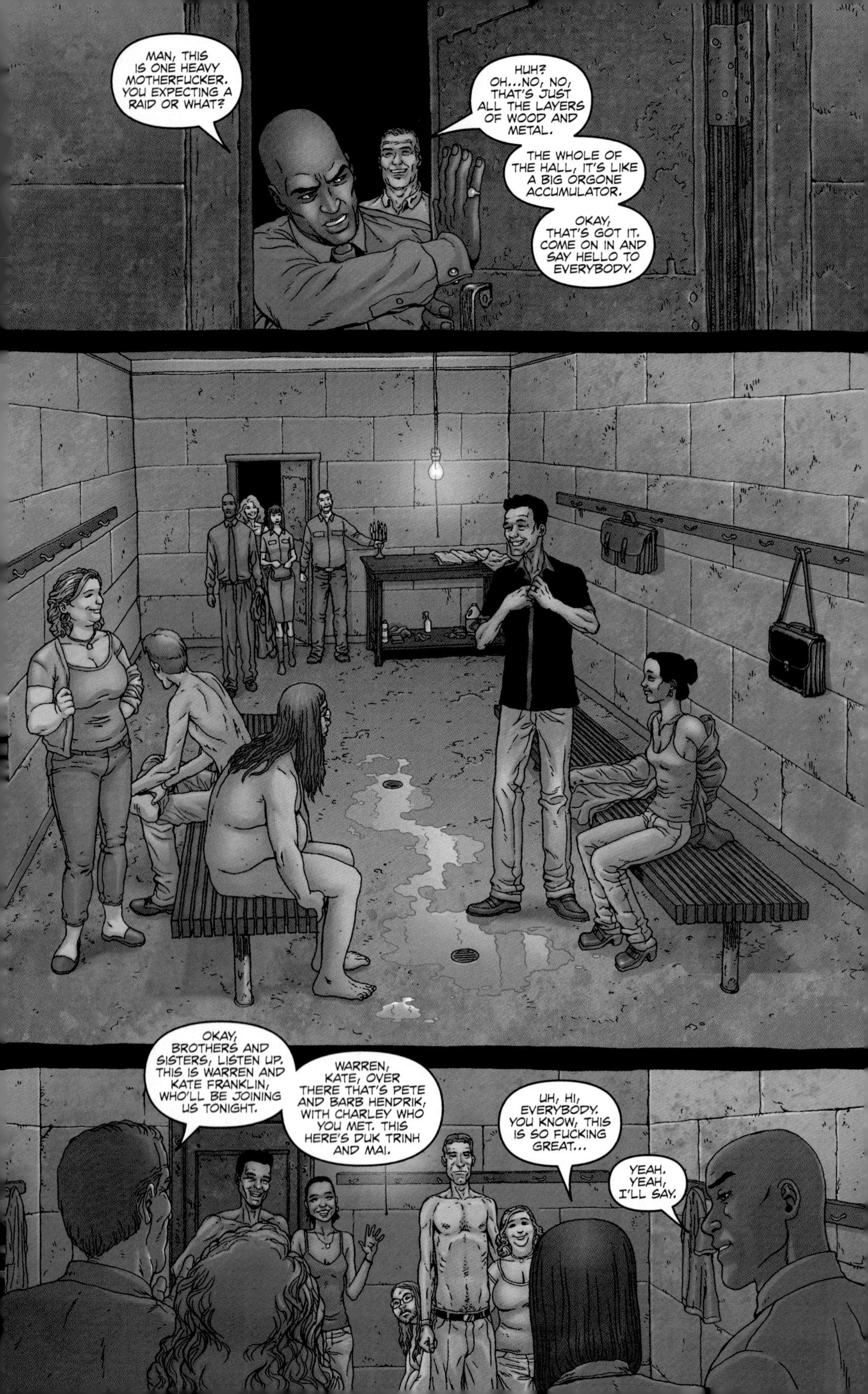
MAN, THIS IS ONE HEAVY MOTHERFUCKER. YOU EXPECTING A RAID OR WHAT?
HUH? OH...NO, NO, THAT'S JUST ALL THE LAYERS OF WOOD AND METAL.
THE WHOLE OF THE HALL, IT'S LIKE A BIG ORGONE ACCUMULATOR.
OKAY, THAT'S GOT IT. COME ON IN AND SAY HELLO TO EVERYBODY.
OKAY, BROTHERS AND SISTERS, LISTEN UP. THIS IS WARREN AND KATE FRANKLIN, WHO'LL BE JOINING US TONIGHT.
WARREN, KATE, OVER THERE THAT'S PETE AND BARB HENDRIK, WITH CHARLEY WHO YOU MET. THIS HERE'S DUK TRINH AND MAI.
UH, HI, EVERYBODY. YOU KNOW, THIS IS SO FUCKING GREAT...
YEAH. YEAH, I'LL SAY.

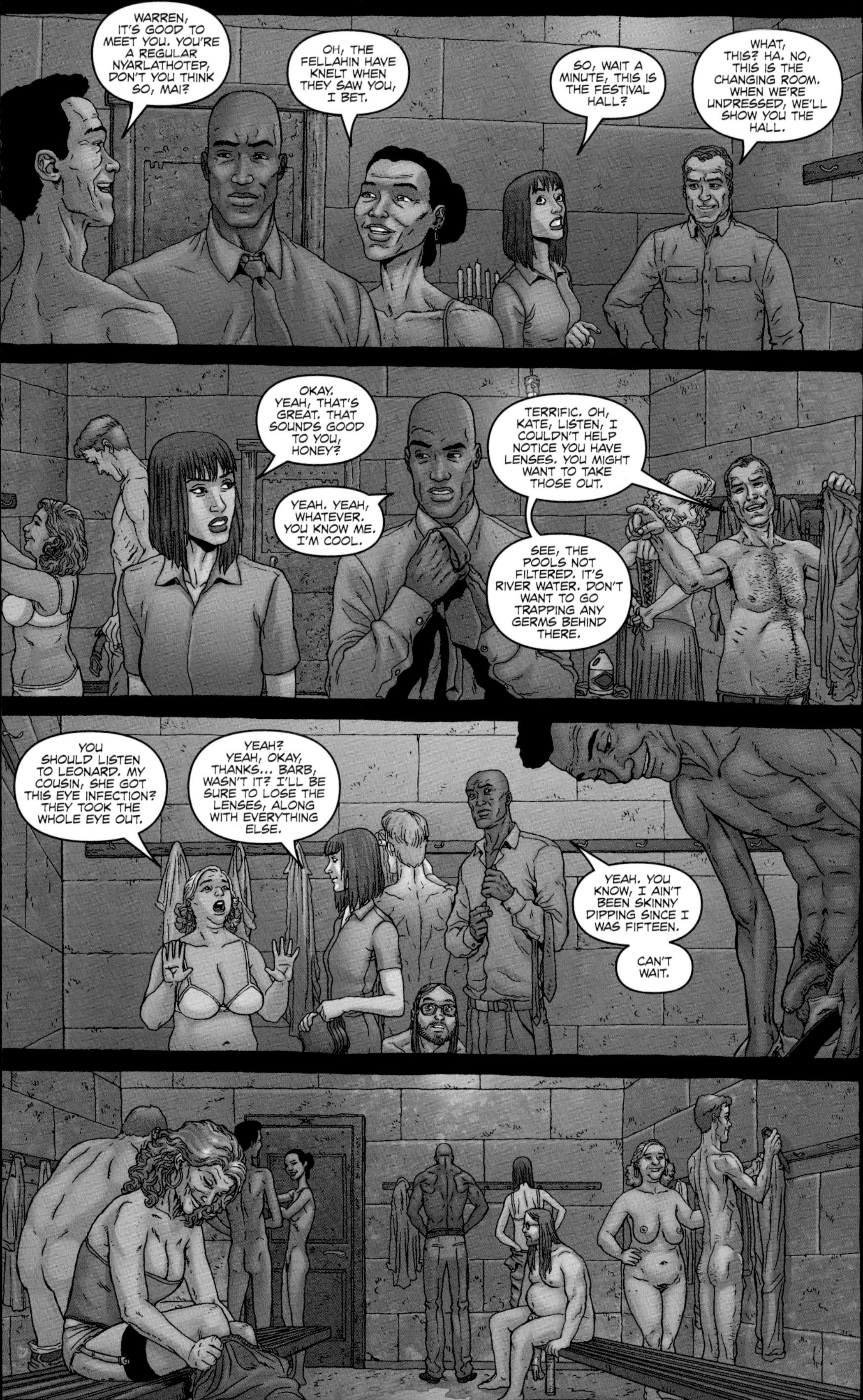
WARREN, IT'S GOOD TO MEET YOU. YOU'RE A REGULAR NYARLATHOTEP, DON'T YOU THINK SO, MAI?
OH, THE FELLAHIN HAVE KNELT WHEN THEY SAW YOU, I BET.
SO, WAIT A MINUTE, THIS IS THE FESTIVAL HALL?
WHAT, THIS? HA. NO, THIS IS THE CHANGING ROOM. WHEN WE'RE UNDRESSED, WE'LL SHOW YOU THE HALL.
OKAY. YEAH, THAT'S GREAT. THAT SOUNDS GOOD TO YOU, HONEY?
YEAH. YEAH, WHATEVER. YOU KNOW ME. I'M COOL.
TERRIFIC. OH, KATE, LISTEN, I COULDN'T HELP NOTICE YOU HAVE LENSES. YOU MIGHT WANT TO TAKE THOSE OUT.
SEE, THE POOLS NOT FILTERED. IT'S RIVER WATER. DON'T WANT TO GO TRAPPING ANY GERMS BEHIND THERE.
YOU SHOULD LISTEN TO LEONARD. MY COUSIN, SHE GOT THIS EYE INFECTION? THEY TOOK THE WHOLE EYE OUT.
YEAH? YEAH, OKAY, THANKS... BARB, WASN'T IT? I'LL BE SURE TO LOSE THE LENSES, ALONG WITH EVERYTHING ELSE.
YEAH. YOU KNOW, I AIN'T BEEN SKINNY DIPPING SINCE I WAS FIFTEEN.
CAN'T WAIT.

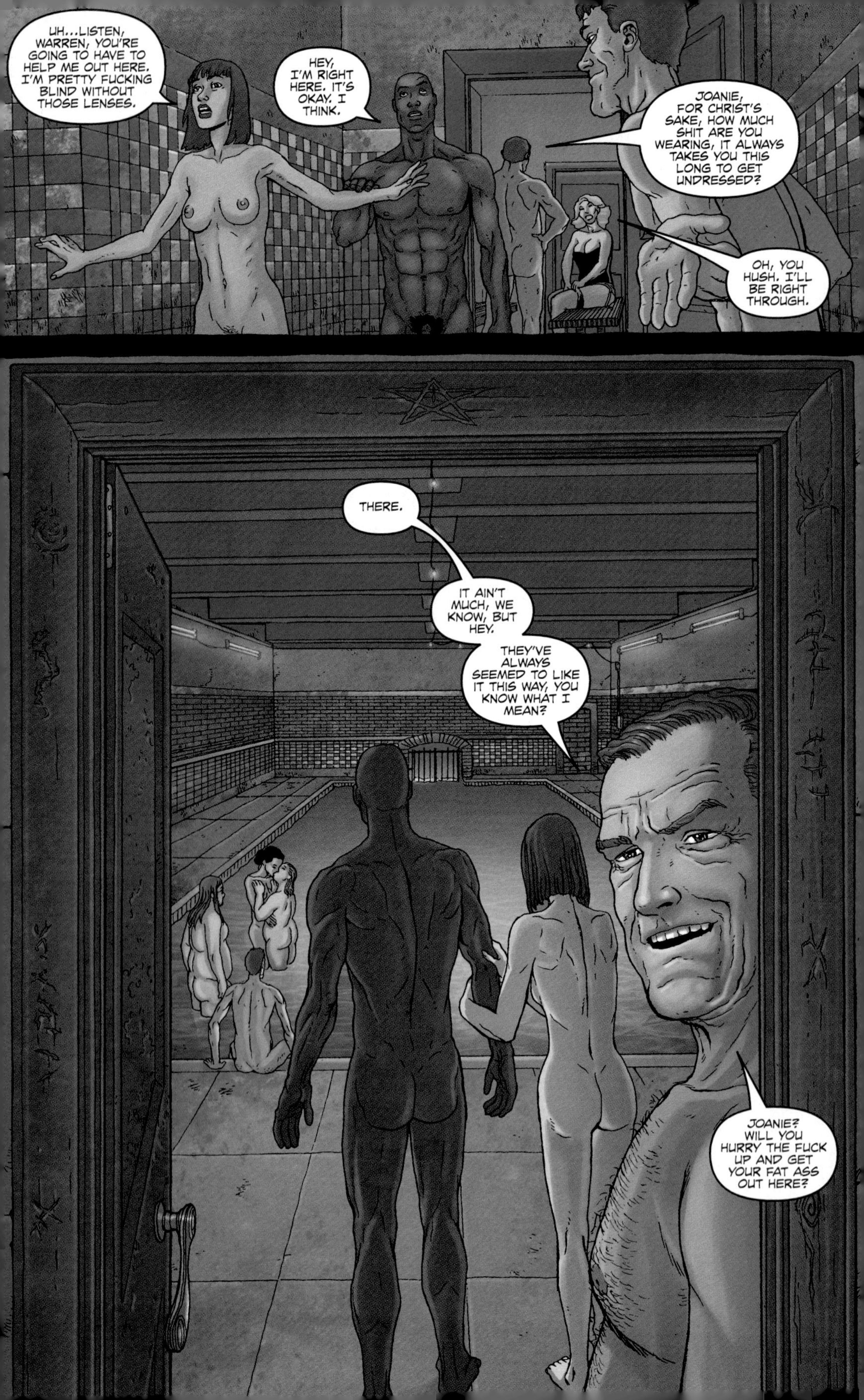
UH...LISTEN, WARREN, YOU'RE GOING TO HAVE TO HELP ME OUT HERE. I'M PRETTY FUCKING BLIND WITHOUT THOSE LENSES.
HEY, I'M RIGHT HERE. IT'S OKAY. I THINK.
JOANIE, FOR CHRIST'S SAKE, HOW MUCH SHIT ARE YOU WEARING, IT ALWAYS TAKES YOU THIS LONG TO GET UNDRESSED?
OH, YOU HUSH. I'LL BE RIGHT THROUGH.
THERE.
IT AIN'T MUCH, WE KNOW, BUT HEY.
THEY'VE ALWAYS SEEMED TO LIKE IT THIS WAY, YOU KNOW WHAT I MEAN?
JOANIE? WILL YOU HURRY THE FUCK UP AND GET YOUR FAT ASS OUT HERE?

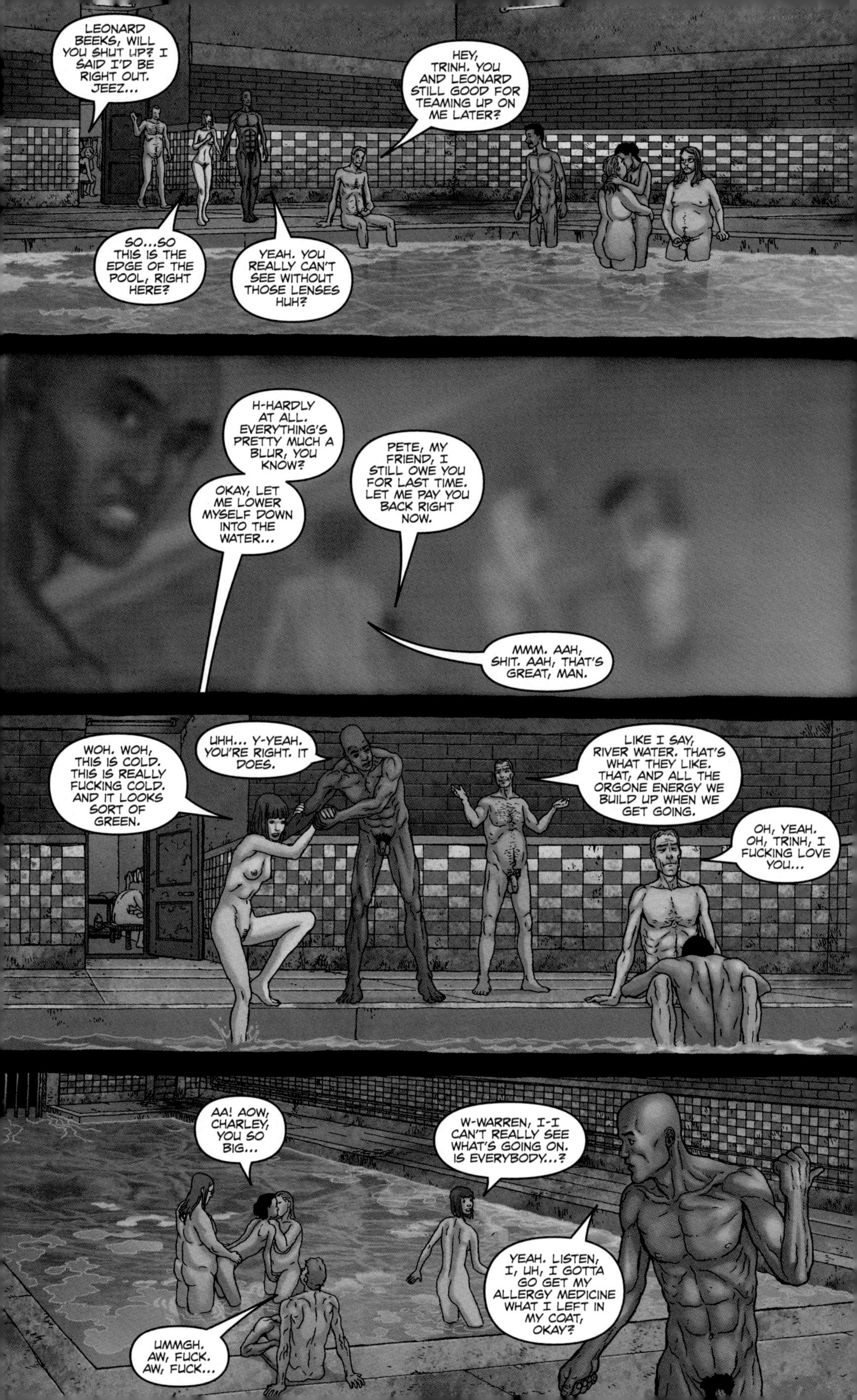
LEONARD BEEKS, WILL YOU SHUT UP? I SAID I'D BE RIGHT OUT. JEEZ...
HEY, TRINH. YOU AND LEONARD STILL GOOD FOR TEAMING UP ON ME LATER?
SO...SO THIS IS THE EDGE OF THE POOL, RIGHT HERE?
YEAH. YOU REALLY CAN'T SEE WITHOUT THOSE LENSES HUH?
H-HARDLY AT ALL. EVERYTHING'S PRETTY MUCH A BLUR, YOU KNOW?
OKAY, LET ME LOWER MYSELF DOWN INTO THE WATER...
PETE, MY FRIEND, I STILL OWE YOU FOR LAST TIME. LET ME PAY YOU BACK RIGHT NOW.
MMM. AAH, SHIT. AAH, THAT'S GREAT, MAN.
WOH. WOH, THIS IS COLD. THIS IS REALLY FUCKING COLD. AND IT LOOKS SORT OF GREEN.
UHH... Y-YEAH. YOU'RE RIGHT. IT DOES.
LIKE I SAY, RIVER WATER. THAT'S WHAT THEY LIKE. THAT, AND ALL THE ORGONE ENERGY WE BUILD UP WHEN WE GET GOING.
OH, YEAH. OH, TRINH, I FUCKING LOVE YOU...
AA! AOW, CHARLEY, YOU SO BIG...
W-WARREN, I-I CAN'T REALLY SEE WHAT'S GOING ON. IS EVERYBODY...?
YEAH. LISTEN, I, UH, I GOTTA GO GET MY ALLERGY MEDICINE WHAT I LEFT IN MY COAT, OKAY?
UMMGH. AW, FUCK. AW, FUCK...

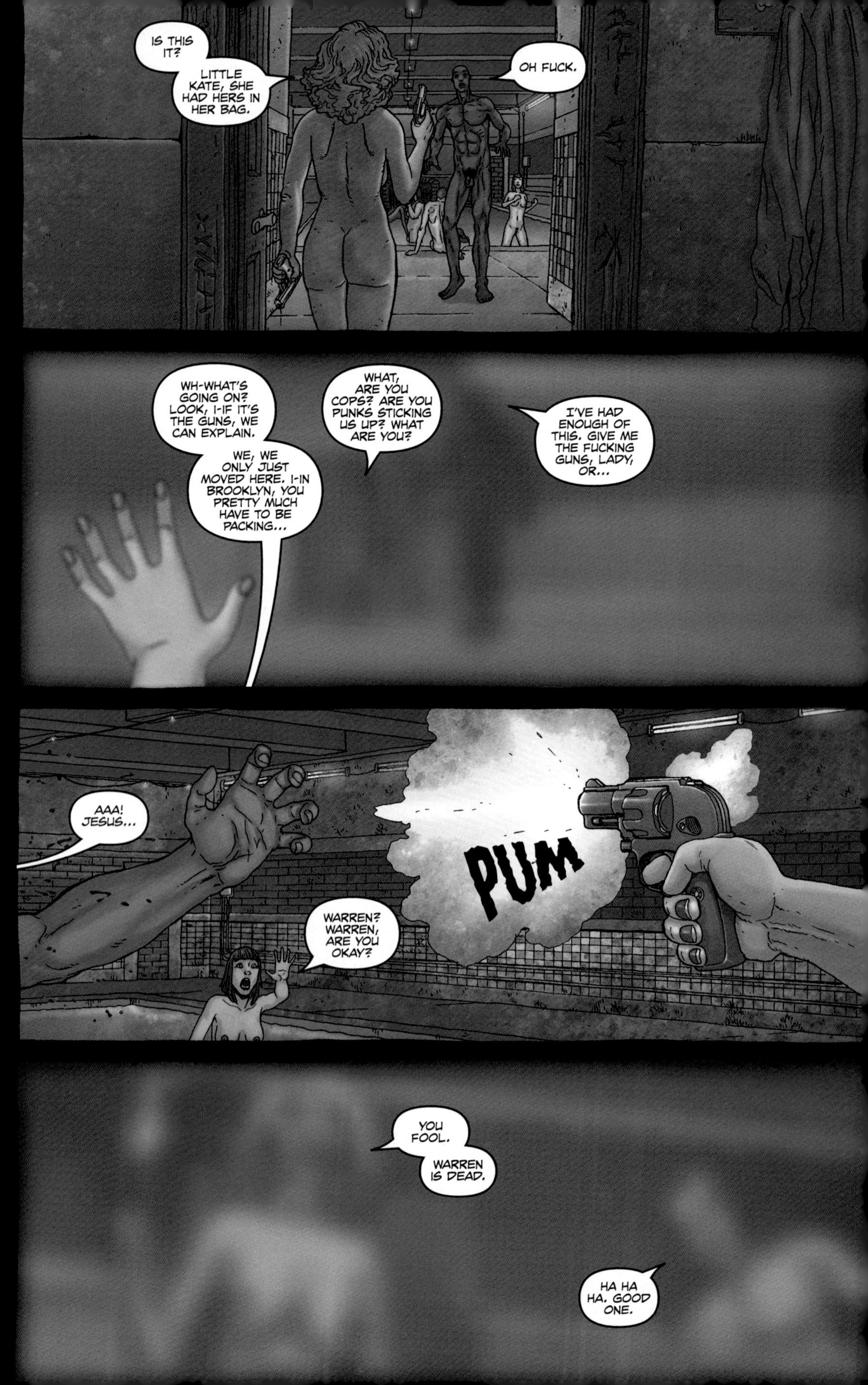
IS THIS IT?
LITTLE KATE, SHE HAD HERS IN HER BAG.
OH FUCK.
WH-WHAT'S GOING ON? LOOK, I-IF IT'S THE GUNS, WE CAN EXPLAIN.
WE, WE ONLY JUST MOVED HERE. I-IN BROOKLYN, YOU PRETTY MUCH HAVE TO BE PACKING...
WHAT, ARE YOU COPS? ARE YOU PUNKS STICKING US UP? WHAT ARE YOU?
I'VE HAD ENOUGH OF THIS. GIVE ME THE FUCKING GUNS, LADY, OR...
AAA! JESUS...
PUM
WARREN? WARREN, ARE YOU OKAY?
YOU FOOL.
WARREN IS DEAD.
HA HA HA. GOOD ONE.

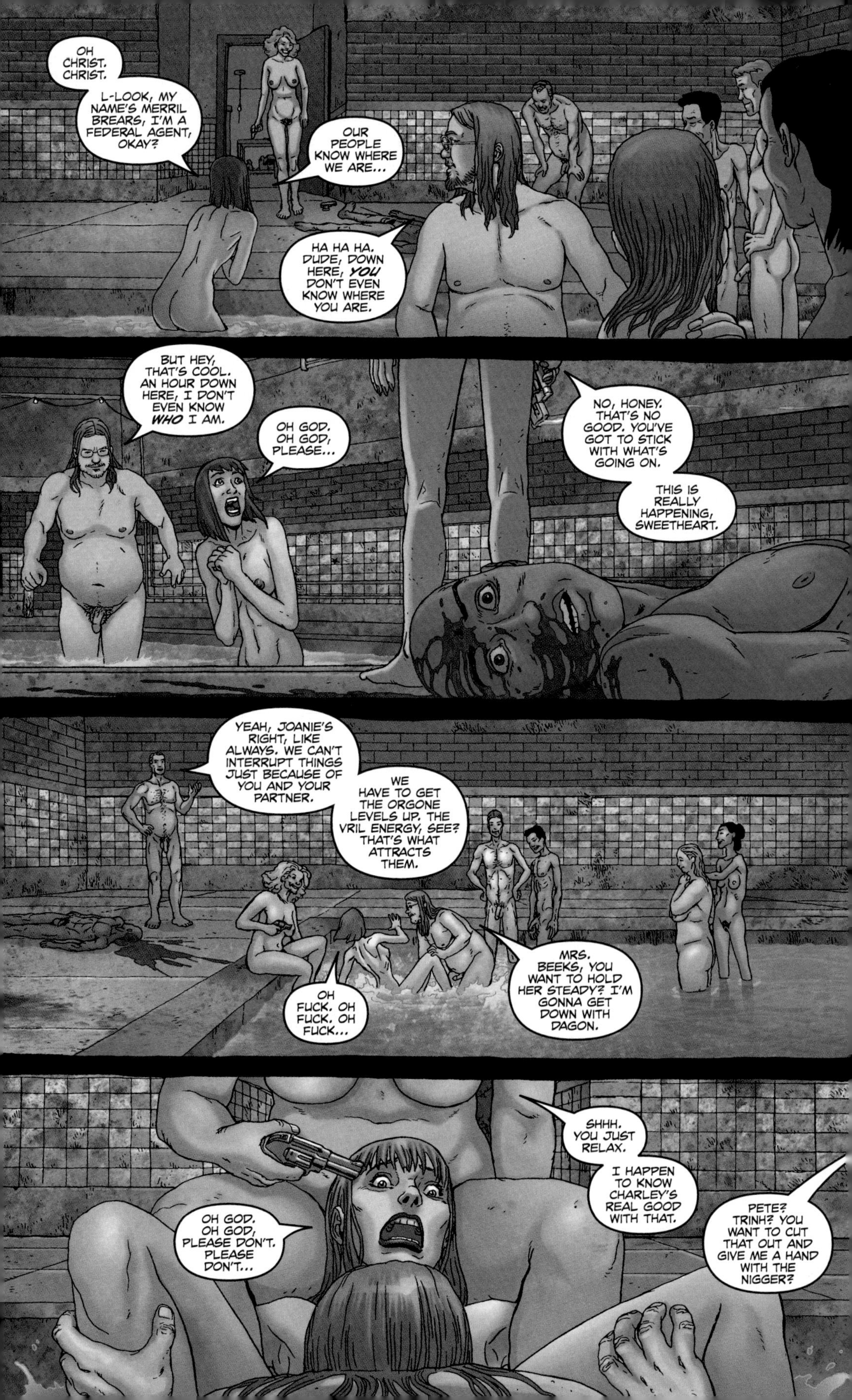
OH CHRIST. CHRIST.
L-LOOK, MY NAME'S MERRIL BREARS, I'M A FEDERAL AGENT, OKAY?
OUR PEOPLE KNOW WHERE WE ARE...
HA HA HA. DUDE, DOWN HERE, YOU DON'T EVEN KNOW WHERE YOU ARE.
BUT HEY, THAT'S COOL. AN HOUR DOWN HERE, I DON'T EVEN KNOW WHO I AM.
OH GOD. OH GOD, PLEASE...
NO, HONEY. THAT'S NO GOOD. YOU'VE GOT TO STICK WITH WHAT'S GOING ON.
THIS IS REALLY HAPPENING, SWEETHEART.
YEAH, JOANIE'S RIGHT, LIKE ALWAYS. WE CAN'T INTERRUPT THINGS JUST BECAUSE OF YOU AND YOUR PARTNER.
WE HAVE TO GET THE ORGONE LEVELS UP. THE VRIL ENERGY, SEE? THAT'S WHAT ATTRACTS THEM.
OH FUCK. OH FUCK. OH FUCK...
MRS. BEEKS, YOU WANT TO HOLD HER STEADY? I'M GONNA GET DOWN WITH DAGON.
SHHH. YOU JUST RELAX.
I HAPPEN TO KNOW CHARLEY'S REAL GOOD WITH THAT.
OH GOD. OH GOD, PLEASE DON'T. PLEASE DON'T...
PETE? TRINH? YOU WANT TO CUT THAT OUT AND GIVE ME A HAND WITH THE NIGGER?

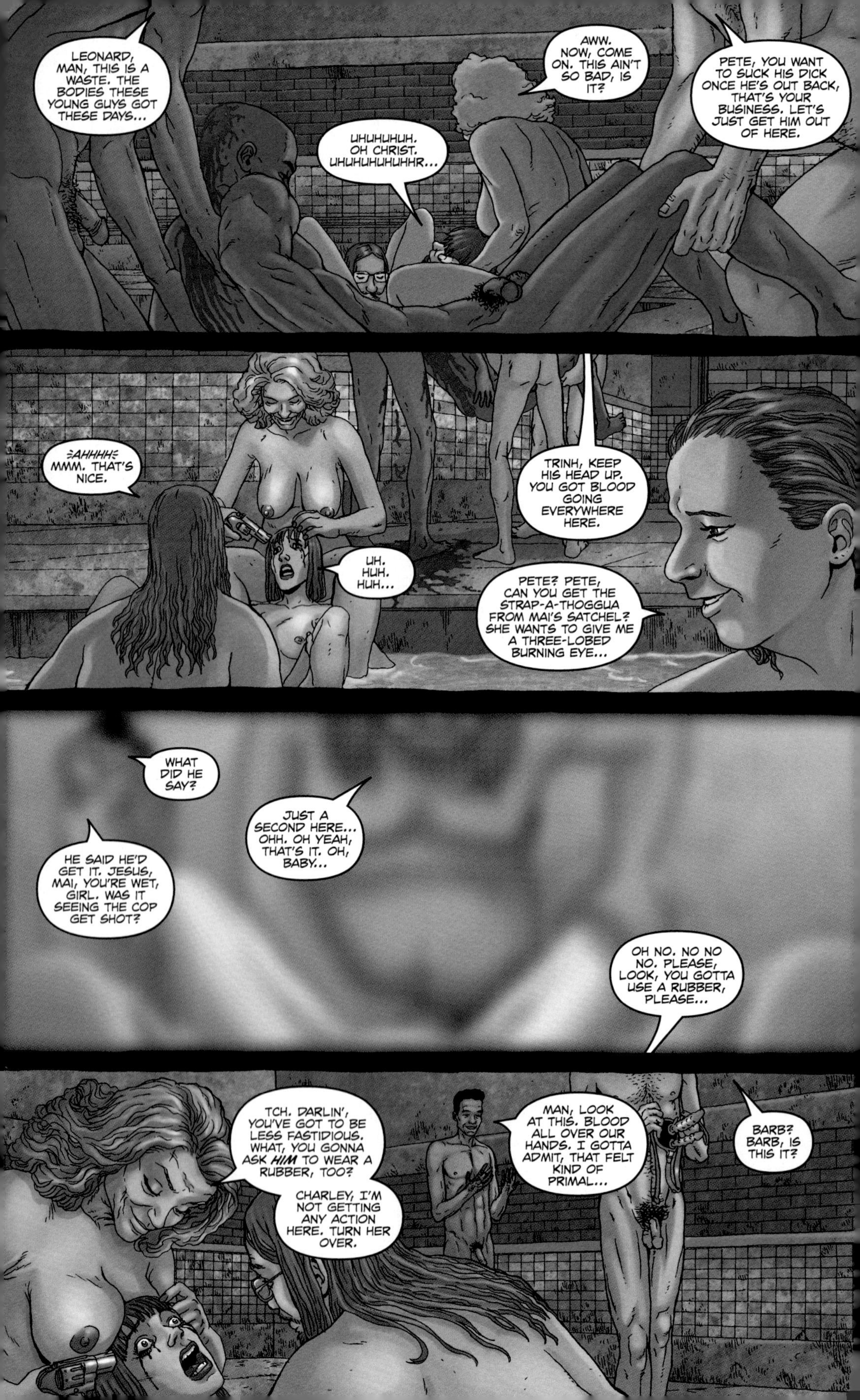

LEONARD, MAN, THIS IS A WASTE. THE BODIES THESE YOUNG GUYS GOT THESE DAYS...
UHUHUHUH. OH CHRIST. UHUHUHUHUHHR...
AWW. NOW, COME ON. THIS AIN'T SO BAD, IS IT?
PETE, YOU WANT TO SUCK HIS DICK ONCE HE'S OUT BACK, THAT'S YOUR BUSINESS. LET'S JUST GET HIM OUT OF HERE.
AHHHH MMM. THAT'S NICE.
UH. HUH. HUH...
TRINH, KEEP HIS HEAD UP. YOU GOT BLOOD GOING EVERYWHERE HERE.
PETE? PETE, CAN YOU GET THE STRAP-A-THOGGUA FROM MAI'S SATCHEL? SHE WANTS TO GIVE ME A THREE-LOBED BURNING EYE...
WHAT DID HE SAY?
JUST A SECOND HERE... OHH. OH YEAH, THAT'S IT. OH, BABY...
HE SAID HE'D GET IT. JESUS, MAI, YOU'RE WET, GIRL. WAS IT SEEING THE COP GET SHOT?
OH NO. NO NO NO. PLEASE, LOOK, YOU GOTTA USE A RUBBER, PLEASE...
TCH. DARLIN', YOU'VE GOT TO BE LESS FASTIDIOUS. WHAT, YOU GONNA ASK *HIM* TO WEAR A RUBBER, TOO?
CHARLEY, I'M NOT GETTING ANY ACTION HERE. TURN HER OVER.
MAN, LOOK AT THIS. BLOOD ALL OVER OUR HANDS. I GOTTA ADMIT, THAT FELT KIND OF PRIMAL...
BARB? BARB, IS THIS IT?

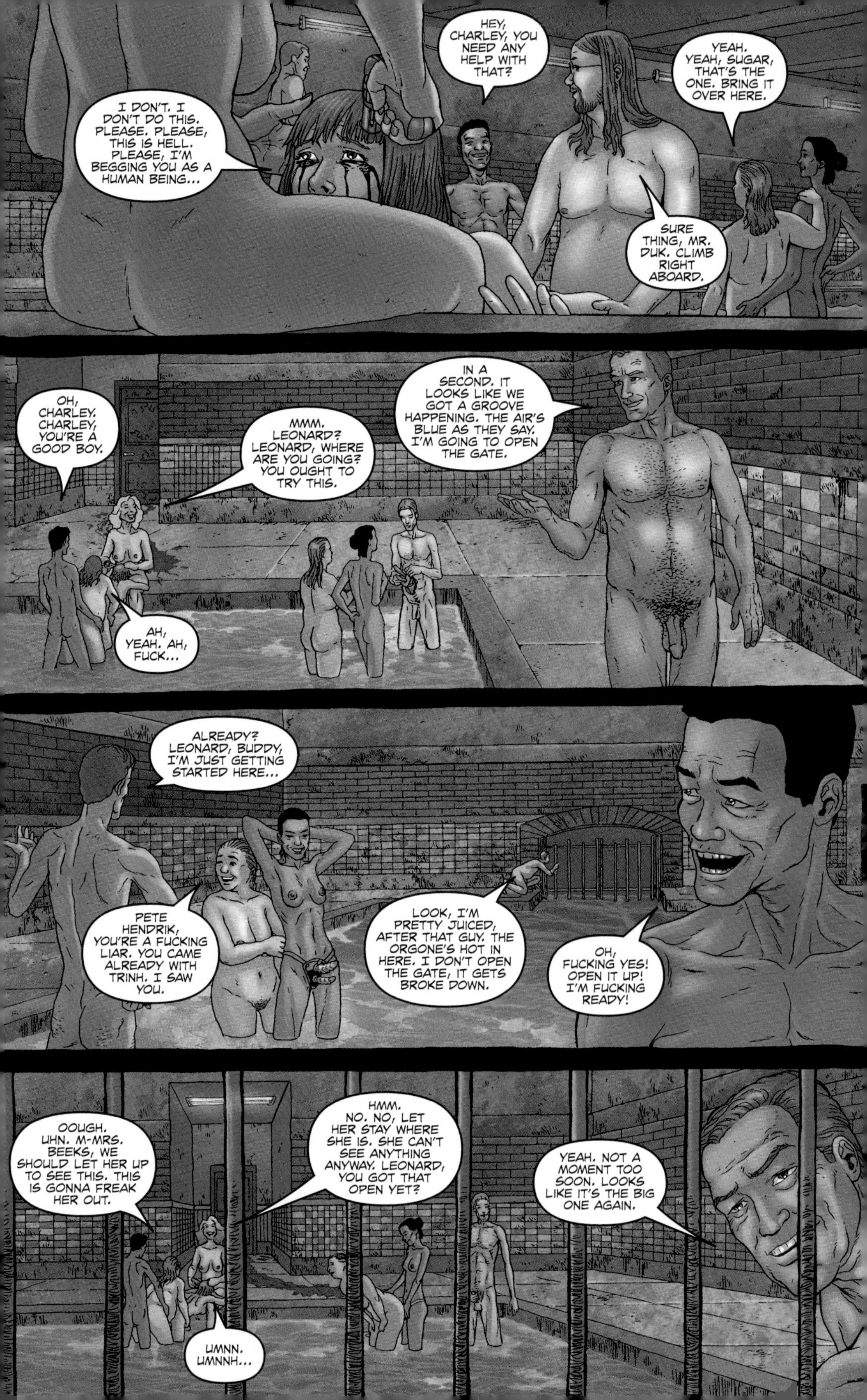

HEY, CHARLEY, YOU NEED ANY HELP WITH THAT?
I DON'T. I DON'T DO THIS. PLEASE. PLEASE, THIS IS HELL. PLEASE, I'M BEGGING YOU AS A HUMAN BEING...
YEAH. YEAH, SUGAR, THAT'S THE ONE. BRING IT OVER HERE.
SURE THING, MR. DUK. CLIMB RIGHT ABOARD.
OH, CHARLEY. CHARLEY, YOU'RE A GOOD BOY.
MMM. LEONARD? LEONARD, WHERE ARE YOU GOING? YOU OUGHT TO TRY THIS.
IN A SECOND. IT LOOKS LIKE WE GOT A GROOVE HAPPENING. THE AIR'S BLUE AS THEY SAY. I'M GOING TO OPEN THE GATE.
AH, YEAH. AH, FUCK...
ALREADY? LEONARD, BUDDY, I'M JUST GETTING STARTED HERE...
PETE HENDRIK, YOU'RE A FUCKING LIAR. YOU CAME ALREADY WITH TRINH. I SAW YOU.
LOOK, I'M PRETTY JUICED, AFTER THAT GUY. THE ORGONE'S HOT IN HERE. I DON'T OPEN THE GATE, IT GETS BROKE DOWN.
OH, FUCKING YES! OPEN IT UP! I'M FUCKING READY!
OOUGH. UHN. M-MRS. BEEKS, WE SHOULD LET HER UP TO SEE THIS. THIS IS GONNA FREAK HER OUT.
HMM. NO. NO, LET HER STAY WHERE SHE IS. SHE CAN'T SEE ANYTHING ANYWAY. LEONARD, YOU GOT THAT OPEN YET?
YEAH. NOT A MOMENT TOO SOON. LOOKS LIKE IT'S THE BIG ONE AGAIN.
UMNN. UMNNH...

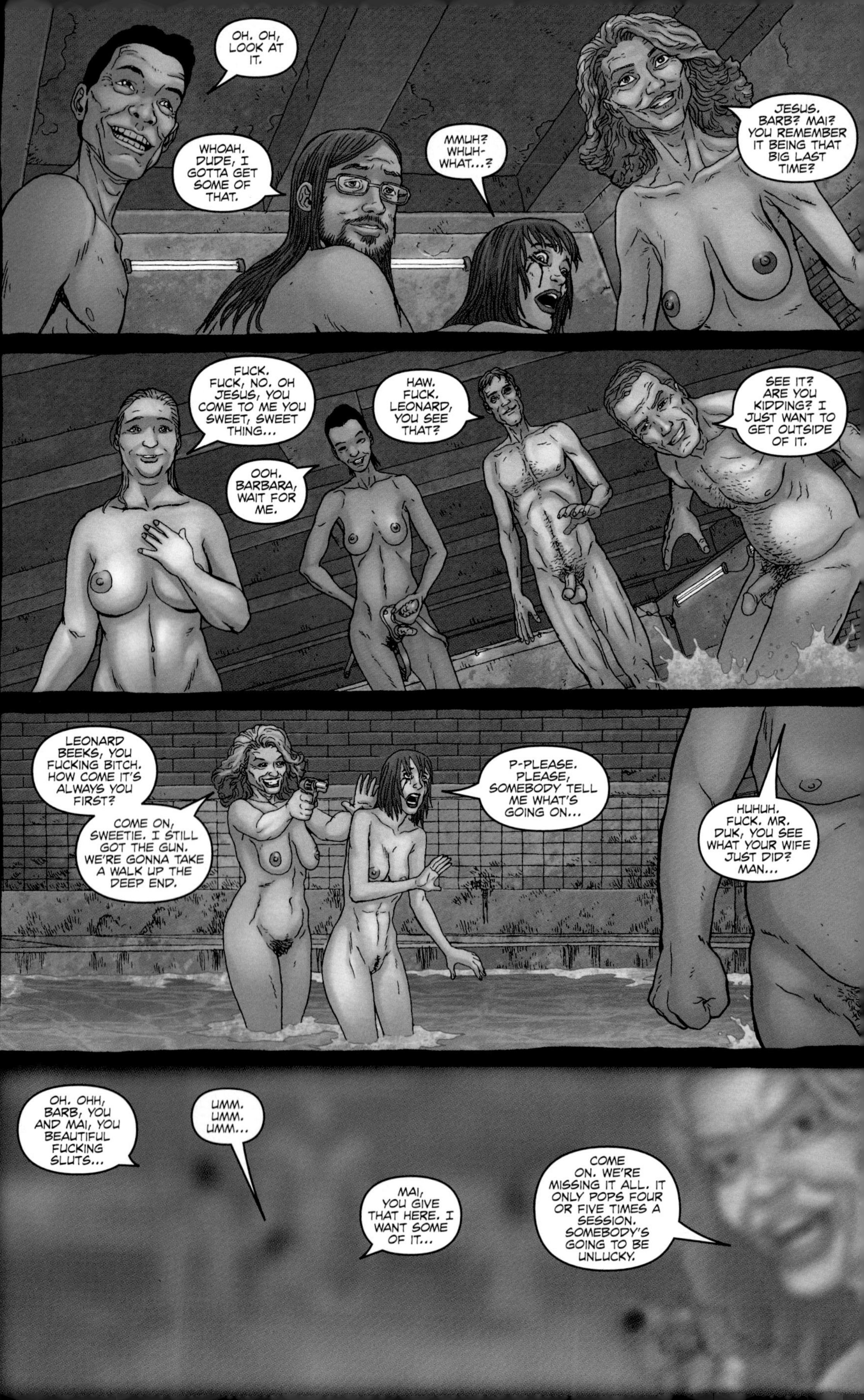
OH. OH, LOOK AT IT.
WHOAH. DUDE, I GOTTA GET SOME OF THAT.
MMUH? WHUH-WHAT...?
JESUS. BARB? MAI? YOU REMEMBER IT BEING THAT BIG LAST TIME?
FUCK. FUCK, NO. OH JESUS, YOU COME TO ME YOU SWEET, SWEET THING...
OOH. BARBARA, WAIT FOR ME.
HAW. FUCK. LEONARD, YOU SEE THAT?
SEE IT? ARE YOU KIDDING? I JUST WANT TO GET OUTSIDE OF IT.
LEONARD BEEKS, YOU FUCKING BITCH. HOW COME IT'S ALWAYS YOU FIRST?
COME ON, SWEETIE. I STILL GOT THE GUN. WE'RE GONNA TAKE A WALK UP THE DEEP END.
P-PLEASE. PLEASE, SOMEBODY TELL ME WHAT'S GOING ON...
HUHUH. FUCK. MR. DUK, YOU SEE WHAT YOUR WIFE JUST DID? MAN...
OH. OHH, BARB, YOU AND MAI, YOU BEAUTIFUL FUCKING SLUTS...
UMM. UMM. UMM...
MAI, YOU GIVE THAT HERE. I WANT SOME OF IT...
COME ON. WE'RE MISSING IT ALL. IT ONLY POPS FOUR OR FIVE TIMES A SESSION. SOMEBODY'S GOING TO BE UNLUCKY.

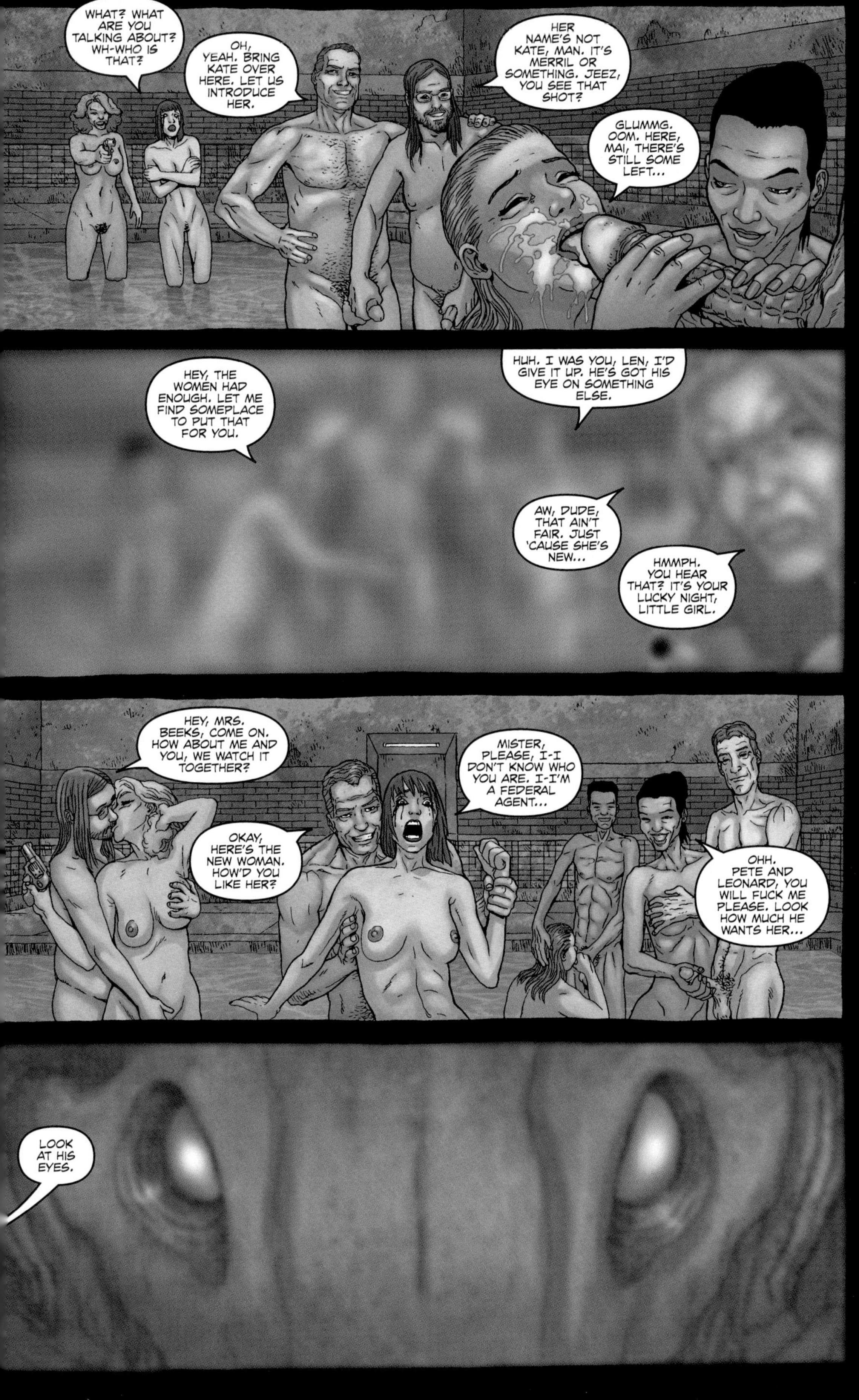
WHAT? WHAT ARE YOU TALKING ABOUT? WH-WHO IS THAT?
OH, YEAH. BRING KATE OVER HERE. LET US INTRODUCE HER.
HER NAME'S NOT KATE, MAN. IT'S MERRIL OR SOMETHING. JEEZ, YOU SEE THAT SHOT?
GLUMMG. OOM. HERE, MAI, THERE'S STILL SOME LEFT...
HEY, THE WOMEN HAD ENOUGH. LET ME FIND SOMEPLACE TO PUT THAT FOR YOU.
HUH. I WAS YOU, LEN, I'D GIVE IT UP. HE'S GOT HIS EYE ON SOMETHING ELSE.
AW, DUDE, THAT AIN'T FAIR. JUST 'CAUSE SHE'S NEW...
HMMPH. YOU HEAR THAT? IT'S YOUR LUCKY NIGHT, LITTLE GIRL.
HEY, MRS. BEEKS, COME ON. HOW ABOUT ME AND YOU, WE WATCH IT TOGETHER?
OKAY, HERE'S THE NEW WOMAN. HOW'D YOU LIKE HER?
MISTER, PLEASE, I-I DON'T KNOW WHO YOU ARE. I-I'M A FEDERAL AGENT...
OHH. PETE AND LEONARD, YOU WILL FUCK ME PLEASE. LOOK HOW MUCH HE WANTS HER...
LOOK AT HIS EYES.

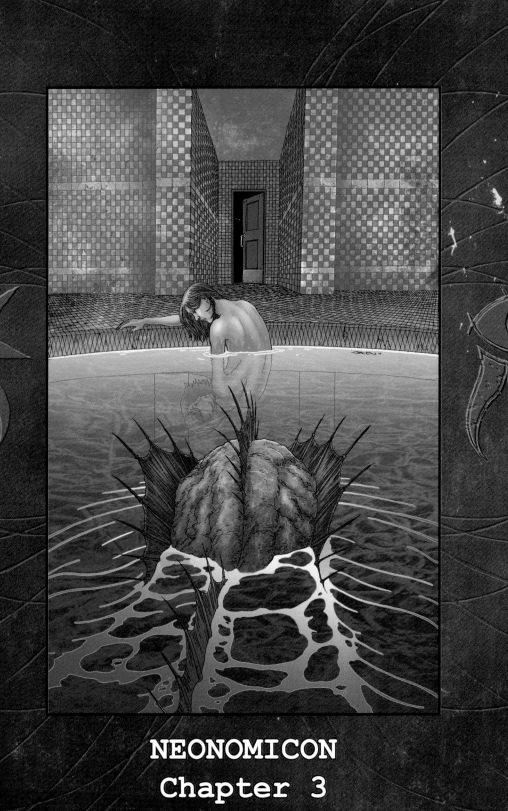

NEONOMICON
Chapter 3

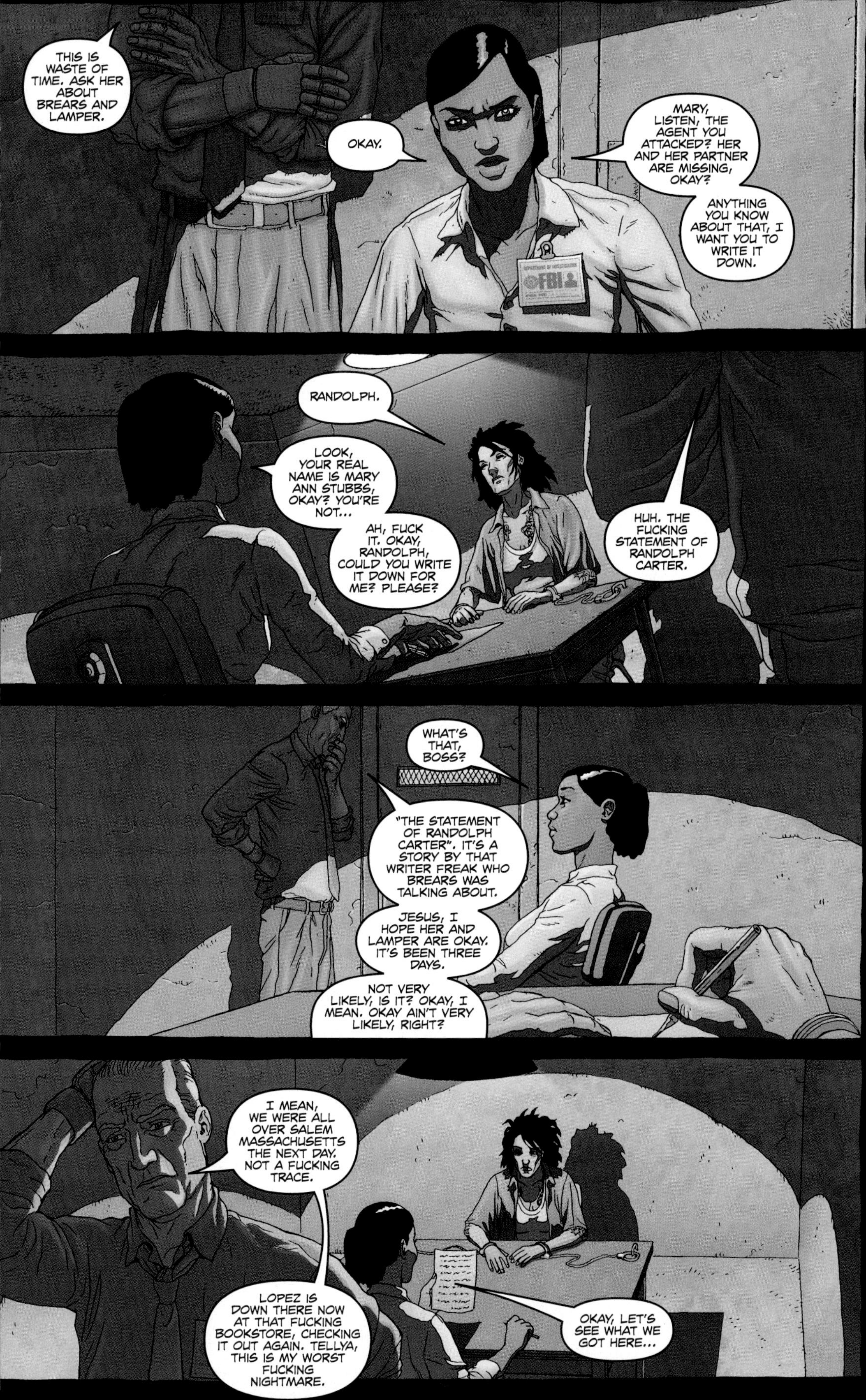
THIS IS WASTE OF TIME. ASK HER ABOUT BREARS AND LAMPER.
OKAY.
MARY, LISTEN, THE AGENT YOU ATTACKED? HER AND HER PARTNER ARE MISSING, OKAY?
ANYTHING YOU KNOW ABOUT THAT, I WANT YOU TO WRITE IT DOWN.
FBI
RANDOLPH.
LOOK, YOUR REAL NAME IS MARY ANN STUBBS, OKAY? YOU'RE NOT...
AH, FUCK IT. OKAY, RANDOLPH, COULD YOU WRITE IT DOWN FOR ME? PLEASE?
HUH. THE FUCKING STATEMENT OF RANDOLPH CARTER.
WHAT'S THAT, BOSS?
"THE STATEMENT OF RANDOLPH CARTER". IT'S A STORY BY THAT WRITER FREAK WHO BREARS WAS TALKING ABOUT.
JESUS, I HOPE HER AND LAMPER ARE OKAY. IT'S BEEN THREE DAYS.
NOT VERY LIKELY, IS IT? OKAY, I MEAN. OKAY AIN'T VERY LIKELY, RIGHT?
I MEAN, WE WERE ALL OVER SALEM MASSACHUSETTS THE NEXT DAY. NOT A FUCKING TRACE.
LOPEZ IS DOWN THERE NOW AT THAT FUCKING BOOKSTORE, CHECKING IT OUT AGAIN. TELLYA, THIS IS MY WORST FUCKING NIGHTMARE.
OKAY, LET'S SEE WHAT WE GOT HERE...

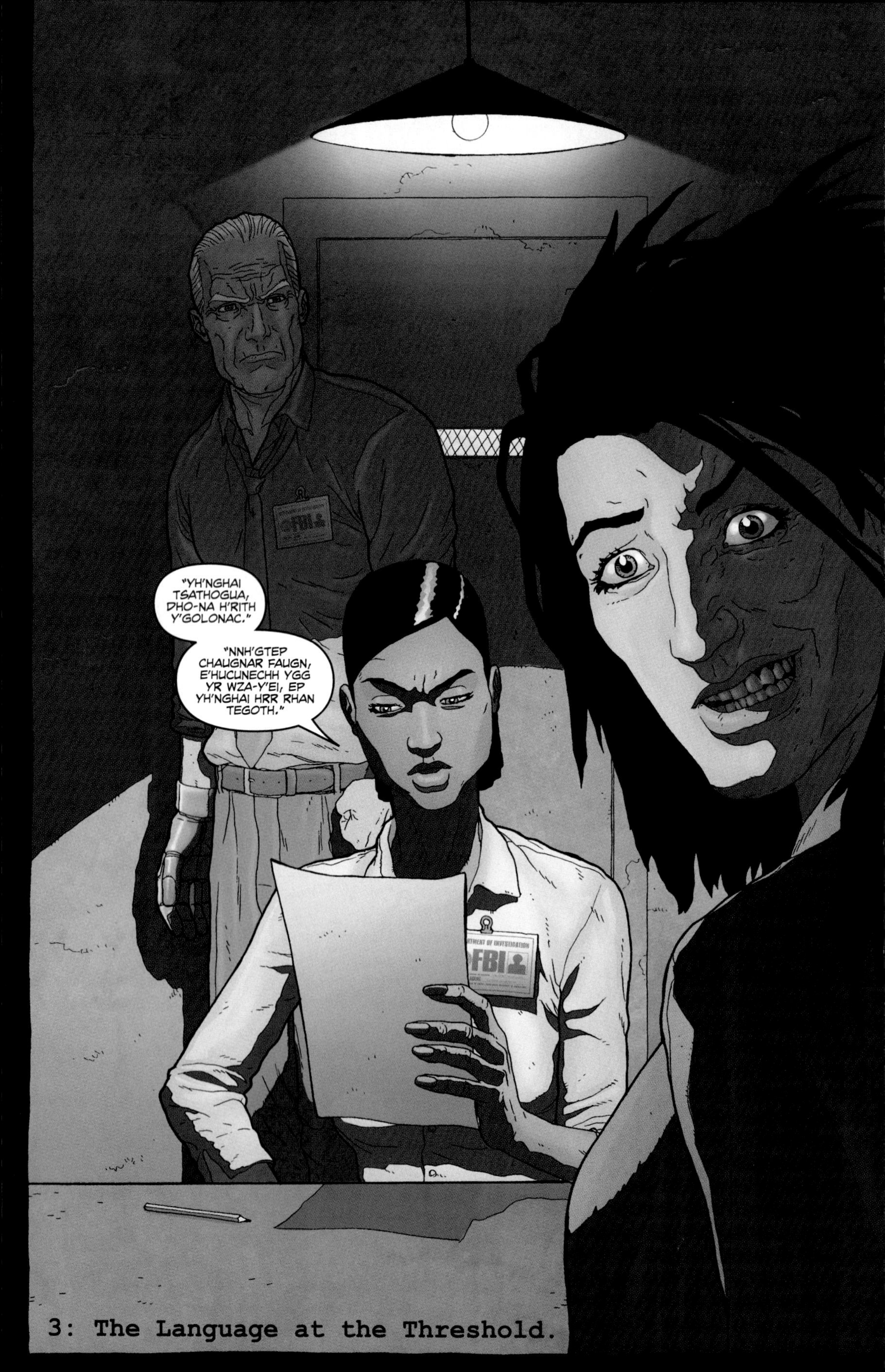
"YH'NGHAI TSATHOGUA, DHO-NA H'RITH Y'GOLONAC."
"NNH'GTEP CHAUGNAR FAUGN, E'HUCUNECHH YGG YR WZA-Y'EI, EP YH'NGHAI HRR RHAN TEGOTH."
3: The Language at the Threshold.

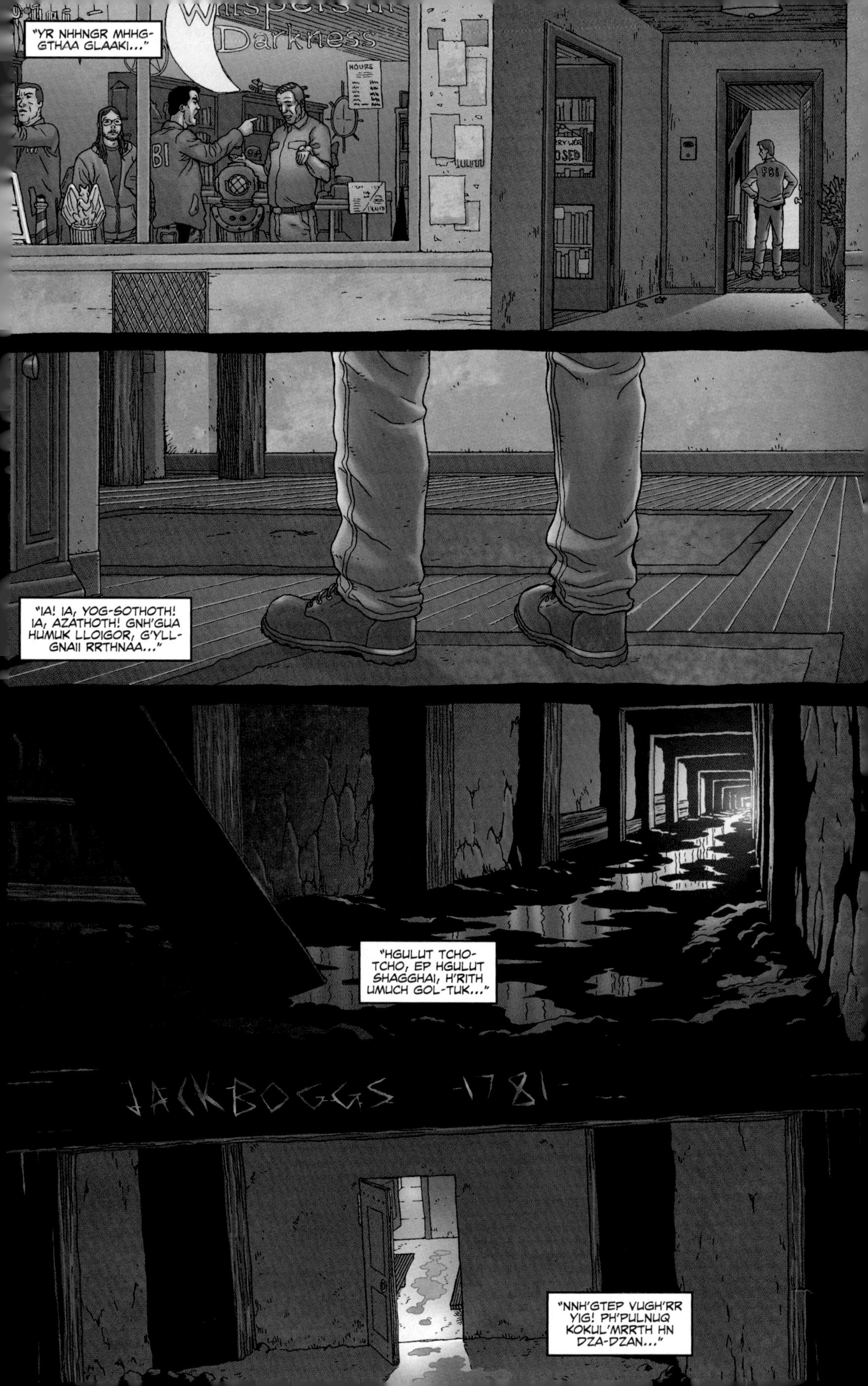
"YR NHHNGR MHHG-GTHAA GLAAKI..."
Darkness
HOURS
"IA! IA, YOG-SOTHOTH! IA, AZATHOTH! GNH'GUA HUMUK LLOIGOR, G'YLL-GNAII RRTHNAA..."
"HGULUT TCHO-TCHO, EP HGULUT SHAGGHAI, H'RITH UMUCH GOL-TUK..."
JACKBOGGS -1781-
"NNH'GTEP VUGH'RR YIG! PH'PULNUQ KOKUL'MRRTH HN DZA-DZAN..."

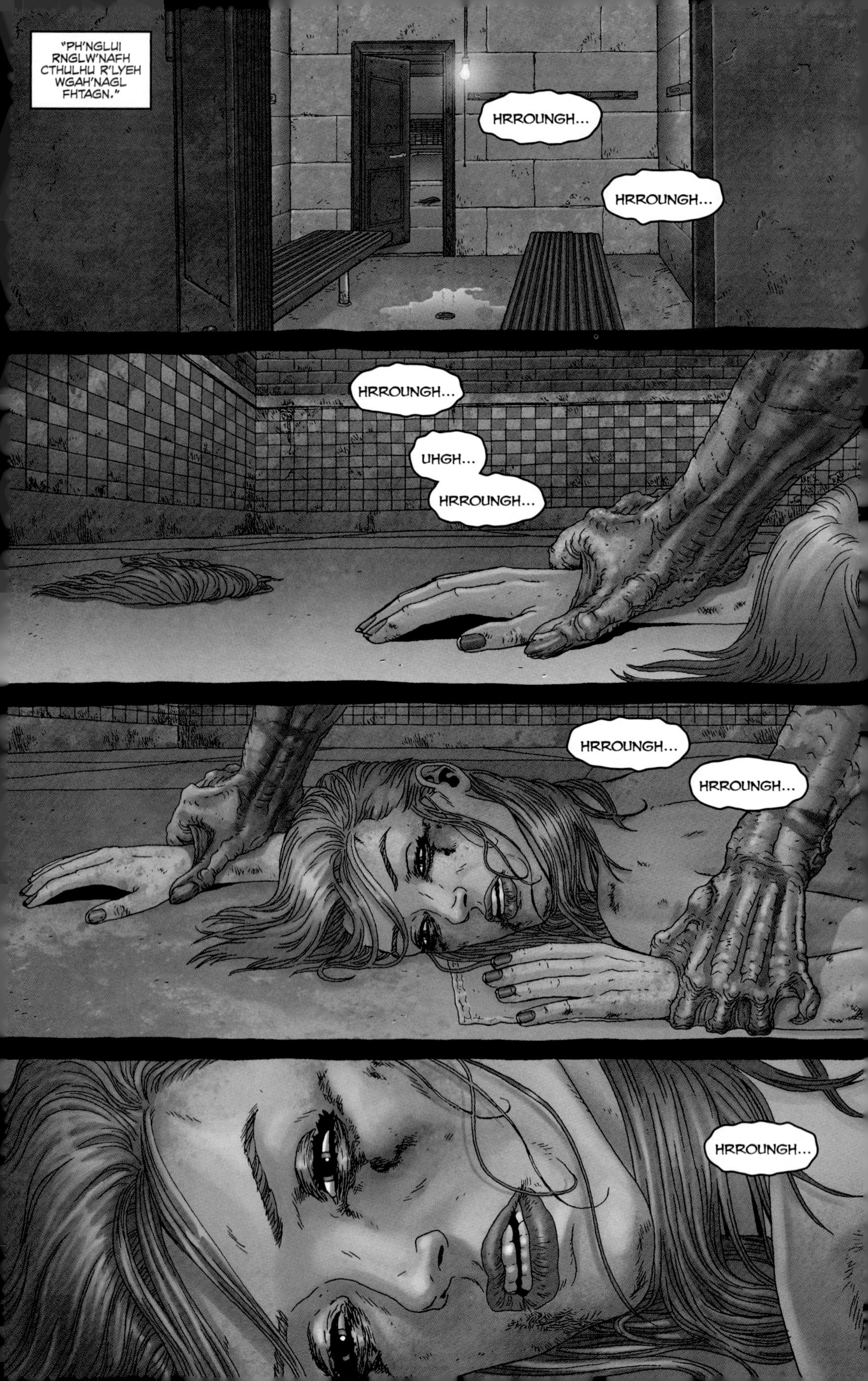
"PH'NGLUI RNGLW'NAFH CTHULHU R'LYEH WGAH'NAGL FHTAGN."
HRROUNGH...
HRROUNGH...
HRROUNGH...
UHGH...
HRROUNGH...
HRROUNGH...
HRROUNGH...
HRROUNGH...

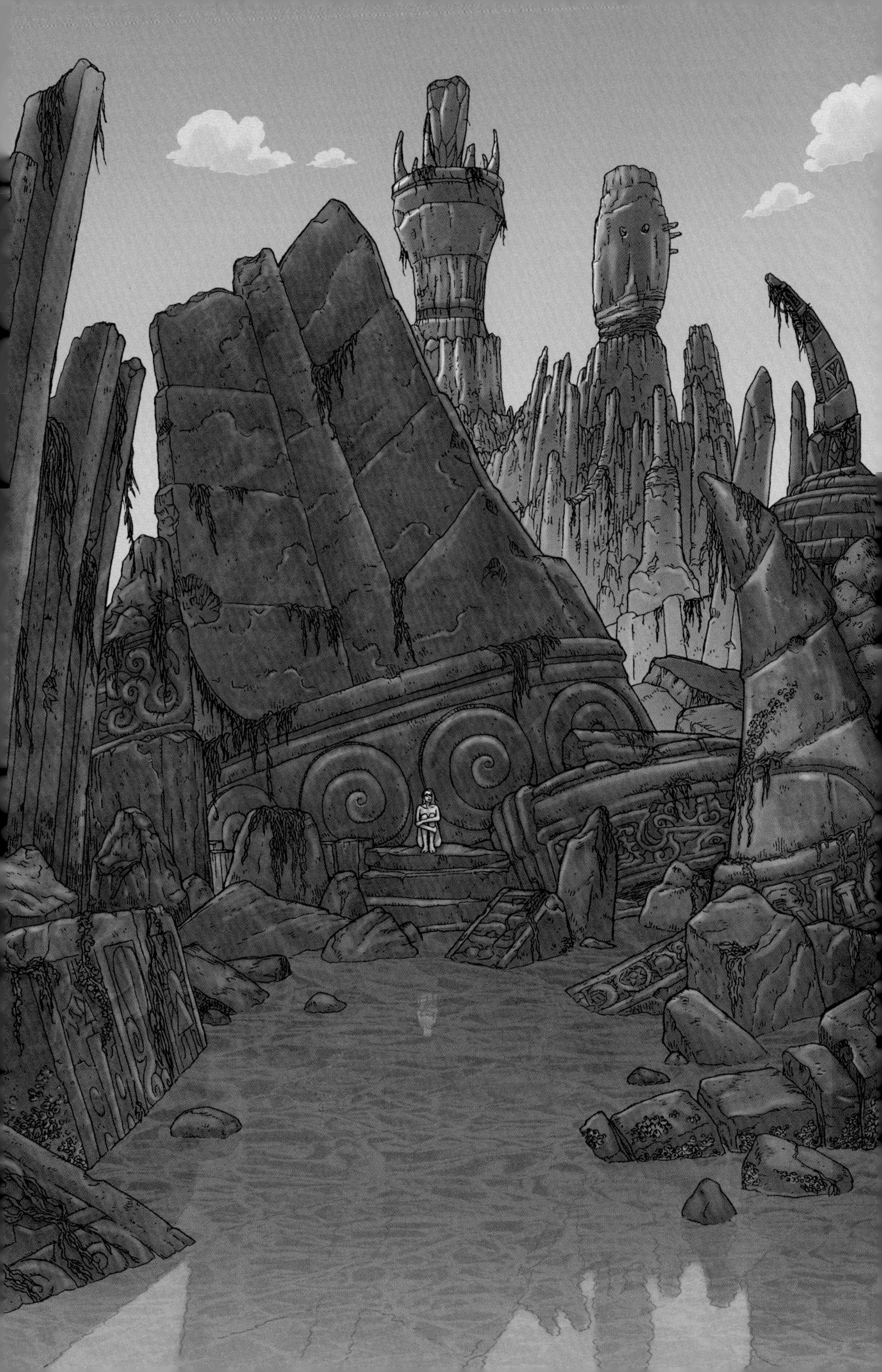

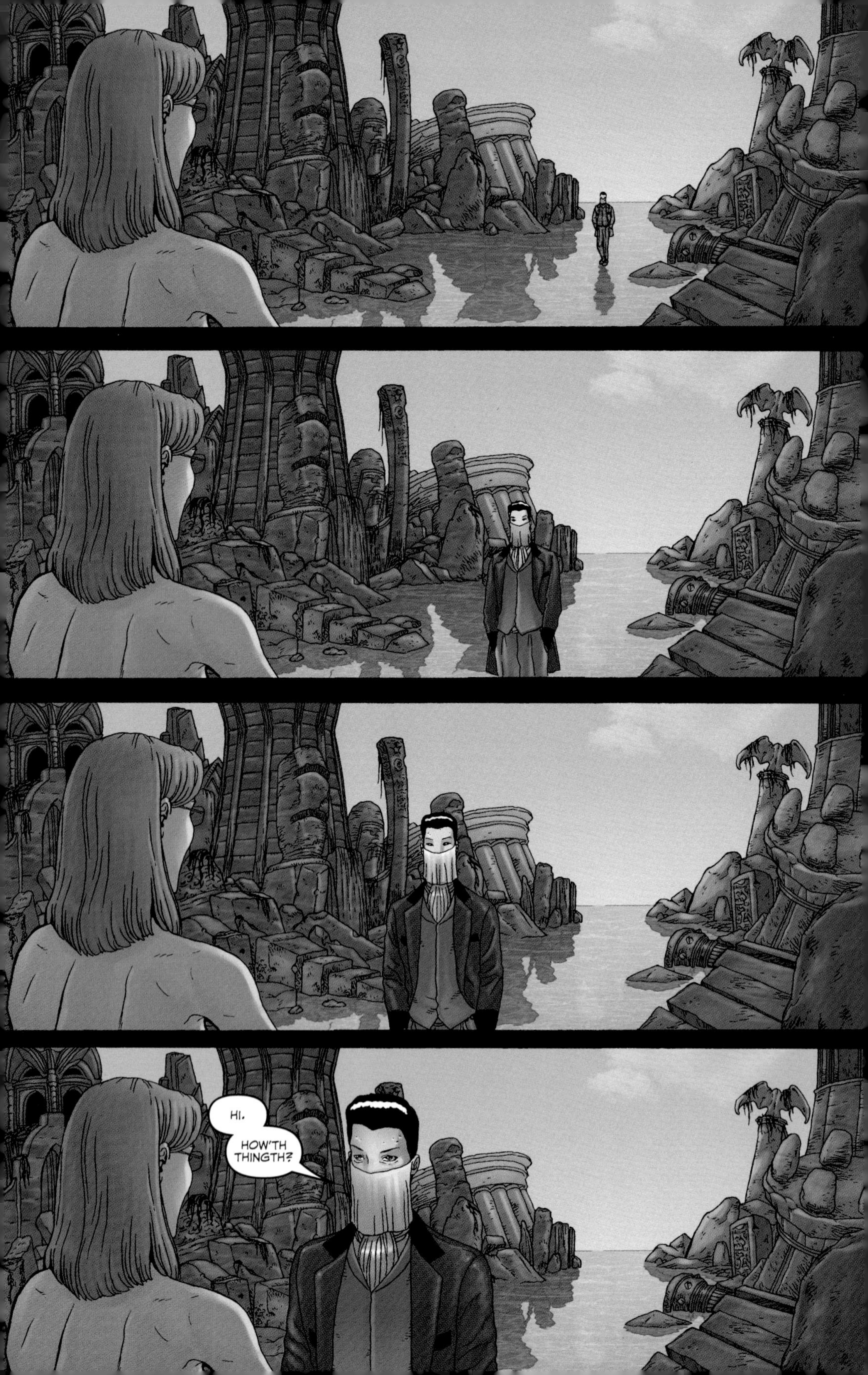
HI.
HOW'TH THINGTH?

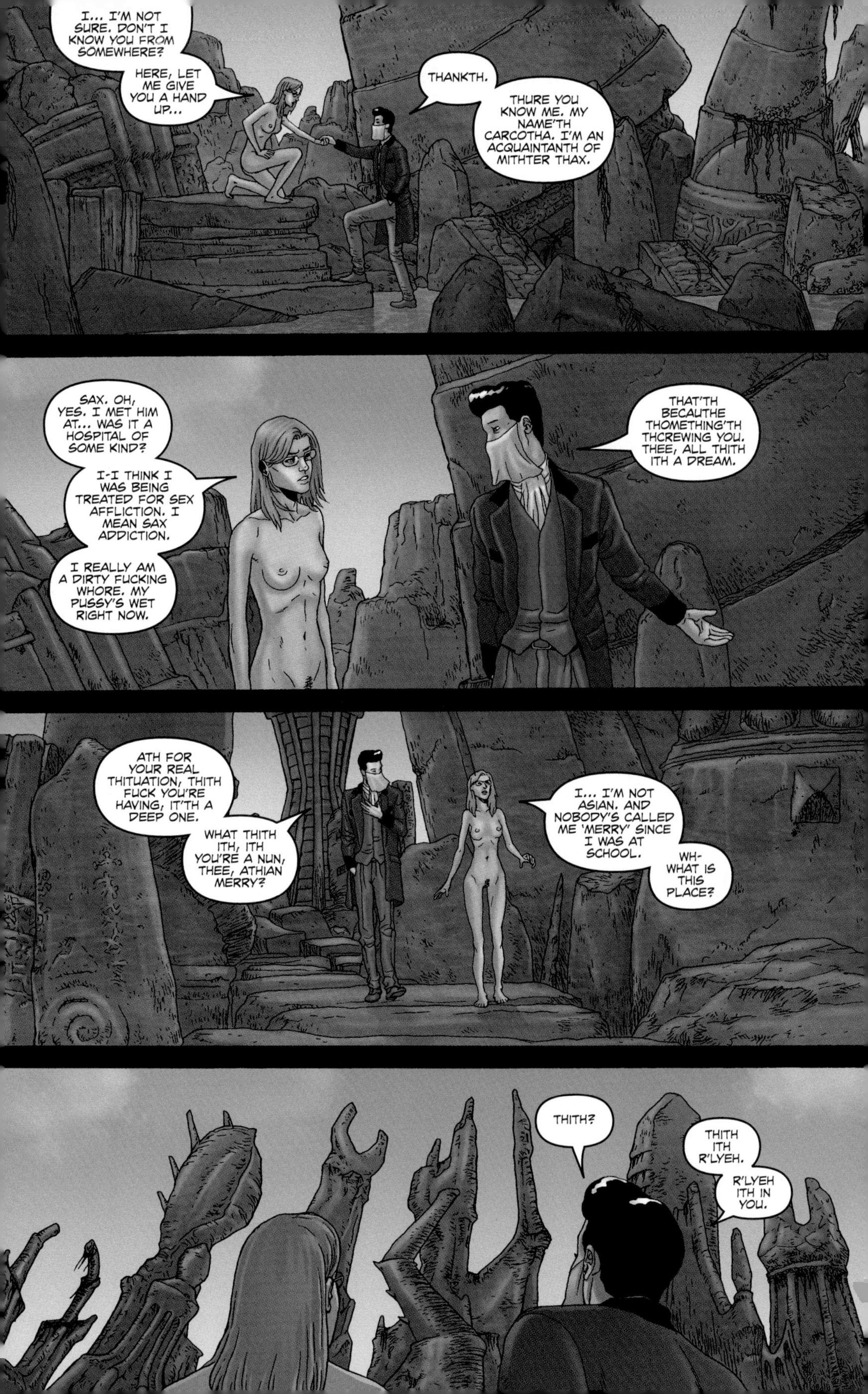
I... I'M NOT SURE. DON'T I KNOW YOU FROM SOMEWHERE?
HERE, LET ME GIVE YOU A HAND UP...
THANKTH.
THURE YOU KNOW ME. MY NAME'TH CARCOTHA. I'M AN ACQUAINTANTH OF MITHTER THAX.
SAX. OH, YES. I MET HIM AT... WAS IT A HOSPITAL OF SOME KIND?
I-I THINK I WAS BEING TREATED FOR SEX AFFLICTION. I MEAN SAX ADDICTION.
I REALLY AM A DIRTY FUCKING WHORE. MY PUSSY'S WET RIGHT NOW.
THAT'TH BECAUTHE THOMETHING'TH THCREWING YOU. THEE, ALL THITH ITH A DREAM.
ATH FOR YOUR REAL THITUATION, THITH FUCK YOU'RE HAVING, IT'TH A DEEP ONE.
WHAT THITH ITH, ITH YOU'RE A NUN, THEE, ATHIAN MERRY?
I... I'M NOT ASIAN. AND NOBODY'S CALLED ME 'MERRY' SINCE I WAS AT SCHOOL.
WH-WHAT IS THIS PLACE?
THITH?
THITH ITH R'LYEH.
R'LYEH ITH IN YOU.

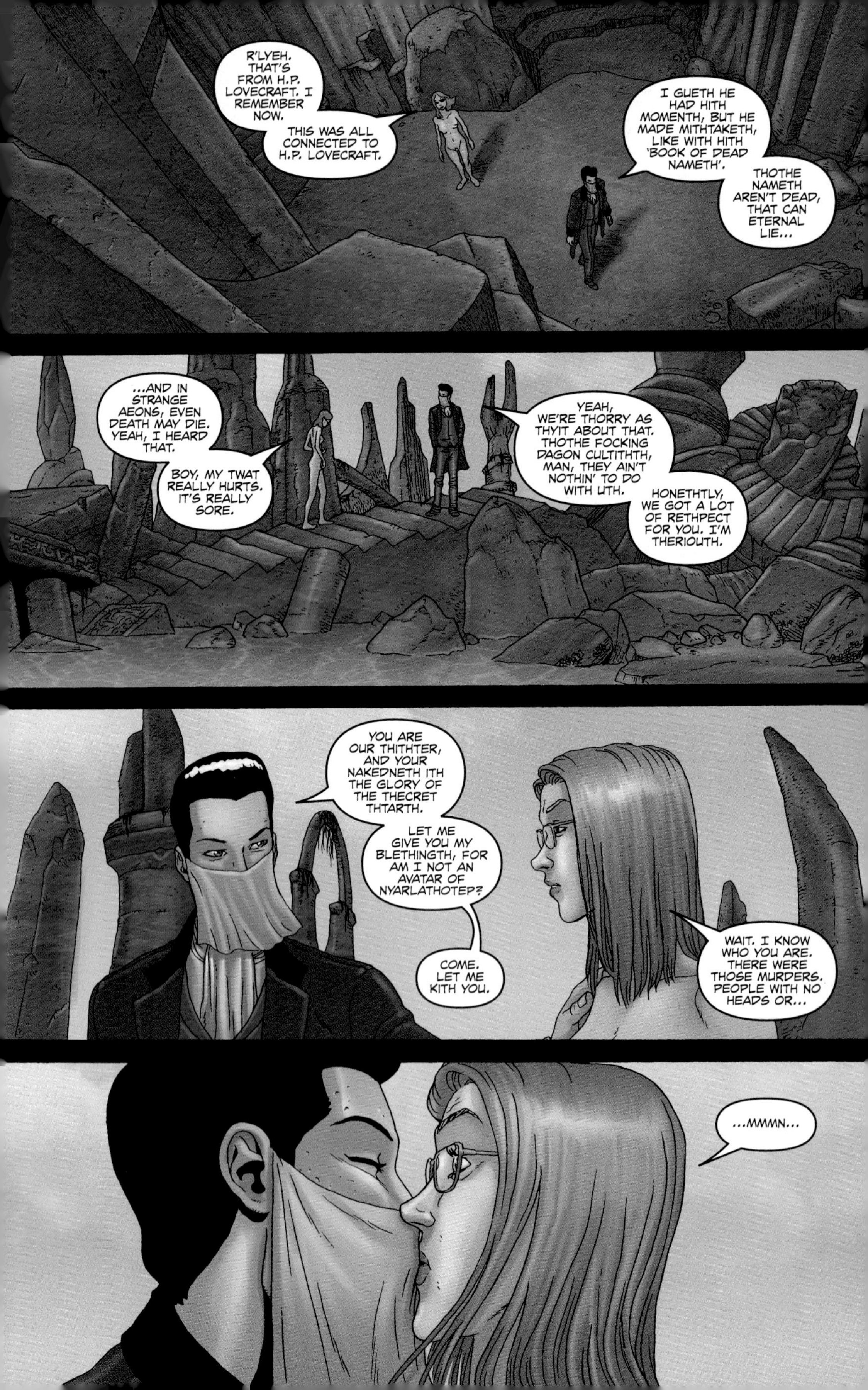
R'LYEH. THAT'S FROM H.P. LOVECRAFT. I REMEMBER NOW.
THIS WAS ALL CONNECTED TO H.P. LOVECRAFT.
I GUETH HE HAD HITH MOMENTH, BUT HE MADE MITHTAKETH, LIKE WITH HITH 'BOOK OF DEAD NAMETH'.
THOTHE NAMETH AREN'T DEAD, THAT CAN ETERNAL LIE...
...AND IN STRANGE AEONS, EVEN DEATH MAY DIE. YEAH, I HEARD THAT.
BOY, MY TWAT REALLY HURTS. IT'S REALLY SORE.
YEAH, WE'RE THORRY AS THYIT ABOUT THAT. THOTHE FOCKING DAGON CULTITHTH, MAN, THEY AIN'T NOTHIN' TO DO WITH UTH.
HONETHTLY, WE GOT A LOT OF RETHPECT FOR YOU. I'M THERIOUTH.
YOU ARE OUR THITHTER, AND YOUR NAKEDNETH ITH THE GLORY OF THE THECRET THTARTH.
LET ME GIVE YOU MY BLETHINGTH, FOR AM I NOT AN AVATAR OF NYARLATHOTEP?
COME. LET ME KITH YOU.
WAIT. I KNOW WHO YOU ARE. THERE WERE THOSE MURDERS. PEOPLE WITH NO HEADS OR...
...MMMN...

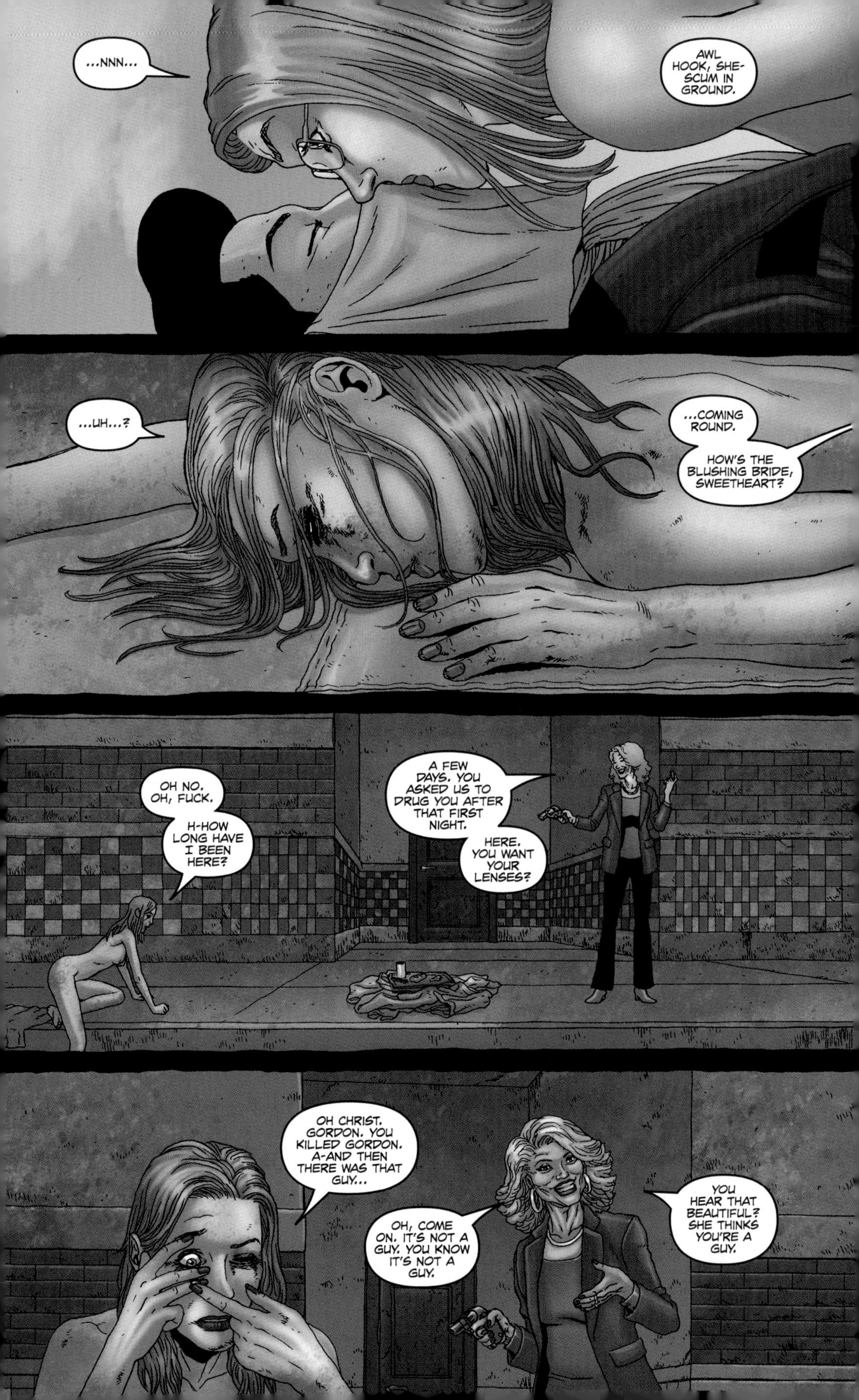
...NNN...
AWL HOOK, SHE-SCUM IN GROUND.
...UH...?
...COMING ROUND.
HOW'S THE BLUSHING BRIDE, SWEETHEART?
OH NO. OH, FUCK.
H-HOW LONG HAVE I BEEN HERE?
A FEW DAYS. YOU ASKED US TO DRUG YOU AFTER THAT FIRST NIGHT.
HERE. YOU WANT YOUR LENSES?
OH CHRIST. GORDON. YOU KILLED GORDON. A-AND THEN THERE WAS THAT GUY...
OH, COME ON. IT'S NOT A GUY. YOU KNOW IT'S NOT A GUY.
YOU HEAR THAT BEAUTIFUL? SHE THINKS YOU'RE A GUY.

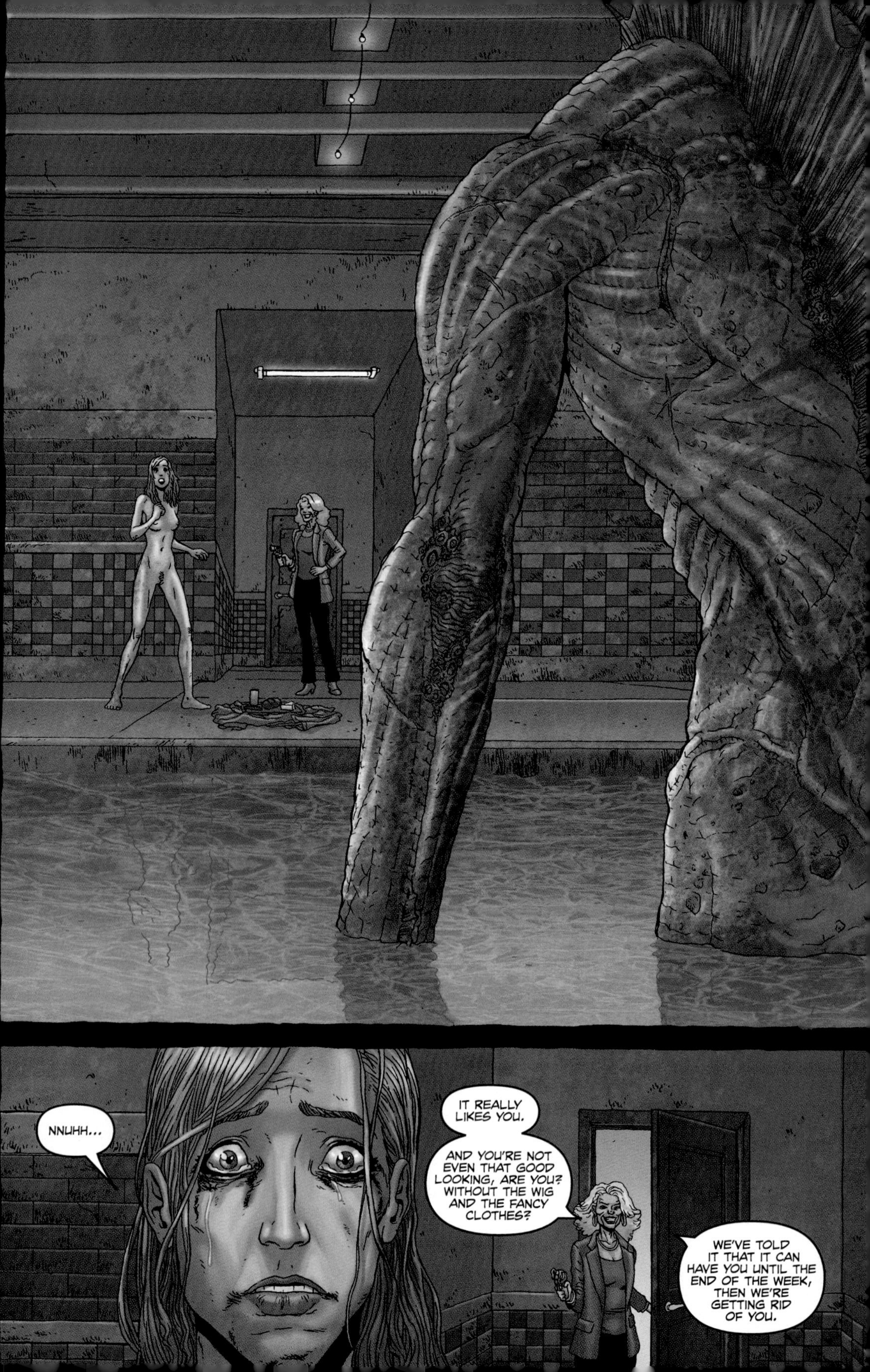
NNUHH...
IT REALLY LIKES YOU.
AND YOU'RE NOT EVEN THAT GOOD LOOKING, ARE YOU? WITHOUT THE WIG AND THE FANCY CLOTHES?
WE'VE TOLD IT THAT IT CAN HAVE YOU UNTIL THE END OF THE WEEK, THEN WE'RE GETTING RID OF YOU.

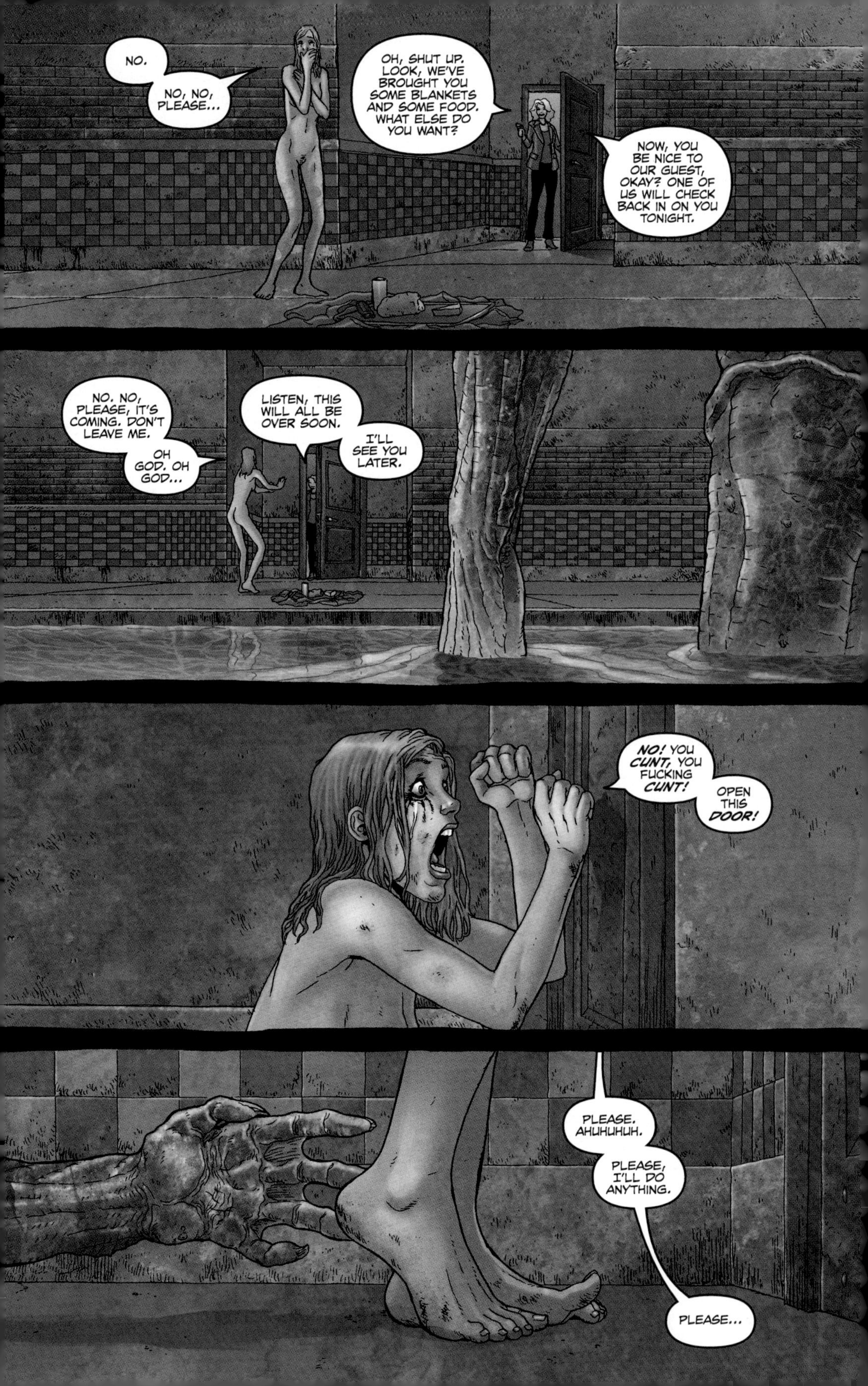
NO.
NO, NO, PLEASE...
OH, SHUT UP. LOOK, WE'VE BROUGHT YOU SOME BLANKETS AND SOME FOOD. WHAT ELSE DO YOU WANT?
NOW, YOU BE NICE TO OUR GUEST, OKAY? ONE OF US WILL CHECK BACK IN ON YOU TONIGHT.
NO. NO, PLEASE, IT'S COMING. DON'T LEAVE ME.
OH GOD. OH GOD...
LISTEN, THIS WILL ALL BE OVER SOON.
I'LL SEE YOU LATER.
NO! YOU CUNT, YOU FUCKING CUNT!
OPEN THIS DOOR!
PLEASE. AHUHUHUH.
PLEASE, I'LL DO ANYTHING.
PLEASE...

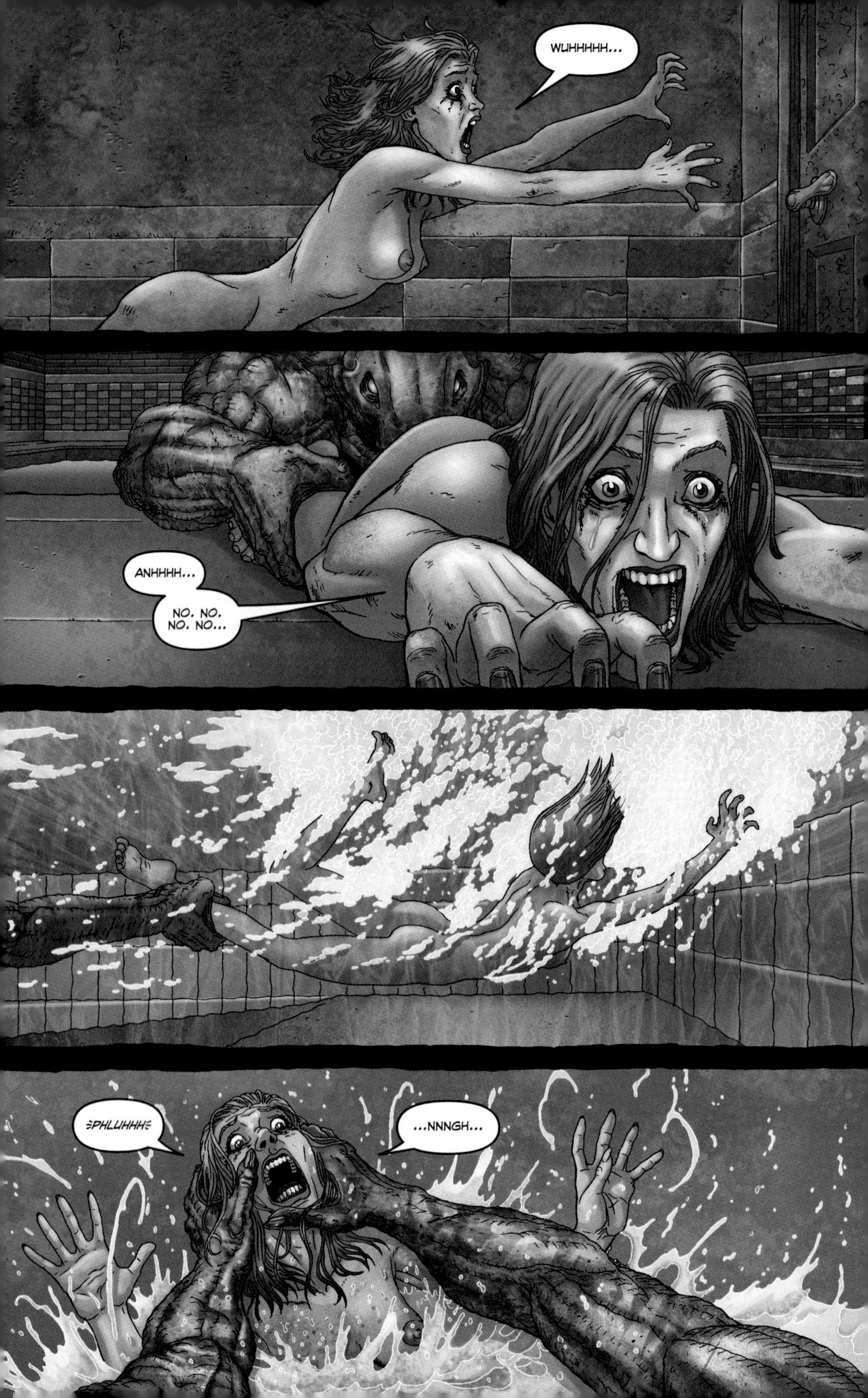
WUHHHHH...
ANHHHH...
NO. NO. NO. NO...
≈PHLUHHH≈
...NNNGH...

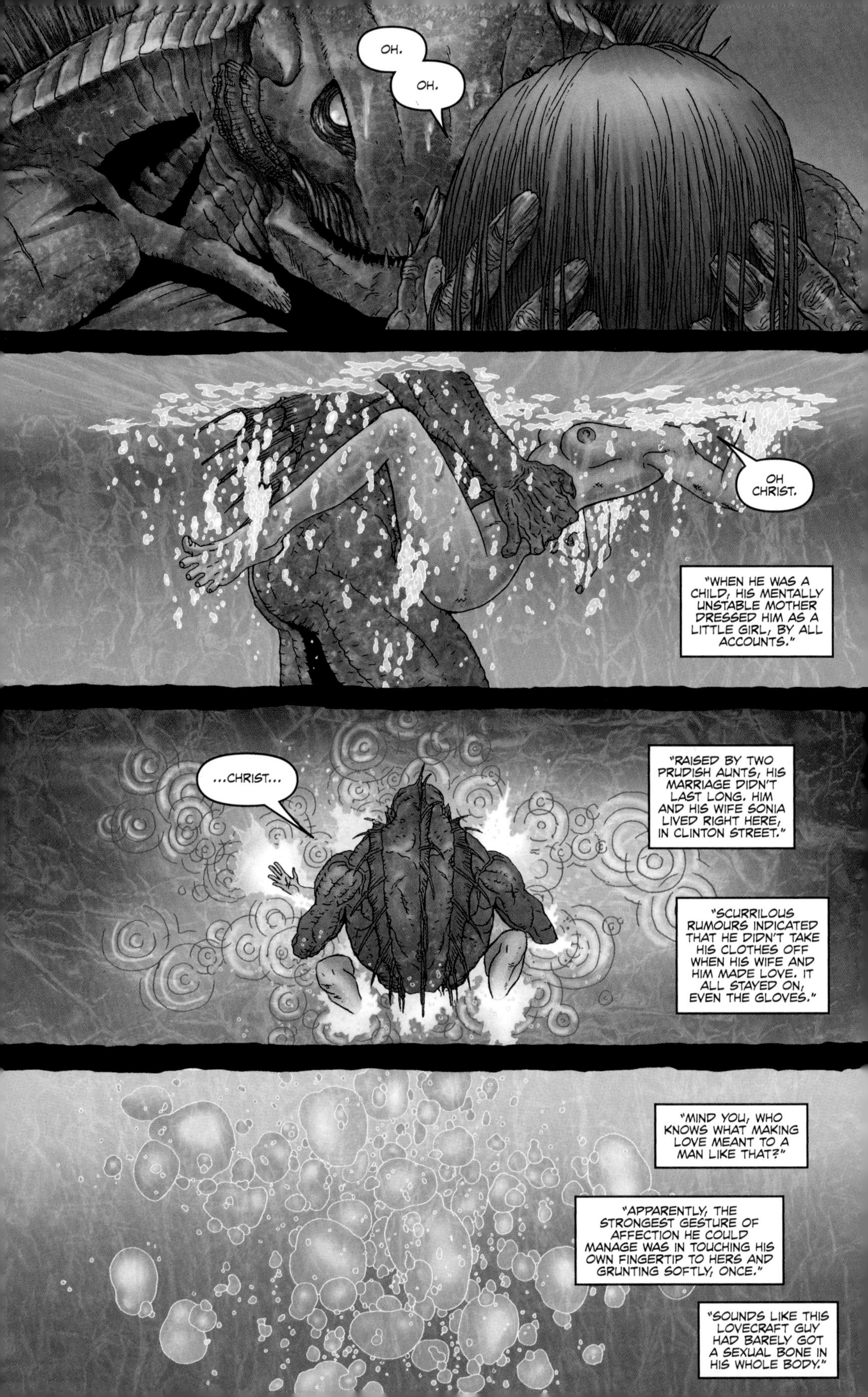

OH.
OH.
OH CHRIST.
"WHEN HE WAS A CHILD, HIS MENTALLY UNSTABLE MOTHER DRESSED HIM AS A LITTLE GIRL, BY ALL ACCOUNTS."
...CHRIST...
"RAISED BY TWO PRUDISH AUNTS, HIS MARRIAGE DIDN'T LAST LONG. HIM AND HIS WIFE SONIA LIVED RIGHT HERE, IN CLINTON STREET."
"SCURRILOUS RUMOURS INDICATED THAT HE DIDN'T TAKE HIS CLOTHES OFF WHEN HIS WIFE AND HIM MADE LOVE. IT ALL STAYED ON, EVEN THE GLOVES."
"MIND YOU, WHO KNOWS WHAT MAKING LOVE MEANT TO A MAN LIKE THAT?"
"APPARENTLY, THE STRONGEST GESTURE OF AFFECTION HE COULD MANAGE WAS IN TOUCHING HIS OWN FINGERTIP TO HERS AND GRUNTING SOFTLY, ONCE."
"SOUNDS LIKE THIS LOVECRAFT GUY HAD BARELY GOT A SEXUAL BONE IN HIS WHOLE BODY."

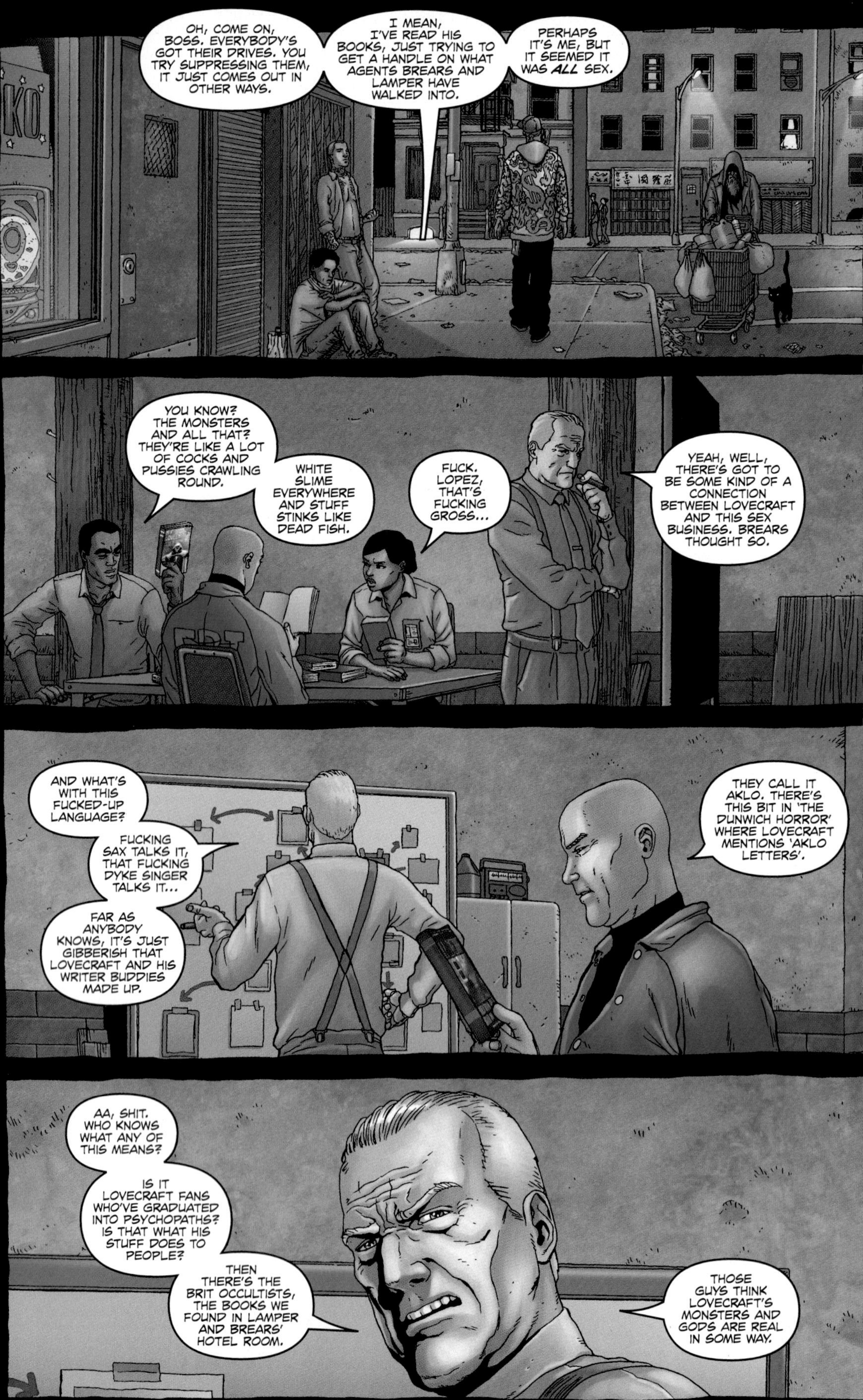
OH, COME ON, BOSS. EVERYBODY'S GOT THEIR DRIVES. YOU TRY SUPPRESSING THEM, IT JUST COMES OUT IN OTHER WAYS.
I MEAN, I'VE READ HIS BOOKS, JUST TRYING TO GET A HANDLE ON WHAT AGENTS BREARS AND LAMPER HAVE WALKED INTO.
PERHAPS IT'S ME, BUT IT SEEMED IT WAS *ALL* SEX.
YOU KNOW? THE MONSTERS AND ALL THAT? THEY'RE LIKE A LOT OF COCKS AND PUSSIES CRAWLING ROUND.
WHITE SLIME EVERYWHERE AND STUFF STINKS LIKE DEAD FISH.
FUCK. LOPEZ, THAT'S FUCKING GROSS...
YEAH, WELL, THERE'S GOT TO BE SOME KIND OF A CONNECTION BETWEEN LOVECRAFT AND THIS SEX BUSINESS. BREARS THOUGHT SO.
AND WHAT'S WITH THIS FUCKED-UP LANGUAGE?
FUCKING SAX TALKS IT, THAT FUCKING DYKE SINGER TALKS IT...
FAR AS ANYBODY KNOWS, IT'S JUST GIBBERISH THAT LOVECRAFT AND HIS WRITER BUDDIES MADE UP.
THEY CALL IT AKLO. THERE'S THIS BIT IN 'THE DUNWICH HORROR' WHERE LOVECRAFT MENTIONS 'AKLO LETTERS'.
AA, SHIT. WHO KNOWS WHAT ANY OF THIS MEANS?
IS IT LOVECRAFT FANS WHO'VE GRADUATED INTO PSYCHOPATHS? IS THAT WHAT HIS STUFF DOES TO PEOPLE?
THEN THERE'S THE BRIT OCCULTISTS, THE BOOKS WE FOUND IN LAMPER AND BREARS' HOTEL ROOM.
THOSE GUYS THINK LOVECRAFT'S MONSTERS AND GODS ARE REAL IN SOME WAY.

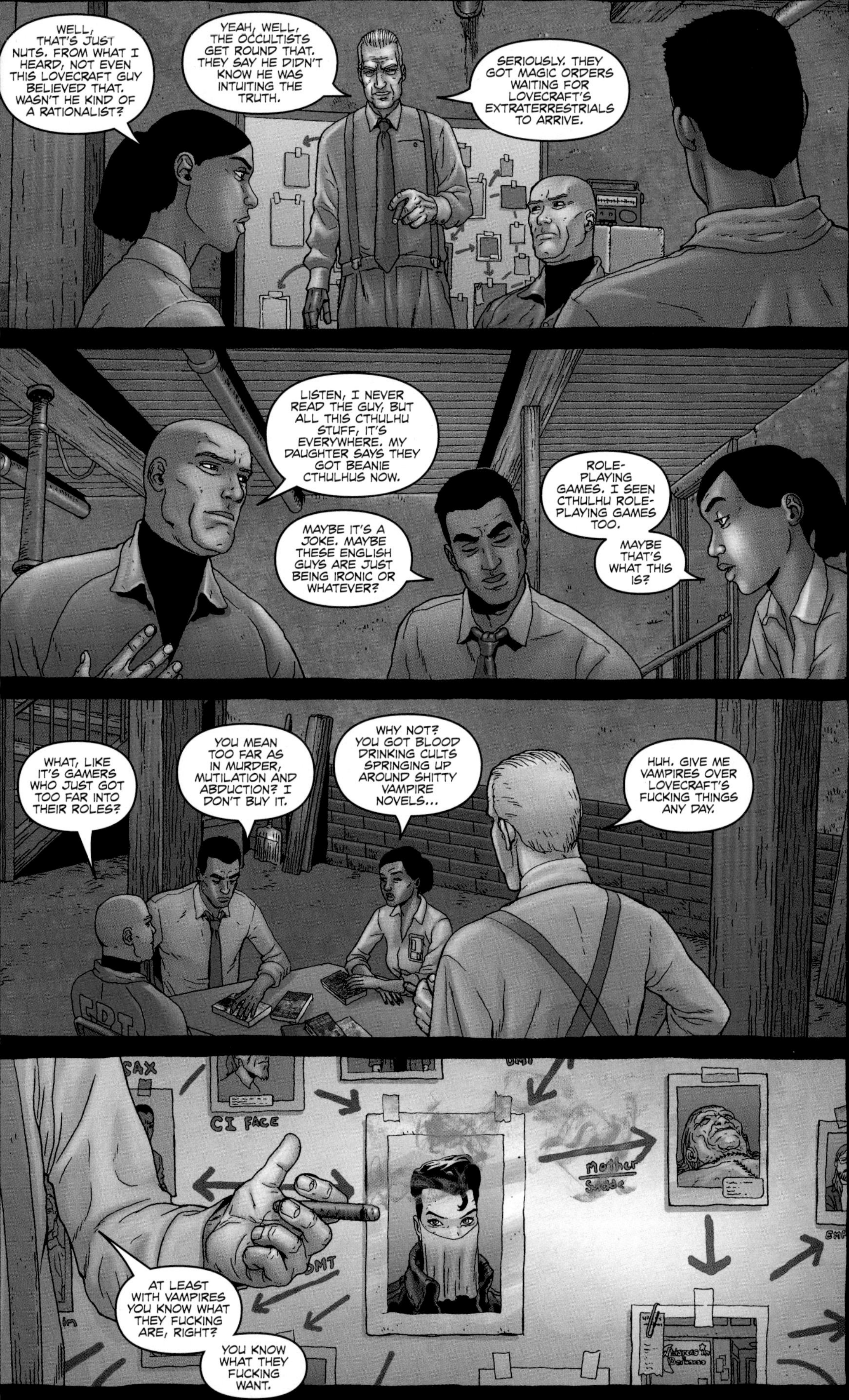
WELL, THAT'S JUST NUTS. FROM WHAT I HEARD, NOT EVEN THIS LOVECRAFT GUY BELIEVED THAT. WASN'T HE KIND OF A RATIONALIST?
YEAH, WELL, THE OCCULTISTS GET ROUND THAT. THEY SAY HE DIDN'T KNOW HE WAS INTUITING THE TRUTH.
SERIOUSLY. THEY GOT MAGIC ORDERS WAITING FOR LOVECRAFT'S EXTRATERRESTRIALS TO ARRIVE.
LISTEN, I NEVER READ THE GUY, BUT ALL THIS CTHULHU STUFF, IT'S EVERYWHERE. MY DAUGHTER SAYS THEY GOT BEANIE CTHULHUS NOW.
MAYBE IT'S A JOKE. MAYBE THESE ENGLISH GUYS ARE JUST BEING IRONIC OR WHATEVER?
ROLE-PLAYING GAMES. I SEEN CTHULHU ROLE-PLAYING GAMES TOO.
MAYBE THAT'S WHAT THIS IS?
WHAT, LIKE IT'S GAMERS WHO JUST GOT TOO FAR INTO THEIR ROLES?
YOU MEAN TOO FAR AS IN MURDER, MUTILATION AND ABDUCTION? I DON'T BUY IT.
WHY NOT? YOU GOT BLOOD DRINKING CULTS SPRINGING UP AROUND SHITTY VAMPIRE NOVELS...
HUH. GIVE ME VAMPIRES OVER LOVECRAFT'S FUCKING THINGS ANY DAY.
CI FACE
AT LEAST WITH VAMPIRES YOU KNOW WHAT THEY FUCKING ARE, RIGHT?
YOU KNOW WHAT THEY FUCKING WANT.

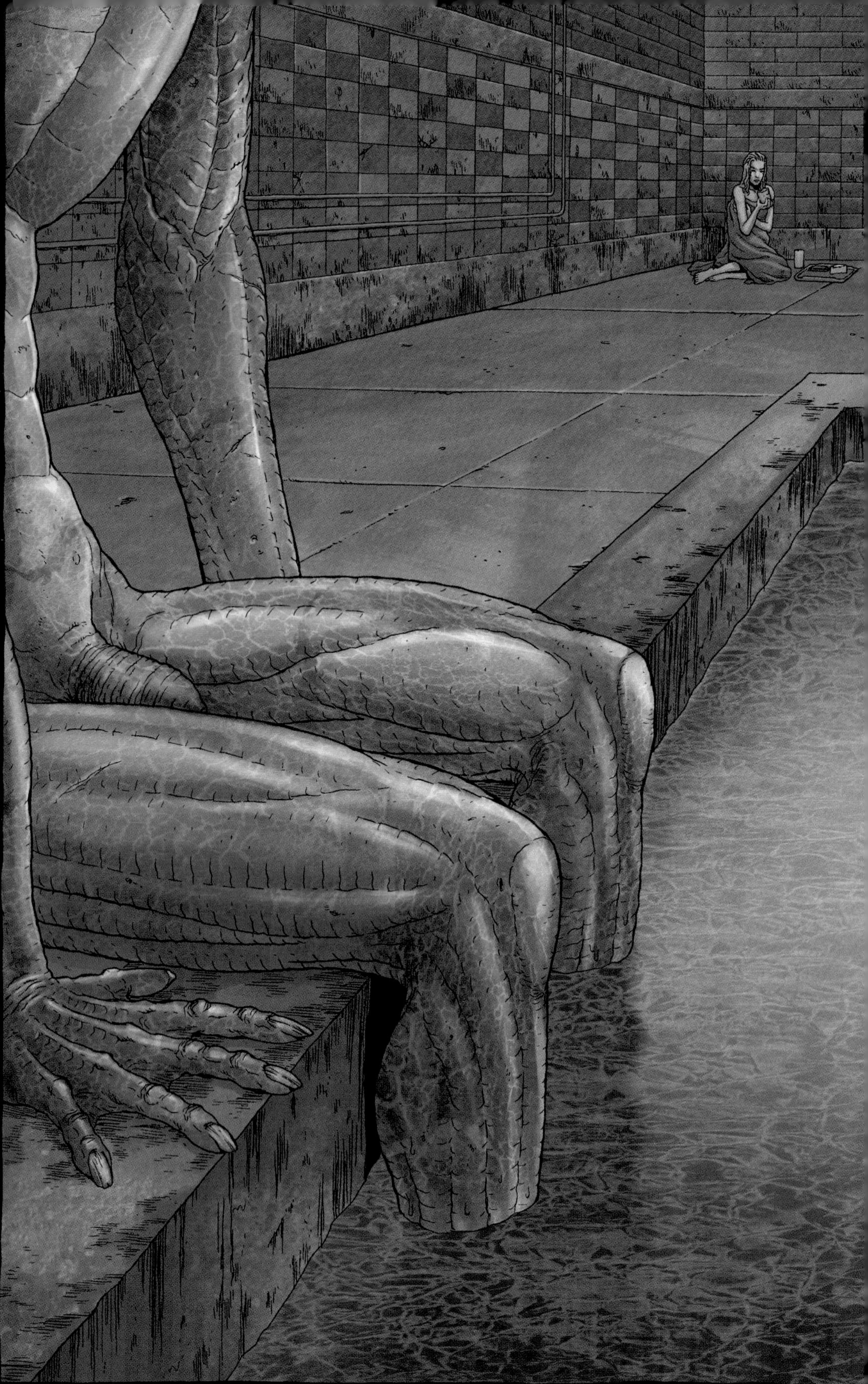

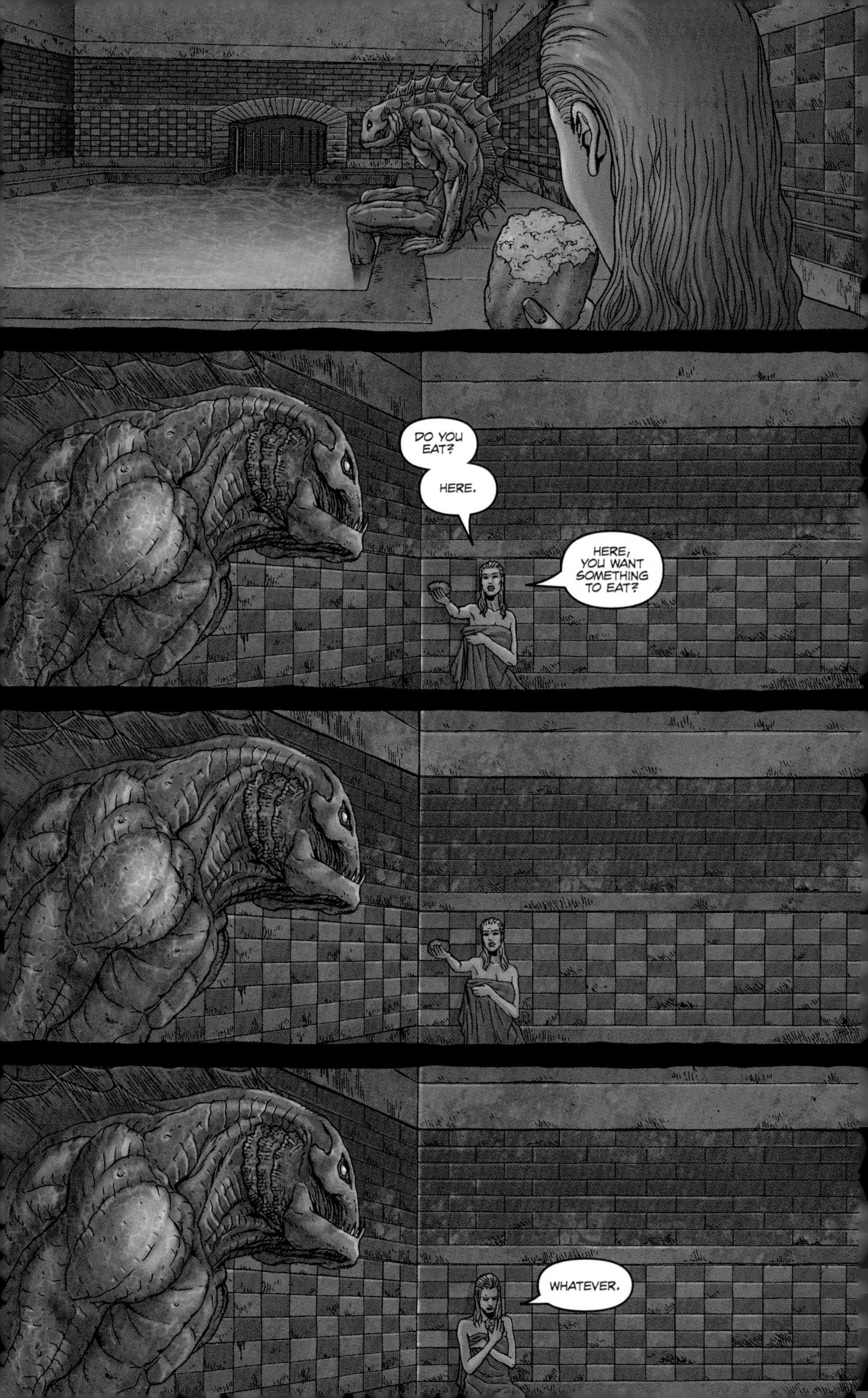
DO YOU EAT?
HERE.
HERE, YOU WANT SOMETHING TO EAT?
WHATEVER.

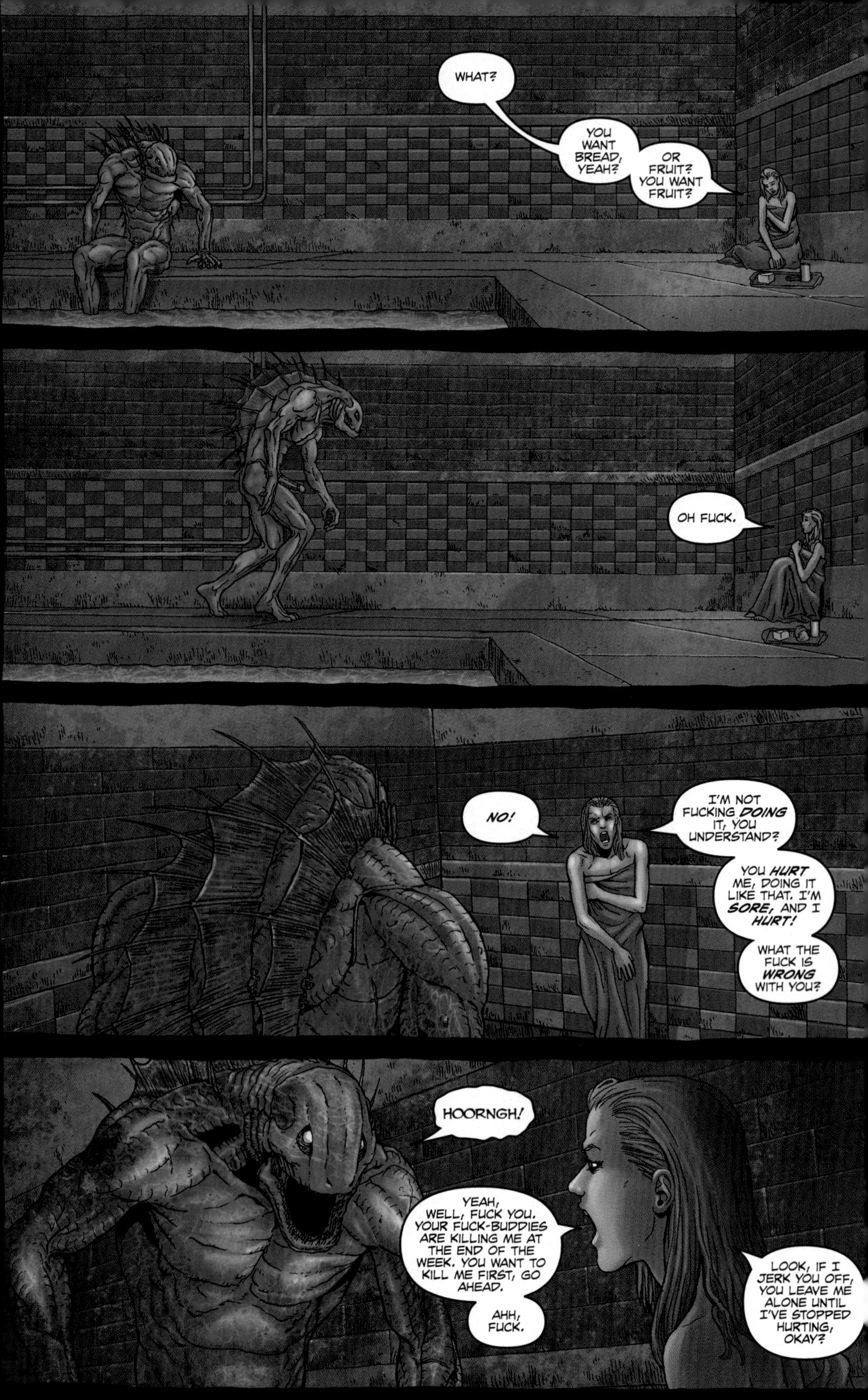
WHAT?
YOU WANT BREAD, YEAH?
OR FRUIT? YOU WANT FRUIT?
OH FUCK.
NO!
I'M NOT FUCKING DOING IT, YOU UNDERSTAND?
YOU HURT ME, DOING IT LIKE THAT. I'M SORE, AND I HURT!
WHAT THE FUCK IS WRONG WITH YOU?
HOORNGH!
YEAH, WELL, FUCK YOU. YOUR FUCK-BUDDIES ARE KILLING ME AT THE END OF THE WEEK. YOU WANT TO KILL ME FIRST, GO AHEAD.
AHH, FUCK.
LOOK, IF I JERK YOU OFF, YOU LEAVE ME ALONE UNTIL I'VE STOPPED HURTING, OKAY?

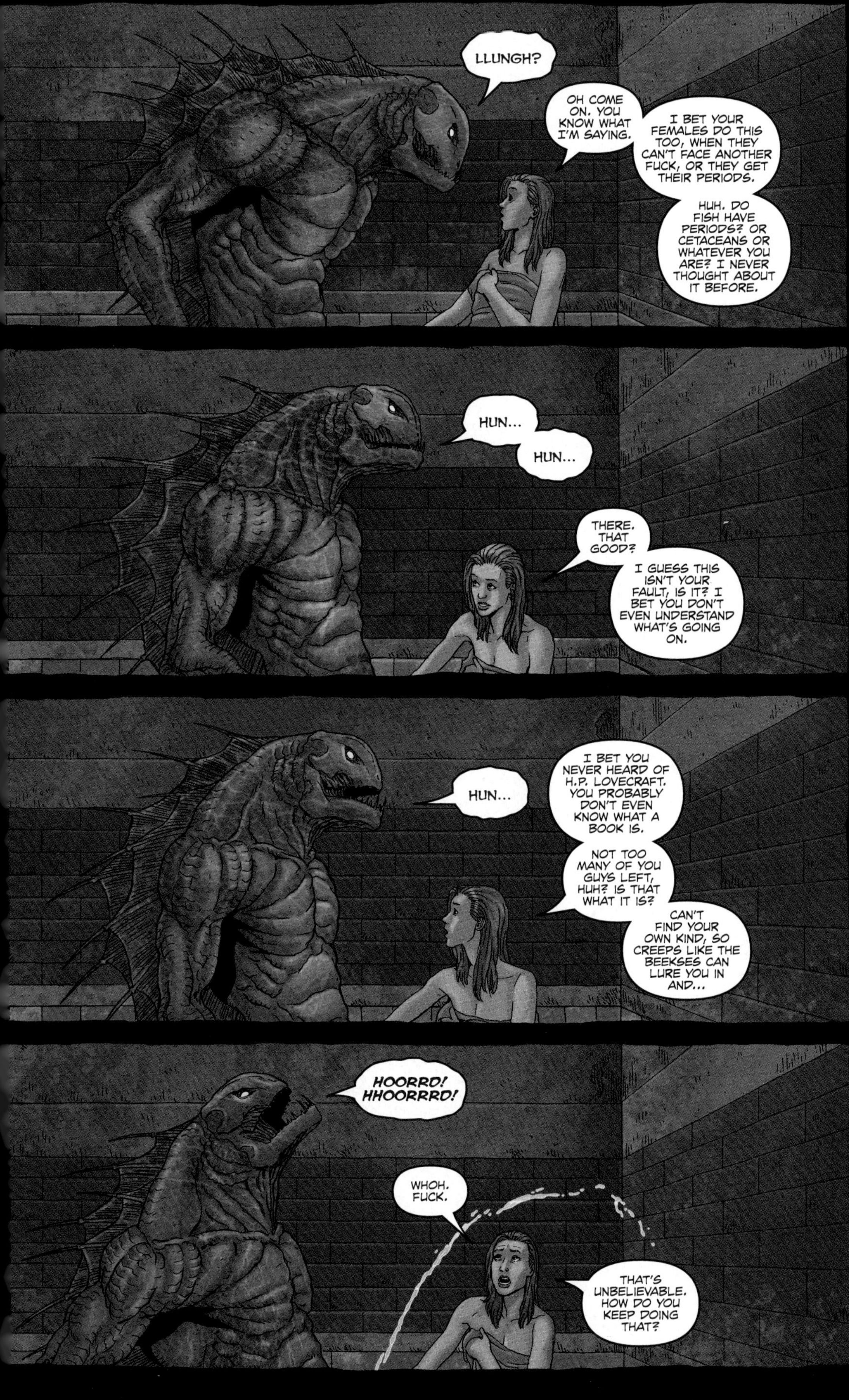
LLUNGH?
OH COME ON. YOU KNOW WHAT I'M SAYING.
I BET YOUR FEMALES DO THIS TOO, WHEN THEY CAN'T FACE ANOTHER FUCK, OR THEY GET THEIR PERIODS.
HUH. DO FISH HAVE PERIODS? OR CETACEANS OR WHATEVER YOU ARE? I NEVER THOUGHT ABOUT IT BEFORE.
HUN...
HUN...
THERE. THAT GOOD?
I GUESS THIS ISN'T YOUR FAULT, IS IT? I BET YOU DON'T EVEN UNDERSTAND WHAT'S GOING ON.
HUN...
I BET YOU NEVER HEARD OF H.P. LOVECRAFT. YOU PROBABLY DON'T EVEN KNOW WHAT A BOOK IS.
NOT TOO MANY OF YOU GUYS LEFT, HUH? IS THAT WHAT IT IS?
CAN'T FIND YOUR OWN KIND, SO CREEPS LIKE THE BEEKSES CAN LURE YOU IN AND...
HOORRD! HHOORRRD!
WHOH. FUCK.
THAT'S UNBELIEVABLE. HOW DO YOU KEEP DOING THAT?

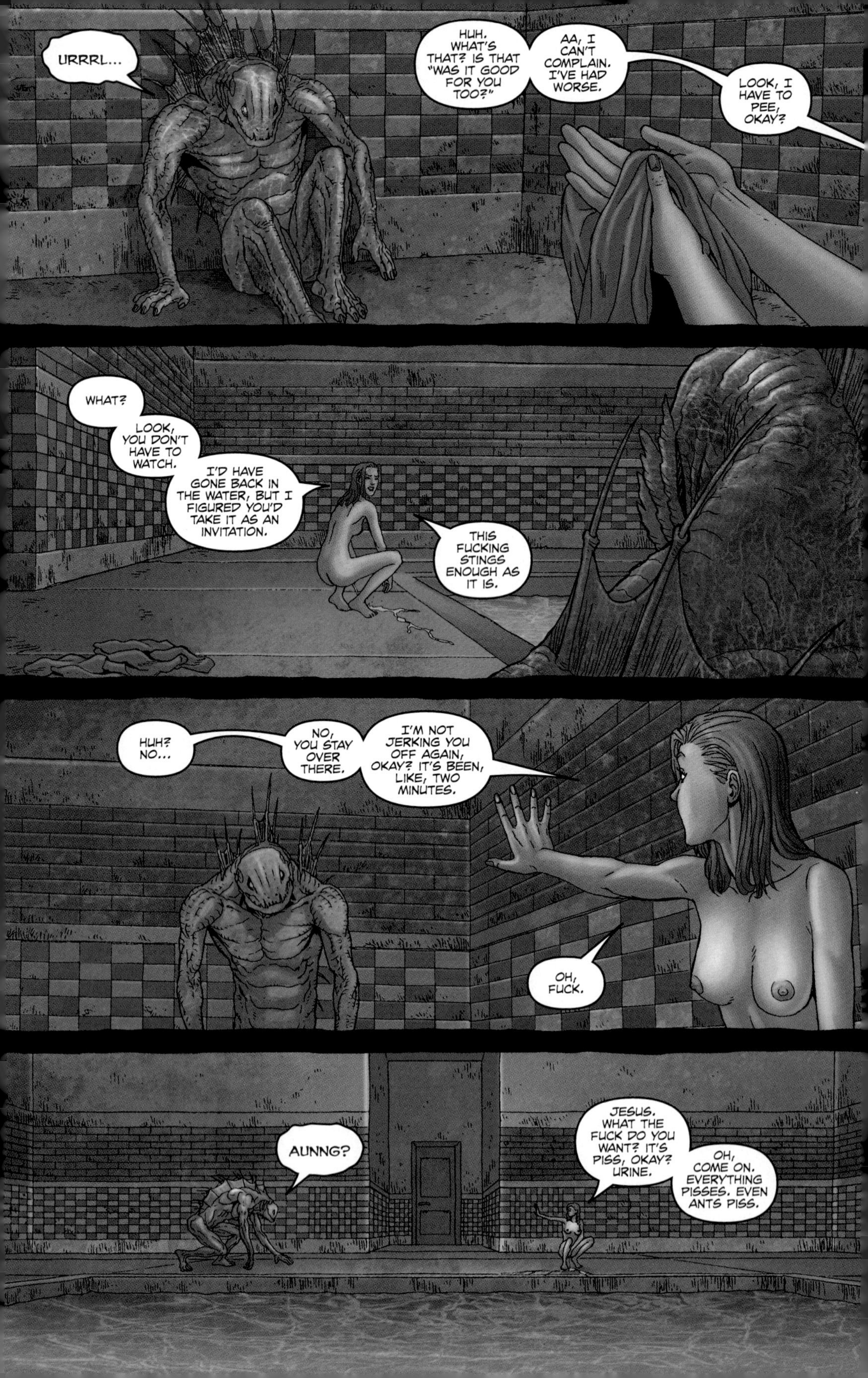
URRRL...
HUH. WHAT'S THAT? IS THAT "WAS IT GOOD FOR YOU TOO?"
AA, I CAN'T COMPLAIN. I'VE HAD WORSE.
LOOK, I HAVE TO PEE, OKAY?
WHAT?
LOOK, YOU DON'T HAVE TO WATCH.
I'D HAVE GONE BACK IN THE WATER, BUT I FIGURED YOU'D TAKE IT AS AN INVITATION.
THIS FUCKING STINGS ENOUGH AS IT IS.
HUH? NO...
NO, YOU STAY OVER THERE.
I'M NOT JERKING YOU OFF AGAIN, OKAY? IT'S BEEN, LIKE, TWO MINUTES.
OH, FUCK.
AUNNG?
JESUS. WHAT THE FUCK DO YOU WANT? IT'S PISS, OKAY? URINE.
OH, COME ON. EVERYTHING PISSES. EVEN ANTS PISS.

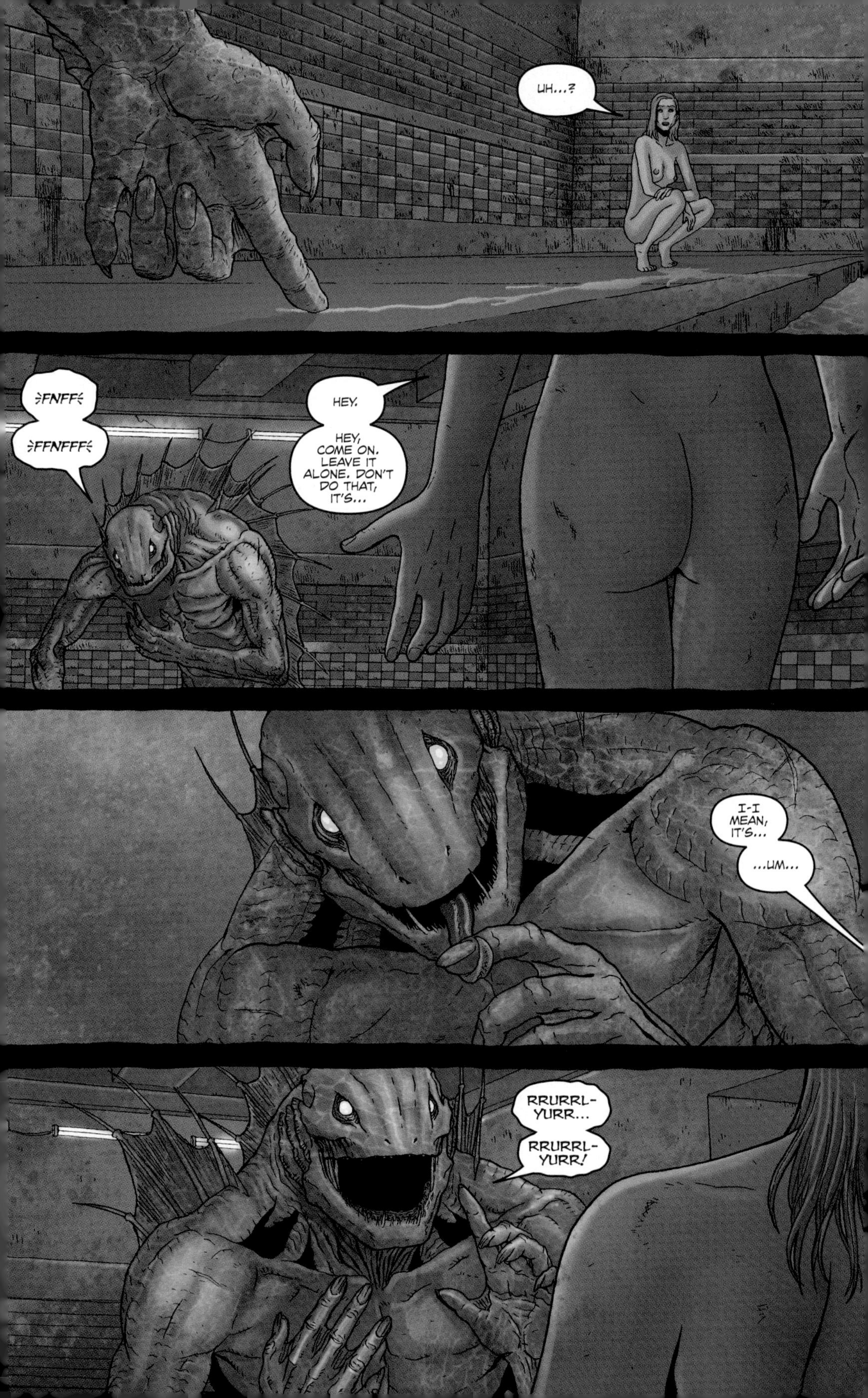
UH...?
≠FNFF≠
≠FFNFFF≠
HEY.
HEY, COME ON. LEAVE IT ALONE. DON'T DO THAT, IT'S...
I-I MEAN, IT'S...
...UM...
RRURRL-YURR...
RRURRL-YURR!

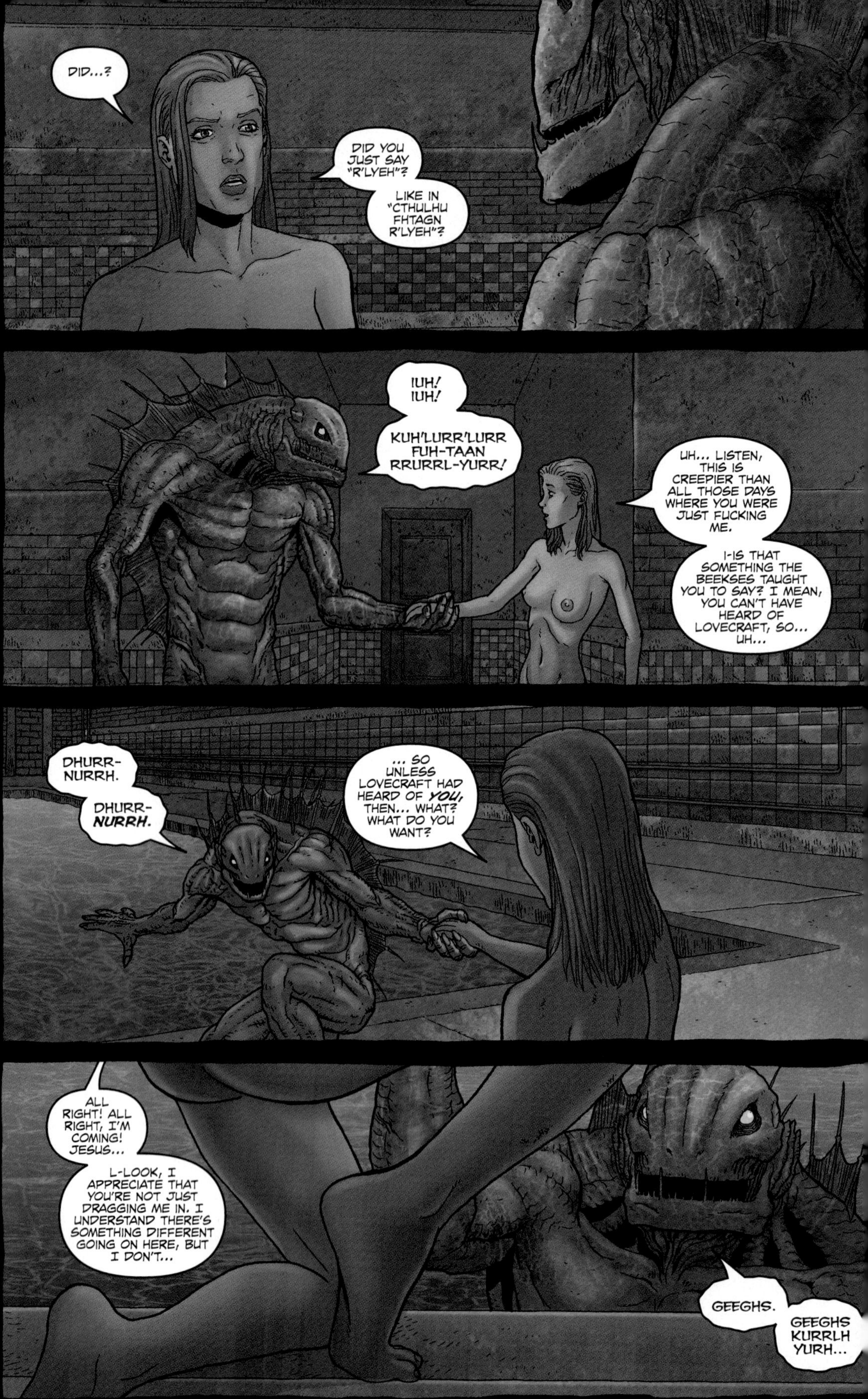
DID...?
DID YOU JUST SAY "R'LYEH"?
LIKE IN "CTHULHU FHTAGN R'LYEH"?
!UH! !UH!
KUH'LURR'LURR FUH-TAAN RRURRL-YURR!
UH... LISTEN, THIS IS CREEPIER THAN ALL THOSE DAYS WHERE YOU WERE JUST FUCKING ME.
I-IS THAT SOMETHING THE BEEKSES TAUGHT YOU TO SAY? I MEAN, YOU CAN'T HAVE HEARD OF LOVECRAFT, SO... UH...
DHURR-NURRH.
DHURR-NURRH.
... SO UNLESS LOVECRAFT HAD HEARD OF YOU, THEN... WHAT? WHAT DO YOU WANT?
ALL RIGHT! ALL RIGHT, I'M COMING! JESUS...
L-LOOK, I APPRECIATE THAT YOU'RE NOT JUST DRAGGING ME IN. I UNDERSTAND THERE'S SOMETHING DIFFERENT GOING ON HERE, BUT I DON'T...
GEEGHS.
GEEGHS KURRLH YURH...

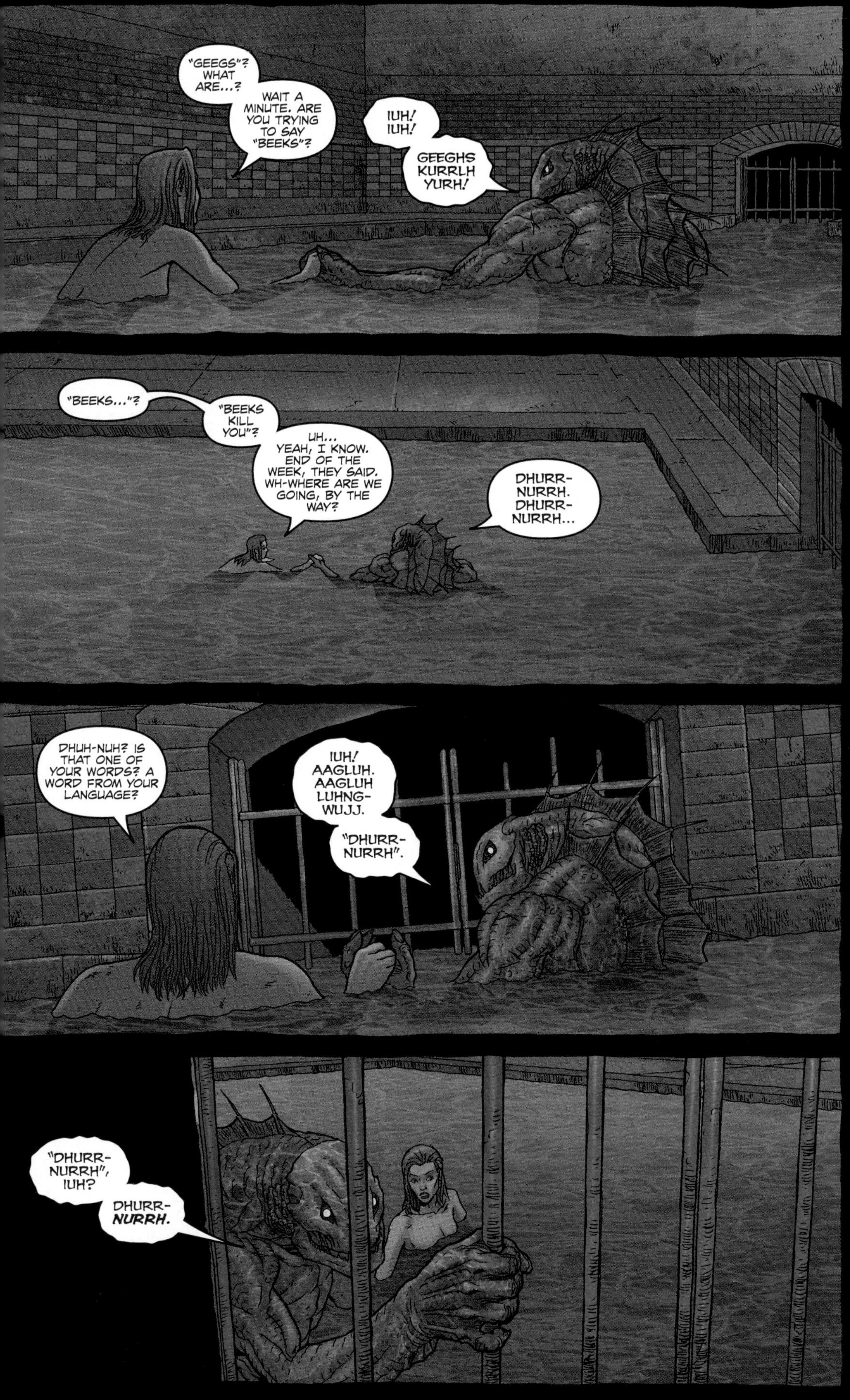
"GEEGS"? WHAT ARE...?
WAIT A MINUTE. ARE YOU TRYING TO SAY "BEEKS"?
!UH! !UH!
GEEGHS KURRLH YURH!
"BEEKS..."?
"BEEKS KILL YOU"?
UH... YEAH, I KNOW. END OF THE WEEK, THEY SAID. WH-WHERE ARE WE GOING, BY THE WAY?
DHURR-NURRH. DHURR-NURRH...
DHUH-NUH? IS THAT ONE OF YOUR WORDS? A WORD FROM YOUR LANGUAGE?
!UH! AAGLUH. AAGLUH LUHNG-WUJJ.
"DHURR-NURRH".
"DHURR-NURRH", !UH?
DHURR-*NURRH.*

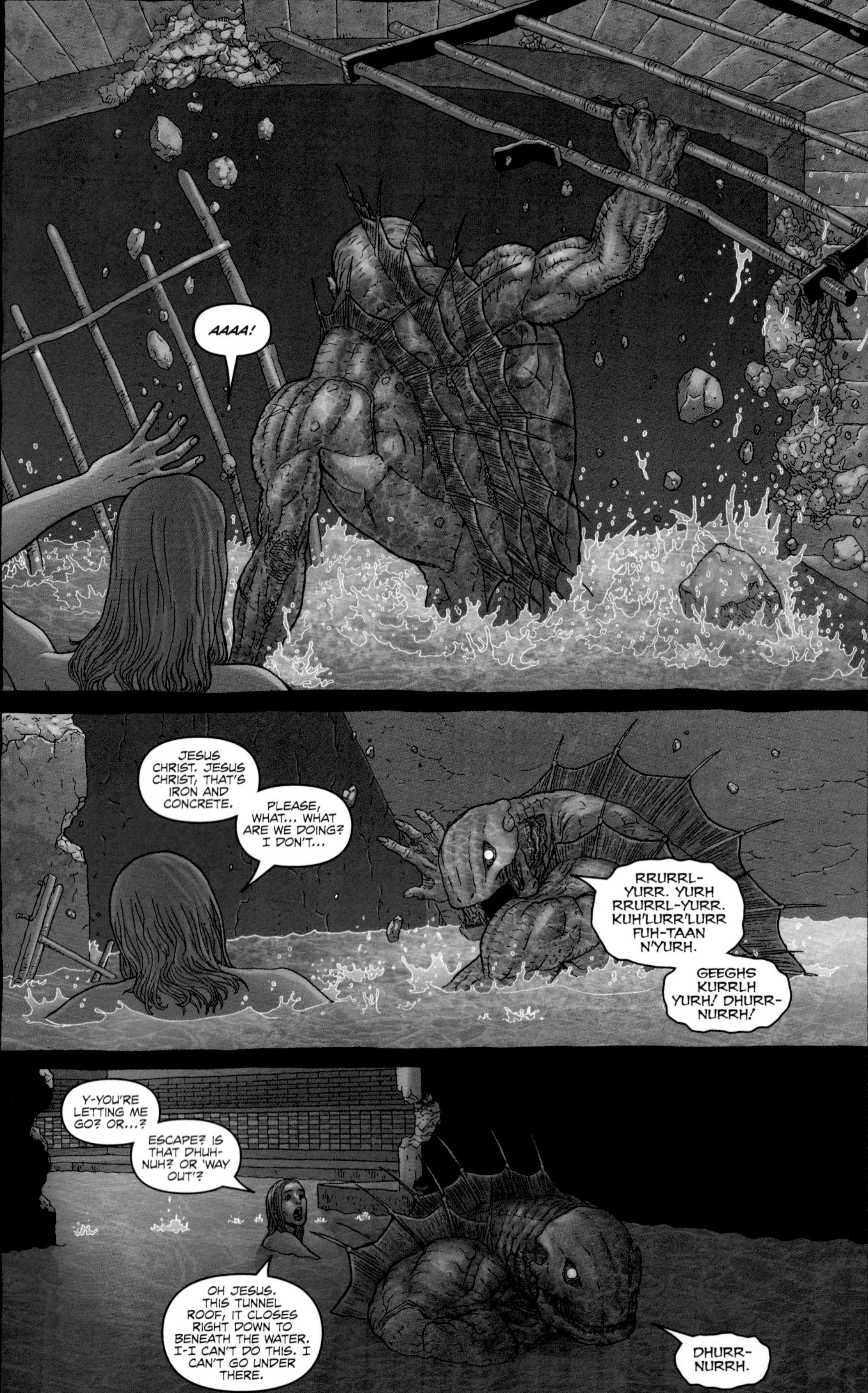
AAAA!
JESUS CHRIST. JESUS CHRIST, THAT'S IRON AND CONCRETE.
PLEASE, WHAT... WHAT ARE WE DOING? I DON'T...
RRURRL-YURR. YURH RRURRL-YURR. KUH'LURR'LURR FUH-TAAN N'YURH.
GEEGHS KURRLH YURH! DHURR-NURRH!
Y-YOU'RE LETTING ME GO? OR...?
ESCAPE? IS THAT DHUH-NUH? OR 'WAY OUT'?
OH JESUS. THIS TUNNEL ROOF, IT CLOSES RIGHT DOWN TO BENEATH THE WATER. I-I CAN'T DO THIS. I CAN'T GO UNDER THERE.
DHURR-NURRH.

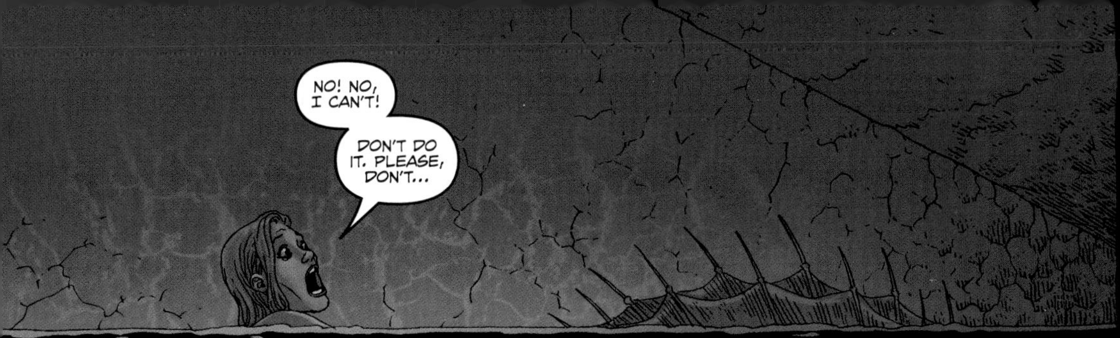
NO! NO, I CAN'T!
DON'T DO IT. PLEASE, DON'T...

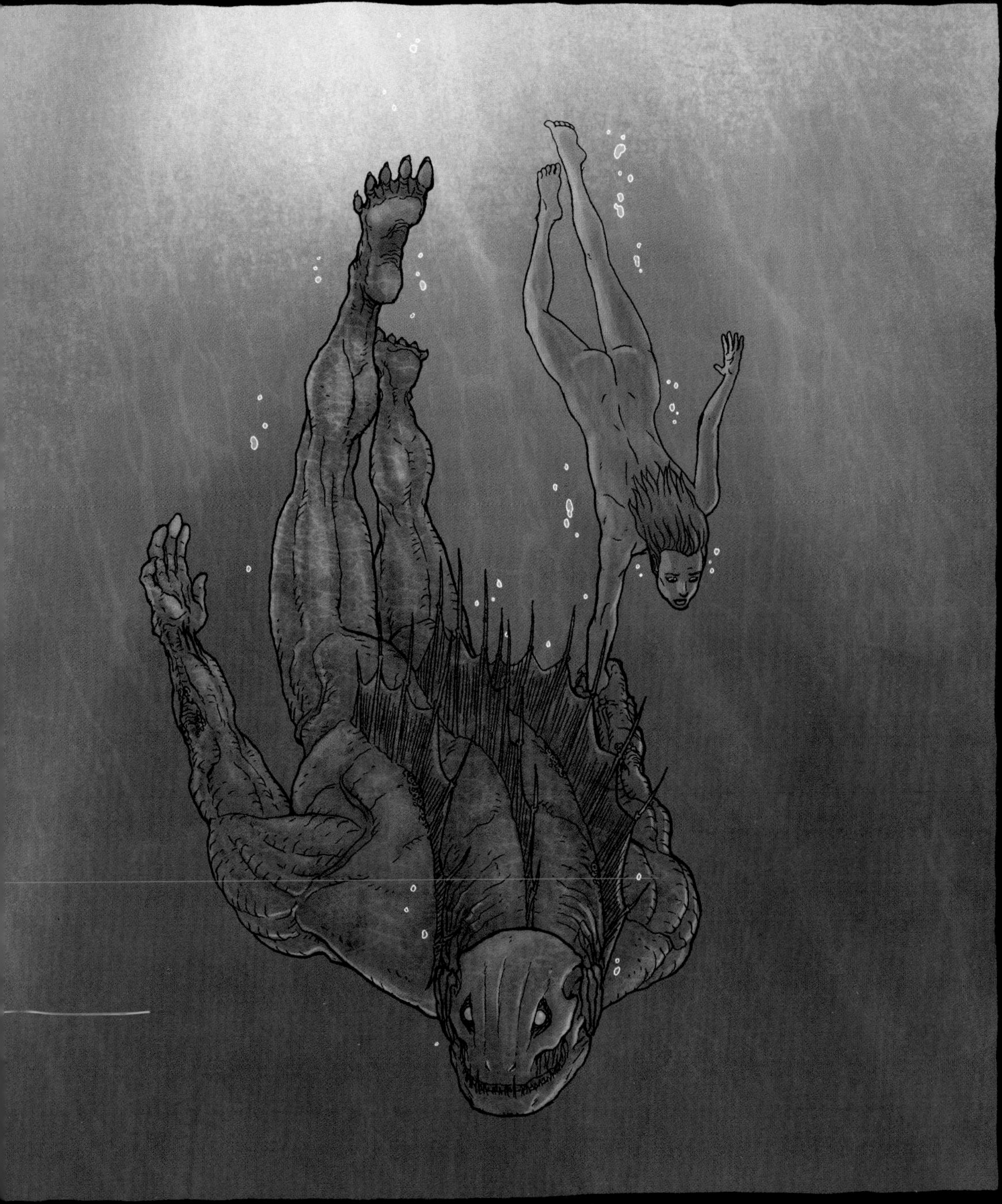

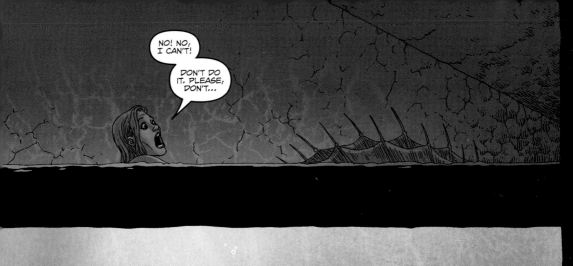

NEONOMICON
Chapter 4

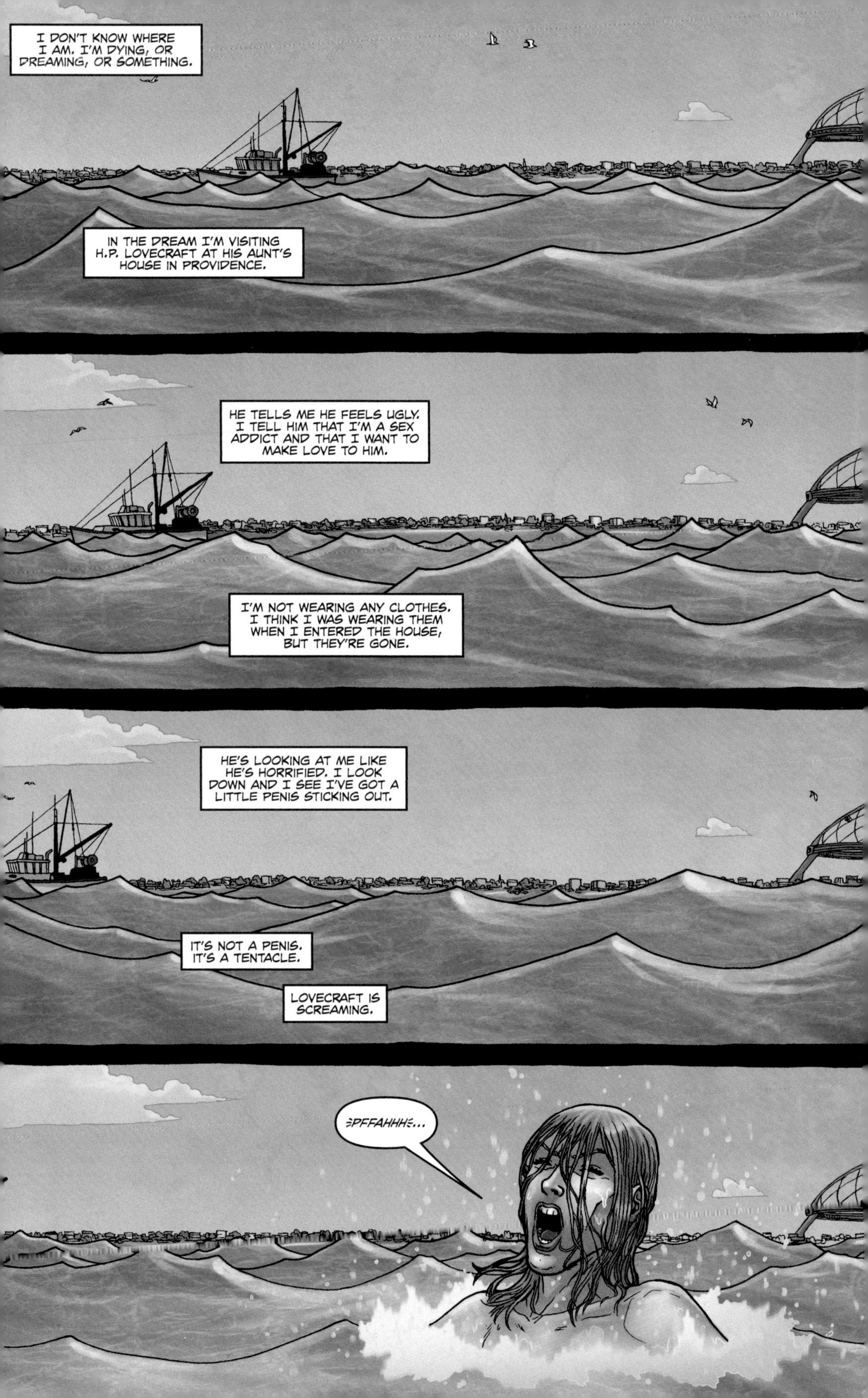
I DON'T KNOW WHERE I AM. I'M DYING, OR DREAMING, OR SOMETHING.
IN THE DREAM I'M VISITING H.P. LOVECRAFT AT HIS AUNT'S HOUSE IN PROVIDENCE.
HE TELLS ME HE FEELS UGLY. I TELL HIM THAT I'M A SEX ADDICT AND THAT I WANT TO MAKE LOVE TO HIM.
I'M NOT WEARING ANY CLOTHES. I THINK I WAS WEARING THEM WHEN I ENTERED THE HOUSE, BUT THEY'RE GONE.
HE'S LOOKING AT ME LIKE HE'S HORRIFIED. I LOOK DOWN AND I SEE I'VE GOT A LITTLE PENIS STICKING OUT.
IT'S NOT A PENIS. IT'S A TENTACLE.
LOVECRAFT IS SCREAMING.
PFFAHHH...

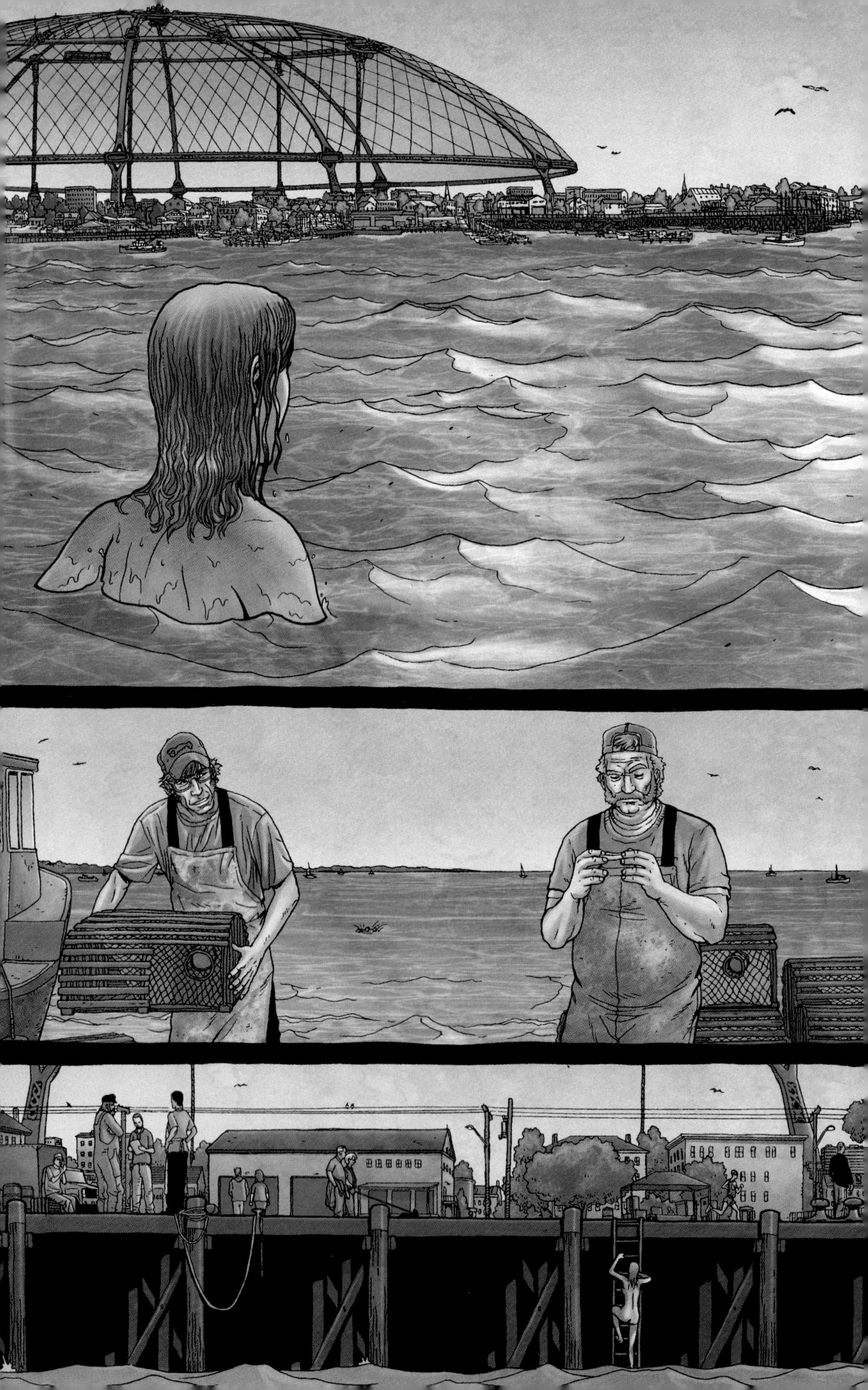

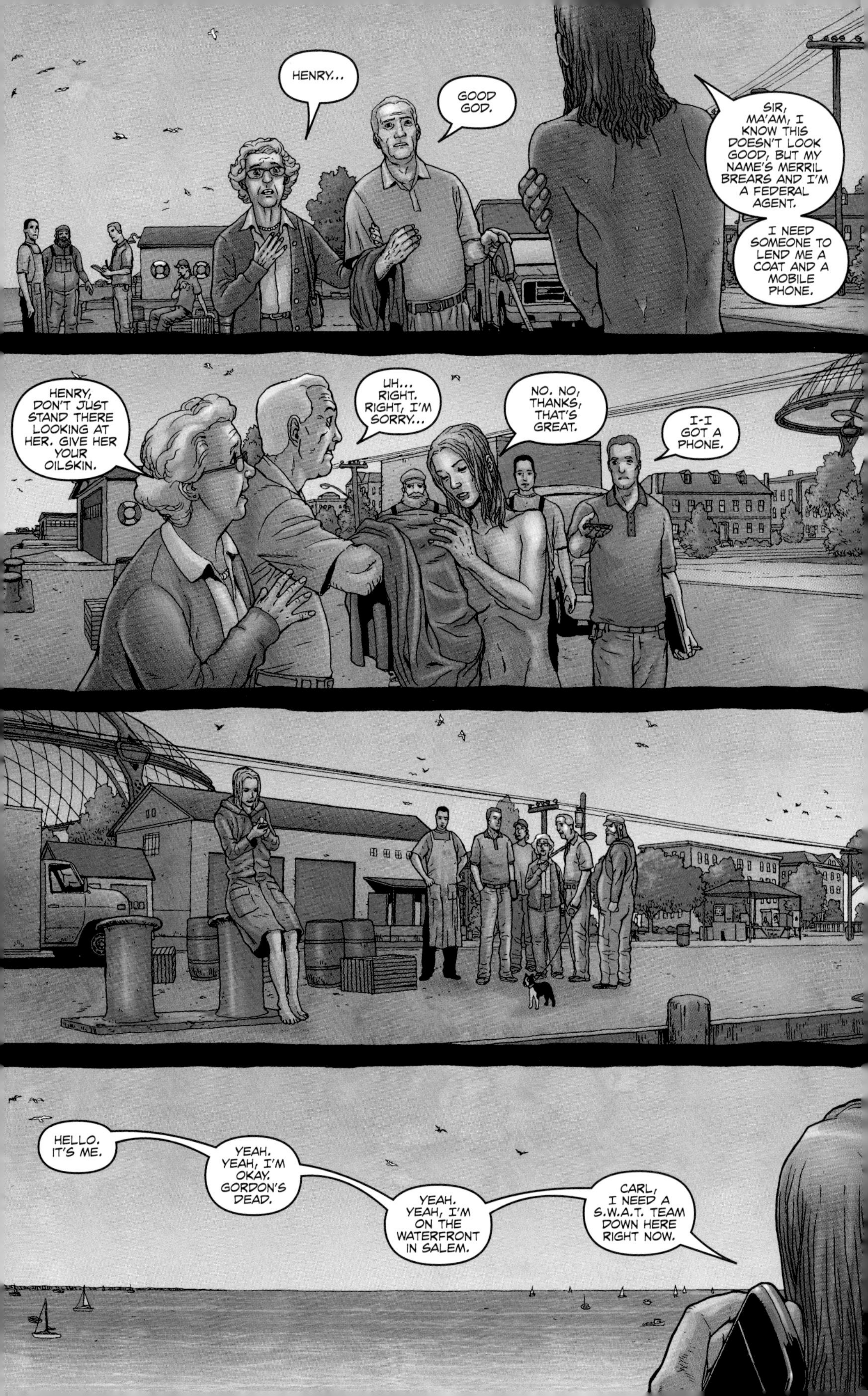
HENRY...
GOOD GOD.
SIR, MA'AM, I KNOW THIS DOESN'T LOOK GOOD, BUT MY NAME'S MERRIL BREARS AND I'M A FEDERAL AGENT.
I NEED SOMEONE TO LEND ME A COAT AND A MOBILE PHONE.
HENRY, DON'T JUST STAND THERE LOOKING AT HER. GIVE HER YOUR OILSKIN.
UH... RIGHT. RIGHT, I'M SORRY...
NO. NO, THANKS, THAT'S GREAT.
I-I GOT A PHONE.
HELLO. IT'S ME.
YEAH. YEAH, I'M OKAY. GORDON'S DEAD.
YEAH. YEAH, I'M ON THE WATERFRONT IN SALEM.
CARL, I NEED A S.W.A.T. TEAM DOWN HERE RIGHT NOW.

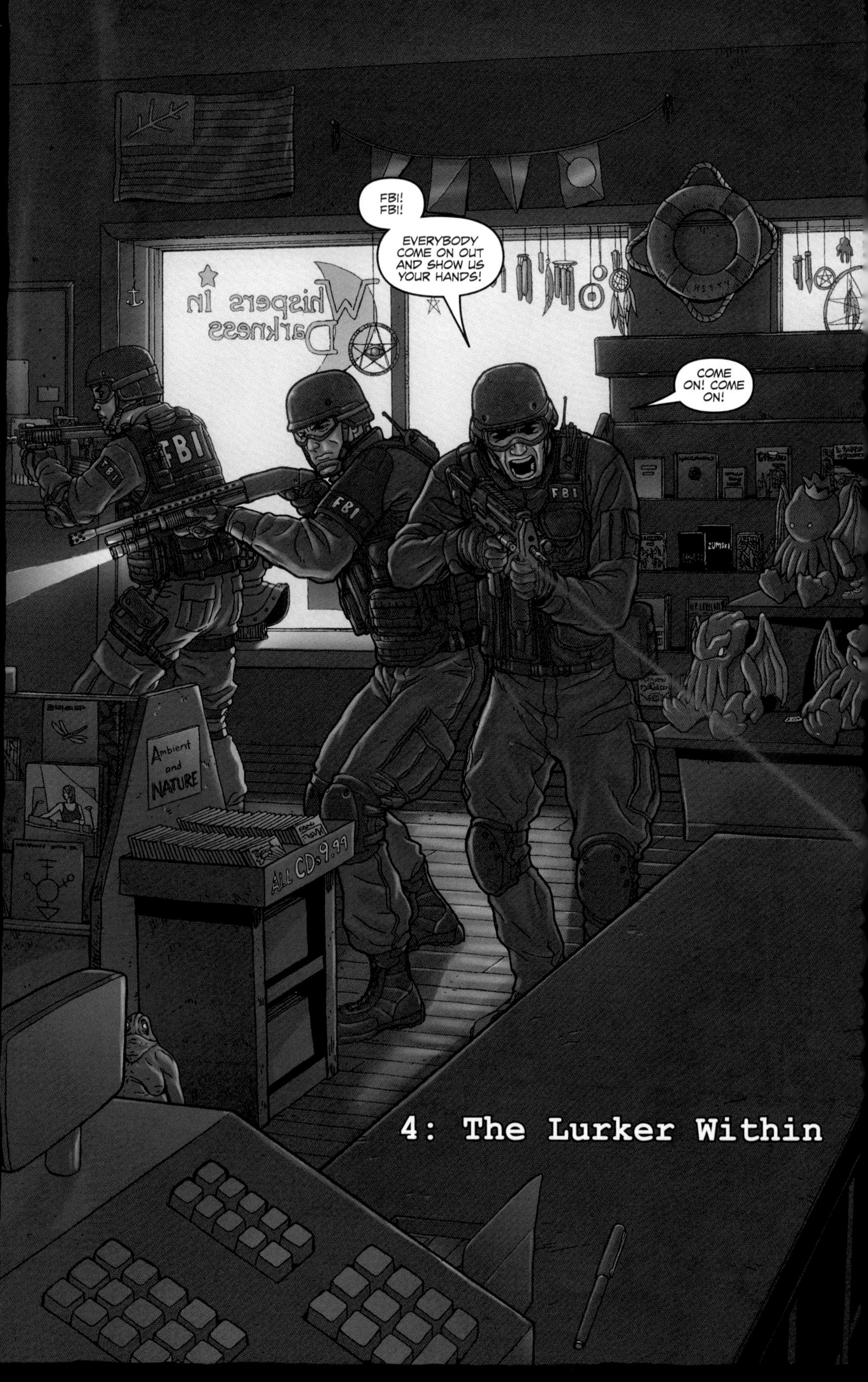
FBI! FBI!
EVERYBODY COME ON OUT AND SHOW US YOUR HANDS!
COME ON! COME ON!
Whispers in Darkness
FBI
Ambient and NATURE
ALL CDs 9.99

4: The Lurker Within

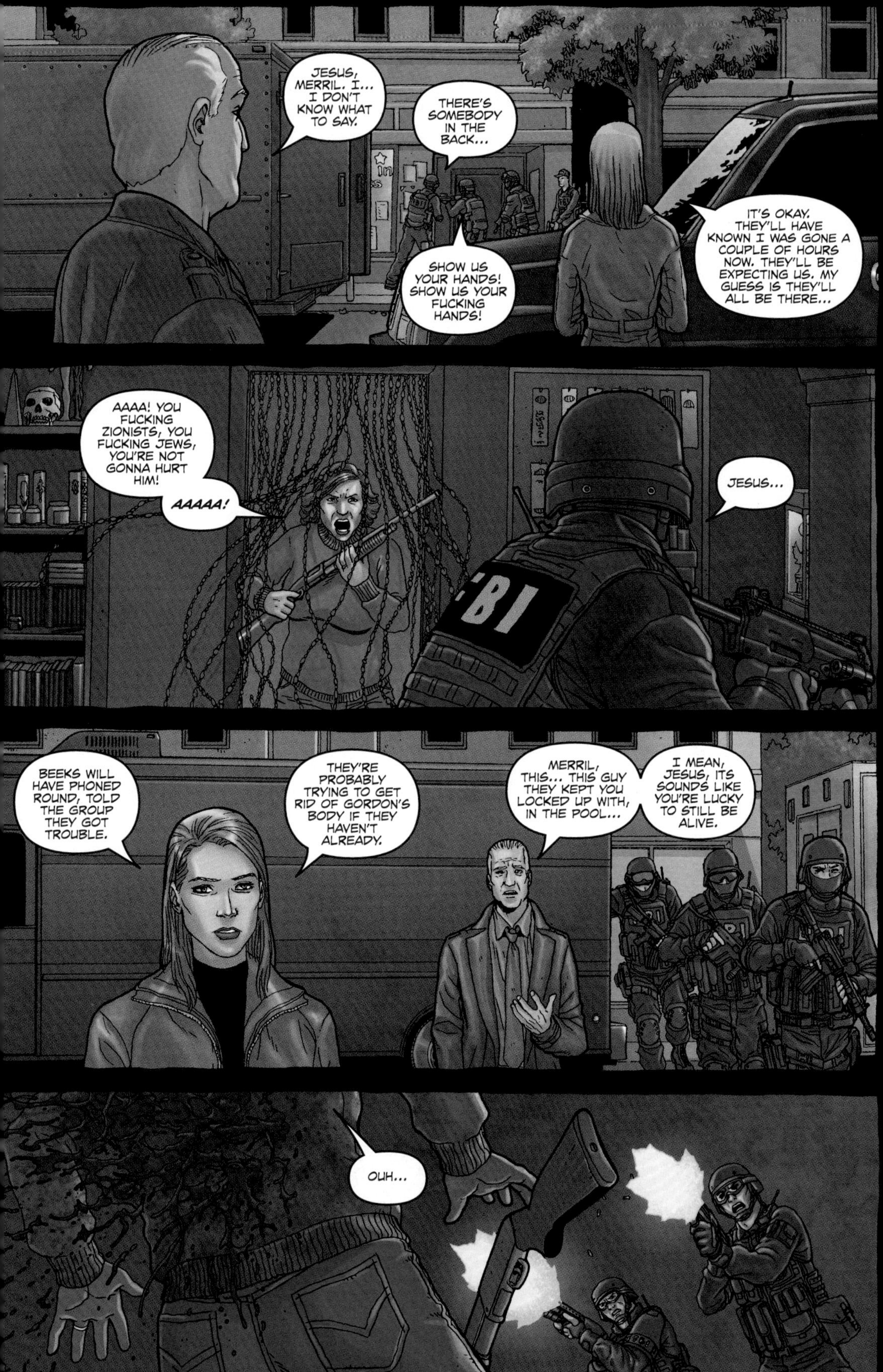
JESUS, MERRIL. I... I DON'T KNOW WHAT TO SAY.
THERE'S SOMEBODY IN THE BACK...
SHOW US YOUR HANDS! SHOW US YOUR FUCKING HANDS!
IT'S OKAY. THEY'LL HAVE KNOWN I WAS GONE A COUPLE OF HOURS NOW. THEY'LL BE EXPECTING US. MY GUESS IS THEY'LL ALL BE THERE...
AAAA! YOU FUCKING ZIONISTS, YOU FUCKING JEWS, YOU'RE NOT GONNA HURT HIM!
AAAAA!
FBI
JESUS...
BEEKS WILL HAVE PHONED ROUND, TOLD THE GROUP THEY GOT TROUBLE.
THEY'RE PROBABLY TRYING TO GET RID OF GORDON'S BODY IF THEY HAVEN'T ALREADY.
MERRIL, THIS... THIS GUY THEY KEPT YOU LOCKED UP WITH, IN THE POOL...
I MEAN, JESUS, ITS SOUNDS LIKE YOU'RE LUCKY TO STILL BE ALIVE.
OUH...

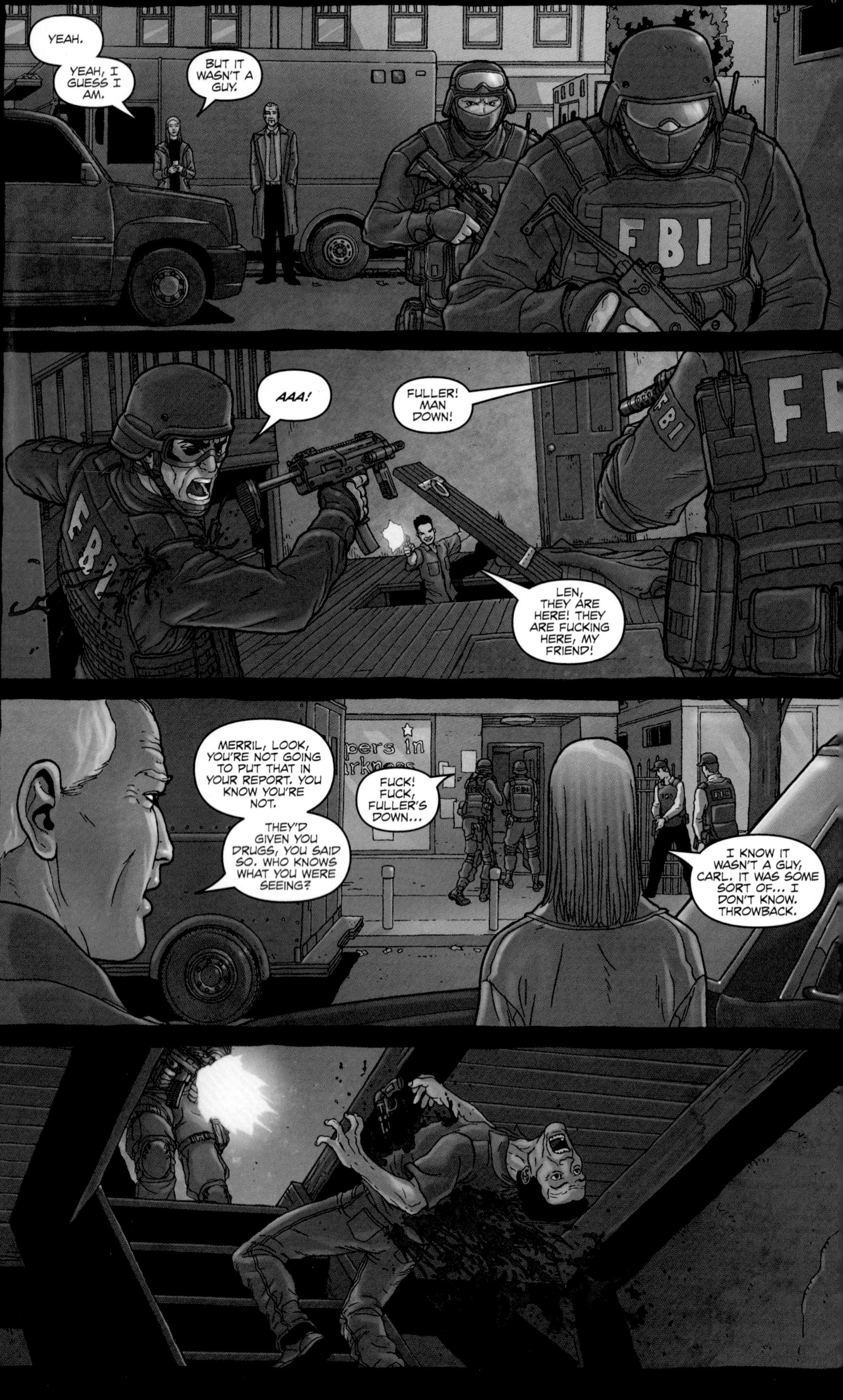
YEAH.
YEAH, I GUESS I AM.
BUT IT WASN'T A GUY.
FBI
AAA!
FULLER! MAN DOWN!
FBI
FBI
LEN, THEY ARE HERE! THEY ARE FUCKING HERE, MY FRIEND!
MERRIL, LOOK, YOU'RE NOT GOING TO PUT THAT IN YOUR REPORT. YOU KNOW YOU'RE NOT.
THEY'D GIVEN YOU DRUGS, YOU SAID SO. WHO KNOWS WHAT YOU WERE SEEING?
FUCK! FUCK, FULLER'S DOWN...
I KNOW IT WASN'T A GUY, CARL. IT WAS SOME SORT OF... I DON'T KNOW. THROWBACK.

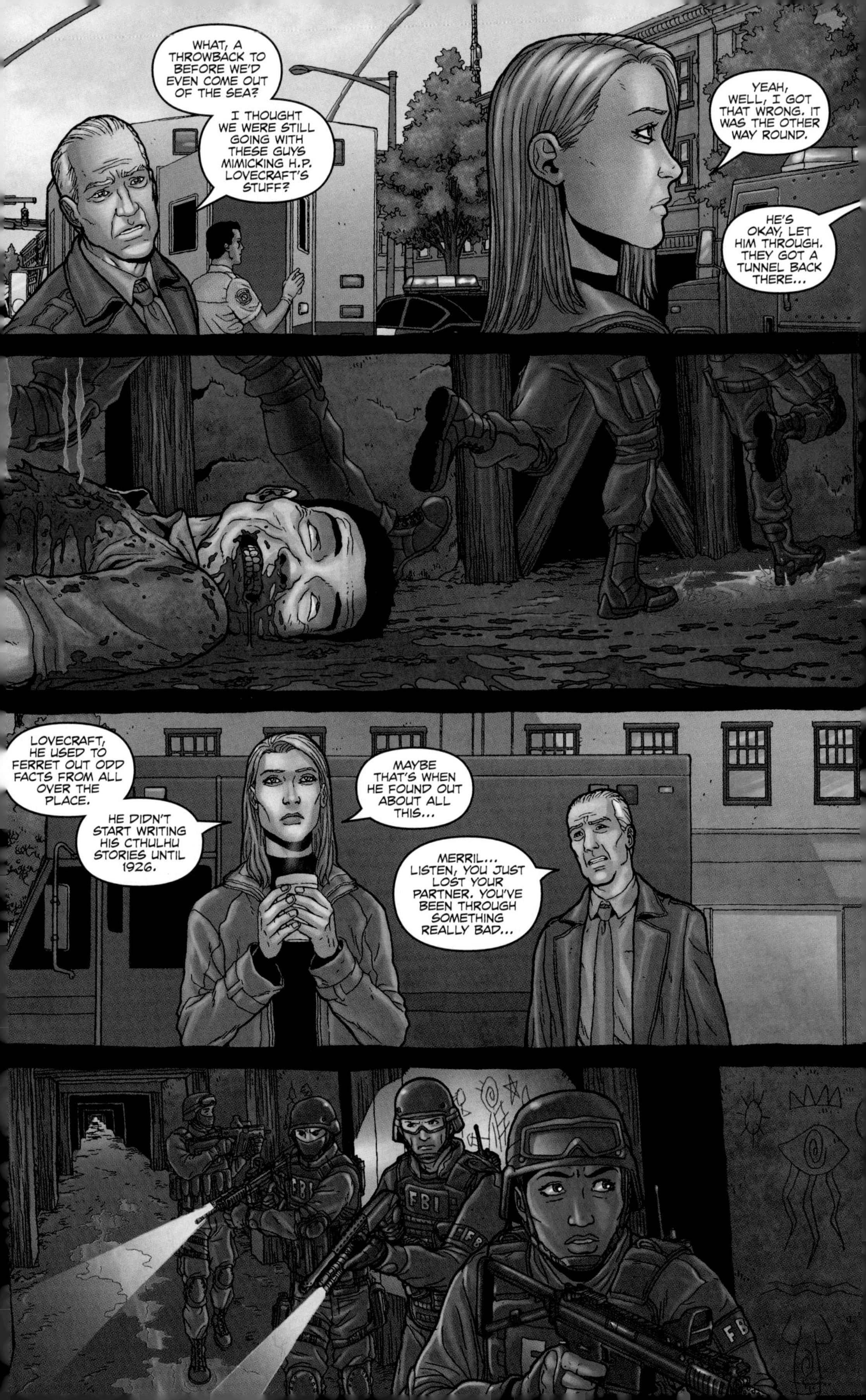
WHAT, A THROWBACK TO BEFORE WE'D EVEN COME OUT OF THE SEA?
I THOUGHT WE WERE STILL GOING WITH THESE GUYS MIMICKING H.P. LOVECRAFT'S STUFF?
YEAH, WELL, I GOT THAT WRONG. IT WAS THE OTHER WAY ROUND.
HE'S OKAY, LET HIM THROUGH. THEY GOT A TUNNEL BACK THERE...
LOVECRAFT, HE USED TO FERRET OUT ODD FACTS FROM ALL OVER THE PLACE.
HE DIDN'T START WRITING HIS CTHULHU STORIES UNTIL 1926.
MAYBE THAT'S WHEN HE FOUND OUT ABOUT ALL THIS...
MERRIL... LISTEN, YOU JUST LOST YOUR PARTNER. YOU'VE BEEN THROUGH SOMETHING REALLY BAD...
FBI
FBI
FBI

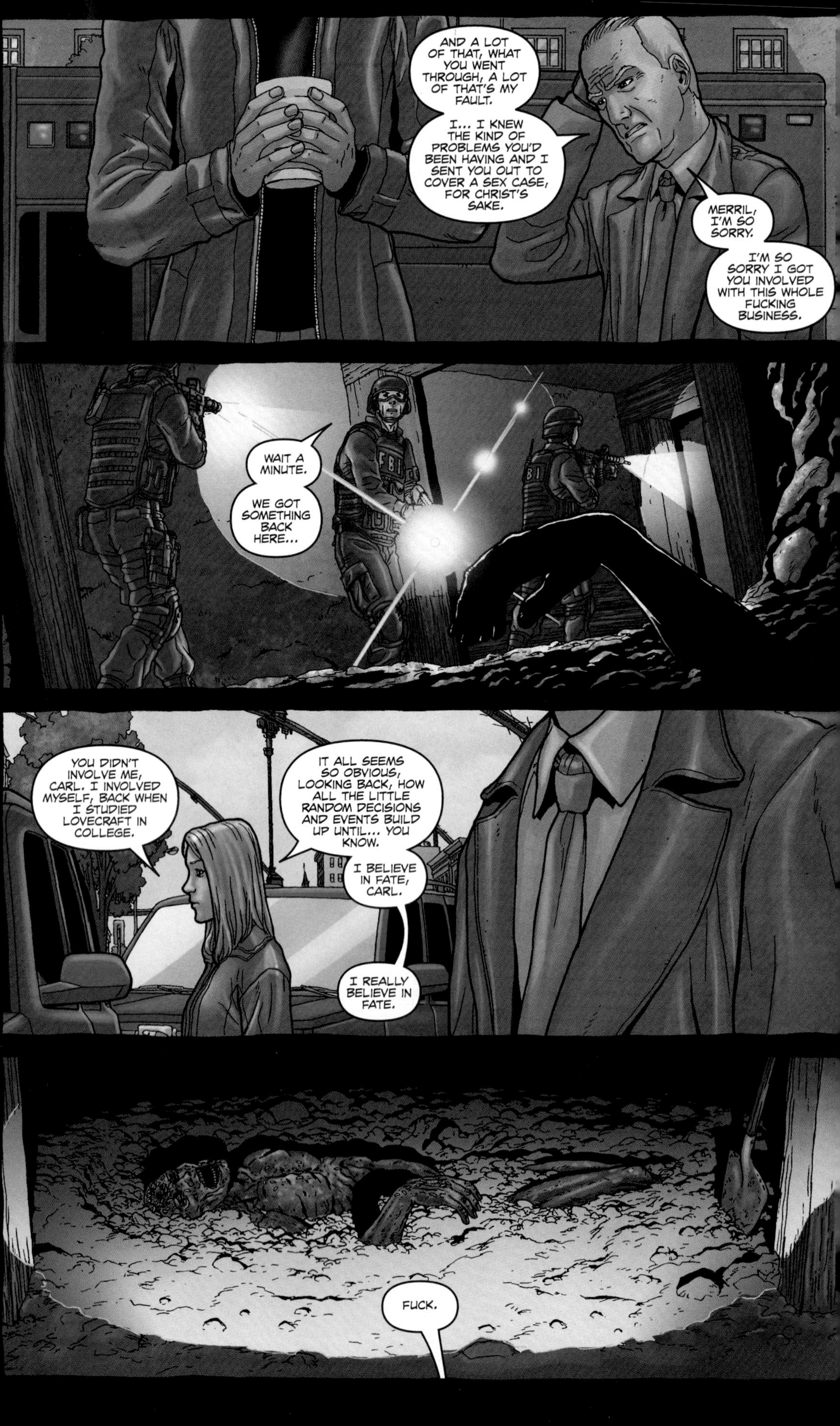
AND A LOT OF THAT, WHAT YOU WENT THROUGH, A LOT OF THAT'S MY FAULT.
I... I KNEW THE KIND OF PROBLEMS YOU'D BEEN HAVING AND I SENT YOU OUT TO COVER A SEX CASE, FOR CHRIST'S SAKE.
MERRIL, I'M SO SORRY.
I'M SO SORRY I GOT YOU INVOLVED WITH THIS WHOLE FUCKING BUSINESS.
WAIT A MINUTE.
WE GOT SOMETHING BACK HERE...
FBI
YOU DIDN'T INVOLVE ME, CARL. I INVOLVED MYSELF, BACK WHEN I STUDIED LOVECRAFT IN COLLEGE.
IT ALL SEEMS SO OBVIOUS, LOOKING BACK, HOW ALL THE LITTLE RANDOM DECISIONS AND EVENTS BUILD UP UNTIL... YOU KNOW.
I BELIEVE IN FATE, CARL.
I REALLY BELIEVE IN FATE.
FUCK.

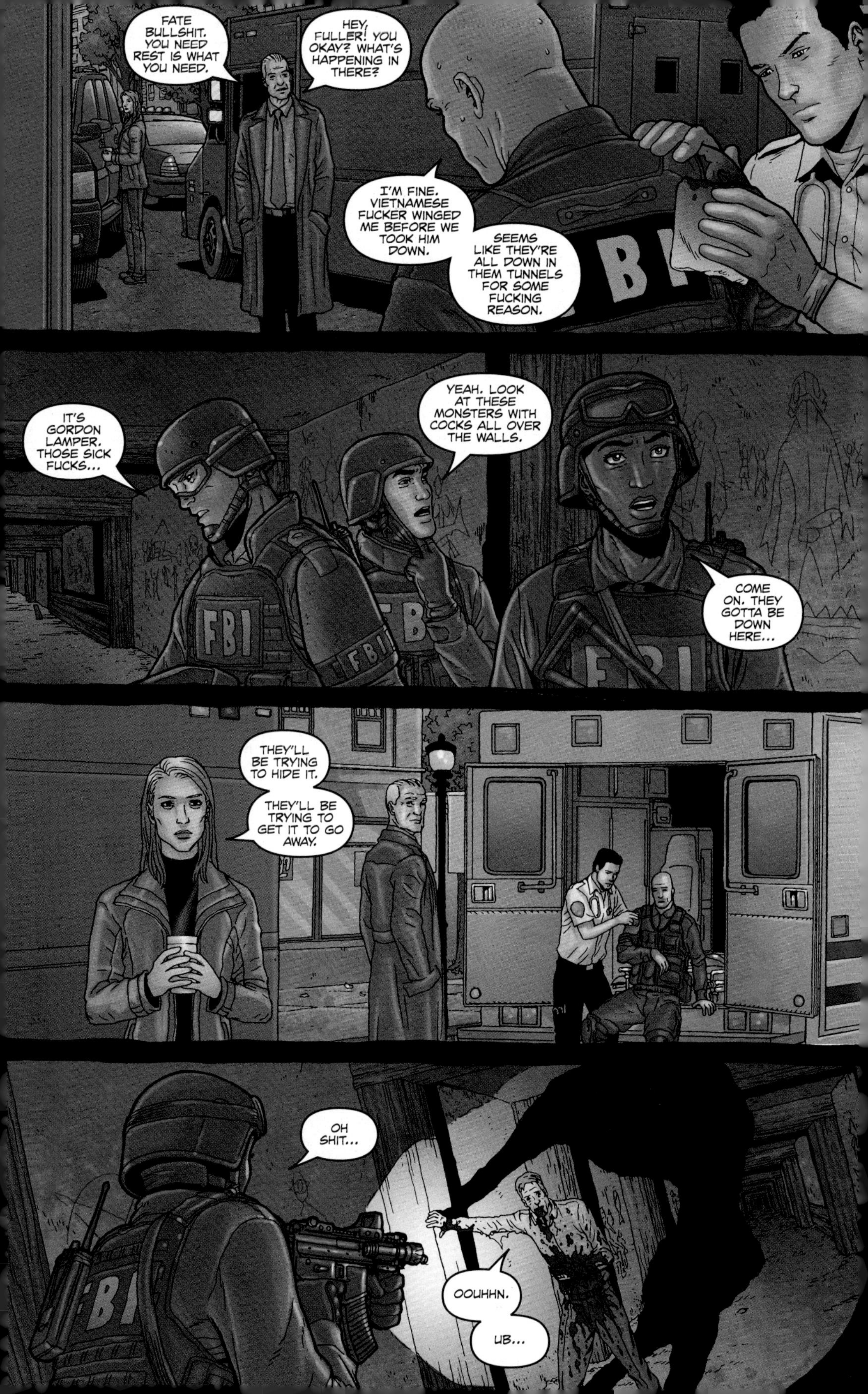
FATE BULLSHIT. YOU NEED REST IS WHAT YOU NEED.
HEY, FULLER! YOU OKAY? WHAT'S HAPPENING IN THERE?
I'M FINE. VIETNAMESE FUCKER WINGED ME BEFORE WE TOOK HIM DOWN.
SEEMS LIKE THEY'RE ALL DOWN IN THEM TUNNELS FOR SOME FUCKING REASON.
IT'S GORDON LAMPER. THOSE SICK FUCKS...
YEAH. LOOK AT THESE MONSTERS WITH COCKS ALL OVER THE WALLS.
COME ON. THEY GOTTA BE DOWN HERE...
THEY'LL BE TRYING TO HIDE IT.
THEY'LL BE TRYING TO GET IT TO GO AWAY.
OH SHIT...
OOUHHN.
UB...

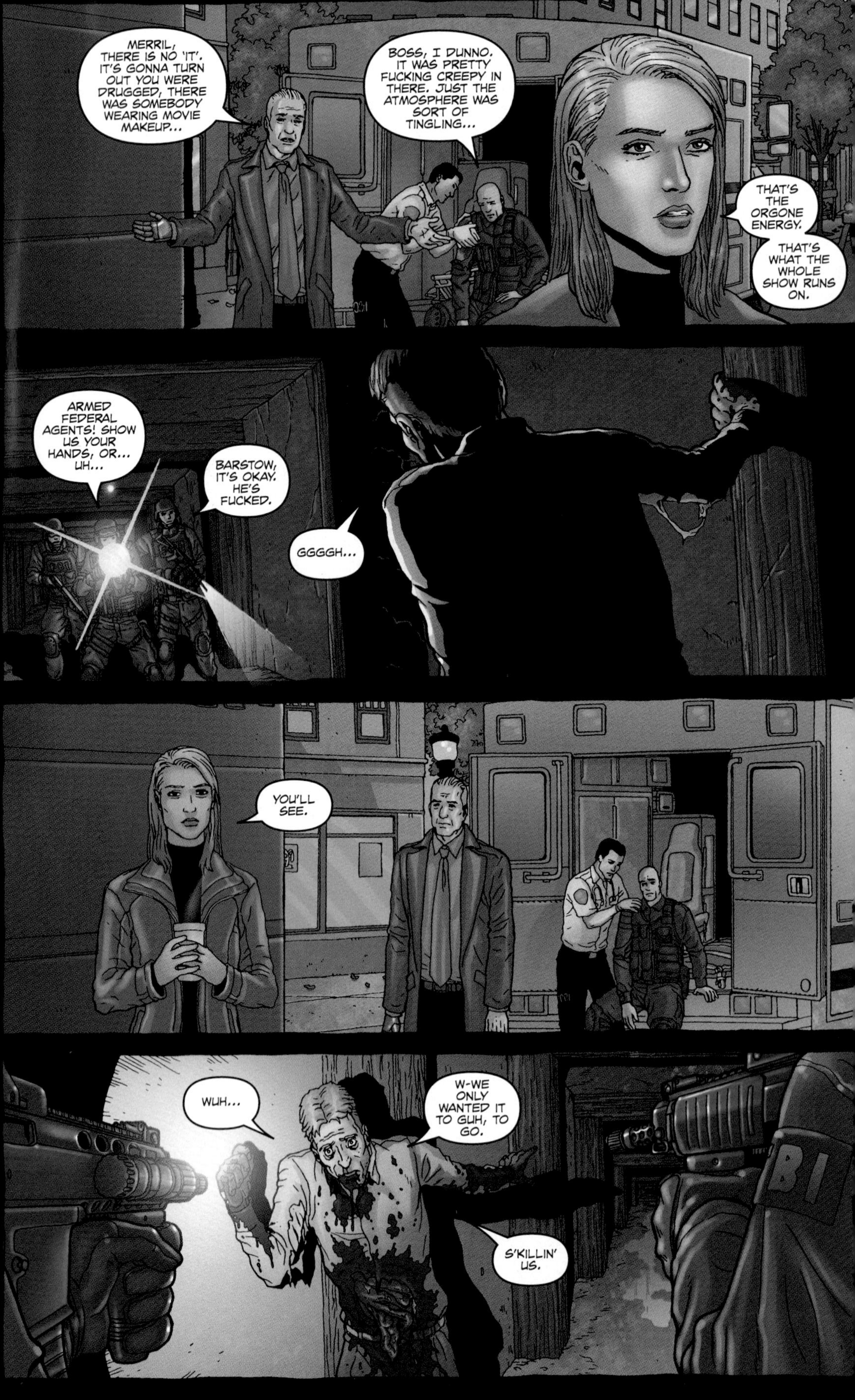
MERRIL, THERE IS NO 'IT'. IT'S GONNA TURN OUT YOU WERE DRUGGED, THERE WAS SOMEBODY WEARING MOVIE MAKEUP...
BOSS, I DUNNO. IT WAS PRETTY FUCKING CREEPY IN THERE. JUST THE ATMOSPHERE WAS SORT OF TINGLING...
THAT'S THE ORGONE ENERGY.
THAT'S WHAT THE WHOLE SHOW RUNS ON.
ARMED FEDERAL AGENTS! SHOW US YOUR HANDS, OR... UH...
BARSTOW, IT'S OKAY. HE'S FUCKED.
GGGGH...
YOU'LL SEE.
WUH...
W-WE ONLY WANTED IT TO GUH, TO GO.
S'KILLIN' US.

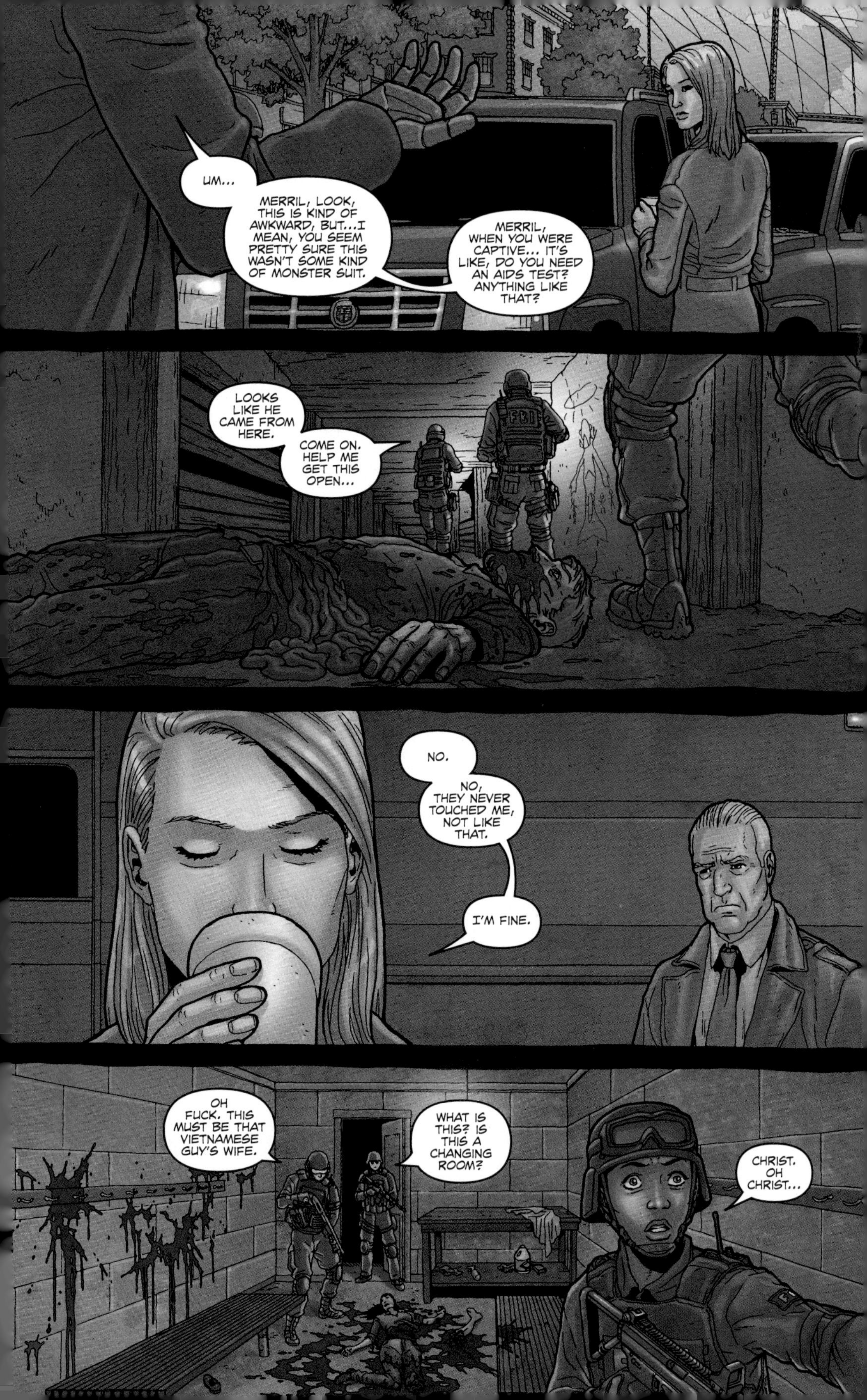
UM...
MERRIL, LOOK, THIS IS KIND OF AWKWARD, BUT...I MEAN, YOU SEEM PRETTY SURE THIS WASN'T SOME KIND OF MONSTER SUIT.
MERRIL, WHEN YOU WERE CAPTIVE... IT'S LIKE, DO YOU NEED AN AIDS TEST? ANYTHING LIKE THAT?
LOOKS LIKE HE CAME FROM HERE.
COME ON. HELP ME GET THIS OPEN...
NO.
NO, THEY NEVER TOUCHED ME, NOT LIKE THAT.
I'M FINE.
OH FUCK. THIS MUST BE THAT VIETNAMESE GUY'S WIFE.
WHAT IS THIS? IS THIS A CHANGING ROOM?
CHRIST. OH CHRIST...

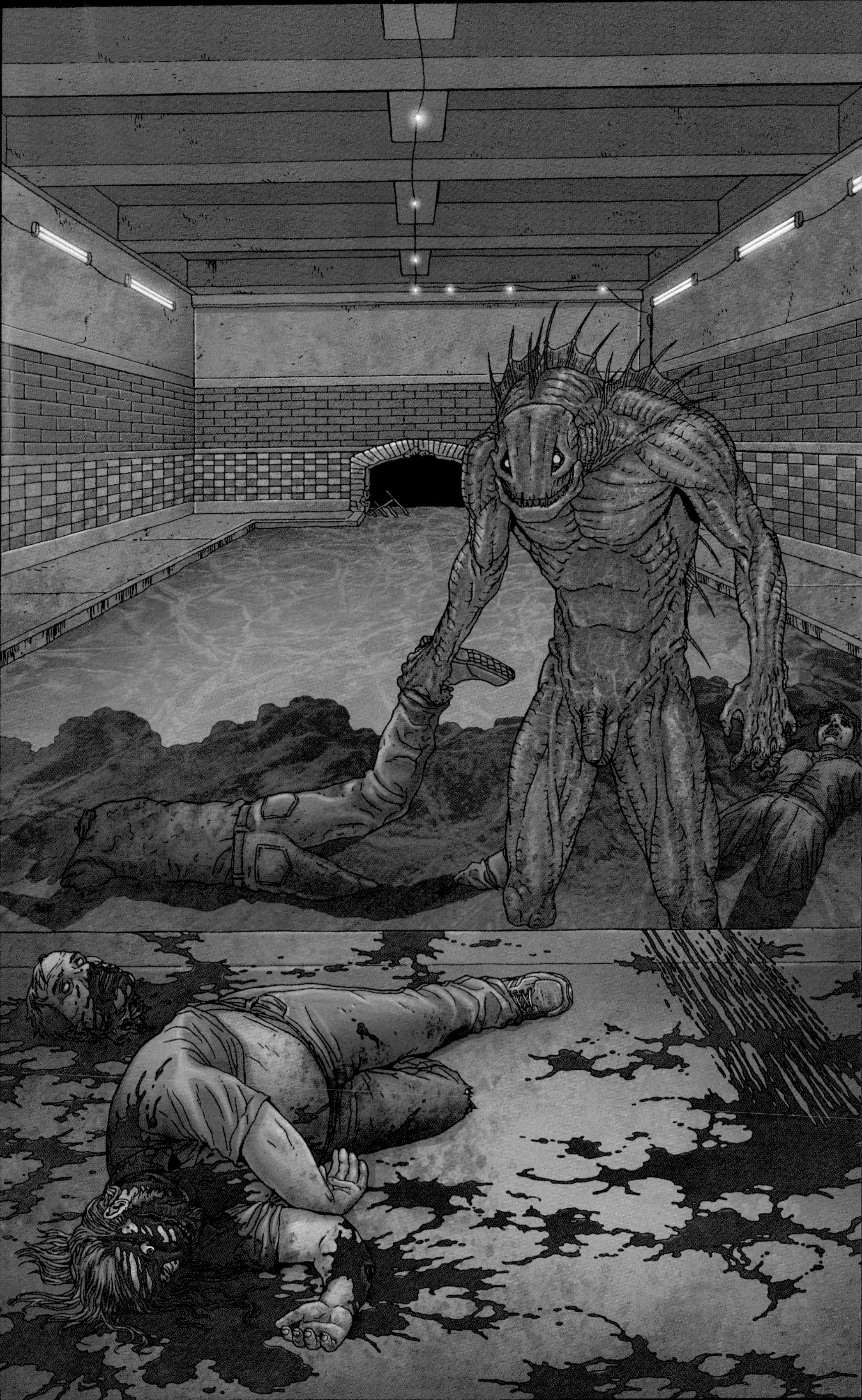

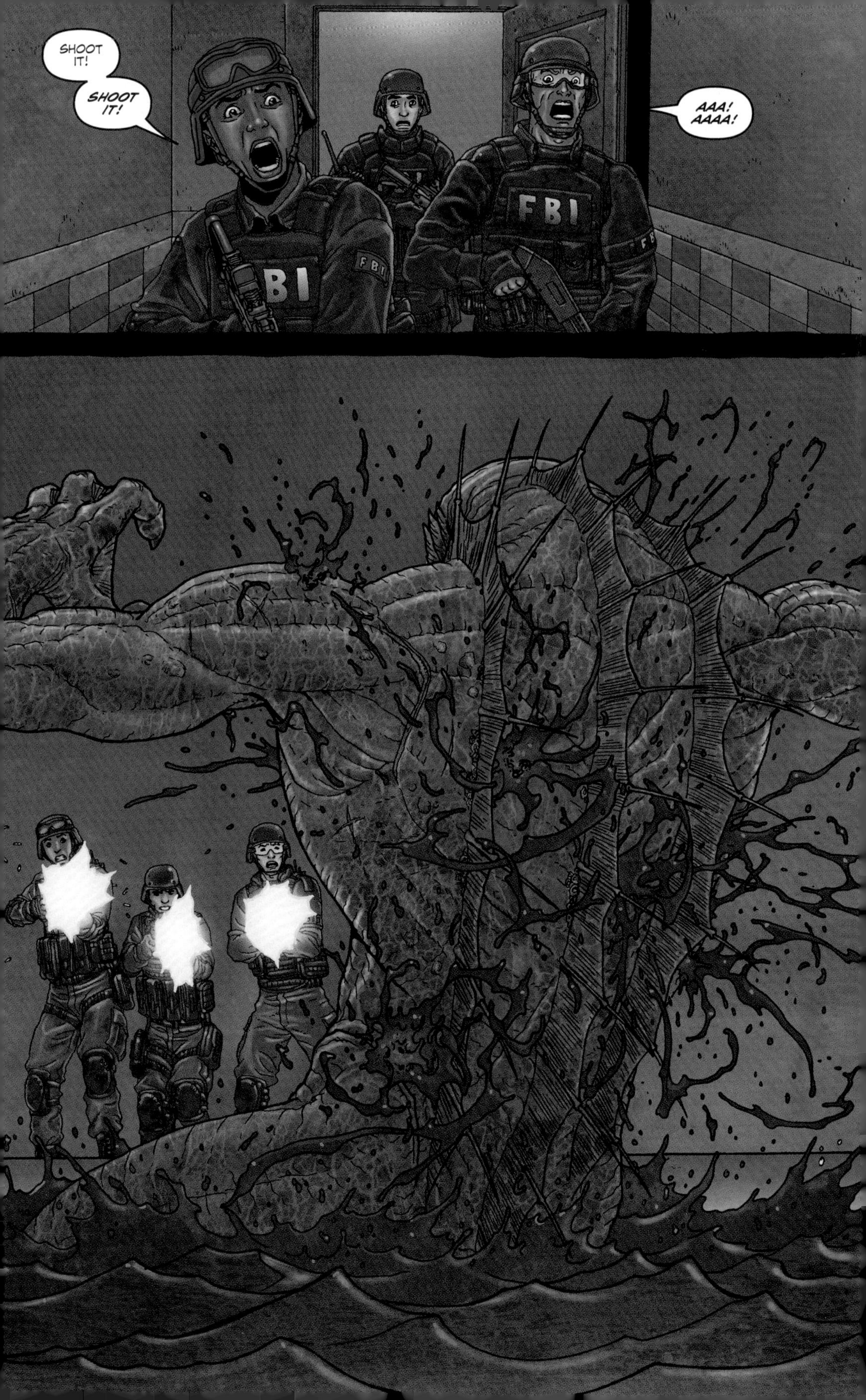
SHOOT IT!
SHOOT IT!
AAA! AAAA!
FBI
FBI

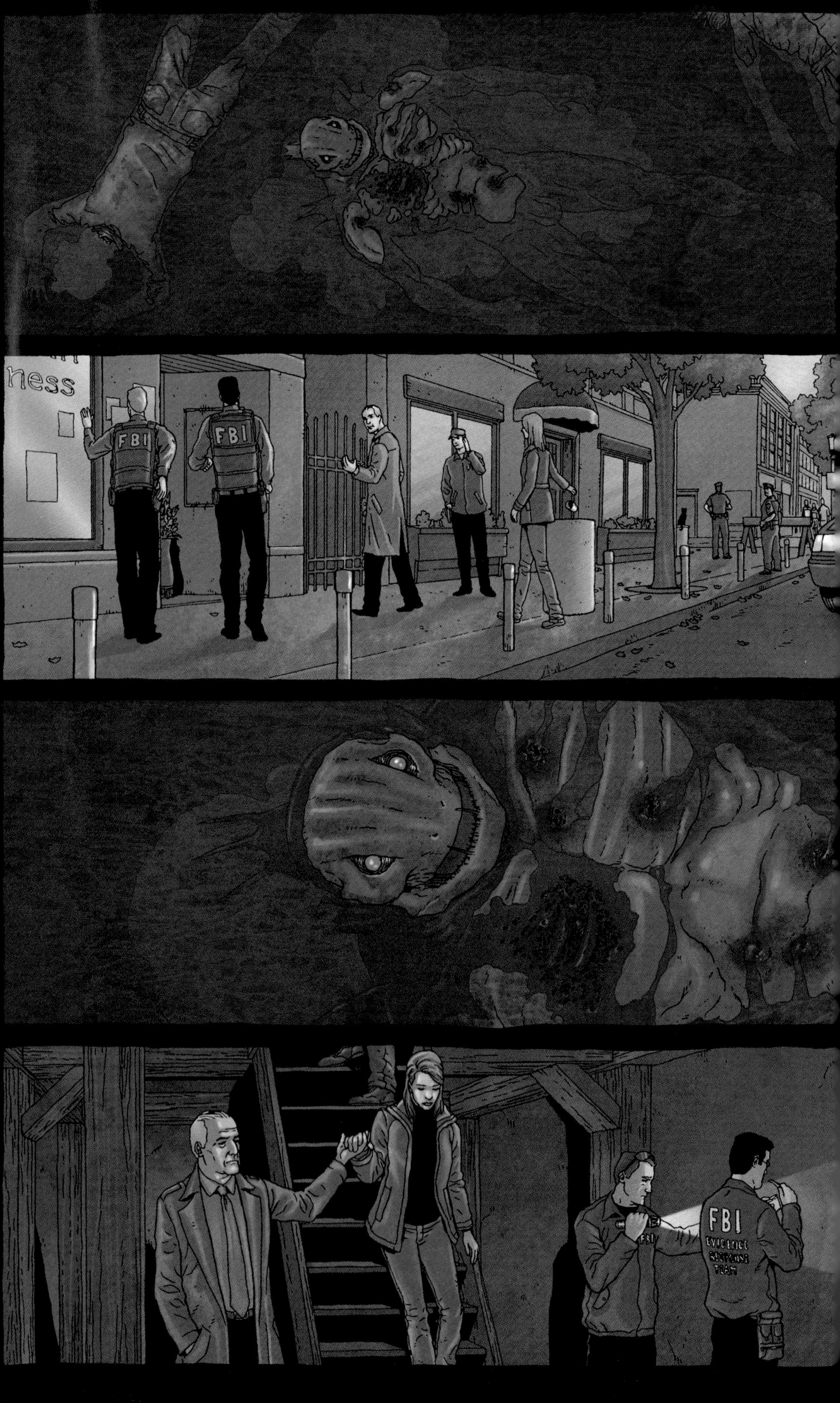
ness
FBI
FBI
FBI

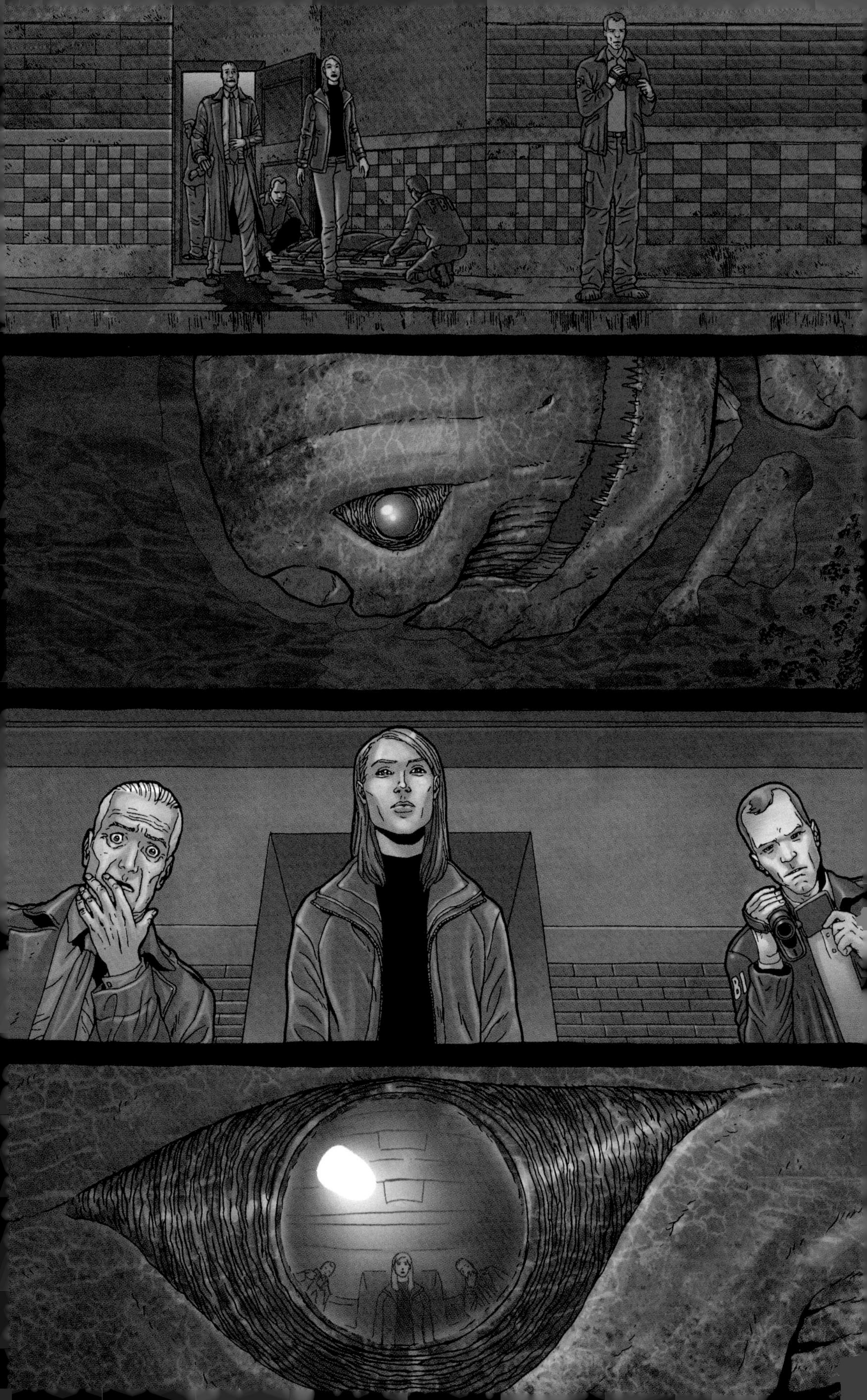

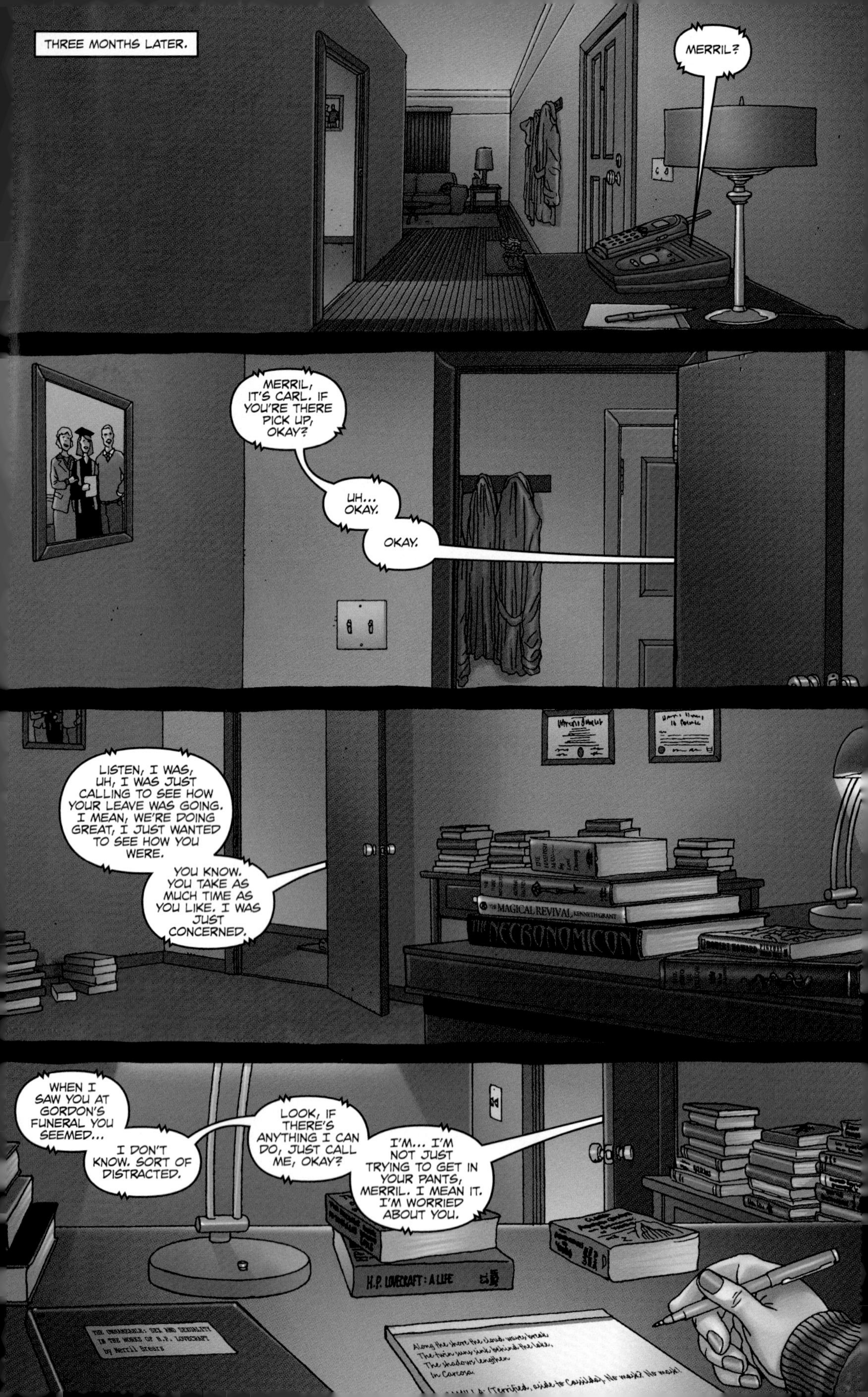
THREE MONTHS LATER.
MERRIL?
MERRIL, IT'S CARL. IF YOU'RE THERE PICK UP, OKAY?
UH... OKAY.
OKAY.
LISTEN, I WAS, UH, I WAS JUST CALLING TO SEE HOW YOUR LEAVE WAS GOING. I MEAN, WE'RE DOING GREAT, I JUST WANTED TO SEE HOW YOU WERE.
YOU KNOW. YOU TAKE AS MUCH TIME AS YOU LIKE. I WAS JUST CONCERNED.
THE MAGICAL REVIVAL KENNETH GRANT
THE NECRONOMICON
WHEN I SAW YOU AT GORDON'S FUNERAL YOU SEEMED...
I DON'T KNOW. SORT OF DISTRACTED.
LOOK, IF THERE'S ANYTHING I CAN DO, JUST CALL ME, OKAY?
I'M... I'M NOT JUST TRYING TO GET IN YOUR PANTS, MERRIL. I MEAN IT. I'M WORRIED ABOUT YOU.
H.P. LOVECRAFT : A LIFE
Along the shore the cloud waves break
The twin suns sink behind the lake,
The shadows lengthen
In Carcosa.

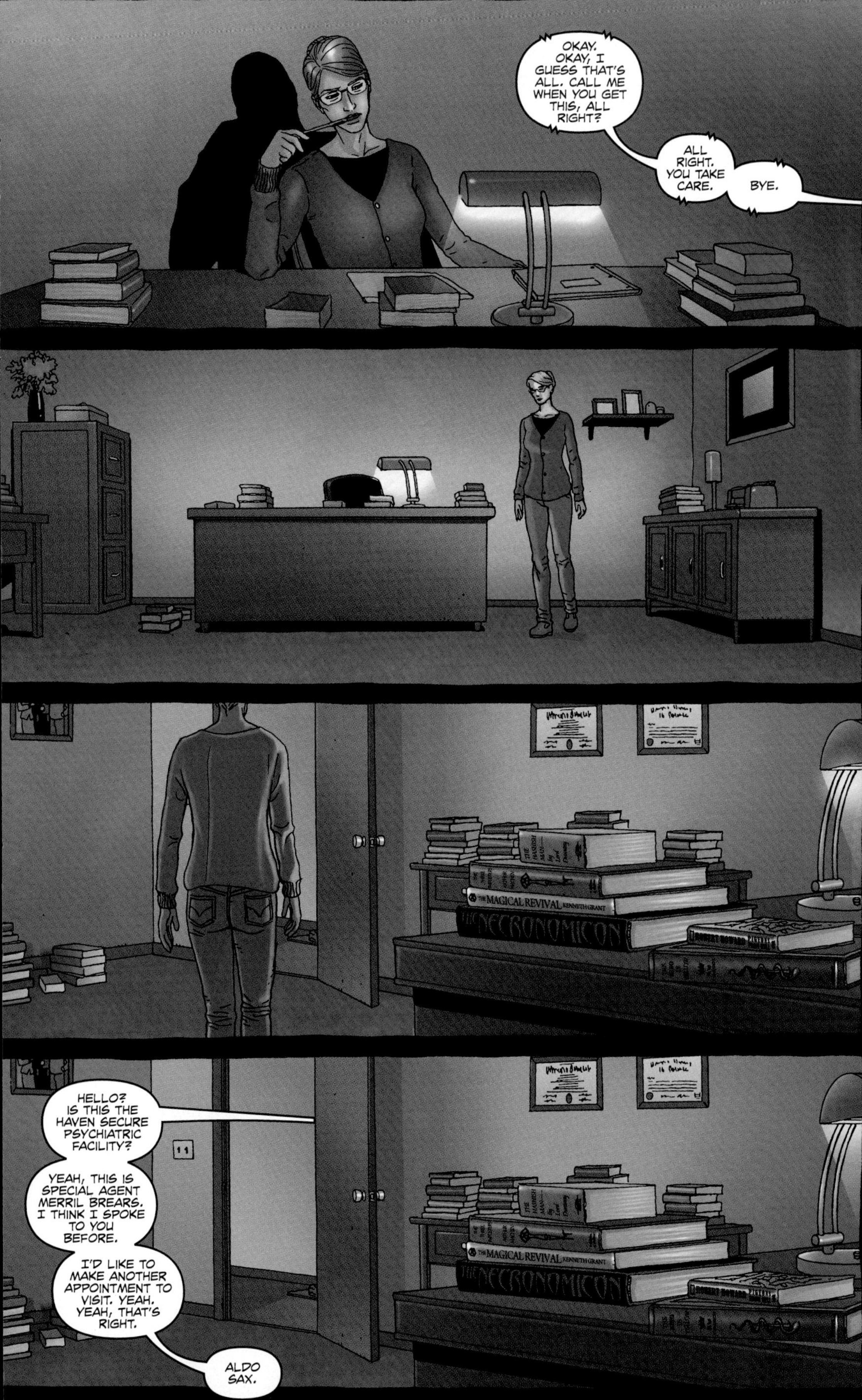
OKAY. OKAY, I GUESS THAT'S ALL. CALL ME WHEN YOU GET THIS, ALL RIGHT?
ALL RIGHT. YOU TAKE CARE.
BYE.
THE MAGICAL REVIVAL KENNETH GRANT
THE NECRONOMICON
HELLO? IS THIS THE HAVEN SECURE PSYCHIATRIC FACILITY?
YEAH, THIS IS SPECIAL AGENT MERRIL BREARS. I THINK I SPOKE TO YOU BEFORE.
I'D LIKE TO MAKE ANOTHER APPOINTMENT TO VISIT. YEAH. YEAH, THAT'S RIGHT.
ALDO SAX.

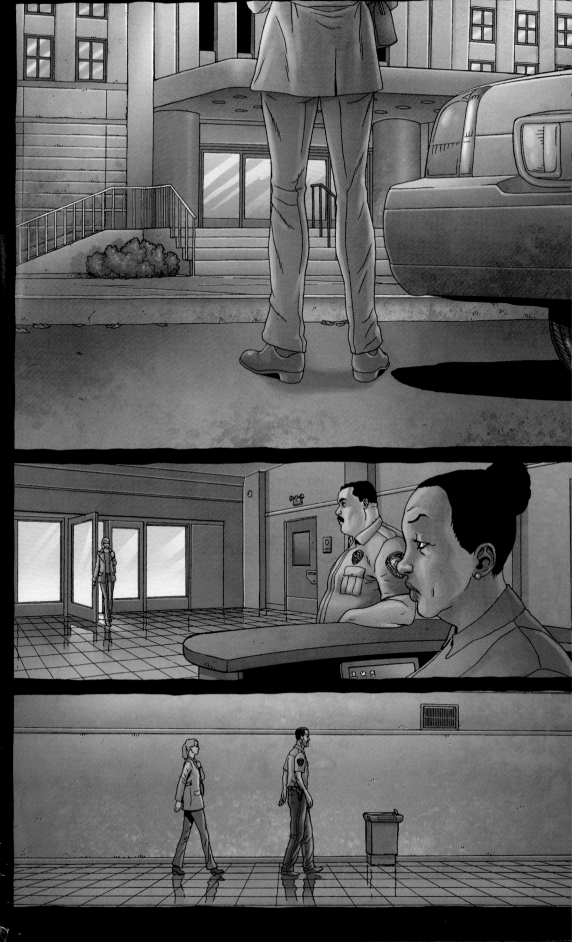

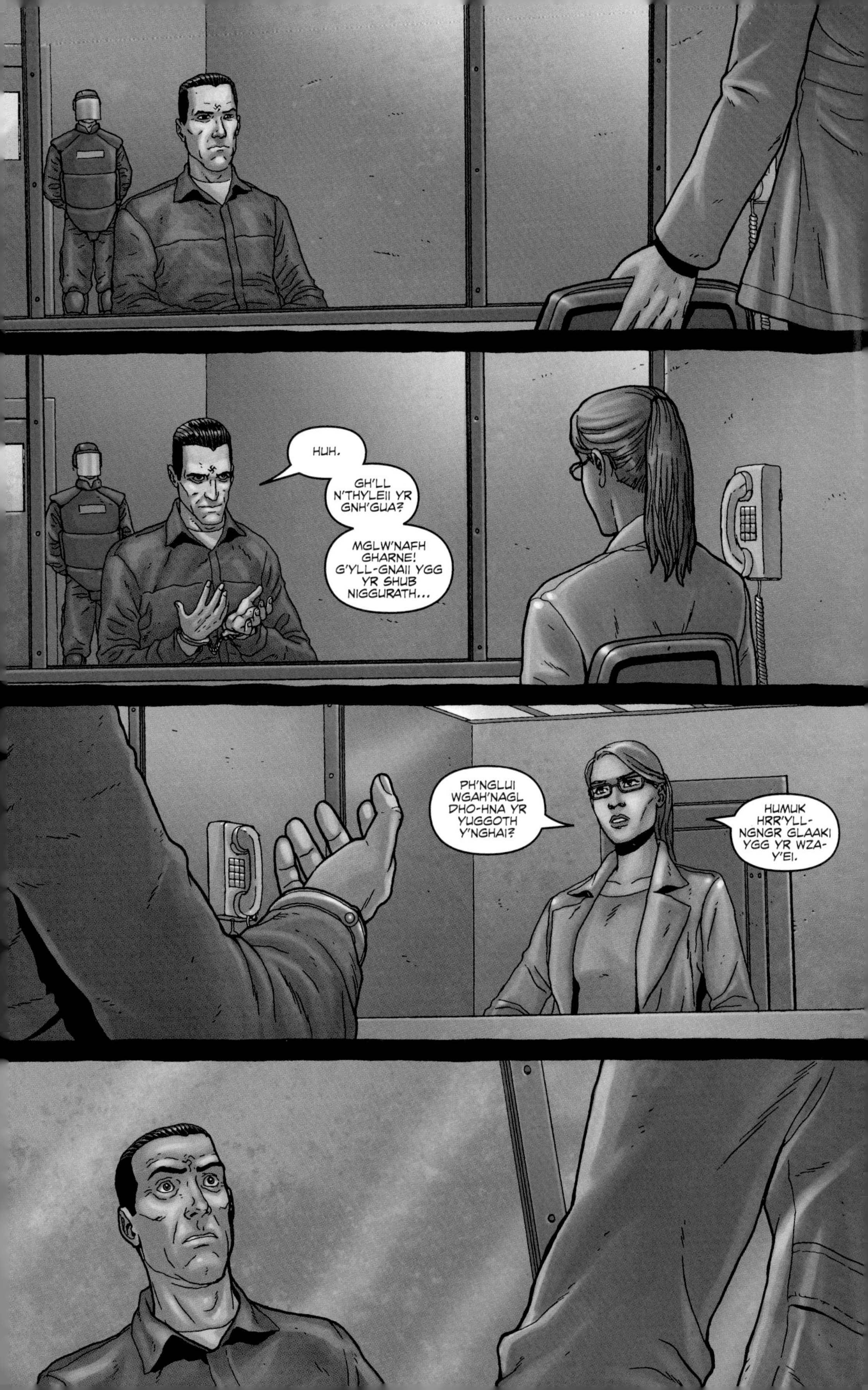
HUH.
GH'LL N'THYLEII YR GNH'GUA?
MGLW'NAFH GHARNE! G'YLL-GNAII YGG YR SHUB NIGGURATH...
PH'NGLUI WGAH'NAGL DHO-HNA YR YUGGOTH Y'NGHAI?
HUMUK HRR'YLL-NGNGR GLAAKI YGG YR WZA-Y'EI.

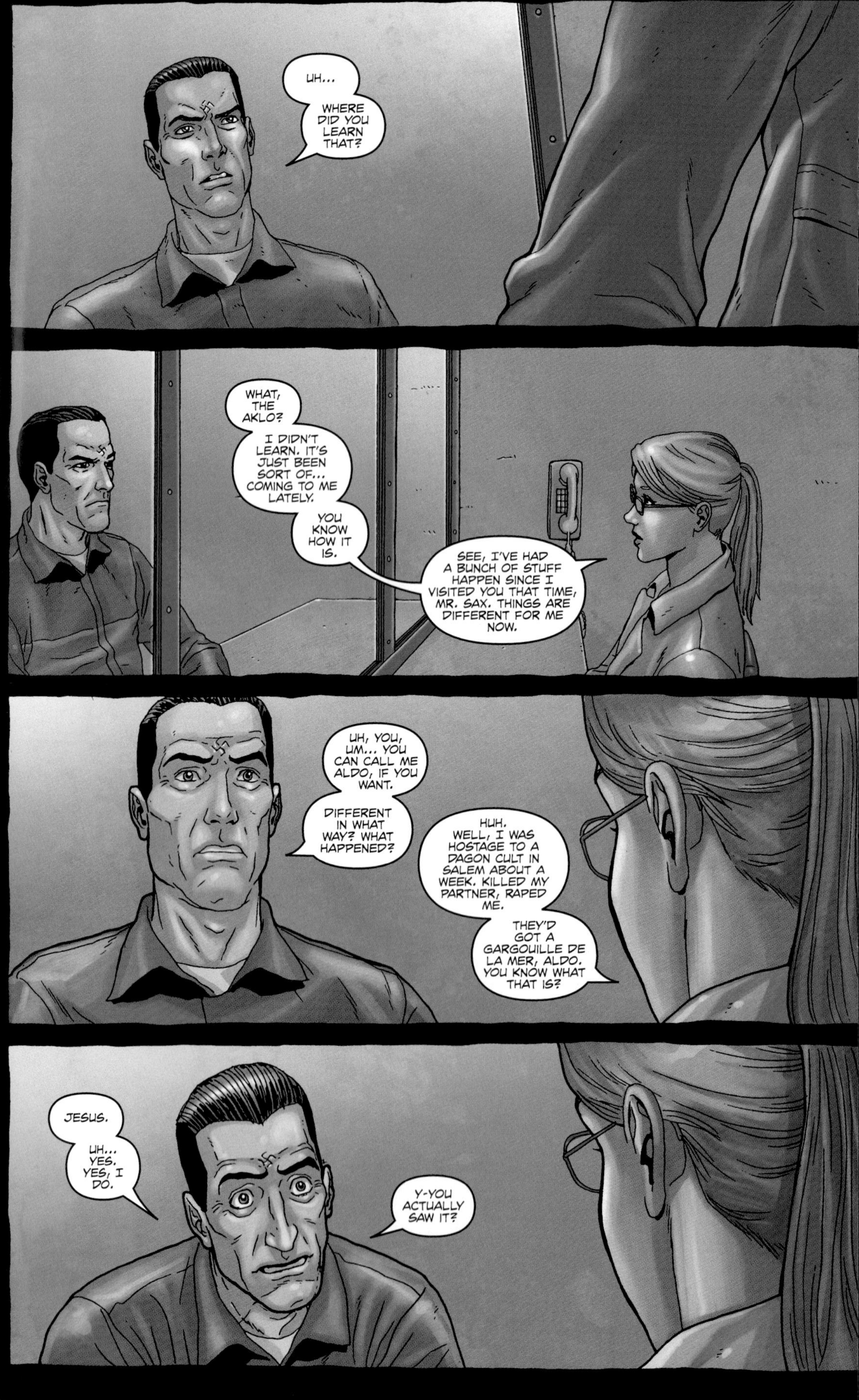
UH... WHERE DID YOU LEARN THAT?
WHAT, THE AKLO?
I DIDN'T LEARN. IT'S JUST BEEN SORT OF... COMING TO ME LATELY.
YOU KNOW HOW IT IS.
SEE, I'VE HAD A BUNCH OF STUFF HAPPEN SINCE I VISITED YOU THAT TIME, MR. SAX. THINGS ARE DIFFERENT FOR ME NOW.
UH, YOU, UM... YOU CAN CALL ME ALDO, IF YOU WANT.
DIFFERENT IN WHAT WAY? WHAT HAPPENED?
HUH. WELL, I WAS HOSTAGE TO A DAGON CULT IN SALEM ABOUT A WEEK. KILLED MY PARTNER, RAPED ME.
THEY'D GOT A GARGOUILLE DE LA MER, ALDO. YOU KNOW WHAT THAT IS?
JESUS.
UH... YES. YES, I DO.
Y-YOU ACTUALLY SAW IT?

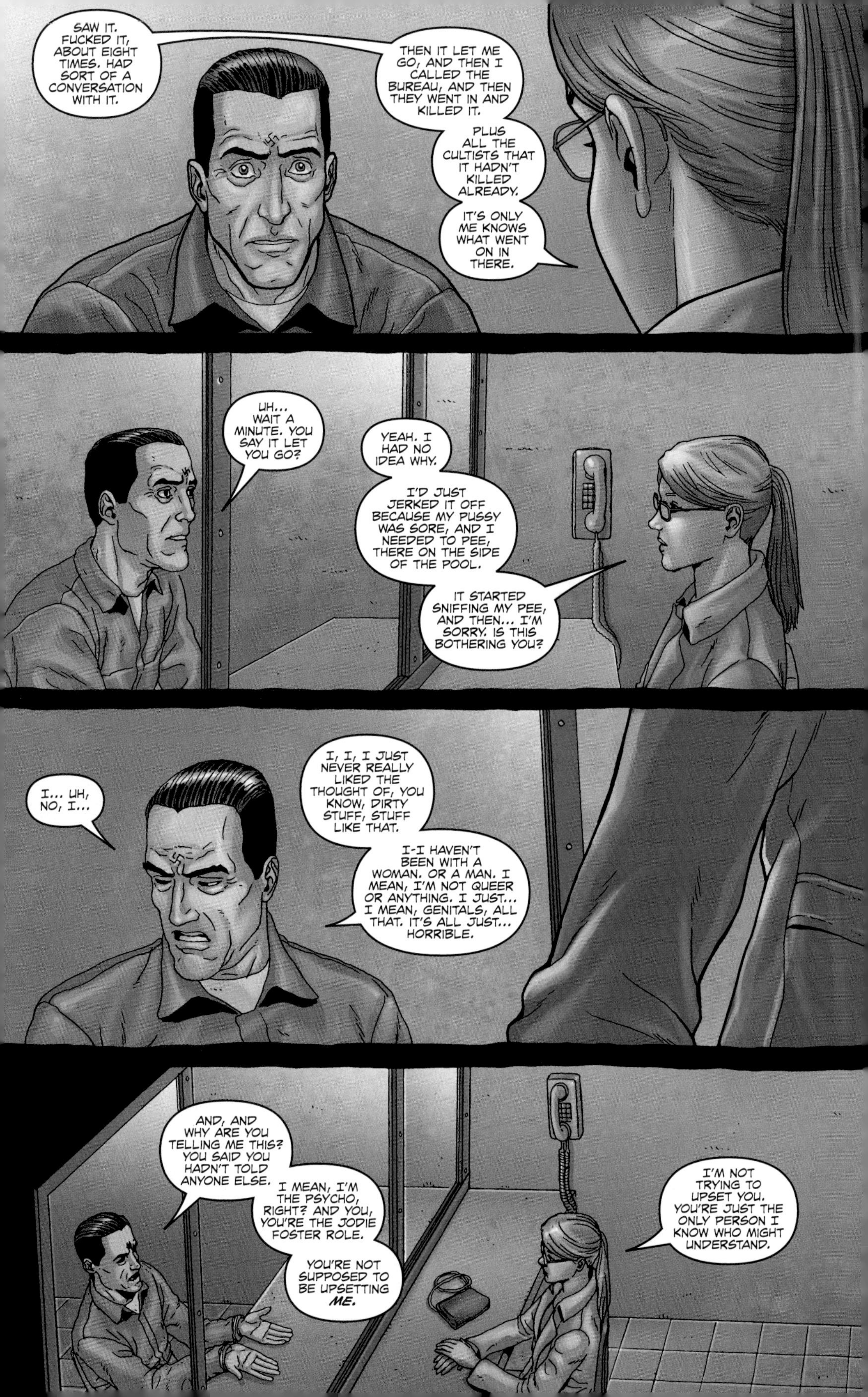
SAW IT. FUCKED IT, ABOUT EIGHT TIMES. HAD SORT OF A CONVERSATION WITH IT.
THEN IT LET ME GO, AND THEN I CALLED THE BUREAU, AND THEN THEY WENT IN AND KILLED IT.
PLUS ALL THE CULTISTS THAT IT HADN'T KILLED ALREADY.
IT'S ONLY ME KNOWS WHAT WENT ON IN THERE.
UH... WAIT A MINUTE. YOU SAY IT LET YOU GO?
YEAH. I HAD NO IDEA WHY.
I'D JUST JERKED IT OFF BECAUSE MY PUSSY WAS SORE, AND I NEEDED TO PEE, THERE ON THE SIDE OF THE POOL.
IT STARTED SNIFFING MY PEE, AND THEN... I'M SORRY. IS THIS BOTHERING YOU?
I... UH, NO, I...
I, I, I JUST NEVER REALLY LIKED THE THOUGHT OF, YOU KNOW, DIRTY STUFF, STUFF LIKE THAT.
I-I HAVEN'T BEEN WITH A WOMAN. OR A MAN. I MEAN, I'M NOT QUEER OR ANYTHING. I JUST... I MEAN, GENITALS, ALL THAT. IT'S ALL JUST... HORRIBLE.
AND, AND WHY ARE YOU TELLING ME THIS? YOU SAID YOU HADN'T TOLD ANYONE ELSE.
I MEAN, I'M THE PSYCHO, RIGHT? AND YOU, YOU'RE THE JODIE FOSTER ROLE.
YOU'RE NOT SUPPOSED TO BE UPSETTING ***ME.***
I'M NOT TRYING TO UPSET YOU. YOU'RE JUST THE ONLY PERSON I KNOW WHO MIGHT UNDERSTAND.

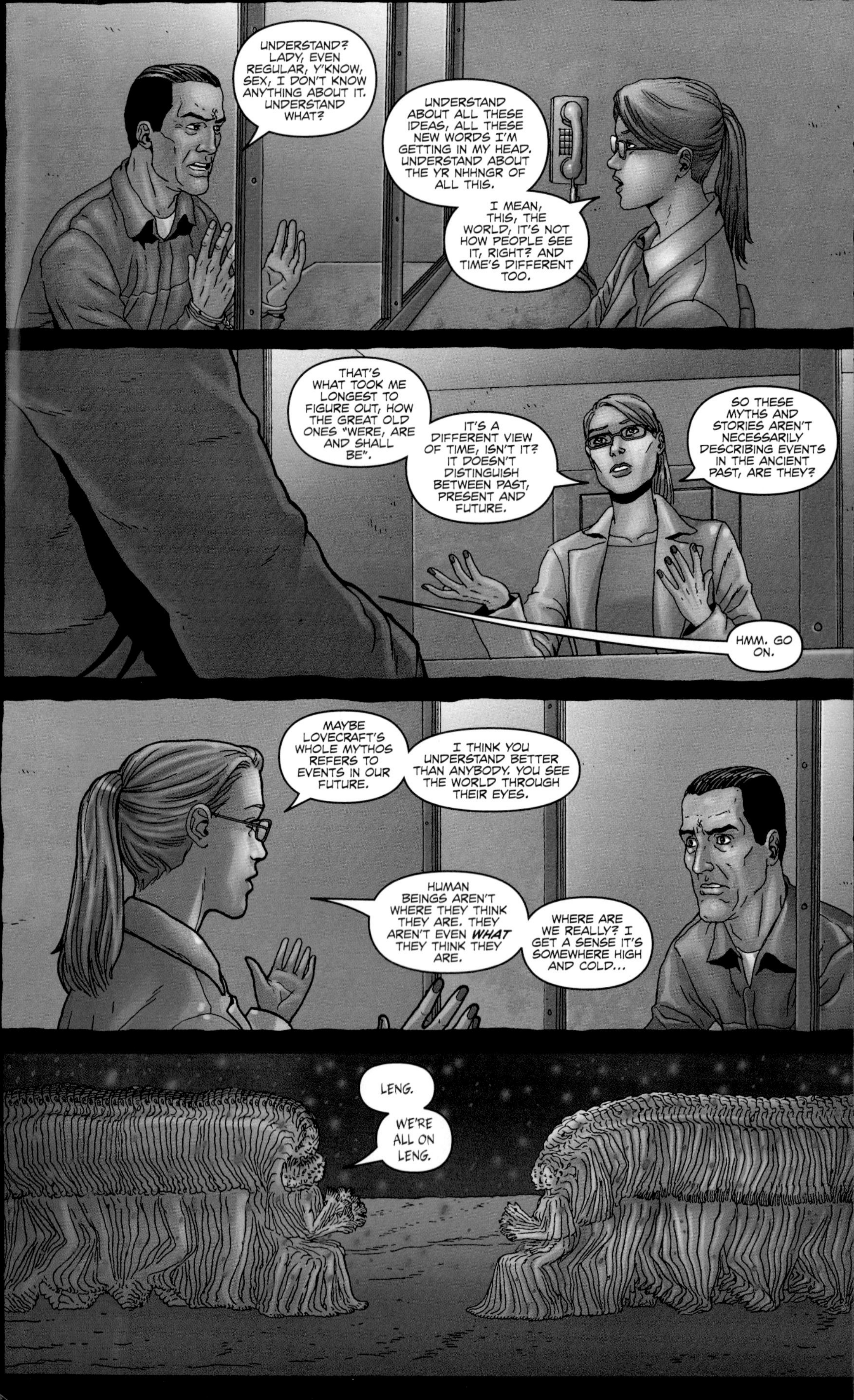
UNDERSTAND? LADY, EVEN REGULAR, Y'KNOW, SEX, I DON'T KNOW ANYTHING ABOUT IT. UNDERSTAND WHAT?
UNDERSTAND ABOUT ALL THESE IDEAS, ALL THESE NEW WORDS I'M GETTING IN MY HEAD. UNDERSTAND ABOUT THE YR NHHNGR OF ALL THIS.
I MEAN, THIS, THE WORLD, IT'S NOT HOW PEOPLE SEE IT, RIGHT? AND TIME'S DIFFERENT TOO.
THAT'S WHAT TOOK ME LONGEST TO FIGURE OUT, HOW THE GREAT OLD ONES "WERE, ARE AND SHALL BE".
IT'S A DIFFERENT VIEW OF TIME, ISN'T IT? IT DOESN'T DISTINGUISH BETWEEN PAST, PRESENT AND FUTURE.
SO THESE MYTHS AND STORIES AREN'T NECESSARILY DESCRIBING EVENTS IN THE ANCIENT PAST, ARE THEY?
HMM. GO ON.
MAYBE LOVECRAFT'S WHOLE MYTHOS REFERS TO EVENTS IN OUR FUTURE.
I THINK YOU UNDERSTAND BETTER THAN ANYBODY. YOU SEE THE WORLD THROUGH THEIR EYES.
HUMAN BEINGS AREN'T WHERE THEY THINK THEY ARE. THEY AREN'T EVEN *WHAT* THEY THINK THEY ARE.
WHERE ARE WE REALLY? I GET A SENSE IT'S SOMEWHERE HIGH AND COLD...
LENG.
WE'RE ALL ON LENG.

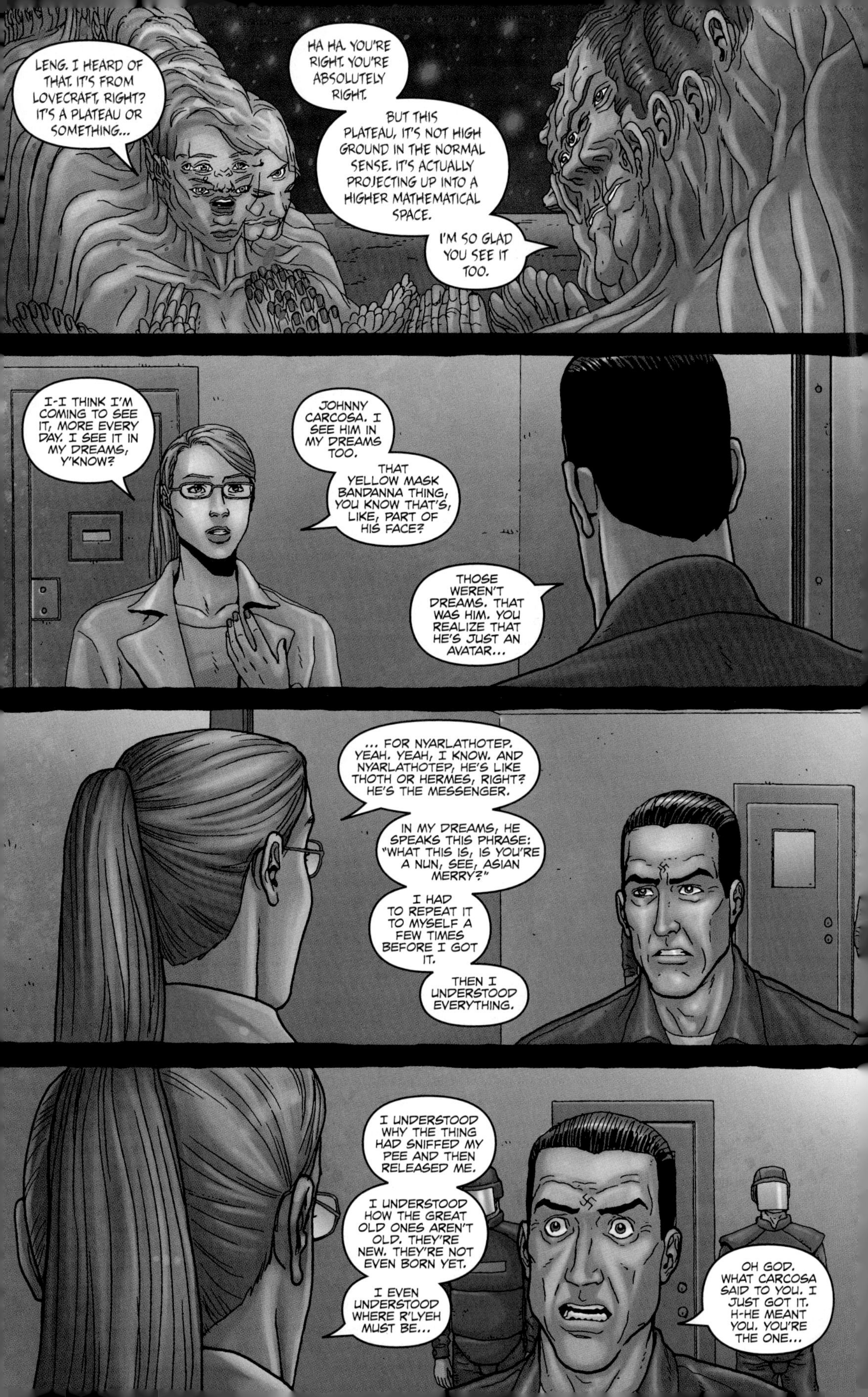
LENG. I HEARD OF THAT. IT'S FROM LOVECRAFT, RIGHT? IT'S A PLATEAU OR SOMETHING...
HA HA. YOU'RE RIGHT. YOU'RE ABSOLUTELY RIGHT.
BUT THIS PLATEAU, IT'S NOT HIGH GROUND IN THE NORMAL SENSE. IT'S ACTUALLY PROJECTING UP INTO A HIGHER MATHEMATICAL SPACE.
I'M SO GLAD YOU SEE IT TOO.
I-I THINK I'M COMING TO SEE IT, MORE EVERY DAY. I SEE IT IN MY DREAMS, Y'KNOW?
JOHNNY CARCOSA. I SEE HIM IN MY DREAMS TOO.
THAT YELLOW MASK BANDANNA THING, YOU KNOW THAT'S, LIKE, PART OF HIS FACE?
THOSE WEREN'T DREAMS. THAT WAS HIM. YOU REALIZE THAT HE'S JUST AN AVATAR...
... FOR NYARLATHOTEP. YEAH. YEAH, I KNOW. AND NYARLATHOTEP, HE'S LIKE THOTH OR HERMES, RIGHT? HE'S THE MESSENGER.
IN MY DREAMS, HE SPEAKS THIS PHRASE: "WHAT THIS IS, IS YOU'RE A NUN, SEE, ASIAN MERRY?"
I HAD TO REPEAT IT TO MYSELF A FEW TIMES BEFORE I GOT IT.
THEN I UNDERSTOOD EVERYTHING.
I UNDERSTOOD WHY THE THING HAD SNIFFED MY PEE AND THEN RELEASED ME.
I UNDERSTOOD HOW THE GREAT OLD ONES AREN'T OLD. THEY'RE NEW. THEY'RE NOT EVEN BORN YET.
I EVEN UNDERSTOOD WHERE R'LYEH MUST BE...
OH GOD. WHAT CARCOSA SAID TO YOU. I JUST GOT IT. H-HE MEANT YOU. YOU'RE THE ONE...

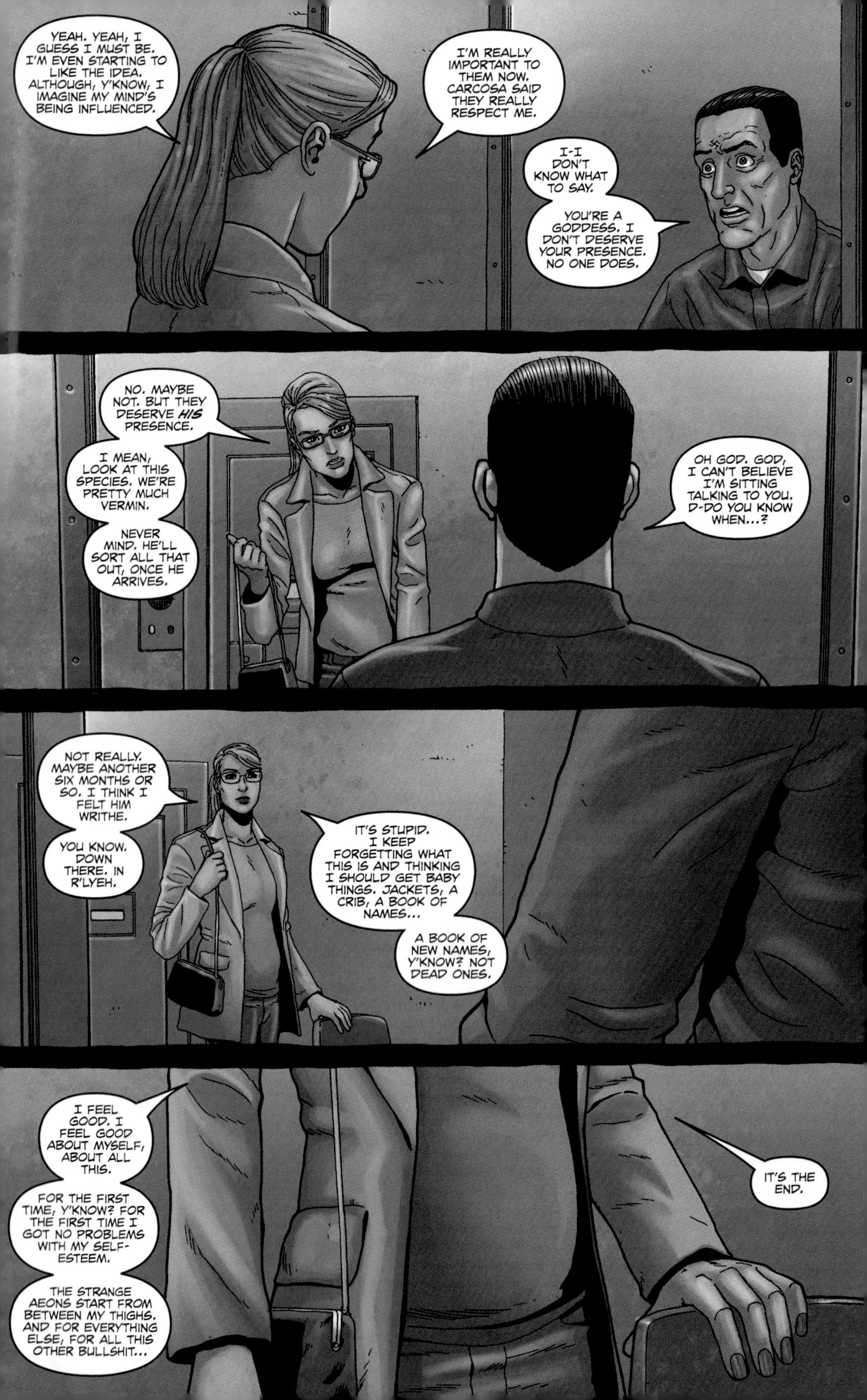
YEAH. YEAH, I GUESS I MUST BE. I'M EVEN STARTING TO LIKE THE IDEA. ALTHOUGH, Y'KNOW, I IMAGINE MY MIND'S BEING INFLUENCED.
I'M REALLY IMPORTANT TO THEM NOW. CARCOSA SAID THEY REALLY RESPECT ME.
I-I DON'T KNOW WHAT TO SAY.
YOU'RE A GODDESS. I DON'T DESERVE YOUR PRESENCE. NO ONE DOES.
NO. MAYBE NOT. BUT THEY DESERVE *HIS* PRESENCE.
I MEAN, LOOK AT THIS SPECIES. WE'RE PRETTY MUCH VERMIN.
NEVER MIND. HE'LL SORT ALL THAT OUT, ONCE HE ARRIVES.
OH GOD. GOD, I CAN'T BELIEVE I'M SITTING TALKING TO YOU. D-DO YOU KNOW WHEN...?
NOT REALLY. MAYBE ANOTHER SIX MONTHS OR SO. I THINK I FELT HIM WRITHE.
YOU KNOW. DOWN THERE. IN R'LYEH.
IT'S STUPID. I KEEP FORGETTING WHAT THIS IS AND THINKING I SHOULD GET BABY THINGS. JACKETS, A CRIB, A BOOK OF NAMES...
A BOOK OF NEW NAMES, Y'KNOW? NOT DEAD ONES.
I FEEL GOOD. I FEEL GOOD ABOUT MYSELF, ABOUT ALL THIS.
FOR THE FIRST TIME, Y'KNOW? FOR THE FIRST TIME I GOT NO PROBLEMS WITH MY SELF-ESTEEM.
THE STRANGE AEONS START FROM BETWEEN MY THIGHS. AND FOR EVERYTHING ELSE, FOR ALL THIS OTHER BULLSHIT...
IT'S THE END.

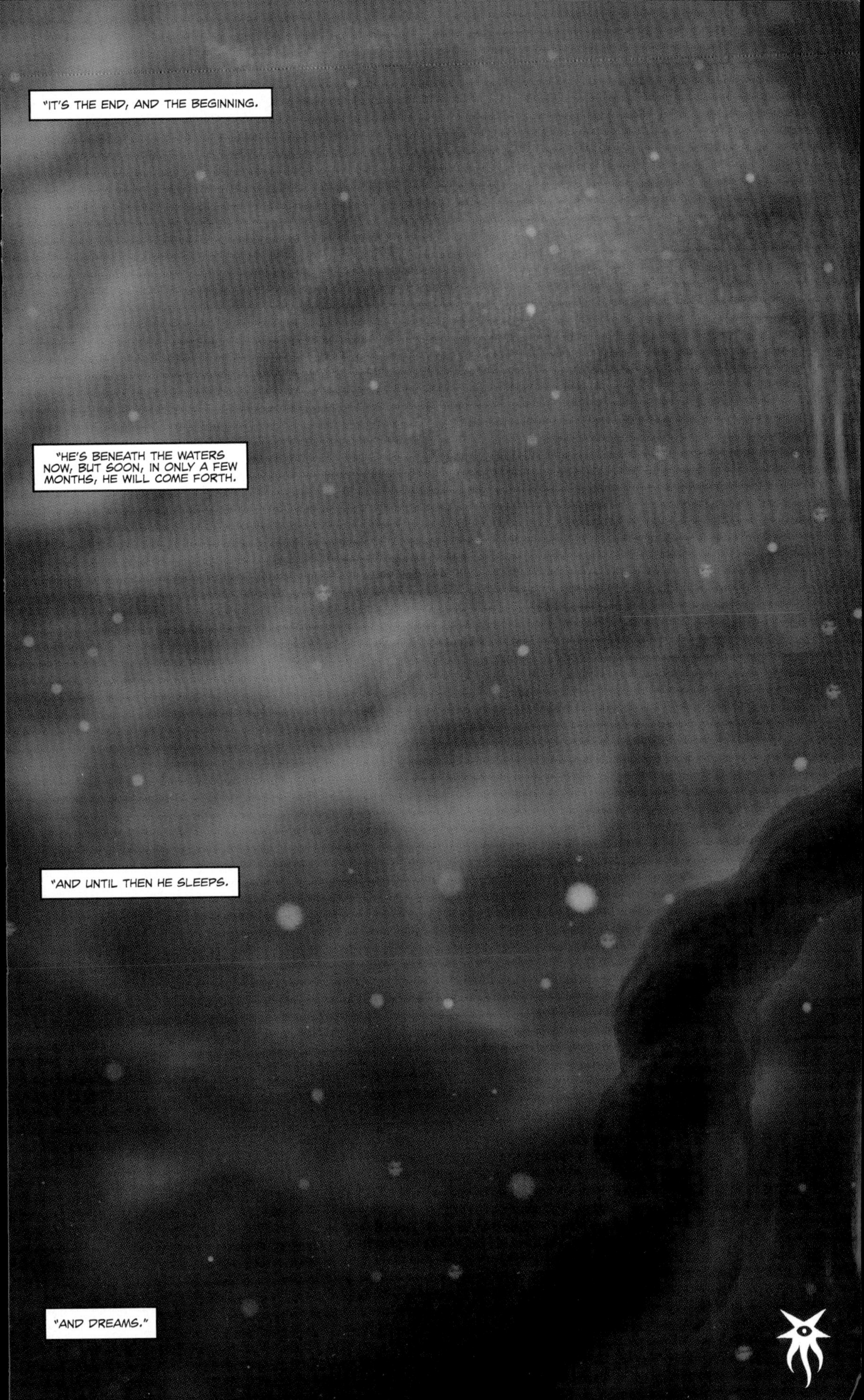
"IT'S THE END, AND THE BEGINNING.
"HE'S BENEATH THE WATERS NOW, BUT SOON, IN ONLY A FEW MONTHS, HE WILL COME FORTH.
"AND UNTIL THEN HE SLEEPS.
"AND DREAMS."

GALLERY

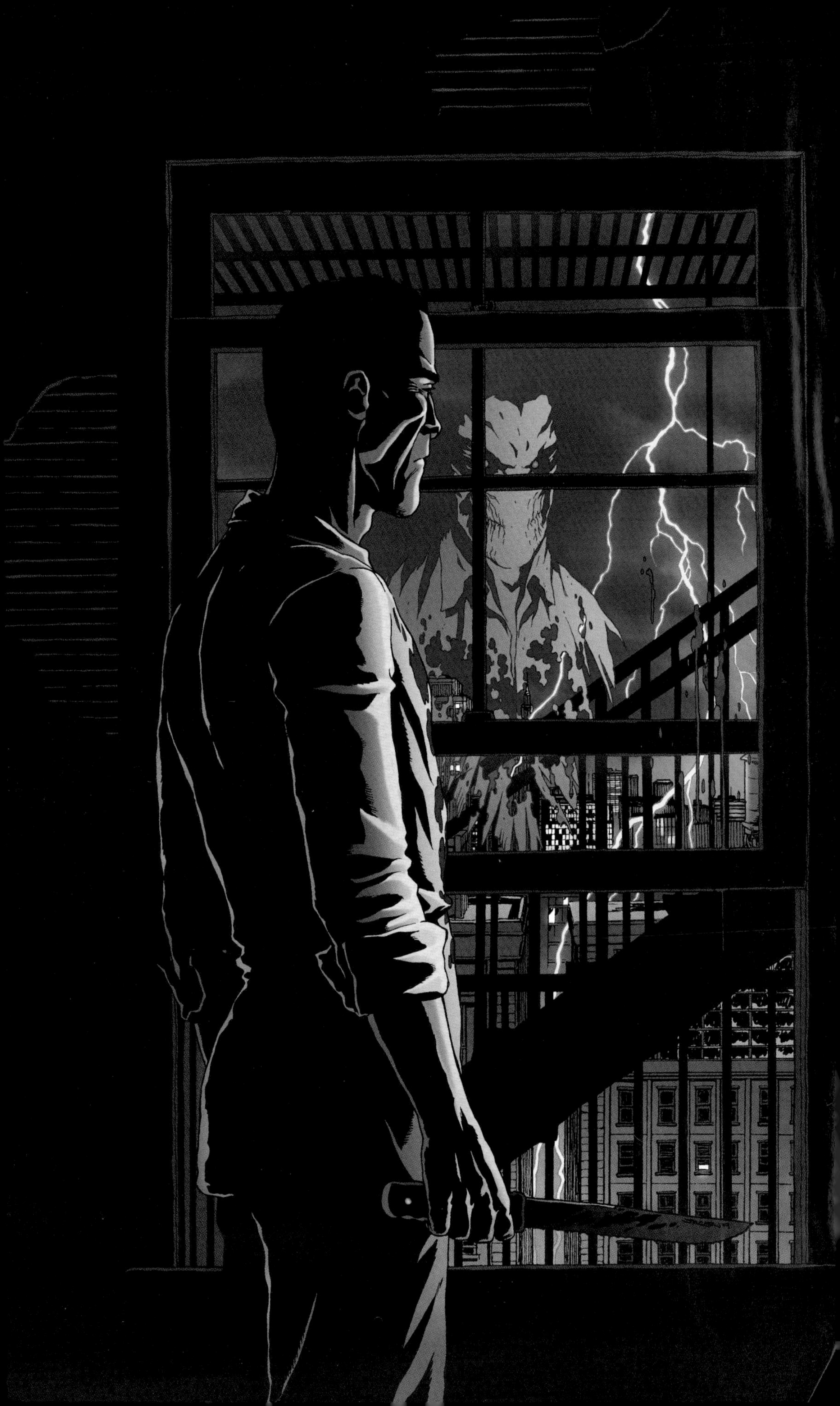

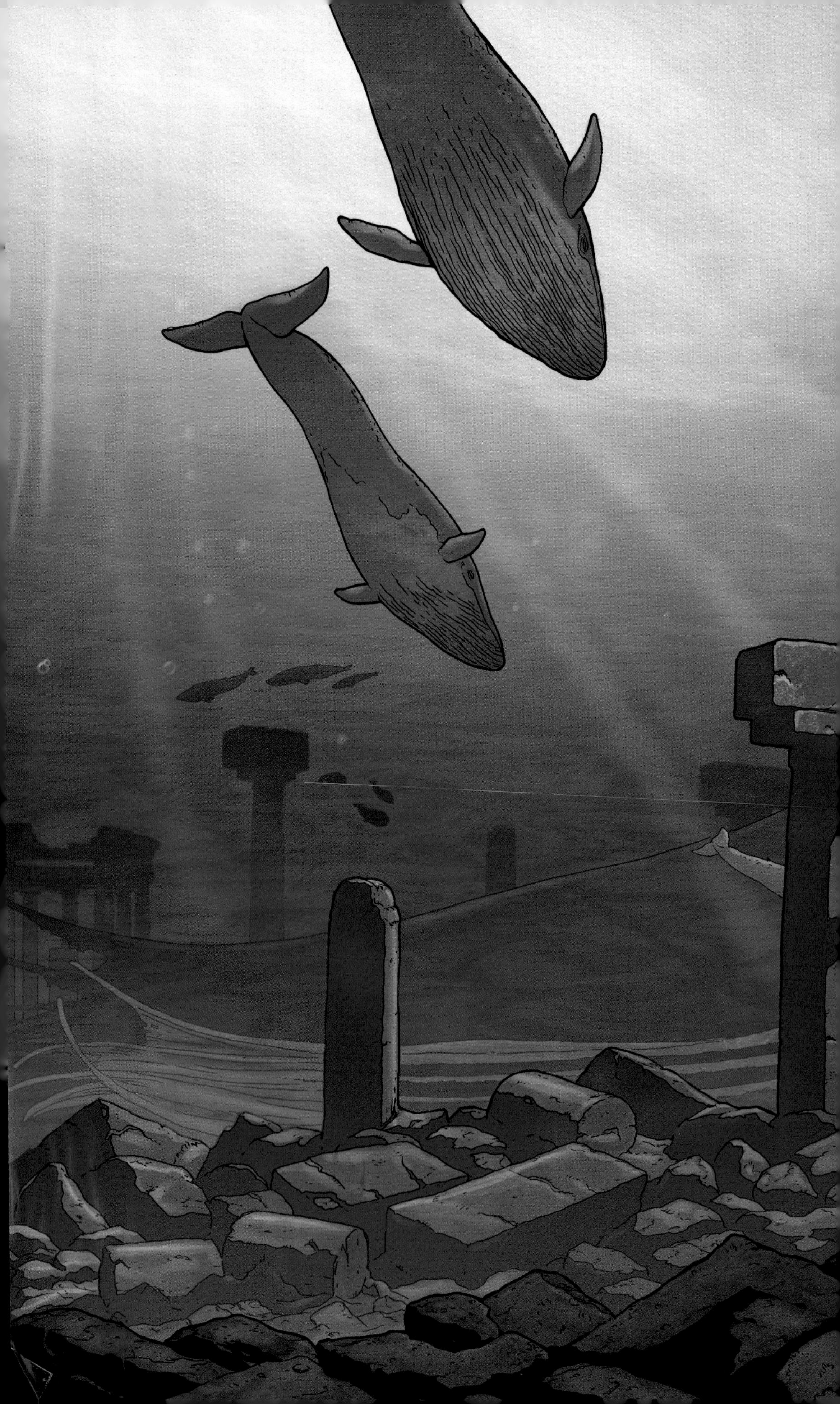

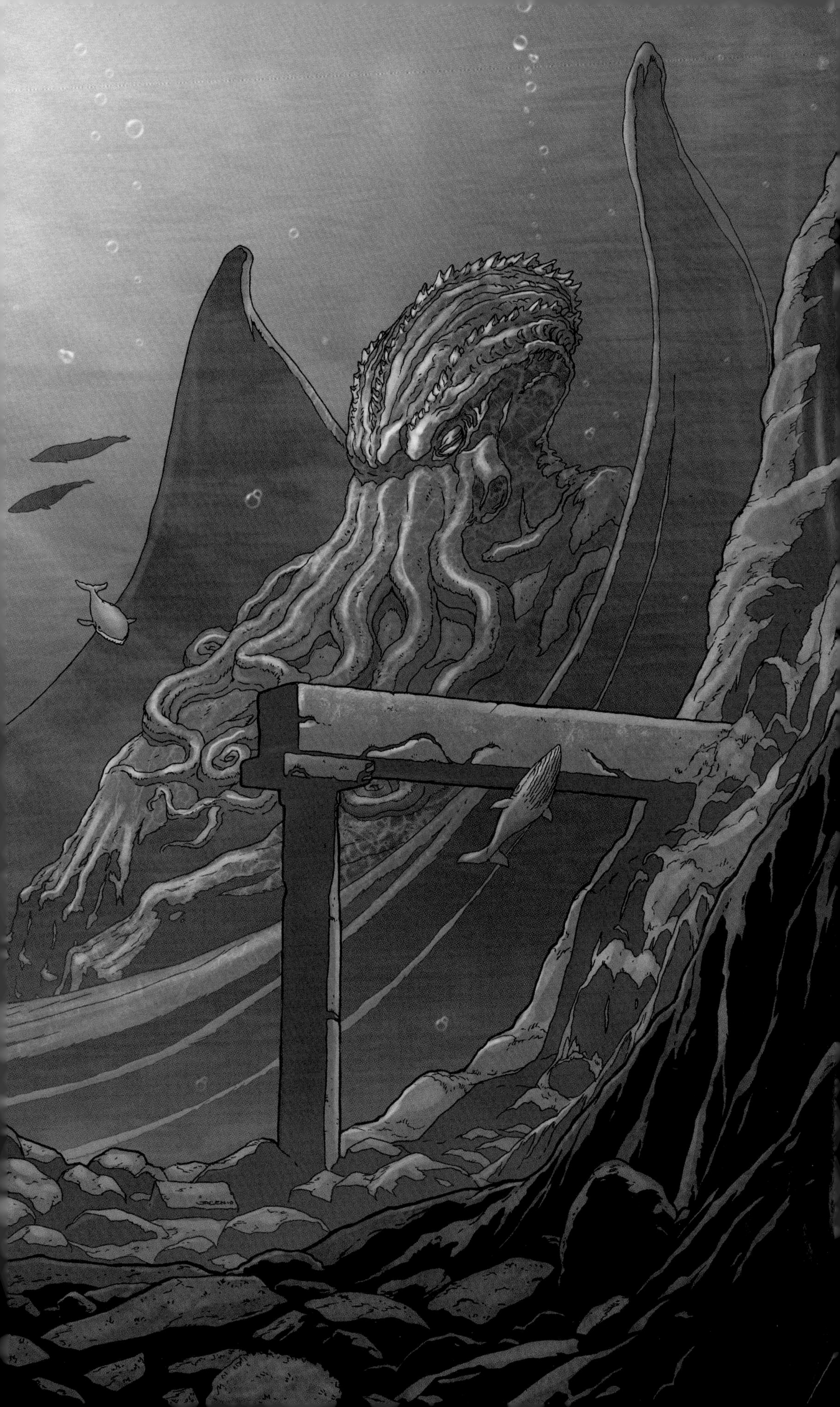

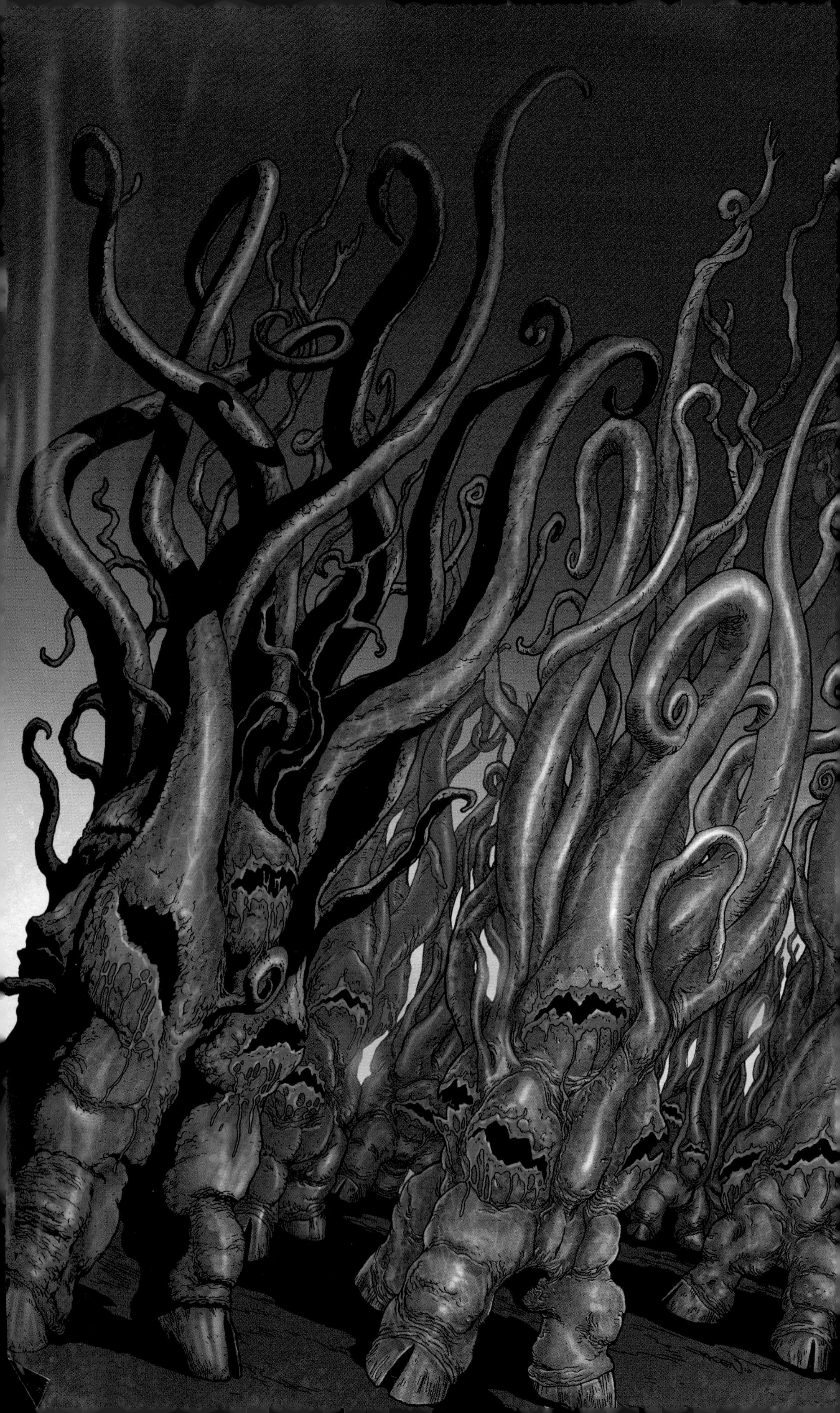

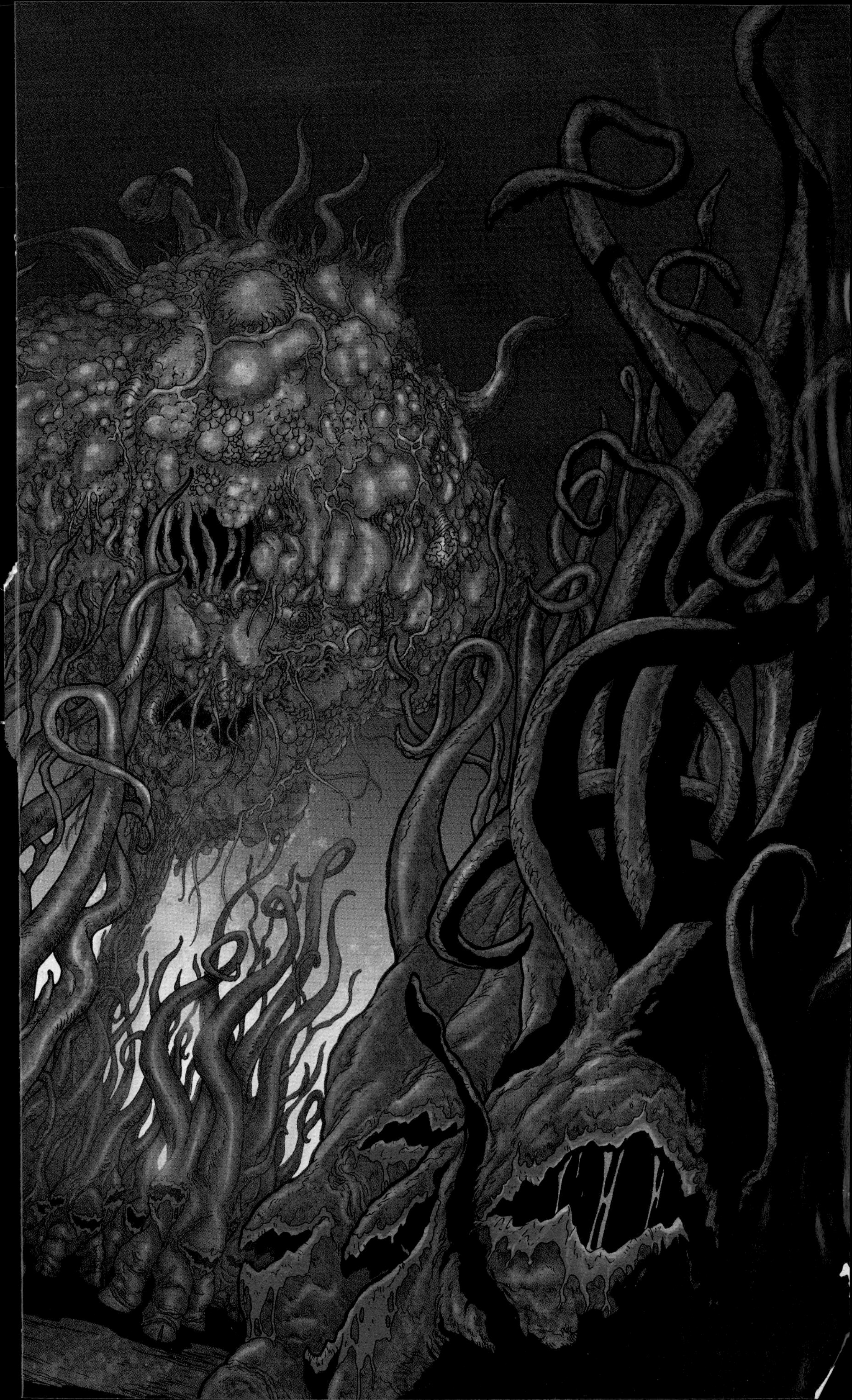

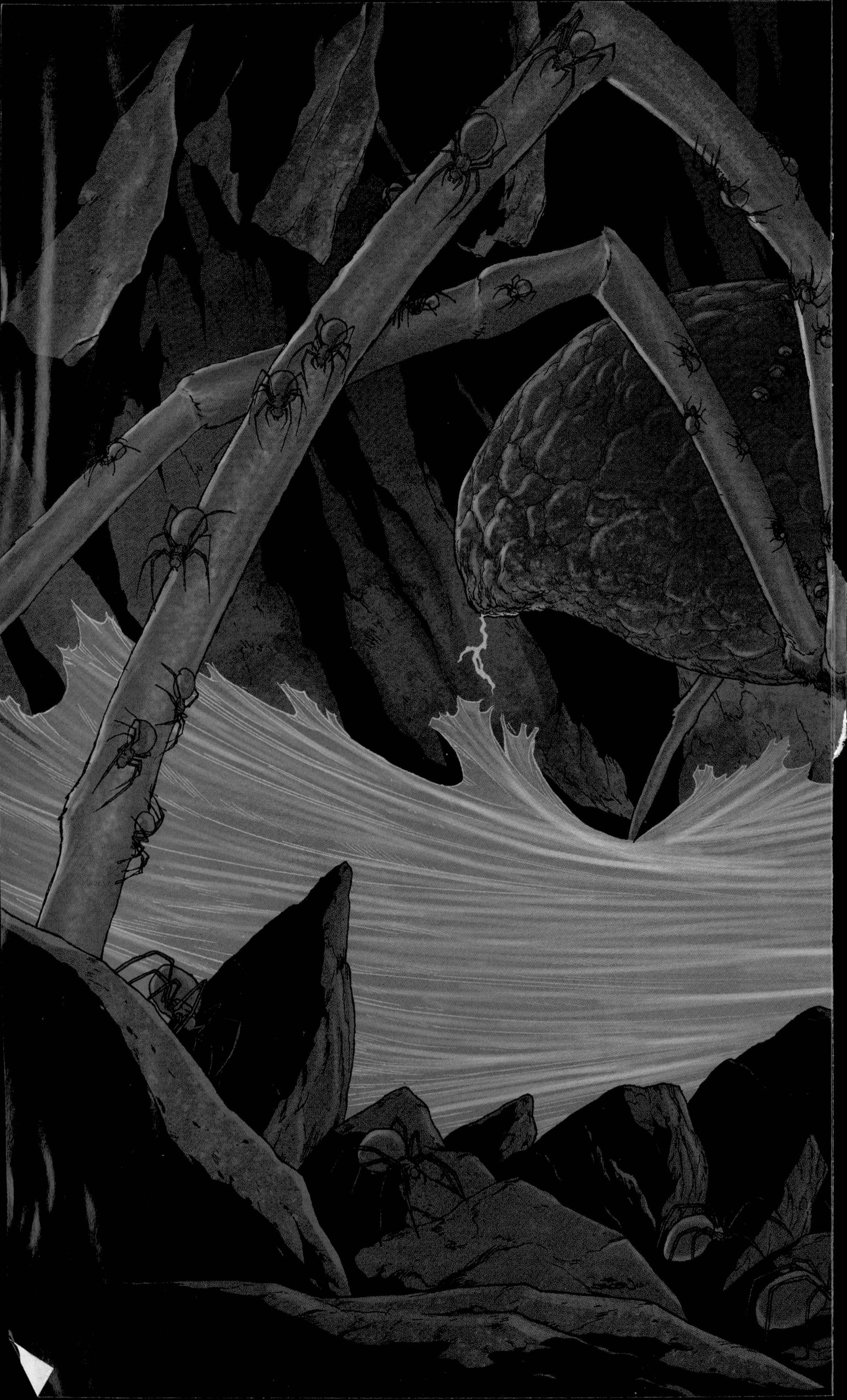

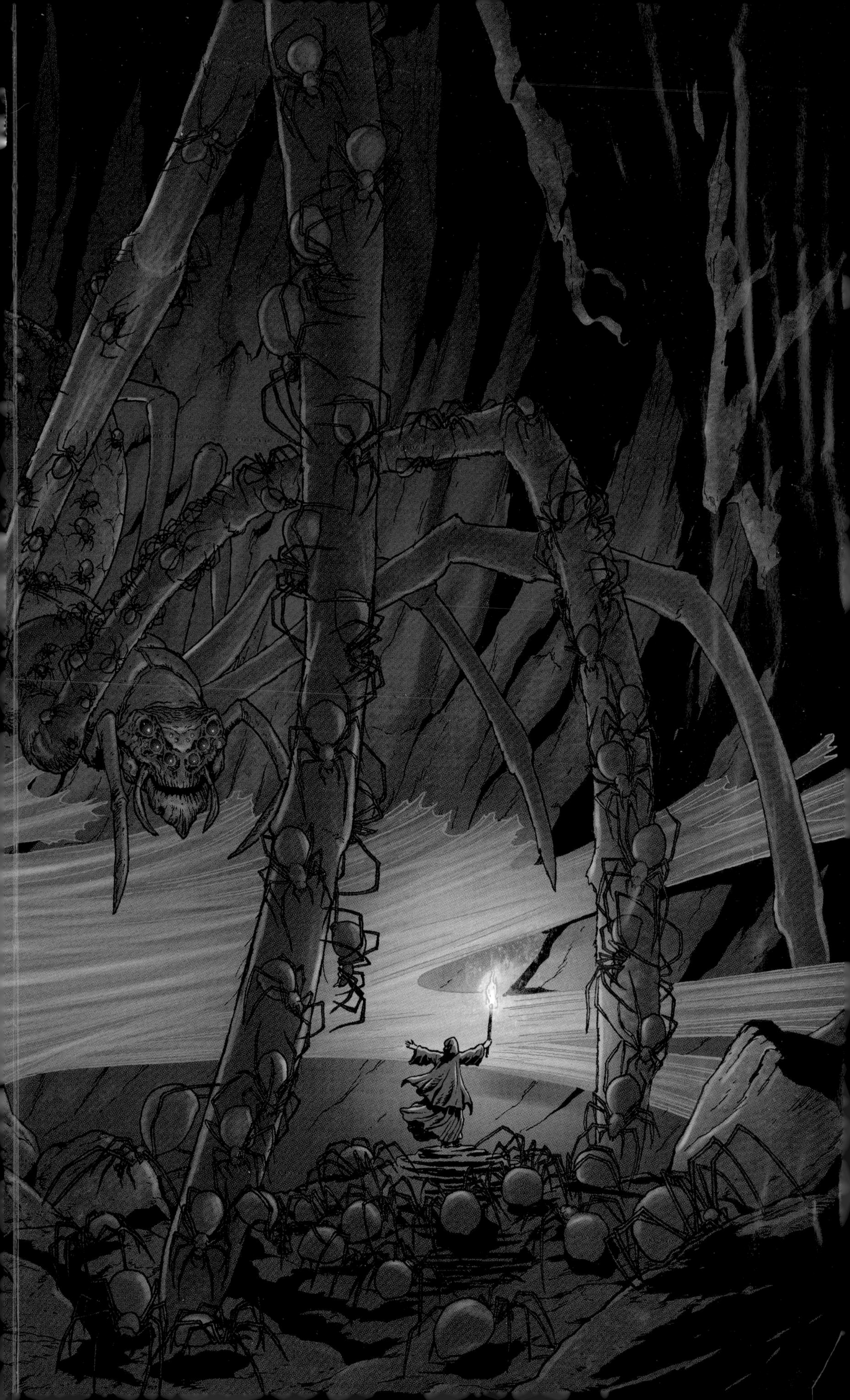

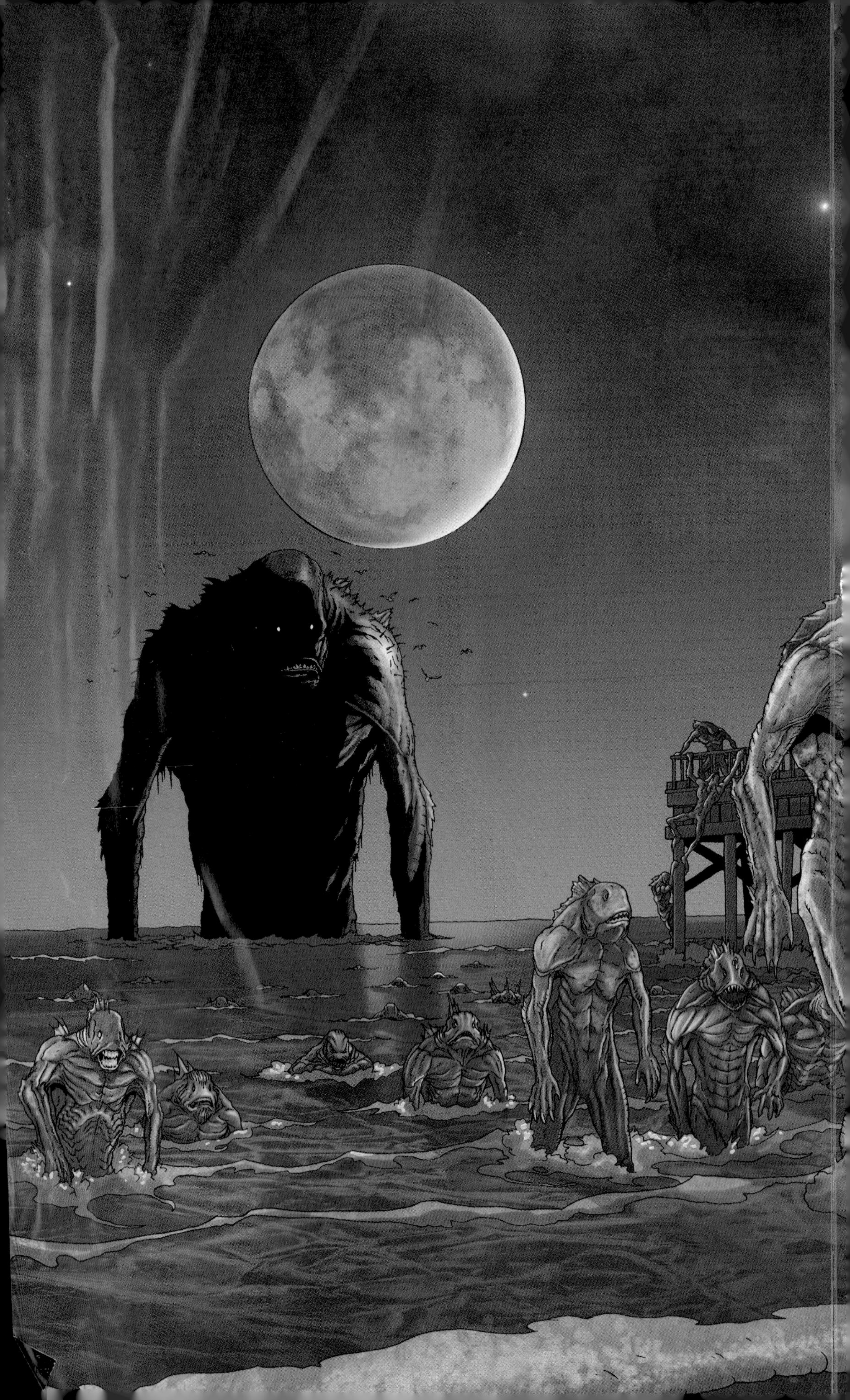

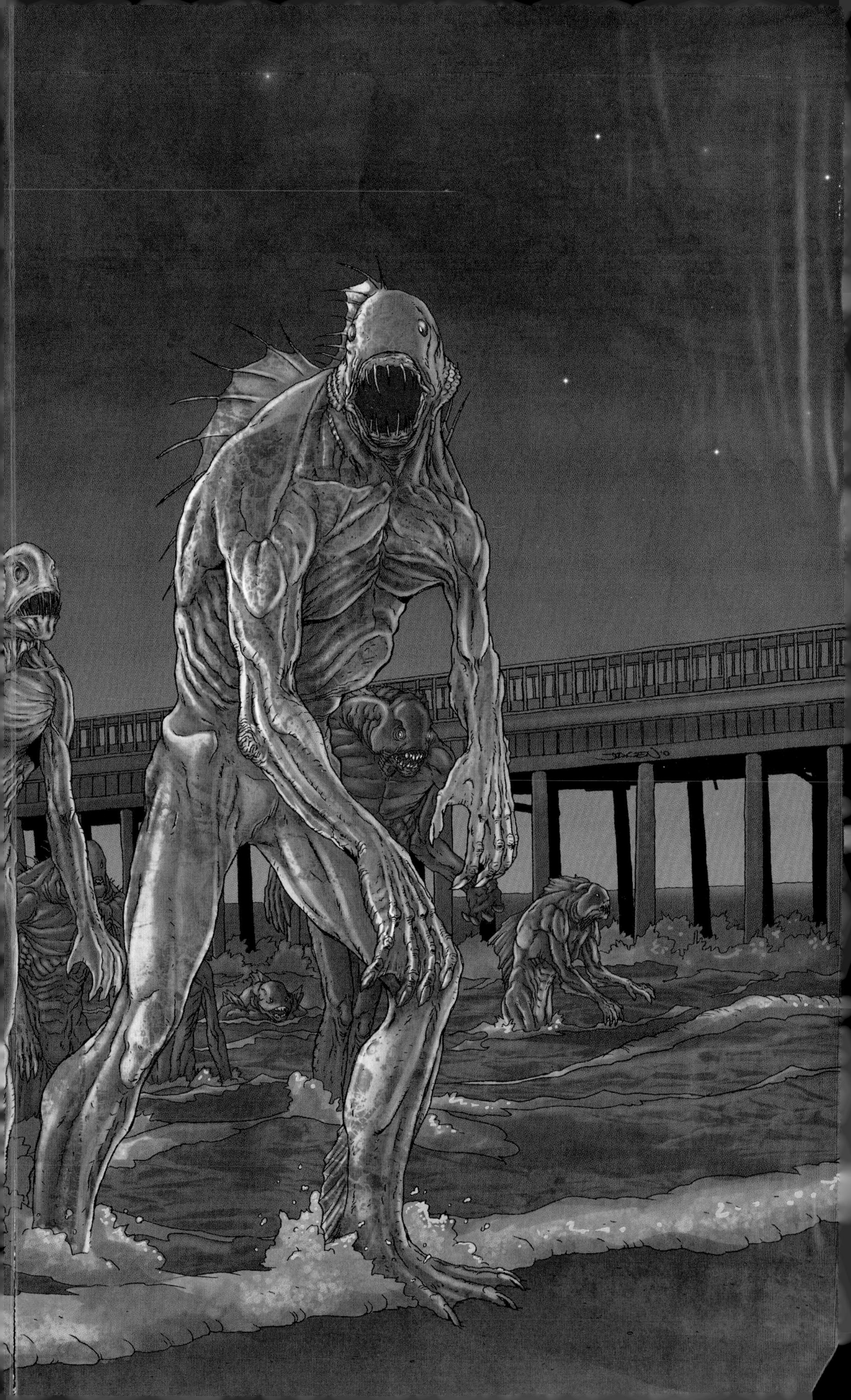

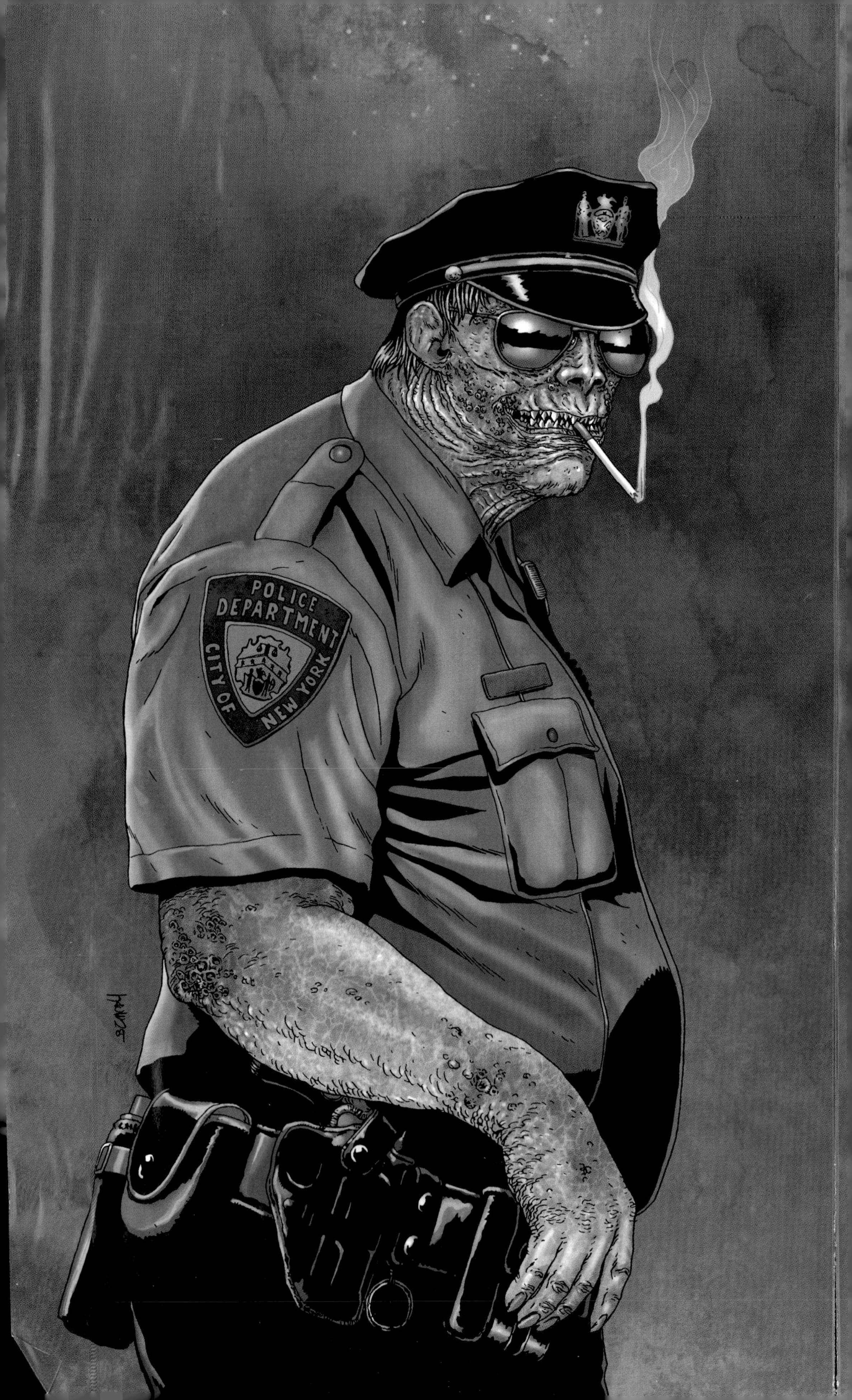
POLICE
DEPARTMENT
CITY OF NEW YORK

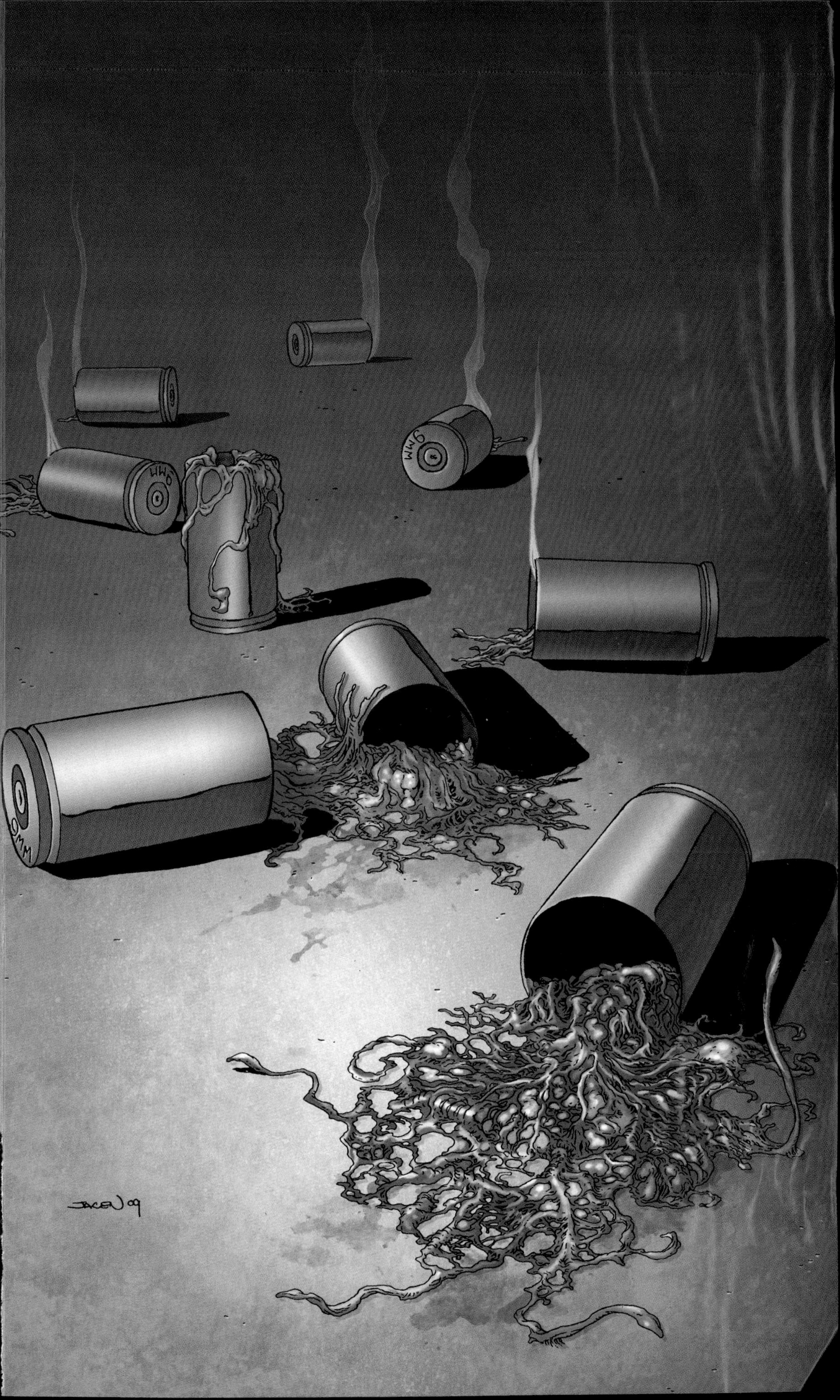
9MM
JACEN 09

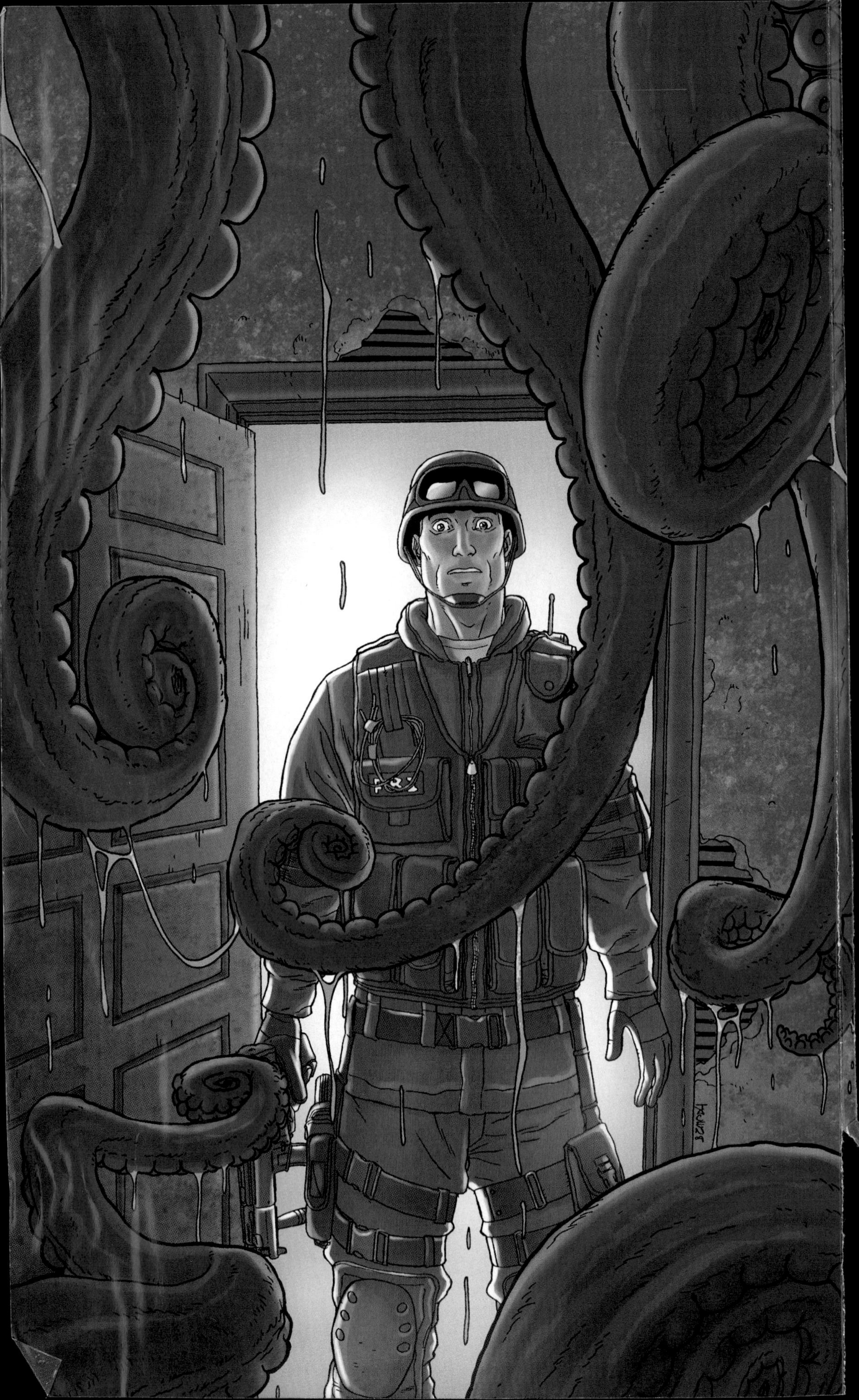

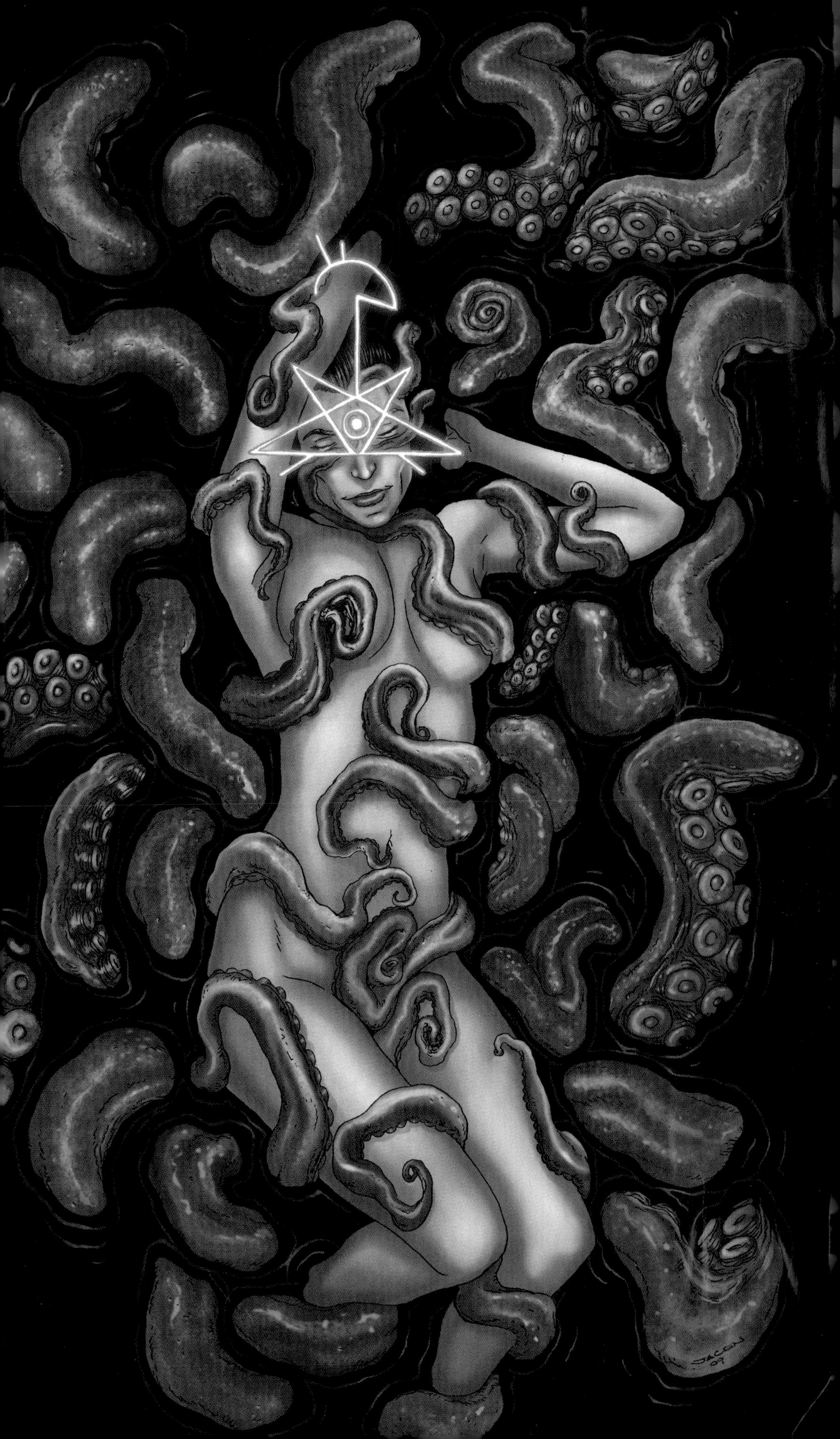

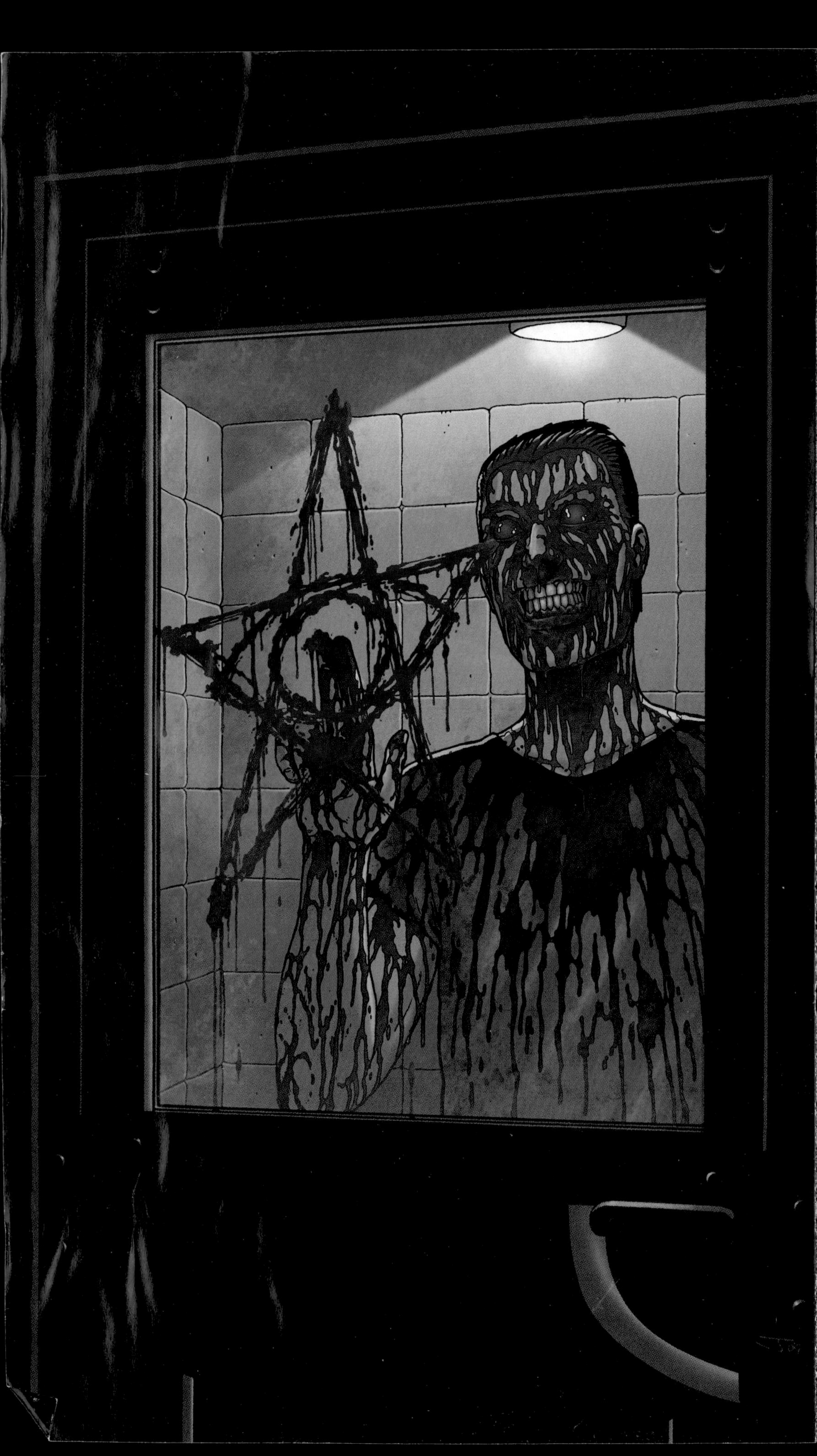